LOOK ME IN THE EYE

Also by Jeremy Isaacs

STORM OVER 4

NEVER MIND THE MOON

COLD WAR (with Taylor Downing)

LOOK ME IN THE EYE

A Life in Television

JEREMY ISAACS

LITTLE, BROWN

LITTLE, BROWN

First published in Great Britain in March 2006 by Little, Brown

Copyright © Jeremy Isaacs 2006

The moral right of the author has been asserted.

A CIP catalogue record for this book
is available from the British Library.

ISBN 0 316 72728 8

Typeset in Palatino by M Rules
Printed and bound in Great Britain by
Clays Ltd, St Ives plc

Little, Brown
An imprint of
Time Warner Book Group UK
Brettenham House
Lancaster Place
London WC2E 7EN

www.twbg.co.uk

For Isabella and Zachary

and

for friends and colleagues along the way

PREFACE

This book is about my time in television, spanning forty years. It does not deal with my briefer spell of song and dance, within that period, at the Royal Opera House; I have written of that in *Never Mind the Moon*. Nor is it a personal or family history; work was always placed at the centre of my life, too single-mindedly so, I now think. Making television programmes can all too easily occupy seven days a week. But family tragedy intersects and turns life and work upside down; it finds a place in these pages.

CONTENTS

I

SMALL, DARK GLASWEGIAN JEW

On 30 June 1950 Lord Reith of Stonehaven, a former pupil, presented the prizes at Glasgow Academy. The ceremony was held at St Andrew's Halls, one of Europe's finest concert venues, where the Scottish Orchestra played on Saturday nights. The prizewinners sat in the front rows, below the concert platform.

Lord Reith had been the founding Director General of the BBC, the ideologue and inventor of public service broadcasting. Its purposes, he decreed, were to 'inform, entertain, educate'. Six feet and a bit tall, his gaunt figure towered over us. One by one we climbed the steps, received our prizes, shook his hand, and stepped down again. Then he spoke. First, a word on shaking hands:

'Whoever he may be, whatever he may be, there are two things for you to do: first, get some sort of an impression of him and, secondly, put some sort of impression of yourself on him . . . It doesn't matter whether you are shaking hands with a convict or a king – take his hand firmly and look him in the eye. You didn't all do that to me today.' Myself, I had looked him in the belly-button.

The speech was extraordinary: 'You will find a lot of humbug and insincerity in daily life and in public affairs, a lack of vision, courage and decision, subordination of principle to popularity and the vote, and inefficiency, irresponsibility and mediocrity on every hand. Well now, what are the Sixth going to do about it? They had better decide what their attitude is going to be.'

That night the Isaacs family took the sleeper to London for a holiday in the West Country. In the mists of morning, ahead of us on the platform at Euston, loomed Reith's imposing figure.

Ten years later he came to Glasgow Academy again. This time he told the boys that, thanks to a young lady, he'd made a new, belated discovery: 'That life's for living. And she was right that I'd never been told it when young, and that I haven't fully learned it yet; but at least I now realise how much I've missed, and how many mistakes I've made.' By then I was at work in broadcasting, at the tail-end of the Reithian era. St Andrew's Halls burned down after a boxing match in 1962.

Merton College, Oxford, would fit me for life, but not for work. Few of us reading arts subjects had any idea what we intended to do. I read Classics, *Literae Humaniores*: Latin and Greek language and literature, ancient history and philosophy. I mentioned to my tutor that I chose to read philosophy because through it, above all other subjects, I should come to understand the universe. 'Nowadays', I was told, 'we don't think that is what philosophy does.' It was too late to change. 'Mr Isaacs', my tutor reported to the Warden at Responsions, 'thinks of philosophical issues as arguments to be won, rather than puzzles to be understood.'

Future lawyers, doctors, scientists, knew what they would do to earn a living. I didn't want to teach, or enter the Civil Service. Politics? I had been Chairman of the Labour Club and President of the Union, but found it hard to believe that undergraduate activity in any way qualified me for a political career. This self-assessment was corroborated when I had an interview with the General Secretary of the Scottish Labour Party. 'What do you know about?' asked Willie Marshall. The answer was: Very little. What I enjoyed at Union debates was not conviction but argument; Michael Foot or Dick Crossman would make a devastating case, and Quintin Hogg up-end it. Or vice versa. I relished hearing both sides.

Politics had come naturally to me in my father's house. Isidore Isaacs kept a small jeweller's shop in the Cowcaddens. He was a reader and a thinker – 'a scholar and a gentleman', as a watchmaker who worked for him wrote to me when he died. His bookshelves boasted a sequence of maroon covers: the volumes of the Left Book Club, founded in response to the chronic unemployment and total-itarian threat of the thirties. Before the war, he had supported the League of Nations. In the summer of 1945, on holiday at Llandudno in North Wales, we learned the result of the general election that swept Labour into power from an RAF man behind barbed wire at a radar station on Great Ormes Head. In the Jewish boarding house where we were staying, hungry guests queued at the dining-room door, waiting for the gong that summoned us to meals. All rejoiced at Labour's landslide victory, except for one gloomy refugee couple who shook their heads and spoke darkly of their fear of socialism. At the pitch-and-putt course the proprietor feared his business would be taken over by Christmas.

My mother, Sally Jacobs, was a general practitioner who had graduated in medicine at Glasgow University in 1923. (Half the entrants in 1918 had been women, so great a toll had the Great War taken of the young men.) In student cabaret she appeared in top hat, white tie and tails, stick in hand, as 'Burlington Bertie, I rise at ten-thirty, Burlington Bertie from Bow'. In the 1923 gradu-ates' yearbook, beneath her picture, the editors put:

Where Sally goes, it's always spring
Her presence brightens everything.

and

Words, words, words . . .

Sally had a clear voice, and enjoyed using it. In synagogue she sang out boldly; in the garden she relished the Latin names of flowers, and would roll the vowels round her tongue; po-ten-till-a; cal-ce-o-la-ri-a. If my father loved books, my mother loved music, and made sure that we heard lots. Together they saw their three sons had the best education possible.

We had good newspapers at home, the *Glasgow Herald* and the *Manchester Guardian*, and my father took also a weekly *Hansard* which I avidly devoured, starting with parliamentary questions. I don't know why he subscribed to *Hansard*, except to whet my interest in politics. Perhaps he was prompted by a letter he'd had years before, from Mr Campbell, headmaster of the village school in Rhonehouse, Kirkcudbrightshire, which suggested that one day I could be Prime Minister.

At Glasgow Academy I was the only boy in my class to support Labour, and enjoyed gleeful triumphs as, from 1945 to 1951, the party successfully contested by-election after by-election. On our first visit to London, Dad took us on Sunday morning to Hyde Park Corner, where a regular gaggle of eloquent eccentrics held forth on soap boxes, living testimony to Britain's commitment to free speech. As many aimed to amuse as to inspire or convert. One orator, having entertained us for an hour, complained that in the Royal Park he was not allowed to pass the hat round. 'They say it's indecent,' he told us, 'against the law. There are things go on in this park which Havelock Ellis and Krafft-Ebing know nothing about, and I'm not allowed to accept a coin from you. So I'll go out through that gate and stand on the pavement. If you care to meet me there, shake my hand and cross my palm with silver, I shall be very glad to see you.'

Bearsden, outside Glasgow, where we lived from 1945, was comfortably middle class; Clydebank, where they built the liners *Queen Mary* and *Queen Elizabeth*, solidly working class – Red Clydeside. Both were in the constituency of Dunbarton Burghs (later East Dunbartonshire), with Davie Kirkwood as sitting

Labour member. In 1950, at election meetings in Bearsden Town Hall, I heard Walter Elliott, MP for the Scottish Universities and a member of Churchill's wartime government, lay into Labour with a will. Asked from the floor, 'What is your policy then?' he answered, 'When a car is being driven towards a precipice, the first thing to do is stop it.' I did not hear Kirkwood speak. Instead, in the same genteel Bearsden venue, I heard our next-door neighbour in Strathview Gardens. This was Rosslyn Mitchell, a quietly-spoken, silver-haired solicitor with a ravishing and much younger French wife. Mitchell had been an MP, defeating Asquith at Paisley in 1923; but the good people of Bearsden did not want to hear him now, and barracked him noisily. Delicately but firmly, he reproved them for their bad manners and refused to go on unless they stopped. They wouldn't. He did. Kirkwood won easily.

Looking back, it was the young Conservative candidate in the constituency who was to mean most to me in the end. He had wartime service in the Scots Guards to his credit and his election address made much of the golf blue he had won at Cambridge. He had an attractive wife and four beautiful blonde daughters. He was William Whitelaw. On Clydeside, the shipworkers gave him quite as rough a time as Rosslyn Mitchell had in Bearsden. 'Away home, son; you don't know what you're talking about.' Willie learned from his going-over. At the heart of Red Clydeside, 'his illustrious opponent' – Davie Kirkwood – treated him, he tells us, 'with kindness and generosity'. There might be two Britains, one rich, one poor; but Willie Whitelaw was a 'One-Nation Conservative'.

I went up to Oxford to sit the scholarship exam on an icy winter's day in 1950. A man fell off his bicycle on Magdalen Bridge and bellowed, as his bum hit the road, 'Blast and damn this bloody government.' Labour's days were numbered.

Successive Labour Club chairmen vied to lure the bigwigs of Labour government to speak in Oxford. Our biggest catch was

Clement Attlee, whose wife drove him to meet us at the Randolph Hotel. He spoke in a packed Union Society debating chamber; the audience rose to applaud the modest statesman who had moved to grant independence to India, Pakistan and Burma. Could we get Nye Bevan, also? At a meeting she addressed at the MacLellan Galleries in Glasgow, I solicited help from his wife, Jennie Lee. 'Away you go, son,' she told me, 'and sell some *Tribunes*.'

After Oxford I still had National Service to do; so I continued my education at Maryhill Barracks, Glasgow. 'Why don't you put the boys in the kilt, Isidore?' my father's friends asked. 'I will if you'll show me an Isaacs tartan,' he would answer. I never regretted the months I spent in the Highland Light Infantry, or later, commissioned, in the Royal Scots Fusiliers, though at twenty-three I was something of a misfit sharing a barrack-room with streetwise eighteen-year-olds. Allowed out after the first few weeks' basic training, we togged ourselves out in kilt and sporran, Balmoral bonnet and highly polished brogues, whited gaiters over red-and-white diced hose, shining gilt badges and upright plume. Outside the guardroom we walked across the mirror embedded in the tarmac, supposedly to ensure we wore nothing under the kilt. No one cared, but the clippie on the tram outside the gate, standing on the rear platform, would call out, 'Plenty of room inside . . .' and then, cocking her head upwards, 'HLI upstairs.' Returned after a chaste evening at my parents' home, I listened to my companions comparing notes: 'Did you get yer hole?' Some did.

At Eaton Hall Officer Cadet School in the summer of '56, the platoon commander stood us easy: 'Gentlemen, I have good news for you. Nasser has nationalised the Suez Canal. You may yet have the privilege of serving your Sovereign in action.' One lad from my platoon did indeed land at Port Said. He took a wrong turning in the souk, was abducted and returned, lifeless, in a trunk. Tony Howard was part of the invading forces, reporting, pseudonymously, on what he saw for the *New Statesman*. I never left these shores. Commissioned, I asked to be posted to Africa, and was sent instead to Churchill Barracks, Ayr, regimental head-quarters and training depot for the Royal Scots Fusiliers.

When I finished my stint in autumn 1957 and came to London to seek my fortune, I attended the founding meeting of CND at Central Hall, Westminster, with my cousin, the virologist Alick Isaacs. Alick, who identified the presence in our bodies of inter-feron, a vital part of the immune system, had brought with him a colleague from the Soviet Union. Bertrand Russell, J. B. Priestley, Michael Foot, A. J. P. Taylor spoke, Taylor denouncing both the Prime Minister, Harold Macmillan, and the Labour leader, Hugh Gaitskell, as 'murderers'. At the halfway point of the meeting, Canon John Collins appealed for funds. 'This I do not like,' said the Russian scientist. 'In my country, the government finds money for all good causes such as this.' Afterwards the audience walked round to Downing Street to continue the protest outside the Prime Minister's windows at Number Ten. We went too. The street was packed. A couple next to me started chanting: 'Eden must go!' Eden had gone some months previously; the Prime Minister whose sleep we were disturbing was Macmillan. I realised that the demonstrators, exchanging fond looks and digging each other in the ribs, were actually remembering happy days protesting over Suez. I was observing, not participating. It seemed a proper basis on which to pursue a career in current affairs television.

Established in the comforts of a hospitable flat in St John's Wood, and drawing the dole at the Lisson Grove labour exchange, I looked around. I applied to the BBC to join its general traineeship scheme and was interviewed by a senior personnel officer, Sir Herbert Thompson, formerly of the Indian Civil Service, then rowing cor-respondent of the *Sunday Times*. This went well, but it was only the beginning of a lengthy process. For the general traineeship, and for a junior post that came up in Outside Broadcasts, I was seen by others in Appointments. N. S. Holmes was impressed. His brief note begins: 'Small, dark Glaswegian Jew. Very much alive.' It ends: 'Outstandingly good personality. To be invited to Board.' D. Salt was impressed also: 'His shrewdness is tempered with a quick sense of humour and he seems to have that cosmopolitan flexibility of mind common to many of his race.' Would that today be thought 'incorrect'? Reading these verdicts after nearly fifty years, I am amazed above all at my own capacity for bullshit and at the leisured thoroughness of the BBC's procedures.

I was still unemployed. ITV? But how did you get in? Tony Howard suggested I ask Bernard Levin, then excoriating ITV weekly in the *Guardian*, to advise. In the Mortimer Arms near the *Spectator*'s Gower Street office, Bernard mentioned three names – the only three ITV people, I understood, of whom he thought anything at all. One of them was Mary Hewat, at Granada. She returned my calls, and said she would see me.

I knew nothing of television; indeed, I'd scarcely seen it. On Coronation Day in 1953, when the nation tuned in and the medium caught on, I was playing cricket in the rain in Oxfordshire. (Not a ball was bowled.) I once saw Aneurin Bevan on *Press Conference*. At the time of the Suez crisis, since Ayr was only 30 miles down the road from my parents' home in Renfrewshire, I'd seen both Anthony Eden and, to Eden's fury, Hugh Gaitskell, address the nation on television as our troops slowly headed towards Egypt. At the Oxford Union, I'd spoken in debate against the introduction of commercial television. No one there had denounced it in the ferocious terms Quintin Hogg, and Reith himself, used in the House of Lords, damning it as a 'bubonic plague' menacing the national culture, though Christopher Mayhew turned up to oppose, bringing with him the chimpanzee J. Fred Muggs, symbol of his campaign to preserve the BBC's monopoly. Muggs had appeared on CBS in the United States during their Coronation coverage. We voted, I remember, to keep the commercial swine well away from the lucrative advertising trough. But in Parliament the legislation went through, and in 1955 ITV came on air, first in London and the Midlands, then, at intervals, across the country. Granada, which held the weekday franchise for the North of England and North Wales, first broadcast in 1956. Its first evening's schedule included, at the behest of the company's founder and driving force, Sidney Bernstein, a tribute to the BBC. This gesture – quirky as it seemed, like Arsenal saluting Chelsea, or Liverpool, Everton – was no mere flourish, but a signal of lofty intent: Granada, too, would shoulder the broadcaster's social and cultural responsibilities.

In February 1958, as I waited for the postman or the telephone to ring, Granada announced a broadcasting first: it would cover a by-election to be held at Rochdale. The BBC at that time made a point, stressed in its annual report, of not covering elections, in case anything it broadcast should influence the result. At an early meeting between chairmen and directors general of the two authorities, the BBC solemnly invited the brash newcomer, ITV, to subscribe to this self-denying ordinance. Sir Robert Fraser, for the Independent Television Authority (ITA), flatly refused. Now Granada, on its own initiative, persuaded the three candidates in the by-election to take part in television programmes, and their respective party headquarters to allow them.

The Liberal candidate at Rochdale was a broadcaster, Ludovic Kennedy. He promptly agreed. Labour's candidate, Jack McCann, seemed willing also. The party's General Secretary, Morgan Phillips, took a canny approach, putting McCann through his paces first in a makeshift studio at Transport House; then he assented. The Conservatives and their candidate, John Parkinson, reluctantly fell into line. Granada's programmes were modest enough; the candidates debated topics and answered questions. The count was broadcast live: McCann came home well in front, Kennedy second, the Tories (to whom the seat had previously belonged) a humiliating third. As important as the result was the broadcaster's agenda. Television, Bernstein's Granada was saying, has a role to play in the democratic process.

The Rochdale programmes were not broadcast in London, only in Granadaland. I watched a feed from the North to Granada's offices behind Oxford Street. Excitedly, I told Mary Hewat, 'It's your Rochdale coverage that makes me want to come to Granada. I don't want to join a company that does quizzes and westerns.'

'We show the best westerns and make the best quiz games on the network,' Mary answered.

Before the BBC summoned me to the next stage of their selection process, I was called in and told, by Mary's husband, Tim Hewat, that I had a job. The salary was £18 a week; he broke this to me apologetically, but it was more than many started at in those days. First, however, I must go to Manchester and be looked over by the news department. In some trepidation, I went north.

In January that year London's bus drivers had gone on strike for higher pay. I reported on the episode for *Forward*, a right-wing Labour weekly whose editor was George Thomson, later to be Commonwealth Secretary and Chairman of the IBA. I went to the Cricklewood depot and persuaded a driver to take me home to his wife, who broke down their weekly budget for me, item by item. Happily, the piece appeared in print; I had it in my pocket for the visit to Manchester. When I entered his office, Barrie Heads, in overall charge of news and local currrent affairs, gave me a critical look; what was he to do with a toffee-nosed Oxford graduate in his newsroom? But the *Forward* piece pleaded my case.

So did George Singleton, proprietor of the Cosmo in Rose Street, Glasgow, whose son Ronald was a schoolfriend of mine. It was at the comfortable Cosmo that I had wallowed most in movies, wept at *Poil de Carotte*, laughed at *Marius* and *La Kermesse Heroique*, gawped at Signoret in *Casque d'Or*; at *A Night at the Opera* I fell out of my seat laughing. At Clouzot's *Les Diaboliques*, when Signoret, with a weak heart, got out of bed to investigate the creaky corridor and find a supposed corpse in the bath whose rolling eyes would terrify and kill, the woman in front of me exclaimed to her neighbour: 'The puir soul, has she no' got a dressing gown? She'll catch her death.' Singleton wrote on my behalf to his fellow cinema-owners, the Bernsteins, and his letter helped; it was seen by Denis Forman. I could start in May. So, having left Glasgow for London, I prepared to move to Manchester. And Tamara would come with me.

The previous November, in the interval of Giraudoux's *The Trojan War Will Not Take Place* at the Piccadilly Theatre, I had rung home with some good news.

'You've got a job.'

'No, but I've met the woman I'm going to marry.'

My parents plainly thought I had things in the wrong order, but were mightily relieved that Tamara was a well-brought-up Jewish girl from Muizenburg in the Cape, and were bowled over when they met her. Now that I did have a job, we could plan a summer wedding.

Tamara had acted at Cape Town's Little Theatre with Nigel Hawthorne and had worked as an announcer for SABC, South African radio. She had fine secretarial skills, was working at Penguin when we met, and soon found a job with BBC Manchester, working with Roy Speer, producer of *The Goon Show*. I found the transition to work far more daunting than that from school to university, or from Oxford to the army. What if I failed? No Lady Macbeth, Tamara was with me through trials and testing times ahead, a loved and loving support to me, and adoring mother of John and Kate. When she died, after twenty-eight years of marriage, I was Chief Executive of Channel Four. I would never have made it without her.

David Plowright was Granada's News Editor. He sent me to a horticultural show; I brought back a paragraph on an enormous prize marrow. I wrote the weather forecast. 'We don't use words like anti-cyclone here,' he said. 'It's either going to be wet, or dry.'

The daily magazine programme *People and Places* was appalling, and we knew it. The researchers, whose task it was to find material to fill it, were a mixed bunch. Pat Owtram was an extremely capable journalist; another old hand refused to answer the telephone in case of being dunned for debt; Margaret Owen was flamboyant, full of wild enthusiasms, resolute in pursuit. Then there was me. I was willing enough to work, but fearful, reluctant to knock on doors to persuade whoever answered to come into the studio and answer three short questions from Bill Grundy. The studio was a frightening place to anyone who'd never been in one before. Under glaring lights, heavy cameras lumbered across the floor; the microphone hovered close overhead or, on a stand, under your nose. 'Relax,' the floor manager counselled. 'Don't let any of this bother you. Be your natural self.' Quick questions, hesitant answers, and the ordeal was over: 'I'm sorry, that's all we've got time for.'

People and Places rarely got out of the studio. I suggested we film one day at Burton Manor on the Wirral, a further education college run by a friend from Oxford. Burton Manor had been Gladstone's home, with tree stumps to prove it. Features of interest there, surely, and tales to tell; chuck in a few visiting Japanese, and we had a story. Or did we? Director and camera crew followed me there. The director took one look around and another at me; 'Nothing to film here. Wasted trip.'

Clueless as I was, it wasn't the researchers that were the problem. *People and Places'* mistake was never to plan ahead, but always to cobble everything together on the day. I recall one evening after transmission being alone in the tepid hospitality room with Pat Owtram, looking forlornly at empty teacups and tired paste sandwiches. (No alcohol was allowed. Granada had been dry since, legend had it, someone had thoughtfully put a bottle of whisky in the dressing room of each member of Humphrey Lyttelton's band. One day, preparing with Bill Grundy to interview Sir John Wolfenden on his report on the law affecting homosexuals, I urged that I must offer our guest a drink. A half-empty bottle of sherry was produced, and one glass. 'I've marked the bottle,' said the production manager as he reluctantly produced two more glasses.) Pat and I, on our own that week, confirmed before going home that we had nothing for tomorrow. The programme lasted only half an hour, but no item ever ran longer than two and a half minutes. Ten items, at least, to find. We would search for inspiration in the morning papers. Hopeless.

Eventually the programme's producer went on holiday and Tim Hewat took over. 'Five items a day only,' he decreed. 'Everything will run twice as long.' Even so, *People and Places* could still mess it up. When Leonard Bernstein's *West Side Story* had its British première at The Opera House up the road, Bill Grundy interviewed the producer Jerome Robbins. Grundy told viewers, citing the *Daily Express*, that the lyrics of 'Gee Officer Krupke' were rude, and asked, 'Why are you purveying this filth?' Robbins walked out.

No one at Granada was allotted only one task. In my very first week I was sent to get an old journalist pal of Sidney Bernstein's, Quentin Reynolds, out of the pub. A famous correspondent in his day, Reynolds had presented Granada's opening night two years before. He had been drunk then, and he was drunk now – or at any rate, drinking hard – as the hour of live transmission neared. 'Quent' was in the Baulking Donkey, a gloomy pub with a surly landlord, but closest to the studio; I was sent to see that he didn't have a drink and bring him back. What he was supposed to be doing in the pub if not drinking, I never discovered. In any case I failed, falling for the oldest trick in the book. At the bar, Reynolds made room for me and, after a moment or two, indicated that there was something behind me of interest. I looked back, for an instant only. In that flash the landlord, well used to these procedures, poured and 'Quent' lifted and downed another hefty snort. He got through the programme, just, but was replaced soon after by a skilled professional, the Canadian Elaine Grand.

In *Youth Wants to Know*, four sixth-formers interviewed men and women of substance and achievement. I helped choose the interviewing panel, travelling with the director Mike Scott across the North of England to audition schoolboy or schoolgirl interrogators. Mike Scott was tall, handsome and utterly charming; he set the sixth-formers instantly at their ease, both when we met them and again when they did their turn on live television. What we were after was not politeness, but thoughtfulness, spirit and daring. We were seldom let down.

The researcher's other duty was to write the brief, sent in advance to the chosen panel. We didn't suggest the line of questioning; that was up to them. But we burrowed in libraries, and cuttings, and summarised the subject's life story. Charles Laughton, an old friend of Sidney Bernstein's, came to Manchester in a play by Jane Arden, *The Party*. He was invited to take on *Youth Wants to Know* but, wily old bird, agreed to do it only if we would also quiz a young actor, a local boy, who would make his debut in the play, Albert Finney. Finney was too new to have cuttings about him; I went to his home in Salford to talk to his proud mother and father, and to his headmaster. They spoke highly of Albert. The programme went well.

The episodes I best remember of *Youth Wants to Know* each involved politicians. Morgan Phillips was looking pretty confident as he faced his first question from a sixteen-year-old. 'Mr Phillips, as General Secretary of the Labour Party, what would you say was the worst mistake you've made in your life?' His jaw dropped; there was a long pause. Finally, Transport House's generalissimo confided that, as the party's servant, he took no decisions himself and, therefore, could make no mistakes. Later, when the programme was over, he said he should have advised far more strongly against Clem Attlee's decision, faced with an exhausted Cabinet and a tiny majority, to call a general election in October 1951. We should have hung on, he said; Labour could have continued to govern.

But the biggest come-uppance was R. A. Butler's. In 1958 Butler was Home Secretary, second only to Prime Minister Harold Macmillan in the political hierarchy. He was tackled by four young girls who wanted to know what the government was doing to reduce unemployment, particularly in Lancashire. One, with a strong accent, led the attack:

Q: Mr Butler, what are you doing to reduce unemployment?

A: Well, the national average is just over two per cent. I hope we can get it down again below that.

Q: Mr Butler, the figure here in Lancashire is nearly six per cent. What about that?

A : Yes, well there are historical reasons for that, and we're conscious that . . .

Q: Mr Butler, I come from Bolton, and we've got over seven per cent unemployment. What are you going to do about it?

A : I do understand your concern, and I share it. What we must hope is . . .

Q: Mr Butler, my dad is a weaver, and he's been out of work now for over twelve months . . .

A : Yes, well, as I say, we're doing what we can . . .

Q: Mr Butler, we mustn't be complacent, must we?

A : [Gulp]

A general election loomed. Granada had reported the Rochdale by-election; what would it do now? Two extensions followed logically from the Rochdale experience. First, the political parties, as well as delivering homilies of their own devising in party political broadcasts, should debate issues on radio and television with each other. If the party leaders would not debate, at least let them face questioning, on air, as in those days they still did on the hustings. Television – the BBC, jolted into activity partly by Granada's example – would this time mount programmes in which the parties' representatives would take part. Granada had a proposal or two of that sort. But there was another lesson from Rochdale. Granada's coverage was, supposedly, aimed not at viewers but at voters. No matter what others might think of the candidates' performance, the point was: what did voters in the Rochdale constituency think? If Granada was serious, then it followed that, at a general election, all voters in Granadaland should have the same chance to inspect and evaluate those seeking their votes.

Sidney Bernstein saw the point. To general amazement, and with some indrawing of breath, Granada announced that however much airtime it occupied, at whatever hours of the day or night, all the candidates in all the constituencies in all the areas where Granada broadcast – Lancashire, Yorkshire, Cheshire, parts of North Wales – would be invited to present their cases to their electorates, and would each have two minutes of valuable airtime to do it in. This project would be called *Election Marathon*. With others' help, I was to make it happen.

All the candidates, in all those constituencies, had to be contacted and offered appointments in Manchester or Leeds. The workload was trimmed by candidates who refused to take part; if only one refused, invitations to the others in that constituency lapsed. Some, with large majorities, turned us down point-blank. Others, after a little cajoling, came along. The slots they were offered ranged from afternoon to late at night; nobody appeared in peak time. The potential for administrative slip-ups on my part seemed horrendous. In the end 229 candidates took part. By some miracle, all of them turned up in the right place, at the right time.

No one made history; no one disgraced him- or herself. One woman addressed the camera in mid-afternoon: 'Now, children, go and fetch your mum. Tell her there's a lady here wants to speak to her.' Was democracy served? Yes, up to a point. The company was proud of *Marathon*. It was on offer again in 1964.

Granada had a mixed result with another election offering. *Last Debate* was a three-way discussion in our biggest studio, filled with an invited audience of party supporters. John Selwyn Lloyd, Conservative Foreign Secretary, Barbara Castle for Labour and, for the Liberals, Arthur Holt, MP for Bolton West, conducted a lively debate. The studio audience kept up a din of boos and cheers and whistles. The protagonists were sure their voices were drowned; furious, they vowed they'd never venture into such a bear-pit again. Actually, in spite of the noise in the studio, no one at home perceived the programme as a shouting match. The politicians, carefully miked, were perfectly audible.

The last days of the campaign were devoted in Manchester to Sidney Bernstein's attempts to secure access to the count. The BBC had long since negotiated entry for its cameras; Granada had left it late, but now claimed a legal right to be there too. Democracy again! Sidney was a fierce litigant in this sort of cause. At the last minute, justice prevailed.

It had been, we thought, a closely fought campaign. Suez, three years before, had marked a low point in Britain's foreign policy and standing in the world. Failure, and illness, brought down Anthony Eden, his lies mocked by Aneurin Bevan in Trafalgar Square: 'If he is sincere – and he may be, he may be; if he is sincere, he is too stupid to be Prime Minister.' Surely the electorate would remember the fiasco, and the UK's humiliation by the United States? Might not Labour, led by Hugh Gaitskell, just squeak home? Granada threw a lavish party on a studio floor to watch the results. The UK's voters, feeling better off, gave Macmillan a handsome victory; Gaitskell conceded, graciously. Sidney's guests, tucking into lobster, tut-tutted over the electorate's deplorable materialism.

I needed a break. Next day, Tamara and I set off for Venice.

2

WHAT THE PAPERS SAY

In the first days of November 1956 Brian Inglis presented the first edition of *What the Papers Say*. It seemed simple enough; a weekly review of the press. But as the date of transmission neared, a natural anxiety grew: what if there were nothing interesting in the papers that week? Then the British and French, colluding with the Israelis, invaded Egypt; in Hungary, Soviet tanks crushed a rebellion against foreign, communist rule. From Budapest came anguished pleas to the West to come to the freedom fighters' aid. The cries went unanswered.

And it was Guy Fawkes time. Walking across from Water Street to the studio at Quay Street, Inglis passed bonfires alight on the waste ground in between; fireworks exploded, echoing larger explosions in the wider world. *What the Papers Say* took less than a quarter of an hour of airtime – twelve and a half minutes to be precise. Nearly fifty years have passed since the programme first went out; it is still on the air. Denis Forman remembers proposing it simply as an account of how the press had reported the week's events. Sidney Bernstein had in mind A. J. Liebling's 'The Wayward Press' in the *New Yorker*, which delighted in pointing up discrepancies of fact in news reports.

In any case, *What the Papers Say* offered an overview of the week's events, and savoured the attitudes with which Fleet Street – from *The Times* to the *News of the World* – had tackled them. The programme employed only the simplest of means: a commentator, always a journalist, who spoke to camera; and, to illustrate the argument, extracts from the printed page, mounted on cards and read out by announcers or actors. When it started, and until *World in Action* came along six years later, *Papers* was Granada's only regular factual programme to be networked to London. There it reached both a general and a particularly interested audience: journalists. After my avoidance of cock-up in organising *Marathon*, I was given the job of producing *What the Papers Say*. I did so, week after week, for three years. It was more fun than any other programme I ever worked on, and it helped change my life.

For one thing, it could not easily be produced from Manchester. The script, written by a busy Fleet Street journalist, had to be composed on Wednesdays in London. So the producer – before fax, before email – had to be there too, to agree on the text and approach with the presenter. To ensure that the script reached Manchester in time for graphics to be prepared ahead of transmission late on Thursday evening, it was carried up by sleeper on Wednesday night. This could have been achieved by a Manchester-based producer going down to London; Granada proclaimed that its programmes were made in Manchester by men and women who lived in Manchester, or anyway in the North. Exceptions were rare. But, for whatever reason, I was allowed to make the change. We moved to London. Tamara left her job at the BBC for another in London. Later, when I was given charge of a second networked programme, *All Our Yesterdays*, I commuted up and down to Manchester, twice a week.

Reading newspapers – and I now had to read all the dailies and all the Sundays – was and has remained one of the great pleasures in my life. And journalists were pleasant company. But the programme also raised an issue of broadcasting policy and principle which immediately preoccupied me. Should television programmes say anything?

The Broadcasting Act 1955 insisted that every programme tackling an issue of current industrial or political controversy should do so with 'due impartiality'. It is easy to see why the legislation embodied this stipulation: television franchise holders, licensed to make money, were not to be allowed – nor should they have been, then or now – to ram the proprietor's opinions down the audience's throats. Virtually no one in the industry ever wanted to do this, or sought authority to do it; Rupert Murdoch is the sole evident exception. Yet it still seems odd to me that a commentator, presenting an account of a week's events, should not be allowed some latitude, some hint of attitude or opinion.

The issue arose between Granada and the regulatory body, the ITA, even before *What the Papers Say* went to air. To guard against breach of the Act, Granada proposed to rotate presenters of the left, right and centre, ensuring balance over a three-week span, in case of undue partiality in any one week. The programmes were to be presented by journalists of known, contrasting views: Kingsley Martin, doyen of the left, Editor of the *New Statesman*; for the hard-headed right, Donald Tyerman, Editor of the *Economist*; and in the centre, Brian Inglis, former leader-writer and diarist of the *Irish Times*, and shortly to be Editor of the *Spectator*. Neither Martin nor Tyerman was happy in the role, or any good at it. Why indeed should they, steeped in print, have felt at home in this new world? Brian Inglis, though, swam like a fish in water. J. P. W. 'Bill' Mallalieu, a Labour MP with an interest in sport and the navy – he'd written an admired and popular book on his war service, *Very Ordinary Seaman* – did a longish stint in the left-hand seat; John Connell, a combative columnist on London's *Evening News*, was a regular on the right. After he went, that spot was always hard to fill adequately. In fact, the programme's choice of presenter – for the princely fee of £25, later raised to £35 – became more eclectic: Bernard Levin and Michael Frayn were two of those

I most enjoyed working with; Clement Freud and Malcolm Muggeridge took a turn also. I used foreigners to vary the mix, inviting the correspondents of the *New York Herald Tribune*, *Le Monde* and *Izvestia* to contribute. Katharine Whitehorn came to an audition, but not a single woman did the show in my time. Women got disgracefully few opportunities in those days.

The technique of *What the Papers Say* was to use the smallest studio and three cameras, one pointed at the presenter, the other two at two easels bearing caption cards. As soon as a caption cleared – the PA intoning a litany in the gallery, 'Twenty-one on two,' 'Twenty-three on three,' 'Twenty-five on two,' 'Twenty-seven on three' – stage hands whipped it off the stand, exposing the next. The director cut either to the next caption, if one ran into another, or back to the presenter, whose next utterance gave time to ready the next caption. At least, that was the theory.

What the Papers Say went out live. Any error made was immediately evident on air. We had rehearsed and timed the script, of course, but still, as the minutes and seconds of transmission ticked away, the PA counting down, there was concern in the gallery whether we'd get out on time. If there was a doubt, the director would kill the credits, going straight to the Granada caption. When this happened it distressed my mother, who watched transmissions like a hawk. Even if my name appeared she would sometimes remark that 'Producer: Jeremy Isaacs' had not been up for as long as usual; was I all right?

The director who did more editions of *What the Papers Say* than anyone else was Peter Mullings, a stickler for detail who used cheerfully to say, 'I'm the sort of person who, if you ask me the time, will tell you how a clock works.' In the gallery, he stuck to the point. The director who first held a beginner's hand, and then became a loved guide and mentor, was Mike Wooller, who had an eye for design that could find full expression only in a more demanding show. He was nevertheless a superb director for us because he so enjoyed getting it right, live. As our partnership progressed, I became aware that he positively relished making transmission more exciting by cramming in yet more shots. This was done not by complicating what the presenter had to do – he might proceed at just as stately a pace – nor by adding irrelevant visuals, but by including the headline as a separate shot, or breaking a paragraph into three shorter captions. Carrying eighty captions, we were up to ten shots a minute; Mike Wooller never missed a beat.

Just how good he was, and how fortunate I was, I realised later, after videotape was introduced and video-recording permitted to us. The Bernsteins were painfully aware of profligacy in the film industry caused by retakes, and for years set their face against the use of film in what was a live medium. When videotape was introduced, they were against our being allowed to edit. If you were pre-recording a show on video, and something went wrong, you were supposed to accept the error and crack on, as if live. Few with any pride in their work were happy to agree. If we really did need to go again, we must first get permission from an executive director of the company.

One week I had flu and simply could not get to the studio. On this occasion the programme was to be recorded not in Manchester, but in Studio 10, the old Chelsea Palace music hall in the King's Road. (There Granada's classy variety show *Chelsea at Nine* was put together. On air, the announcer would declaim: 'It's half-past eight. From the North, Granada presents *Chelsea at Nine*.') It was to be directed by an experienced hand, a Canadian called Max Morgan-Witts.

The presenter that evening was making his debut: Jocelyn Stevens, proprietor and editor of *Queen* magazine. I had helped him prepare his script before retiring to my sick-bed. At ten-thirty on the Thursday evening I hauled myself out of bed, put on a dressing-gown and got ready to watch the programme. At first all went well; Jocelyn looked his useful ebullient self. Then, a very loud crash, followed by visual chaos. A caption stand had fallen over, spilling its contents. What Jocelyn was saying no longer related in any way to the visuals we saw on the screen; unintelligible tosh continued until the end. Had this really been live, I could have borne it. What could anyone have done to restore synchronicity? Nothing. But the programme had been recorded, dammit. They could have stopped, and started again. Jocelyn was able to go home to watch himself on screen, which normally he couldn't have done. 'Is it always like this?' he asked. But his cleaning lady enjoyed having him in her living room. What did he think of her new curtains? she wanted to know. She had put them up specially.

Brian Inglis was the most dependable of the regular presenters, not only prompt in writing a script, but a quiet joy to work with. His calm reticence on screen, verging on anonymity, prolonged his career. He poked fun, or expressed scepticism, with an eyebrow. When I was stuck, over a bank holiday weekend, he would come to the rescue – indeed, he became a bank holiday specialist, relishing the contrast between what holidaymakers hoped for and what they got: foul weather, traffic jams, mods-and-rockers' punch-ups on the beach. Once I teased him at the read-through by putting last year's bank holiday script on the teleprompt. He was halfway through it before he realised.

One Easter, with no one yet booked to do the show on Thursday, I was saved by a beginner. As the Aldermaston march, calling for nuclear disarmament, was nearing Trafalgar Square on Easter Monday 1960, Ronald Segal, Editor of *Africa South* and a cogent and outspoken critic of apartheid, arrived by air in London. I had read *Africa South* and knew from Tamara what an eloquent fellow Ronald was. I made contact and asked him to do the programme, clearing this *fait accompli* with the Bernsteins later.

Ronald, who had never been in a television studio before, was very good. Characteristically, he inverted one of the programme's most cherished nostrums, its scornful highlighting of discrepancies. A huge crowd had gathered on Easter Monday at Trafalgar Square, and, sure enough, estimates of the numbers differed considerably. The *Daily Mail*, against CND, thought 30,000; the *News Chronicle*, for unilateral disarmament, claimed 250,000. Everyone else was for something in between. Ronald Segal did not take the obvious point. Instead, he was glad to note these divergences; for in South Africa, from which, an exile, he'd just departed – or, more accurately, escaped – there would have been no discrepancy. The South African press, Nationalist or Liberal, Afrikaans or English, would most probably all have based their stories on one report from the South African Press Agency, quoting one official tally, the police estimate. He preferred variety.

But Segal's eager manner did not go down well. He had given the impression of being committed, a touch frenetic; I was not to use him again. The same veto dented the prospects of another talent I introduced, and used once only: Clement Freud. Clement, omnivorous in his appetites, was a glutton for sport, on which he reported for the *Financial Times*. Back in 1954 he'd tipped off Tim Hewat at the *Daily Express* to send a reporter to Iffley Road, Oxford, to see Roger Bannister become the first man in history to run a mile in under four minutes. (Later that evening, at the Oxford Union Society, I moved, on a point of procedure, that 'This House adjourn for a token period of three minutes, fifty-nine point four seconds, in tribute to this historic achievement.' The President did not know what I was talking about. The house insisted. It made a paragraph on the front of the *Express*.) Clement Freud also loved to gamble. The week he was to cover for *Papers* included the first Saturday of the football season. Here, he proposed, was an opportunity to have some fun. In those days popular newspapers set enormous store by the service they provided punters, tipping results for the football pools: 'The *Daily Blah* has the best pools tipster in Britain'; 'For pools' pointers, choose the *Beast*', etc. Clement's idea was to report what they forecast and compare that with the results. To win the pools, you need to forecast draws; the fewer there are, the higher the dividend. Twelve or thirteen draws, correctly forecast, might win you a fortune. But draws were usually hard to find. Fate played into our hands. On that first Saturday of the season, there were far more draws than usual, and far, far more than anyone had forecast. Not only that, but all the matches the tipsters forecast as likely draws had ended in clear-cut victories; and, although so numerous, none of the actual draws had been forecast by any of the tipsters. It was a wipe-out – Tipsters, Nil. What made this contretemps memorable, however, was a twist in our presentation. When football results are given, even today, there's a notable change of intonation on the announcer's part according to whether it's a home win, an away win, or a draw. We announced the victories as if they were draws. This is not easy; it's like rubbing one hand across your stomach while passing the other in a circle round your head. I'm not sure, though, how many viewers saw the joke.

Too much attention was paid in those days to what people looked like on screen. It helped to be good-looking, or at least inoffensively nondescript, or at any rate not peculiar. Clement Freud looked like a mournful spaniel, begging for a bone. (Indeed, he later earned a fortune from this impersonation.) But it was one facial too far for Sidney's brother, Cecil Bernstein, who commented that Freud had looked strange, even frightening. We should remember that our programmes were watched by older people, some of a nervous disposition.

I could never take Cecil's strictures of this sort to heart. He had once supervised a programme I did in London for Christmas transmission, in which we visited, in their homes, old people who would be alone over Christmas. The research was sound; the results, shocking. The conditions in which these isolated and impoverished pensioners lived were filthy, smelly, cramped, utterly deplorable. In one room, the stench was such that the cameraman vomited on the stairs. The old folk told us how they got by from one Christmas to the next. I thought the point well made to the rest of us, tucking into turkey, exchanging presents. Cecil, who in fact was a thoughtful and kindly soul, nevertheless had a view as to what constituted suitable family viewing: 'I would not have wanted any of those old people in my home over Christmas.'

Working with Clement Freud, even once only, was an extraordinary experience. Clement came into Golden Square, as pre-arranged, on the Wednesday afternoon to write his script. He finished by six o'clock. 'What are you doing, Clement,' I asked, 'between now and your coming to Manchester? I may need to talk to you when we've seen tomorrow's papers.' He was going first, he told me, to a tobacconist's shop he owned near the British Museum; then to the Open Air Theatre at Regent's Park, where he had the catering concession; then to the nightclub he owned and managed in Sloane Square above the Royal Court Theatre; then he would drive to the studios of Southern Television in Southampton, and perhaps get a couple of hours' sleep before starting rehearsals for a cookery programme he presented there, recording it by midday. He would then drive to Heathrow and fly to Manchester, arriving in time to rehearse *Papers* in the early evening.

We agreed I'd telephone him in Southampton between the dress rehearsal and the recording of the cookery show.

Taking all this in his stride, he turned up in Quay Street, rehearsed, and then – first time he'd ever done it – presented a tricky *What the Papers Say* live. After the programme ended at 11 p.m., we had supper at the Midland Hotel. At this point the ego, or perhaps the strains and tension of the day, began to tell. In the role of gourmet and wine connoisseur, Clement became noisily critical of the kitchen, the food, the service. Well after midnight, he demanded vintage port, not a glass or two but a half-bottle ordered from the list. The bottle was encrusted by age, and the waiter could not get the cork out. 'Let me do it,' said Clement, 'as it should be done.' Wrapping a napkin round his hand, he karate-chopped the neck of the bottle, breaking it cleanly. We drank.

To bed? No. 'Where is the action in this town?' he demanded at the hall porter's desk. Mesmerised, I went with him by taxi to a gambling saloon where, to our surprise, the clientele wore Wild West gear – high boots, frilled shirts and Stetsons. Freud won £25, and we left. There was no taxi. We walked back to the Midland.

'How do you keep up this pace?' I asked. 'And why? How long will you go on like this?'

'I want to be famous,' he replied. 'I want my face to be as well known as Eamonn Andrews's.'

He left a call with the night porter for 6 a.m.; he would catch the first plane south in the morning.

The most frightening image I was responsible for on *What the Papers Say* was of Bernard Levin, in close-up, with his eyes crossed. We did it while at Blackpool in 1961 for the Labour Party conference. I was staying at the Norbreck Hydro, not the best hotel in the world – there were notices in bedrooms saying 'Guests are forbidden to use the windows as a means of egress.' The high point of the conference would be the debate on Europe.

We rehearsed.

'Bernard, you say: "There are some people here in Blackpool for joining Europe; and some here against." And you gesture to either side.'

'Yes.'

'"There are some sitting on the fence looking this way, and some sitting on the fence looking that way." And you gesture again.'

'Yes.'

'And then you say, "There are some sitting on the fence looking both ways."'

'Yes.'

'Bernard, when you say that, could you possibly cross your eyes?'

'Like this, you mean?'

'Aaaagh!'

Old ladies wrote to complain.

There was something special about doing *Papers* not in the

Manchester studio but as an outside broadcast. Harry Evans, then Editor of the *Northern Echo*, did it live, in the open air outside the town hall, when we had cameras there for a by-election at Stockton. He was good. And Henry Fairlie did the programme from Scarborough, during the Labour Party conference of 1960 when Gaitskell, losing the vote against the left and unilateralist nuclear disarmers, pledged himself to 'fight and fight and fight again, to save the party we love'. I had urged that, in addition to broadcasting the entire event live as part of our normal conference coverage, we should put out an hour of edited highlights at peak time. This was agreed. The rest of the ITV network would never take it, of course. Granada would go it alone. Early on the Wednesday morning I went over the moors to Manchester to ready an hour of excerpts for transmission at eight o'clock.

The debate was of riveting quality; there were so many speeches that counted, so much high drama, I was spoilt for choice. With minutes to spare, we got to air. After supper we were driven, drained and exhausted, through mist and fog, slowly back to Scarborough. Henry Fairlie had promised the script for *Papers* would be ready when I returned. At three in the morning, I knocked on the door of the Royal Hotel. When the night porter opened to us, there, lying on the floor of the lobby, was Henry, asleep. There was no script. He went off to his lodgings, saying he'd make an early start on the next day's papers. Henry was quite right not to have started; there was nothing to say about the conference until, the debate over, the next day's copy was written and in print.

The press of which *Papers* then offered a critique was a richer mess of pottage than today's. *The Times* was then a paper of record. The *Guardian* was the *Manchester Guardian*; the *Herald*, the *Glasgow Herald*. The *Sunday Dispatch*, which serialised *Forever Amber*, the *Sunday Pictorial* and *Reynolds News* were still with us; so was the *Daily Sketch*, living down its proprietor's pre-war flirtation with Mosley's Blackshirts. The *News Chronicle*'s liberal light still glowed; it went out in October 1960. Over at Odhams, the

Daily Herald's Labour readership aged, and died off. Then the *Daily Herald* died too. Euthanasia was arranged for a Saturday. The same staff who produced the paper on the Friday night had one day off only before coming in again on the Sunday to give birth to its successor, which rose next day: the *Sun*, still a broadsheet. Odhams could not make that work, even with Hugh Cudlipp in charge. The *Sun* was later sold to Rupert Murdoch. The *Sunday Telegraph* arrived in February 1961.

Glasgow, in those days, had three evening papers: *Times, Citizen, News*; London three also: *Standard, News, Star*. Roy Thomson bought the staid, right-wing *Sunday Times* from Lord Kemsley. On my watch one week a new banner proclaimed: '*The Sunday Times* is an independent newspaper of the centre.' On *Papers*, Brian Inglis commented, 'Lord Kemsley must be turning in his grave.' Lord Kemsley in fact was watching television in the south of England. We grovelled.

Newspaper production was a bastion of union restrictive practices. Complacent managements were too frightened to take them on: stoppages meant lost sales. The proprietors' association kept paying Danegeld. The wealthier papers could afford it; the poorer could not. The *Economist*, in a famous study, denounced the inefficiencies of Fleet Street. We varied our usual format to interview Max Aitken, owner of the *Daily Express*. The Granada crew crammed into a boardroom at the art-deco Black Lubianka.

'How do you justify the over-manning?' we asked.

'Before I answer that question,' said Aitken, 'I'll count the number of people in this room.'

We were two on camera, two on sound, a couple of sparks, an interviewer, a director, a researcher, a production assistant, and a producer. *Touché*. The coming reckoning for ITV was far ahead.

There was much to admire in newspapers at that time. The broadsheets maintained a clear distinction between news given straight on news pages, and opinion on editorial pages. Their features dealt with large matters of political and social interest, unobsessed by the cult of celebrity, disdaining synthetic yelps of mob fury or outrage. The family newspapers – the *Daily Mail*, the *Express*, the *News Chronicle*, the *Daily Herald*, prided themselves on their foreign coverage. Many newspapers maintained correspondents in Paris and Bonn and Washington. They sent star reporters to trouble spots. Radio and television were not yet the nation's prime source of news. Newspapers were.

In the popular papers in those days there was, I think, less personality-oriented trivia and less malice. The *News of the World* – All Human Life Is There – reported sexual peccadilloes through meticulous court reporting, as the *Daily Telegraph* did in divorce cases. The *People* got up to all sorts of tricks, its reporters exposing prostitution rackets in Soho – 'I made an excuse, and left.' (I never read a story by a reporter who stayed.) Murray Sayle, in an hilarious Fleet Street novel, *A Crooked Sixpence*, told of his exploits on the *People*, exposing vice and interviewing murderers' families before they hanged. It was too close to the knuckle for the Editor, Sam Campbell. An injunction was sought, and *A Crooked Sixpence* withdrawn from sale. But newspapers did not routinely pay people for their stories then; there was little kiss and sell. And they did not stake out, set up and denounce footballers or politicians cheating on their wives as assiduously as they do today. When Lord Denning reported on the Profumo affair, no one named in print, or went into overdrive to identify, other ministers and MPs around whose ankles scandal lapped. Brothel-keepers were fair game. Others' lives, and lifestyles, stayed private.

The paper that interested me most was the *Daily Mirror*, as Harold Wilson, promising to introduce the white heat of new technology, got after the Tories. Left of centre, edited by Hugh Cudlipp with force and flair and wit, the *Mirror* at the beginning of the 1960s had a circulation of nearly 5 million, the highest daily sale in the world. It was written in a manner George Orwell might have admired: simply, pithily, clearly. Editorial opinion was delivered crisply. Occasionally the *Mirror* would crusade for a cause with a shock issue, successive pages using big black-and-white photographs and bold print to drive a social message home. But the staple of the paper conveyed information, intelligibly and entertainingly. The Political Editor, Sidney Jacobson, led an attempt to interest *Mirror* readers in foreign affairs. This began boldly, and was kept up for a while. Then, day by day, the space allotted dwindled. Within a few months 'Foreign Spotlight' had vanished. I grieved to note the *Mirror* drawing in its horns. Ahead lay the ferocious competition afforded by Murdoch's new *Sun*. But the *Mirror* set an example that counted. If it tackled big subjects in simple images and prose, reaching audiences of millions, so could we.

It was Cudlipp's front-page splashes I most enjoyed. No one else used print alone to fill the page as he did, making it almost an art form; today, he might have won the Turner Prize. When Nikita Khrushchev, complaining of the US's overflying Soviet airspace, abusively disrupted his Paris summit with Eisenhower in May 1960, the *Mirror*'s front page had this:

That year we launched what became the annual *What the Papers Say* awards. On the back of its serious, inventive exuberance, and citing particularly the Paris summit front page, Henry Fairlie announced that the *Daily Mirror* was our Newspaper of the Year. The *Daily Mail* was not amused. Henry, who had an aversion to abroad, had been due to report on the summit for the *Mail*. He drew the expenses, but did not go. Looking at Fleet Street from the outside, I knew nothing of this fracas, and did not feel very clever when it was pointed out.

Producing *What the Papers Say*, however pocket-sized a pro- gramme, brought me into regular contact with the men who had charge and oversight of Granada's output: Denis Forman, one level up, and then, over him, Cecil and Sidney Bernstein. There were no hierarchies at Granada. Or rather, there was only one hierarchy: at the top, the Bernsteins; below them, everybody else. I was new, as junior as could be; yet I answered directly to the owner and pro- prietor, Sidney Bernstein, submitting the *Papers* script for approval to Denis only if neither Bernstein was there. Denis always saw the script, but would never express a view of it if Sidney was around. It took time, therefore, to get broadcast clearance; this made Thursday afternoons tenser than they need have been.

When Sidney read the script, he would often propose quite minor changes, but what he commented on more than anything else was the way the actors read the extracts we quoted. They were always too mannered for his taste, always over-acting. He would ring late, after transmission, to give me his notes to this effect, urging me to employ some distinguished directorial figure to put this glaring weakness right. But talented directors of major drama had quite enough on their plates.

Another obsession of Sidney's was Orson Welles; why didn't I get him to present *Papers*? The fact that he was in Los Angeles or New York or Paris at the time never deterred Sidney from press- ing this on me – indeed, if Orson was in Paris, he said, he might easily come over. It never occurred to him that Orson was far too big a beast to perform in this little patch of the jungle, and that, however much I urged or pleaded, he would not come. I ignored Sidney's suggestion, but sometimes could not, day after vital day, get permission to use another presenter instead. More than one was drafted in as late as Wednesday evening to get the programme out of the hole.

Sidney Bernstein was a litigious man, often engaged in costly legal skirmishing with one newspaper group or another, usually Beaverbrook's *Express*. There was no explicit written instruction not to comment on this or that, just a general injunction to be careful. I was expected, on Thursday afternoons, to read the *Papers* script over the phone to the lawyer who advised on these matters, Arnold Goodman, who would say: 'You may broadcast all of that,' or 'No, you may not include that,' or 'You may broadcast that, but there is risk attached. It is Mr Bernstein's decision.' In this last case, I would enquire, 'How much of a risk?' He would say, 'Perhaps a one in four chance that the *Express* will sue.'

This I would report to Sidney. More than once, he said, 'Go ahead.'

On one occasion, Arnold Goodman said: 'You may not broadcast any of that. If you have evidence to support the allegations you make in this script, you must take them at once to the police. It is your duty to do so.'

In February 1962 James Hanratty was sentenced to death at Bedford Assizes for the 'A6 murder': the killing of Michael Gregsten and the rape and shooting of his lover Valerie Storie, which left her paralysed for life. The crimes were committed in a layby on the A6, but began in a cornfield in Buckinghamshire when a gunman tapped on the window of a car in which Gregsten and Storie were making love. At first Valerie Storie identified another suspect, Peter Louis Alphon, as Gregsten's killer – he seemed to fit the description she first gave the police. Later, however, she positively identified Hanratty, and stuck to that throughout the trial. Hanratty was hanged in April.

In an article the *Observer* published after the conviction, Louis Blom-Cooper, while not disputing the verdict, argued that the trial never even asked key questions which a different sort of inquiry would have interested itself in. How was it that a petty urban criminal, who had never used a gun, came to be in the field, tap on the window of a closed motor-car and enter, with horrific consequences, the lives of people he had never met? Who sent the murderer to the cornfield? A French murder inquiry would have sought an answer; we did not. I asked my colleague Alex Valentine to consider what else the papers were saying about the A6 murder case, and report what he could find.

I lived then at Swiss Cottage, where several characters in the case lived also, and where newspapers reported unexplained sightings of a 'man with staring eyes', later claimed to be Hanratty. One of those sightings was through the window of a bric-a-brac shop in the arcade of Swiss Cottage tube station, two hundred yards from my home. Two days later, Alex Valentine was back. The woman said to have 'recognised' Hanratty through the antique-shop window was Janet Gregsten, the widow of the murdered man; the shop belonged to her brother-in-law William Ewer, who dealt there in secondhand goods. Was this the link with the murderer's presence in the cornfield? Valentine and I put together a *What the Papers Say* script that incorporated Blom-Cooper's questions. It was this that Arnold Goodman vetoed. Page after page was discarded; only a ghostly outline remained.

Partly because those questions went unanswered, partly because the other suspect, Alphon – for reasons not clear – more than once 'confessed' to the A6 crimes, partly because of contradictions and anomalies in the police investigation, journalistic interest in the subject lasted more than forty years. The journalist Paul Foot campaigned for Hanratty's innocence in an important book on the case and acted as consultant to an investigation for the BBC's *Panorama*, which found some corroboration for a last-minute alibi Hanratty put forward at his trial, surprising his own counsel; this put him in Rhyl, rather than on the A6, on the fatal night. The jury did not believe the alibi. Libel laws being what they are, Blom-Cooper's questions are still unanswered. The campaign to clear Hanratty has only recently been finally undermined by DNA evidence. The Hanratty family insisted on the tests in the belief the results would attest his innocence; they showed the opposite.

What the Papers Say was never a heavyweight critic of the press. It sought to inform, and to entertain. Michael Frayn poked fun at the use newspapers made of pictures, pointing, for example, to the *Guardian*'s regular welcome to a new cricket season: empty benches at Lord's. Malcolm Muggeridge professed himself enthralled by the *Times* court page: 'How fascinating to learn that the Duke of Gloucester, Colonel-in-Chief, took the salute at a regimental parade; how equally fascinating to know that he lunched in the officers' mess afterwards.' Granada presented the annual *What the Papers Say* awards at lunches at the Savoy. The menu paid its own tribute to Granadaland: Morecambe Bay shrimps, Lancashire hot-pot, Wensleydale cheese.

3

ONE OF THE FAMILY

Tamara's labour was long, arduous, exhausting: late in August 1960, at the old Charing Cross Hospital, John Daniel was born. Cecil Bernstein wished me 'Mazeltov' and, as we toasted the new arrival, assured me that fatherhood changed everything. I was part of the Granada family. But did I want to be?

Denis Forman had oversight of programmes I might expect to work on. Drama was Sidney's brief; entertainment, Cecil's. Denis, not yet heir apparent to it all, played a waiting game. The Bernsteins, second-guessing him, had imported from Canada an alternative, Stu Griffiths, to whom I was at once introduced. At our first meeting he gave me good advice: 'This is a frustrating business. When you get angry, let it out. Scream. Whatever you do, don't bottle it up; it can kill you otherwise.' Griffiths did not stay long. I screamed a bit, in my time.

Granada picked well; the corridors were hoaching with talent. On my floor, at the far end, there were three screen promotion writers: Geoff Lancashire, who would write comedy series, like *Pardon the Expression* and *The Lovers*; Tony Warren, who invented *Coronation Street*; Jack Rosenthal, who would write *Evacuees, Bar*

Mitzvah Boy and other lyrical, bittersweet joys. Older stagers attended programme meetings – Milton Shulman, Philip Mackie, Peter Wildeblood and Derek Granger: each someone for a novice to look up to.

Derek Granger entered the researchers' office like a Dior model coming to a suburban sewing circle. Tanned and tailored, he plonked a vase of roses on a shared table cluttered with telephones and placed a call to Cecil Beaton. He had been drama critic on the *Financial Times*, dictating fifteen hundred words from a telephone box in Sloane Square, it was said, after the first night of *Look Back in Anger*. He was a typical Sidney signing; he knew nothing of television, but oozed promise. He was at once impishly bold in his judgements. Before very long he took over as producer of *Coronation Street* and was formidably good at it, keeping it taut and unsentimental. With aplomb, he presented *Cinema*. He devised and produced *Country Matters*, assemblies of stories by A. E. Coppard and H. E. Bates which I thought the best of their kind. He brought to the screen, after the stormiest of stormy passages, *Brideshead Revisited*. Whatever he did, Derek buzzed and lifted spirits.

Philip Mackie had been recruited by Denis Forman, like him a veteran of the Second World War Italian campaign and of film documentary. Titles were hard to come by at Granada – there were no controllers or directors – but Philip was reckoned to be head of plays. Or he would have been if Sidney wasn't determined to be head of plays himself, choosing or vetoing choice, authorising budgets, interfering in casting, generally buggering Philip about. He would telephone constantly: 'How can I help?' Philip couldn't stand it, and at last mustered the courage to say, 'You can help best by leaving me alone.' Then Sidney would ring to say, 'Philip, you'll notice I'm leaving you alone.'* Philip left Granada to write, which anyway was his métier. He came up with

*For a fuller account of this see *Persona Granada* by Denis Forman.

and perfected the notion of adapting short stories for the screen – de Maupassant or D. H. Lawrence – and fitting two, or even three of them into one television hour. For Granada he wrote *The Caesars*. For Yorkshire Television he wrote *The Organisation*, an acerbic study of the workings of a company not unlike Granada. And for the short-lived Granada Films he wrote *The Naked Civil Servant*, which everyone else turned down but which, when Verity Lambert brought it to me at Thames, I recognised instantly as something we must do.

Philip found Sidney's interventions harder to take than most did, perhaps because, as producer, he himself ruled with a featherweight touch. I bumped into him once outside the studio in that anxious hour between dress rehearsal and live transmission, when cameras lined up. Philip was calculating what notes he could usefully give the director before the red light came on. He would give very few. 'It's up to him now,' he told me, 'out of my hands.'

Milton Shulman, a Canadian, had caught Beaverbrook's eye with an account of the campaign that ended the Second World War in the West. He caught Sidney's, I suppose, as film critic of the *Evening Standard*. Milton had various tasks, but always exhibited an air of transatlantic experience which made his opinions seem worth attending to, and a slight self-importance which invited joshing. Like Philip, though, Milton refused to take Sidney or Cecil too seriously. His irreverence appealed. He said Cecil had once remarked to him, admiringly, on a film director's attention to detail: the inside of a hatband, within the crown, just visible on screen, was spotlessly clean. This, Cecil thought, made it a good movie.

Granada had an arrangement with London Zoo and its clever director, Desmond Morris, to present *Zoo Time*. An outside broadcast unit was assigned to the zoo; Milton Shulman presided. The broadcasts were popular with children, particularly if they featured a cuddly new arrival – a lion cub or baby polar bear. But Granada always had an eye for economy. After the use of videotape was sanctioned, someone must have realised that an earlier year's *Zoo Times* could well be shown again, particularly if the unit was now needed elsewhere. This led to small Londoners beseeching their parents to be taken at the weekend to see the new arrival. 'Where is Samba?' they would clamour. The keeper would point to a grizzled adult lion: 'That's him over there.' Desmond Morris encouraged a chimpanzee, Congo, to paint; his work hung at Granada's offices in Golden Square, beside Hitchens and Rouault. Congo drew attention to the possibility that abstract expressionism might not be a human invention.

Milton Shulman produced a short weekly programme that bit, and helped shore up Granada's commitment to political impartiality. Three commentators would answer questions on the issues of the day, not in debate, but each addressing the camera and the viewer, scripted, uninterrupted. The three might be Dick Crossman, Charles Curran, Malcolm Muggeridge. Watching this, I always thought how effective speech direct to camera could be.

Milton created another format I much admired. He had the idea of taking a subject, recording opinions of his conduct and character that might never have been expressed to his face, and confronting the heroic victim with what others thought of him. The willing subject would need a thick skin; for the pilot programme, Milton chose Randolph Churchill. He invited me to view it, and was much put out when I opened a notebook and on a blank page wrote 'Faults'. He need not have been huffy; the programme was riveting. Randolph Churchill was a bully, picking on those who found it hard to answer back – taxi drivers, railway attendants, waiters. Now they had their chance to have a go at him, together with Randolph's grand White's Club friends; Lord Stanley of Alderney was particularly frank. Randolph was robust in reply. The programme had no successors. Milton could not persuade others to play. Today, they might be queuing up.

The man who in those years had most influence on me was a brash and ebullient, sharp and domineering, New Zealand-born Australian journalist, Tim Hewat. In Fleet Street he had been

Night Editor of the then flourishing *Daily Express*. It was in response to his brief that Mike Wooller created a look for *Searchlight*. Light came from darkness, as spots lit an image or a graphic on hung caption cards, or picked out in close-up the features of Kenneth Allsop or Bill Grundy punching out the terse text. This was a far cry from loose studio discussion. Without Hewat, there would not have been a *Searchlight*, and probably not a *World in Action* either.

Tim's wife Mary, a Canadian journalist, had been my first contact at Granada. I did not know, and I think then she did not know – if she did, she did not say – that she was suffering from a brain tumour, which not much later killed her. Tim was shattered at her death. Hard drinking deadened the pain only slightly; work would do most of the rest, and he hurled himself into it.

In factual programming, he sought to grab the viewer's attention by any means to hand. For a *Searchlight* on road accident fatalities, 'Slaughter in the Avenue', he closed a broad, tree-lined roadway in north London suburbia and lined it with the impersonated corpses of the slain. In these shows he used film as stills. Writing commentary, battering away at the typewriter as editing proceeded, he would hold out his hands like an angler measuring one that got away, and demand: 'Give me this much of traffic.' Subtle it was not.

In the freezing winter of 1960, when Siberian blizzards swept northern Europe, there was an outbreak of anti-semitic, neo-Nazi incidents in West Germany. The incidents were minor enough individually, but fairly widespread. Was this a Nazi revival? The newspapers wanted to know. For Sidney Bernstein, who had sent Alfred Hitchcock to Belsen to ensure a record was made of Nazi atrocity, this was not an issue to ignore. Hewat took charge. Mike Wooller and I went to Germany. Neither of us spoke German.

To smoothe our path, and guarantee access to the German right, Hewat sent with us Sefton ('Tom') Delmer, the *Daily Express*'s crack pre-war Berlin correspondent, and during the war, with Dick Crossman and Hugh Carleton Greene, a member of the unit that broadcast black propaganda to Germany. Delmer, now retired (getting by, he told me, on stingy Beaverbrook severance pay), welcomed the assignment. He and I took the train at Liverpool Street and went over from Harwich on the night ferry. Next morning, at the Hook of Holland, the great trains were lined up for Hamburg, for Munich and Vienna, for Basle and Milan. We went to Düsseldorf, on the Rhine; rooms awaited us at the Breidenbacher Hof.

A chauffeur-driven Mercedes, at vast cost per kilometre, conveyed us to Cologne to talk to the writer Hans Magnus Enzenberger. We had no lights, so the interview had to be done in the open air; I have never been so cold. We went south, to an inn at Bad Godesberg, to interview Adolf von Thadden, future head of the National-demokratische Partei Deutschlands, the NPD. To Delmer, it was obvious that the subject of our story should be entertained with due ceremony. 'Landlord, your best bottle!' he cried. Otto Skorzeny, the commando whom Hitler sent to parachute in and rescue Mussolini, turned up in the hotel. There too, gingerly, I took the hand of Emmy, widow of Baldur von Schirach, the leader of Hitler Youth who had been tried at Nuremberg and executed. Delmer had known where to find her. Her forearms were punctured and patterned by the pricking of needles.

On this trip Tom Delmer told me that in Berlin in February 1933 his Nazi contacts – he was close to Goebbels – tipped him off to go quickly to the Reichstag as it went up in flames. Whom should he see there but Adolf Hitler, gloating over what may have been the Nazi party's own handiwork (and was certainly to the Nazis' advantage). Delmer telephoned a description to the *Daily Express*, advising that it was front-page stuff. 'No, no, Tom,' was the response. 'Not another fire. We've had two this week already.'

Von Thadden came to very little; the NPD later won seats in the Bavarian regional parliament, but failed nationally. No subsequent prediction of a neo-Nazi renaissance has been realised.

The sense that Granada's current affairs programmes had points to make was giving the regulatory body, the ITA, concern. The Act insisted that, in treating matters of current political or industrial controversy, each and every programme exhibit due impartiality. Did Granada's? Did *Searchlight*? When Granada applied for a franchise, and looked likely to succeed, some Conservatives protested to the ITA that Sidney Bernstein was too left-wing to hold a licence. The ITA Chairman, Sir Kenneth Clark, fended them off, saying that if it could be demonstrated that Sidney was a paid-up, card-carrying communist – which perhaps is what they were alleging – he would deny him the franchise; if not, not. Granada got its licence; after all, it was quite clear what Associated Newspapers' politics were, and they had half – until they panicked and sold – of Associated-Rediffusion. The notion that franchise-holders could be found who would have no politics proved an illusion; the question was not what they privately or publicly believed, but how they conducted themselves. Yet there remained a problem with the Act. Total impartiality in any one programme was hard to achieve; striving to achieve it militated against vivid, lively programming. On honesty and accuracy we were all determined. But balance, as often as not, made for dull viewing.

If treatment of a controversial theme meant evenly balanced studio discussion, then there was no great difficulty. The BBC had once mounted a lucid debate on capital punishment, pre-filmed and meticulously edited, by alternating and juxtaposing arguments from either side. This enabled viewers to see their own prejudices confirmed, or perhaps confounded; the undecided might make up their minds for themselves. It was possible, therefore, but far from easy; no broadcaster, no newspaper certainly, could ever suppose this was the only way to proceed.

With only a small number of channels available to the viewer, no one took the view that any proprietor should be permitted to propagate one political point of view, or social stance or attitude. It might have been argued that, since ITV's roof sheltered several proprietors, of different persuasions, each should be allowed his own utterance within a balanced whole. But this was never the intention; the Act was framed to quite different effect, and rightly so. That still left the problem of how any one simple short programme, a single commentator on *What the Papers Say*, or a *Searchlight* tackling critically a single aspect of the social scene – congested roads, overcrowded classrooms, hospitals in disrepair – could achieve impartiality, particularly if, reaching out to audiences of millions, it proposed a simple message and put it in simple terms.

After one *Searchlight* series, the ITA's Director General, Sir Robert Fraser, read us the riot act. Informally, in a private room at Scott's Restaurant and Oyster Bar in Piccadilly, Fraser told the *Searchlight* team that, in his view, every episode of the series was in breach of the Act, with the possible exception of a programme on cruelty to children; even then, he wasn't sure that we should not have had someone say, 'Cruelty to children is a good thing.' This seemed to me to point more to the absurdities of a flawed Act than to *Searchlight*'s failing. It may not have been intended literally, but that is how the position was formally, repeatedly stated.

I produced a *Searchlight* on hospitals which illustrated the difficulty. No new hospital had been built in Britain since the Second World War; many were then, as some still are, of Victorian origin. The first problem was to gain access for a camera crew. No one would have us. It was not that hospital boards and health authorities were not aware of the situation, or that they were opposed to our shining a *Searchlight* on an eye-catching example. But not, please, on their premises, because of the effect this might have on the morale of patients and families. We pleaded in vain. Then one health authority found a way to help us. There was a newly built hospital, ready for use but not yet open, the Princess Margaret Hospital at Swindon. If we would film that, Thames Valley would grant us entry also to Amersham General Hospital, which consisted of Nissen huts and ancient almshouses.

Amersham General was a good, even a very good hospital:

but its buildings were a disgrace. Converted military Nissen huts housed the surgical and medical wards; geriatric patients were kept in the almshouses, where the stairs to the first floor turned so sharply that patients could not be carried on stretchers in case they were tipped out; they went up sitting in chairs. There were no lifts. The beds were eighteen inches apart. Elsewhere in the hospital there was an operating theatre, but no recovery room; after an operation, patients were wheeled from theatre straight out into the open air – there were paved and covered walkways – back to the wards. Amersham General Hospital's excellence was owed to the staff who, in these unpropitious conditions, did out-standing work. One specialist, a paediatrician called Dermod MacCarthy (brother of the literary critic Desmond MacCarthy), provided spaces in his Nissen huts where parents of sick children could be close to them overnight, at critical phases of their illness. This was wholly innovative, best practice in Britain.

Our film showed all this, and the glittering, still empty Princess Margaret Hospital at Swindon; but we were not allowed to broad-cast it without a stilted contribution from the Minister for Health, who assured viewers that a major new building programme about to be undertaken would alter everything.

More than a decade later I received a circular appeal from the Friends of Amersham General Hospital. They urgently sought funds for a building programme to alleviate the grim conditions in which the staff worked; they needed to provide a recovery room, and to install lifts for geriatric patients in the almshouses. So much for the power of the media.

Tim Hewat was a role model in more than one way. 'Anything in them?' he'd ask each morning of the newspapers. 'Anything for us?' However hard he played outside, in the office only the task in hand mattered; politeness, paperwork, the proprieties of rank, he swept wholly aside. He never wrote memos, or answered them; bureaucracy was the enemy, as were the authorities. What mat-tered, first and last, was the story. And then the next one. If you worked with him, you worked for him and for a cause, willingly, flat out, day and night, seven days a week.

As a former Fleet Street night editor, in effect in charge of getting out the paper, he was an expert in production techniques. Television was in its infancy and techniques were changing fast; this was true of tape in the studio, and of film outside. With part of their business brains the Bernstein brothers feared, and wished to postpone, change; particularly they feared film. Sidney, after all, as well as owning cinemas, had more than dabbled in film production. He had produced several movies Hitchcock made in Britain, and went with him to Hollywood. That had not worked out, and he soon came back. He and Cecil knew one thing about filming: it could be expensive. In the earliest days at Granada the use of film was banned. But news needed film; the film camera had its role to play in current affairs. The next question was: which camera?

The newsreels had used 35mm cameras, heavy and cumbersome; picture quality was high, processing costly. Would 16mm deliver a sharp enough image to register on a domestic TV receiver, the ill-adjusted box in the living-room corner? It would be cheaper; but 35mm buffs poured scorn on 16mm: simply not good enough, they said. Hewat investigated. He talked to Sydney Samuelson, whose family business was film equipment hire. Samuelson rented out cameras to movie-makers; he wanted to rent equipment to TV programme-makers also, and invested in a new, lightweight, easily portable 16mm camera, the Arriflex. Hewat did his homework, then he and Forman proposed that Granada should put their money where Samuelson's mouth was. It was agreed that first *Searchlight*, and soon *World in Action*, should rent Samuelson's new cameras, when they were still on proving trials. Much good followed.

Tim Hewat came to film from print, and that always showed. Yet he was keen to exploit the full potential of celluloid. With director Clive Donner, he made four short films in India; with James Hill in 1961 he went to post-Batista Cuba, revolutionary, but not yet formally Marxist, under Fidel Castro, and again made quickly four short films, *Cuba Sì*. Change was fresh in the air, and cameras caught the positive mood. It was too positive for the ITA; not impartial, they said.

Tim Hewat made one film on which I worked that combined film-making skills with the urgency of daily journalism: *Sunday in September*. CND's Committee of 100, concerned that peaceful marches from Aldermaston were not leading to disarmament, sought to advance their cause by escalating the struggle. What were needed, activists argued, were high-profile acts of civil disobedience, creating nuisance and martyrs. On 17 September 1961 – Battle of Britain Anniversary Sunday – they would sit down in Trafalgar Square and defy police attempts to move them. If arrested, charged and sentenced, some bolder spirits would refuse to pay fines and would go to gaol. The Committee of 100 ensured that some of their most famous supporters, including the aged philosopher Bertrand Russell, would appear in person to lead the protest. To this, Hewat spotted, the anniversary service at Westminster Abbey would make a pointed contrast.

Sunday in September was to be transmitted in the *Searchlight* slot at 10.10 p.m. on Monday. Hewat deployed a dozen camera crews, each briefed to cover the day from a different angle; he would rush the film to the labs, print, view rushes, edit through the night, work on through Monday and, with the movie neg cut and show-printed, the soundtrack laid and dubbed, go to air that evening.

'Early morning', the commentary would say, 'in London; a quiet Sunday in September.' At 6.30 a.m. my cameraman and I were at the Serpentine in Hyde Park. Lovingly we photographed the drip of raindrops framed by a bridge over water. Then to Pimlico, where the stage designer Jocelyn Herbert lived. She and the playwright John Osborne would leave from there for Trafalgar Square. They wouldn't talk to us, but we saw them on their way. There was a vast crowd in the Square. The protesters sat. There was tension and good humour. Photographers jostled, spotting the known and looked-for faces. The sit-down occupied the whole space available. The police asked them to 'move along please'. They didn't budge. Nuisance was deemed to have turned to obstruction. Arrests began, and went on through the night and early morning. In all, 1,374 were arrested. One of our cameramen got too close to the police vans and was himself arrested; he was bailed in the early hours. Hewat edited all the material gathered, against the clock. Decisions as to what to use, what to discard, were taken in good time. *Sunday in September*, a small miracle in its making, went to air. It took Tim Hewat to bring it off.

And it was Tim Hewat who gave us *Seven Up*, interviews with seven-year-olds who are now forty-nine. Every seven years we have met them again, as their lives have, variously, unfolded. Michael Apted's skills have made the series marvellous; Hewat's idea was the origin of it all, the acorn from which this great oak grew.

Based at Granada's offices in Golden Square, we would drink together after work at the Old Coffee House in Beak Street. Buying a drink could be expensive: 'Large Teachers all round.' I could only afford one of those, and that with difficulty, so sloped off home as soon as I could. An after-work drink was always convivial; heavy eating and drinking at lunchtime coincided with periods of frustration at work. Then we ate at the Barcelona, a gloomy Spanish hostelry which, I later found from George Melly's autobiography, had been a haunt of London's surrealists in the thirties. After paella and dark red wine, little work was done. I left Granada before the discovery of an all-day drinking club, the Tattie Bogle, in which others whiled away many hours on the payroll.

In Manchester, Granada patronised the Opera House Tavern. Brian Inglis, presenting *All Our Yesterdays* – a glance back, using British Movietone News, at the events of the week, twenty-five years ago – would come to my office, his script completed, prompt at twelve noon, and tap his wrist meaningfully. Occasionally, on a *What the Papers Say* Thursday evening, I repaired with the presenter to the Pineapple in the other direction.

The proprietress complained that, since there was no exit from Granada's car park on her side, she got no business; could I not speak to Mr Frankenstein, and get him to do something?

All my time there, Granada kept me busy. For a year I produced two weekly networked shows, *What the Papers Say* and *All Our Yesterdays*, each of which was normally written in London and recorded in Manchester. I went up and down twice a week, by rail or air. This was not an ideal way to live.

Television was growing; there was much to do, and few of us to do it. I was given opportunity after opportunity. How could one refuse? But there was such a thing as overload. At one point, overworked to the point of collapse, I went to see Denis Forman's chief aide and gatekeeper, Joyce Wooller (Mike's wife). In addition to the two weekly series, I had fourteen separate projects on the go. She looked at me, unsurprised, and arranged for me to see Denis. I left his office cheered and relieved, the fourteen extra projects were reduced to thirteen.

I was allowed to try my hand at producing two historical documentaries, on *The General Strike* and *The Troubles*. With Brian Inglis, I went to Dublin to report on John F. Kennedy's visit to Ireland and his politically obligatory roots. I produced political interviews: *Power in a Party* with Labour's irascible George Brown, and *The Party in Power* with Tory Rab Butler, done as an outside broadcast from the 1960 party conference at Scarborough. For this I proposed to Conservative Central Office an interviewing panel of three: Paul Johnson, then of the *New Statesman*; Alastair Hetherington, editor of the *Manchester Guardian*; and Henry Fairlie, then a contributor to the *Daily Mail*. My contact at the Conservative Party's press office, Howell Thomas, objected. Henry Fairlie was not acceptable as a Conservative: he had written a critical article in the *Mail* against the materialism – 'You've never had it so good' – which he thought had entered the party's soul. 'Nonsense,' I said. 'Henry thinks for himself, but of course he's a Conservative.' Howell Thomas was still reluctant. Let's ask Rab, I suggested, and was taken to see him. This was the right tactic. Rab was a grandee, taller, more imposing, than I'd realised, and immaculately tailored. He was dismissing from his presence a party agent who had been discussing arrangements for his address the next day to a gathering of all of them. There was a great deal of deferential 'Yes, sir. Of course, sir.' Rab Butler had no qualms about facing my suggested panel. He knew Henry Fairlie; questions from him, he implied, would make it a better programme.

At the recording, the camera first focused on Rab, then panned along the panel. 'Fade up camera one,' said Mike Scott, 'cue sound.'

'*The Party in Power*,' an announcer stated. 'The Rt Hon. R. A. Butler faces questions from Paul Johnson, Alastair Hetherington and Henry Fairlie.'

'Cue Henry.'

Henry looked at the camera and said, 'Good night.' The programme was fine, the false start a gem; it ought to have been preserved for posterity.

Roy Jenkins delivered, solo to camera, a half-hour account of his researches into the affair of the Royal Academy, hard-pressed financially, and the proposed sale of its Michelangelo tondo. Jenkins, then a rising parliamentarian and author, had also turned his hand to journalism, offering lucid accounts of complex events. One, for the *Observer*, caught the eye. It unravelled the detail of ICI's attempt to take over Courtauld's. Denis Forman thought there might be a programme in the Michelangelo, and handed the assignment to me. Roy Jenkins, keen, walked me through the House of Commons, pointing out the statues of the great, and urging me to secure him the most generous fee Granada could afford.

I was impressed by the first treatment he sent in – clear, elegant and full of fresh touches. One Academician, the portrait painter James Gunn, had painted Harold Macmillan for the Carlton Club, Arthur Deakin for the Transport and General Workers' Union, and Field Marshal Montgomery for Field Marshal Montgomery.

And this: 'On that Sunday afternoon at the Ritz Hotel, Charles Wheeler and Humphrey Brooke of the Royal Academy had tea with Edward Boyle and Henry Brooke of the Treasury. (Humphrey Brooke is of course Henry Brooke's brother.)' I rang Forman. 'Roy's script has come in; it's good. He has discovered stuff no one else has. Did you know Henry Brooke was Humphrey Brooke's brother?'

Denis authorised me to proceed to second draft. When this came in, the touches I most admired had vanished. I rang Roy Jenkins to ask why; could he please reinstate them? 'Ah,' he said, 'I'm afraid not. They were untrue. I had to take them out.' This novel method of brightening up a piece had never occurred to me. It remained a decent show. We recorded the programme late on the evening of 30 July 1962, at the Granville studio on Walham Green. I remember the date, the only one I have no need to check, because I was finished in time to be in the delivery room at University College Hospital as Tamara gave birth to Kate.

Granada was a wonderful place to work. In spite of a some-times oppressive paternalism and occasional frustrations and niggles, the whole company, top to bottom, was devoted to making television. I was green, and no doubt naïve, but I never heard 'share price' mentioned, or profit. Very few – certainly no one at my level – had any idea that Sidney had mortgaged the company's profits for four years to John Spencer Wills at Associated-Rediffusion, ensuring Granada's viability when things looked dark, and gaining London exposure for his wares.

Of course the Bernsteins were 'mean'; they were adamant against waste, setting their face against the lavish in programmes and in staff rewards. (*Brideshead Revisited* and *The Jewel in the Crown* were twenty years and more in the future.) But their canniness was good business sense; irksome, but tolerable. The budget I had for *What the Papers Say* was £185 a week. Of that, £25, later £35, went to the writer–presenter. The budget broke down, line by line: £8 10s was available for newspapers, for example. Weekly cost reports showed that *Papers* was brought in consistently within budget, yet if one line was overspent by a pound, I would get a note from the production office, wanting an explanation.

Two great lessons were there for the learning at Granada, both of universal application. First, whoever was billed as producer, everyone's contribution counted. If the stage hand changing *What the Papers Say* caption cards boobed, or an announcer fluffed, the programme suffered. Live transmission made this doubly certain. In the gallery, director, vision-mixer and production assistant worked together as one. For me, 'Thank you, studio,' called out to the floor at transmission's end, was never perfunctory, always heartfelt. The sense of making programmes as a team remained with me when fifty of us, staying together over three years, made series like *The World at War* or *Cold War*.

Second, the tone of any creative organisation is set at the top. At Granada it was set by the owners, Sidney and Cecil Bernstein. Sidney, tall, good-looking, flamboyant, commanding, was at first to me a frightening figure, particularly if pursuing to the end some trivial complaint. He was also an inspiration. Cecil was small, quiet, inconspicuous even; he walked with a limp and a cane, talked with a stutter. Yet his role should not be under-rated; he looked out for and pushed forward inexpensive programmes on which the company's ratings and prosperity depended. Sidney, with a care for Granada's image, would advertise in the posher papers, with eye-catching understatement, a single drama or controversial documentary. Cecil fostered programmes that gained most viewers at low cost: quizzes, comedy, soap opera. Sidney cherished the one-off. Cecil bought in formats that would bear years of repetition.

College Bowl was a razzmatazzy American quiz contest, transformed with a deft wave of Cecil's wand into *University Challenge*. The young, quick-witted, silver-tongued Bamber Gascoigne, who had written a West End hit, *Share My Lettuce*, arrived to present it and never looked back. *University Challenge* has lasted more than forty years. Granada also showed more mercenary quizzes: *Cross-Cross Quiz* and *Twenty-One*. This last, supplied as a completed package by an American production company that controlled the rights, quickly gained a following and ran into trouble. Contestants who enjoyed successive weeks of victory, qualifying them to return next week for more, and raising viewers' interest, admitted they had been coached. The producers were seen to be stage-managing the results. Shock, horror, outcry. The ITA was alerted. Sidney stepped in at once. He commissioned a former Attorney-General, Sir Lionel Heald QC, to investigate. Heald was taken to the Chelsea Palace, Studio Ten, to watch an episode of *Twenty-One* being recorded. The notion of the programme's unmanipulated spontaneity was only slightly called into question when a floor manager held up a placard requiring APPLAUSE. Heald found the production team, not Granada, to be at fault.

Cecil also had comedy under his wing. *The Army Game*, starring Bernard Bresslaw, was an early successful situation comedy. In my office at Golden Square, looking through the window across the inner well, I could see the writers Barry Took and Marty Feldman twiddling their thumbs and gazing out of the window. Every so often, one of them would pick up a pencil and make a mark. They had a view of the doors to the ladies' and gents' lavatories, on separate floors, opposite. They were counting visits and betting on numbers. They were also dreaming up the spun-off successor to *The Army Game*, *Bootsie and Snudge*, with Bill Fraser and Alfie Bass.

Apart from his prudence, Cecil Bernstein's prime contribution to the Granada success story must be his sponsorship of *Coronation Street*.

Early one Friday evening I entered the Golden Square viewing theatre and noticed two colleagues on the drama side sitting quietly at the back: Harry Elton, a Canadian, and Stuart Latham. The core programme committee, at its most senior and serious, were sitting at the front, watching the show on screen. When it finished, Elton and Latham left. I introduced my puny offering, the pilot of a putative current affairs show I had devised, *Look Twice*, in which two reporters, of opposed political viewpoints, would each deliver a separate take on the same subject; this would show the world was more complicated than tabloid simplicities allowed. In this pilot, Bryan Magee and Michael Heseltine reported on landlord and tenant law. Characteristically meddling in detail, Sidney had watched an audition from his office and instructed me that Michael should rise and walk about for his inspection, like a male model. Michael walked.

Mike Wooller, my collaborator in this project, came up with an inventive look for it. *Searchlight* was lit in limbo, pale on dark; the figures in *Look Twice* would be seen against a bright cyclorama, dark on pale. It was characteristic of the Bernsteins to allow me to make the pilot, but Granada had already started *Searchlight* and *World in Action* was in the works: there was no room for more current affairs. The programme committee, who appeared preoccupied, watched *Look Twice* in a silence which endured after it ended. Finally, one of them asked me, 'What did you think of it, Jeremy?' Their mood, I gloomily suspected, had been affected by the programme they had seen previously, piped down from Manchester, which had called for Elton and Latham's attendance. It was Friday, 9 December 1960, and they had been watching transmission of the very first episode of *Coronation Street*.

They did not know what to make of it. The cast of characters appeared grey, the pub interior forbidding. Everyone spoke in an unintelligibly strong Lancashire accent; to their evident distress one formidable virago, Ena Sharples, played by Violet Carson, was dominant. But what could they say or do? Episode one was now out, episode two was even then being recorded and would be broadcast next Wednesday. They were stuck with it – saddled with the most successful British television programme ever; the sure underpinning of Granada's good fortune.

Granada mounted conferences for its programme-makers. At one entitled in Italian 'Avanti' – a typical Forman touch – we were to look to the future with imagination, casting aside conventional notions of slots and schedules, free to begin again. Graeme Macdonald held forth on the alienation effect in drama, to be achieved by the 'Brechtian' use of the camera. It was exhilarating, a bit unreal. Cecil Bernstein summed up the session: 'All very well, but we shouldn't forget that ten years from now, *The Army Game* and *Coronation Street* will still be top of the Top Ten.' He was right, too; at least about *The Street*. Sidney insisted that every office wall carried twin images that defined Granada's contrasting ambitions: Ed Murrow, the great CBS journalist, stood for one; Phineas T. Barnum, the circus showman, for the other. If you put either in the bin, the image on the wall was rapidly replaced.

In the first defining era of ITV's stance and governance three at least of the four major contractors – Associated-Rediffusion being the exception – were run at the top by people imbued with the values of show business. Combining entertainment with an element of journalism, they saw themselves as publishers and as impresarios. This was true of Lew Grade at ATV, himself an ex-Charleston dancer, now in charge and with a stake in the company; true of Howard Thomas at ABC, inventor of *The Brains Trust*, the BBC's popularising wartime winner; and true of the Bernstein brothers, with their love of the arts and their background in cinema. All these people cared about what they put on screen. The Bernsteins owned Granada, yet it was the delivery of programmes that principally concerned them. Profits would follow, no doubt; but profit was not seen as the be-all and end-all. Later generations of chief executives, with shareholders in publicly owned companies to satisfy, easily came to see profit as their goal; for them programmes were means, profits their end.

Persona Granada, Denis Forman's account of working with Sidney Bernstein in the early days of ITV, captures brilliantly the flair and foibles of a remarkable man, seen in close-up over the years. I never saw Sidney that close. Scared stiff of him when I started, I came early to admire him, never quite to love him. I was never exposed to the full force of his wrathful inquisition, as were others. *Papers* he took an interest in, and any one-off I made, but mostly I got on with my job. The truth is that Sidney, who had been closely involved in absolutely everything in Granada's earliest years, was just beginning to withdraw from programme matters in my time. The man who would run the company, and who would later come to personify Granada, certainly for all who worked there, was Denis Forman. That was not yet the case in my day. Tacitus wrote of Galba: *'omnium consensu, capax imperii, nisi imperasset'* – universally thought up to being emperor, until he did the job. Denis's case was the opposite: everyone knew what heights, left to himself, he was capable of; given the chance, he soared beyond them.

There was nothing inward-looking or parochial about Granada in the five years I spent there, 1958 to 1963. We were expected to engage in, and learn from, the outside world. This was Sidney's doing. He cared about the arts, and wanted us to breathe their air. Fine paintings hung on his walls, and in the corridors, for our benefit. The critic John Berger advised him on purchases, and came to Manchester to see them hung and to make programmes. In Theodore Major he unearthed a finer northern artist, I thought, than L. S. Lowry. Associated-Rediffusion, poaching in our patch, secured the services of John Barbirolli and the Hallé. Granada riposted with Thomas Beecham and the Royal Philharmonic. For a Beecham concert, *Sir Thomas at Lincoln's Inn*, Denis equipped himself with the score of Mozart's Linz Symphony before discussing detail. Not everyone at Granada saw the arts as a prime concern for television; a colleague gave me a very odd look when I said how much I enjoyed Huw Wheldon's *Monitor* on the BBC. 'Not for me,' he commented; 'too highbrow.'

We were entitled to, and encouraged to use, theatre tickets – best seats – paid for by Granada. Better yet, producers and directors went off in pairs for two whole weeks to the cultural capitals of Europe – Milan, Budapest, Prague, Madrid – to sample theatre and the arts and enjoy themselves. A brief report only was required of them on return. Sidney was married now to his second wife,

Sandra, who had been Hitchcock's secretary. Hitchcock story-boards were put in front of us for our instruction. We marvelled, as we were meant to, at the meticulous preparation these displayed. On a railway platform late one evening at Oxford Street station, I spotted Derek Granger decanting on to the sleeper Wystan Auden, Christopher Isherwood and Stephen Spender, together with Malcolm Muggeridge. I was unsurprised; the arts mattered.

In the winter of 1960, singled out for notice, I went with Sidney to New York as an aide. I had never been there, and was over the moon with excitement, tempered only slightly by the discovery that, by coincidence, my parents would be there too, attending a cousin's golden wedding. They were at the Roosevelt, down near Grand Central Station. I was uptown, at the Sherry Netherland, at the corner of Fifth Avenue and Central Park South, in unimagined luxury. My room cost $27 a night. Sidney had the penthouse.

I was his gofer, but had no idea what a gofer was expected to do. When a cab took us both to CBS on Madison Avenue, I failed glaringly; I had no loose change in my pocket for the fare. Sidney did not expect to have to carry money with him. I met people he met, and people he wanted me to meet. One famous screenwriter lunched on martinis. I wove my way, zig-zag, back to the hotel, out for the rest of the day. In the evenings I went down to the Village, listening to the new stand-up comics, and to jazz at the Village Gate or Vanguard. 'Seen anyone we might use?' Sidney asked. I'd seen a veteran negro jazz dancer, a virtuoso making a comeback after years of substance-induced oblivion, who I thought was pretty fine, but doubted he was right for us. 'Nonsense,' said Sidney. Ten weeks later, Baby Laurence was on our screen.

With my parents, I heard *Don Giovanni* at the old Met. Performance unmemorable; theatre unforgettable. And then, on the Sunday, there was that golden wedding at the Waldorf Astoria. For this I hired a tux. The bride wore white, her wedding dress of fifty years before. Sidney and Sandra had gone to Canada that weekend, to her parents. The formidable Miss Hazelwood, who guarded his London office and had protected me after the martini debacle, went to stay with friends. In case of emergency, and to check that all was well, I was left the key to the penthouse. Greatly daring, I let myself in. I had hired the tuxedo for the next day's function, but not suitable shoes. My own were unimpressive. I opened the wardrobe and took out a gleaming pair of Sidney's, predictably immaculate. I tried them on; Sidney's shoes were too big for me.

Sidney Bernstein always showed me kindness. Tamara and I, a little tongue-tied, spent a weekend at Coppings, in the Weald of Kent. A big red London bus was parked on a driveway, a toy for one of the children. Later on, meetings were infrequent. In 1981, John Daniel and I were travelling up to Edinburgh. Sidney asked us to dine with him; we needed picking up in Birmingham, and were fetched by a modest private plane. He came to John's twenty-first birthday party at the George. I lunched with him once on a roof-top in Arab Jerusalem. He wrote to me in 1986, when Tamara died, and sent a gift when Gillian and I married. In 1989 I attended his ninetieth birthday, more a gathering than a party. He died in 1993. Together with other friends, I was left £1,000 in his will to remember him by.

Sidney was an inspiration because he had a commitment to his vision of excellence, which he invited us to share and help him realise; precisely, I still think, what a television boss should do.

In the early summer of 1963, he learned I was thinking of leaving Granada to work elsewhere. I had been sounded out by more than one would-be employer. He urged me not to go: 'Jeremy, there's no one else in British television you would want to work for.' He was right, in a way. But I didn't believe him, and I left home.

4

THIS WEEK

'Getting the feel of the ship, Isaacs? Getting your sea-legs, are you?'

Captain Thomas Brownrigg RN, General Manager of Associated-Rediffusion, accosted me at the lifts in Television House, Kingsway. The building, opposite Bush House, where the BBC's World Service was based, had belonged to the Air Ministry. Now it held the offices and central London studio of A-R, the first ITV franchise-holder to go on air, broadcasting to London during the week (ATV took over at weekends); it also housed ITN, Independent Television News. Television House was handy for the Law Courts and Fleet Street, not far from Westminster and Whitehall, and a short walk through Covent Garden to the lunch possibilities of Soho. No more commuting to Manchester; the District Line from Turnham Green would do.

I was wooed into producing *This Week*, then ITV's only true weekly – fifty-two times a year – networked, peak-time current affairs programme, by its incumbent producers Cyril Bennett and Peter Morley, an agreeable, talented double act. They'd been doing it too long, and were seeking their own replacement. Peter

Morley, tall, thoughtful, calm, with dark eyes, a long face and bony jaw, was the child of German Jewish refugees from Hitler; he was the eyes of the duo, a film-maker. Cyril Bennett, another Jew, an East Ender, was a journalist who had started out as a tea-boy; chubby verging on podgy and a smart dresser, he had eyes that gleamed intelligence behind pebble-lensed glasses: very quick, full of jokes, he was the partnership's editorial brains. Together they took me to lunch at L'Escargot in Greek Street. Cyril recommended the *foie gras*.

Although it was held in high regard, I did not admire *This Week*. It was very much a magazine programme; bitty, I thought. On its opening night in January 1956 there had been eight items in its half-hour duration – a half-hour minus three minutes for commercials, at that. In 1963 it still covered three, four, even five disparate topics. One of the regular pieces was a brief, supposedly humorous, commentary by the grouchy American cartoonist Al Capp. The whole was presented and held together by an urbane journalist, Brian Connell. Knowledgeable on world affairs – he had been a foreign correspondent for the *News Chronicle* – bearded and well-tailored, he gave proceedings a safe, authoritative, slightly pompous air.

Some years earlier, during my National Service, I'd been taken while on leave in London – I wore the kilt in Baker Street – into the studio gallery while *This Week* was on the air. My guide was John Heyman, an Oxford acquaintance. Instead of passing law exams at St Edmund Hall, Heyman had assisted Hughie Green in finding contestants for *Double Your Money*, a general-knowledge quiz show for Radio Luxembourg. More than one undergraduate won £32 on that. *This Week* was mostly talk that night. The director, John Rhodes, a quiet, studious figure, seemed not at all put out that two of his studio panel of three were drunk: Randolph Churchill rowdy and boisterous, Frank Owen, a former editor of the *Daily Mail*, wholly incapable, slumped down on the table. Around this shambolic scene the cameras picked their way.

The programme that whetted appetites for current affairs was the BBC's *Panorama*, into which millions tuned on Monday evenings before the *Nine O'Clock News*. '*Panorama*, your window on the world.' This too was a magazine, and a popular one. Since almost anything shown in those early days was seen on television for the first time, the argument for variety, in the studio and out of it, was compelling. *Panorama*'s range of subjects was astonishing; looking up one day the contents of a programme in which Malcolm Muggeridge had interviewed an inebriated Brendan Behan, I found it also included an outside broadcast visit to the Paris Motor Show and a studio item on girls' public schools. The headmistress of one of the grandest of these led a crocodile into the hospitality room at the Riverside Studios, whereupon, hearing Behan's effing and blinding, she executed a smart U-turn and led her chaste lambs straight out again, out of harm's way. This was the occasion, Muggeridge told me with a grin, on which the BBC's Leonard Miall, in overall charge, had argued that Behan could not go on. Muggs argued that he should; viewers should savour genius, warts and all. Miall stipulated: 'If he says fuck, promise you won't smile.'

Panorama in the sixties was made of sterner stuff than formerly. Robin Day reported from the Congo, Jim Mossman from the Yemen; Robert Kee dodged bullets in Algiers. Richard Dimbleby presided. I watched *Panorama* more often than I watched *This Week* and remember admiring, from an earlier period, Christopher Chataway exposing British racial prejudice in action. Marylebone Railway Station advertised for workers; Chataway checked there were jobs available, and sent West Indian immigrants along to apply. They were all turned down: 'No more vacancies, all just filled.' QED. The reporter also talked to dusky Cleo Laine.

'Where are you from, Miss Laine?'

'Southall, Middlesex.'

'And where were you born?'

'Southall, Middlesex.'

'Yes, but where are your parents from?'

'Southall, Middlesex.'

'Where were they born?'

'Southall, Middlesex.'

Watching, I wished I'd done that.

I'm not absolutely sure why Bennett and Morley thought I was right for *This Week*. At Granada I had made what you might call current affairs documentaries. One, on railways, was with the film-maker Mike Grigsby, broadcast to coincide with publication of the Beeching Report which would prune the network. In Norfolk, we filmed empty carriages on the service from Wymondham to Wells-next-the-Sea; that line would go. Another programme was on the police. Henry Fairlie propounded, a little too rosily, the theory and practice of policemen as citizens, members of the community, democratically accountable to it – an analysis that owed much to the Tory philosopher Michael Oakeshott, whom Henry revered. Both films made a modest mark. More controversial, and fraught with legal difficulty, was *Dangerous Medicine*, a report on a powerful drug prescribed for pregnant mothers: 'Your child's life depends on the safety of Distaval.' Distaval contained thalidomide, and caused birth defects. And then there was *Searchlight*; certainly relevant experience. Cyril Bennett continued to press me.

If *This Week* was so attractive an assignment, why was he so keen to unload it? Peter Morley wanted to direct proper films, longer documentaries. Cyril was tired of sending out for successive editions of the *Evening Standard* on Wednesdays, and even Thursdays, to fill a hole. Both of them were fed up with humouring Brian Connell. Dealing with him, Cyril confided, took as much time, and more energy and patience, than any other aspect of the programme. Seeing the film items edited, the studio discussion cast, was taxing enough, yet after all this there remained the most wearisome task of the week: arguing the length of Connell's links. 'I shall need two minutes and forty-five seconds at the top,' Connell would say, 'and a minute at the end.' But did he? That was four minutes gone, nearly a sixth of the running time. To ease the pressure on *This Week*, Cyril offered Connell a separate slot, five minutes weekly to camera, solo, for a commentary on world affairs. Connell insisted he would need velvet drapes, a book-case, a genuine period table in front, a lamp on it, a globe of the world beside him. Cyril had had in mind the presentation booth. The idea was dropped.

This Week was weekly, networked current affairs, in peak time: for me, a golden opportunity. I said I was for longer items and fewer, was against light-hearted make-weights, and would have no more of Al Capp. But I would come. Cyril had to clear it with his superiors: John McMillan, Controller of Programmes, a smart and savvy Australian, and Captain Brownrigg, who would want to see me before giving approval. Brownrigg was the man, Cyril told me, who had come upon him and Peter Morley working together late one evening in the cutting room and asked what they were doing.

'We're editing a documentary for Israel's tenth anniversary,' was the answer. '*Israel Rises*.'

'Ah,' said Brownrigg. 'Must remember one thing: tricky fellow, your Hebrew. Carry on.'

Summoned for interview, I took the short bus trip from Holborn down Kingsway so as not to arrive out of breath. Cyril had instructed me to have my hair cut and my shoes shined. (His were always spotless.) Brownrigg was not given to interfering in programme matters but, Cyril warned, he was likely to suggest that British success in motor-racing was a suitable subject for *This Week*. When he did just that, I undertook not to rule it out, and passed muster.

I gave notice to Granada after five good years, and reported for duty. Gill Morphew, *This Week*'s production manager dynamo, introduced me to my new colleagues. The secretary temporarily assigned to me wore a white two-piece edged with navy-blue piping, with anchors embroidered at the corners. I rang the per-sonnel office:

'May I speak to Mr Northcott?'

'I think you mean Captain Northcott.'

He motioned me to a chair. 'Please excuse me while I finish this; I'm stuck with the guest list for a cocktail party.' He put down his pen. 'I do so hate acting as flag lieutenant.'

Commander Everett, a testy martinet, was in charge of the OB units. Years later, I spotted a newspaper report of court proceedings against him: he had driven several miles on the wrong motorway carriageway, against the flow. When David Windlesham left A-R to go to Grampian, before entering government under Ted Heath, I asked him what he had learned. 'I have learned', he said, 'never under any circumstances to employ in a position of responsibility an ex-naval officer.'

My office boasted a fixture I could have used elsewhere: the window behind me led to a fire escape and bore the words, in large letters, Emergency Exit. At A-R I never needed it. *This Week* had awards to its credit, and was a sure fixture in ITV's schedule. But it cried out for change, though not in personnel. There were capable directors and notable reporters in place, some attached to the programme full-time, others available within A-R's ambit. On the very first Thursday I was there – involved, but not quite yet in charge – Dan Farson, with Bill Morton directing, delivered an interview with James Baldwin, author of *The Fire Next Time* – a bold, dark, supposedly prophetic book by a rare black writer. Civil rights agitation was coming to a head in the US; I welcomed their offering. Soon after, on a Thursday afternoon Eastern Standard Time, Martin Luther King Jr addressed hundreds of thousands at the Washington Memorial. His peroration, 'I have a dream,' floated live by satellite into *This Week*. James Cameron was in attendance for that. The problems were not of talent, but of method, and of structure.

Setting out to film abroad, assigned as late, perhaps, as Friday midday for transmission the following Thursday, director and reporter might sit together on the aeroplane. They came from different worlds, neither of them television. The director, whose background was the film industry, would ask for a script to shoot by. The reporter, a journalist, still reading and thinking, would want to sniff around and talk to people before deciding where to begin. But time was short, so the film crew would occupy itself the morning after they arrived taking general views of Government House, or the street market, or a military band. The notion of getting straight to the action was not an imperative. The crews I inherited were staid in their ways; using the 35mm camera, perhaps they had to be. Besides, the very size of the crew militated against 'action' filming. We sent two on camera, operator and focus-puller; two on sound, recordist and boom handler; a director and a PA, who kept the continuity sheets; a reporter and a researcher. An electrician could be hired locally. This caravan was costly, and counter-productive, but the manning level formed part of the union agreement and was strictly observed. Although exceptions were made for war zones – few were prepared to risk evident danger – the crew size remained constant throughout my time in ITV current affairs. In some circumstances two on camera and two on sound were necessary; in others, I wanted flexibility, the cameraman driving and the assistant rigging lights. ACTT was adamant against. As hard to bear for the series producer was the cost: on journeys over 1000 miles, ACTT insisted all should fly first class. Rome was within the limit; Cairo and Tel Aviv were not. I never succeeded in eliminating this ludicrous obstacle to effective journalism.

It didn't help *This Week* that the weekly agenda was set at the Friday meeting. Assembling the morning after the night before, the team would find there was little in the pipeline for next Thursday. The producer would review the week ahead and ask for suggestions. A discussion followed; then he must decide. On no account, Cyril Bennett advised me, take a decision at that meeting. 'Go back to your office, close the door, think it through again by yourself before deciding.' Before too long I decided to abolish the Friday meeting – or at least its stated purpose of settling the subject of the following week's *This Week*; I wanted it to range more widely.

The notion of operating on brief lead times suited a magazine format; by deploying different units, several short items could be assembled on film or readied for the studio within a week. The BBC's *Tonight* was doing this nightly with brio and conviction. But was this a sensible procedure in current affairs? Could solid items be adequately researched in such a hurry? I doubted it. I also distrusted the studio, where success might hinge on whether a key figure would take part. If he would not and I proceeded, I was instantly settling, I thought, for second best. And if all the A-list were unavailable, or fell out, or refused, what then? I did not admire that sort of television. An interview with the Prime Minister, carefully thought through, by all means; a looser discussion, not for me, except as a last resort. I could see, of course, that people needed to form opinions and hear views canvassed. But with limited airtime available, I preferred information over punditry, film over studio – in so far as the programme budget allowed: film meant cash spent; there was no charge for the studio. To stay within budget for the year, the studio would have to be used, but as seldom, I thought, as possible. Besides, I wanted to hold viewers, not lose them. Even well-cast discussions sag in places, but with film, well edited, it ought to be possible to seize the viewer's attention and keep it throughout; gathering more strong material than was needed to fill the time slot guaranteed, I thought, a watchable half-hour. And viewers could identify more easily with people in the street or the workplace than with pundits in the studio; 'us', not 'them'. We could bring these people, on whom political decisions impacted, into our homes. We were on their side.

Film came courtesy of the camera department, and that was firmly controlled by its ex-cameraman boss, Ted Lloyd. Lloyd was brought up on and devoted to 35mm film; so were all those cameramen he trained, employed, protected, promoted. The camera department owed loyalty to him. Lloyd aimed at 'technical' perfection; anything less was to be discarded, the perpetrator reprimanded. The camera must be kept steady, every corner of the frame correctly exposed; no judder, no softness, only pinpoint clarity and sharpness. These were admirable objectives for film shot under controlled studio conditions; quite impracticable for a street market or a riot or a war zone, and hard to realise in an under-lit slum. At just this time, A-R was switching from 35mm to 16mm – against Ted Lloyd's forcibly voiced concerns and determined rearguard action. He could not prevail – 16mm was considerably cheaper, and more suitable to vivid journalism – but he could make life difficult for those who welcomed change. Every cameraman was instructed that, 35mm or 16mm, the same standards applied. Concerned for their jobs, cameramen preferred to obey their head of department rather than the director; to the reporter they paid no heed at all. This was infuriating to reporters who cared about film – Robert Kee, for example, once of *Panorama*, who joined us in 1964. Not only had Robert always worked with smaller crews, but on *Panorama*, unconstrained by ACTT agreements, he had partnered the amazing one-man band Erik Durschmied, a virtuoso of 16mm, who did everything himself, sound included. Durschmied worked better, faster – in Vietnam, in the Yemen, in Algiers – with Kee or Jim Mossman than any full-strength film crew ever could.

A separate anomaly made insistence on perfect exposure pointless. A-R had bought 16mm cameras and brought them into service, but had not yet replaced editing equipment or re-equipped the dubbing theatre. Thus, *This Week* was shot on 16mm, but then blown up, edited and dubbed on 35mm, fudging definition, magnifying faults.

When I started on *This Week* I knew little of the usages of film. On that first Thursday in the cutting room the editor, Brian West, showed me, for final approval, the cut of the interview to go out that evening. I liked the jump-cuts – 'Godardian', I supposed: *A Bout de Souffle* had just reached London – and complimented him on them. He looked at me pityingly: 'I haven't put the reverses in yet.' Now I was learning, I saw no reason why journalists should not aim to make good films.

Today editing and dubbing are computerised; it takes moments to do what took us hours. An unsung hero of our work then was the dubbing mixer, Freddie Slade. There was no computer; no rock-and-roll. Each roll of film had to be dubbed in one continuous movement, the whole lasting ten minutes – or not dubbed at all. One error of judgement, one finger fluff, even seconds from the end, rendered the whole useless. We had to go back to the beginning. The dubbing mixer's feat was hard enough to pull off at the best of times, with ample rehearsal and no pressure to finish. But Freddie Slade, on Thursday evenings, waited patiently upstairs in the theatre for film and dubbing sheets to reach him. Too often they came at the last possible minute. With fifteen minutes to go before the film was due in telecine, Freddie might start work on a ten-minute roll: the reporter in the booth delivering commentary live, a director flashing a light to cue him, the producer watching anxiously. If Freddie made one mistake, it could not be corrected. His concentration never faltered. Time and time again, he saved our bacon.

Then there was the question mark over Brian Connell. When I left Granada, Denis Forman promised me a bottle of champagne if Connell went. Denis had, he said, the network's interest at heart; he thought *This Week* would be a better programme without him. Granada's *World in Action* would use neither a link man, nor invision reporters. I was wedded to working with reporters; so long as *This Week* made regular use of the studio, it would need someone to introduce it. Connell, I knew, was much given to resigning; I waited for events to take their course.

The moment that brought the issue to a head came soon enough. In April 1963 a book called *The Time Has Come* was published. Its American author, John Rock, was a gynaecologist and a believing Catholic; he wanted the Church to change its position on birth control. He knew that many American Catholics used contraceptives but wanted to stay faithful to the Church; very many others obeyed the Church's teaching and lived in discontent, and even misery and fear, as a result. Denied contraceptives, they would bring into the world more children than they could readily feed or love. In the confessional, some priests were sympathetic, others harshly forbidding. Catholicism, Rock argued, was being torn apart. Rock wrote as a Catholic for Catholics; if the faithful knew that the Church's teaching was wrong for them, they would lose faith in the Church.

Here was a topic for *This Week*. Desmond Wilcox would report on film from the poorest parishes of Liverpool. There would be a brief studio debate, chaired by Connell, who would top and tail the programme.

Wilcox was a resourceful, experienced reporter, with the gift of listening; he drew answers from the timid and distressed. The women he talked to in Liverpool were in despair; some had given birth eight or ten times already. Abstention from intercourse was not an option their husbands would accept, and some had Saturday night bruises to prove it. How would their health, their morale, their faith survive the next baby, or the one or two after that? They had asked the priest for help. He confirmed to Wilcox that he could not give it. Sophisticated middle-class parents might more easily have found an understanding priest. In this working-class parish there was, for the believer, no way out of darkness. The priest insisted, to his flock and to us, that God's law must be obeyed.

The tired, worn faces moved us almost to tears; but the film was poorly exposed and I was told that it was not fit to be transmitted. The ITA set standards of image quality which companies agreed to adhere to, so this was a serious matter; but I overruled the ruling. Then Connell, a Roman Catholic, objected: the subject was not to his taste, he made that evident. He preferred less film, a longer studio debate. And what should he say at the end? How to conclude a programme whose thrust and tone he found unattractive, even unacceptable? I'd have preferred him to say nothing, but he was chairing the debate. 'Say what you think right, Brian,' I said, exasperated. 'Say if you like that the Catholic mother we've seen who has eleven children and makes no complaint is, for you, the one who counts for most.' And that is just what he did. Next day, newspapers and viewers called his summing-up wholly at odds with the tenor of the programme, heartless and offensive. I was ill-placed to criticise him. Then I heard that, unhappy to be associated with a programme so distasteful, Brian Connell had again resigned. I raced to ensure that Cyril Bennett and John McMillan did not ask him to change his mind, as had happened before. His resignation accepted, the way was clear to make *This Week* more engaged with people's lives. We never looked back.

We were now without a fixed presenter. For two weeks Kenneth Harris, another solid, avuncular figure, stood in. Elsewhere in the building it was assumed that he, or someone like him, would replace Connell. But there was another route forward. Reporters addressed the camera and could, at a pinch, hand over to a colleague. The need for the handover would arise only if there were more than one item in the programme. I said that we would manage, somehow, using reporters, singly or in combination, and see how that went. To clear the way, I stood Kenneth Harris down. He retired gracefully. But the real way forward was to be bold; a single-subject programme could be presented by the reporter, and would make more compelling viewing than a magazine. I made the case to Cyril Bennett – now Head of Features – and to David Windlesham and John MacMillan, that that was the road I wanted to go down; with their guarded acquiescence, and soon their enthusiastic support, down it I went.

Sibelius's *Karelia Suite* helped. When I arrived at *This Week*, the title sequence was the iris of a camera shutter opening; it lasted eleven seconds, and was set to a bar or two of Bruckner. But *This Week* had previously been introduced by Sibelius, the march from *Karelia*, stirringly asserting Finland's claims to the territory it disputed with Russia. Conducted by Alexander Gibson with the Scottish National Orchestra, it took thirty seconds to run the theme. We brought it back – it was a brave, emphatic, memorable theme. To match it, for want of any better idea, we filmed the reporters coming off aeroplanes, and cut them to the beat; they enjoyed that, and so did the public. As soon as you heard the tune, you knew we were on. Signature tunes matter; with one exception – Carl Davis's for *The World at War* – *Karelia* was the best I ever had. It lasted *This Week* till the end, more than twenty years on.

On a Friday evening in November 1963 I was in the bar when I heard the news: John Kennedy was dead, assassinated in Dallas. All the TV top brass were at the SFTA's awards ceremony at the Dorchester. I thought we must do something that night, and prepared to ring round for help. I had no need; the *This Week* team dropped whatever they were doing, and came in. Milton Shulman, then retained by A-R, came in too, to lend a hand. After the late news we mounted a special programme; no attempt to guess the how or why, just people talking about Kennedy, and their loss: senior political figures, Americans in London. We could not get the Prime Minister, Sir Alec Douglas-Home, or Harold Wilson, or Jo Grimond; they went on BBC News, and on ITN. We did get Wilson's deputy George Brown, who had been at a constituency party dinner in the East End of London and was well away. One of the Americans who came in was the actor Eli Wallach. I greeted our guests in the green room and then went down to the studio, leaving Milton to act host. Brown, when I returned, seemed fit to broadcast, but in the studio the fierce heat of the TV lights did its work; his speech was slurred as, embarrassingly, he claimed friendship both with John Kennedy and with Lyndon Johnson, now sworn in as President. What no one told me that night was that, while I was in the studio, Wallach, offended by the manner and matter of Brown's speech, took a swing at him. Milton separated the combatants. I had crossed the Atlantic to report the assassination's aftermath before I found out.

This Week, under new management, was getting into its stride. The programme that really moved things on came at the year's end. After Christmas Day and Boxing Day off, I came into work on 27 December 1963, a Friday, mulling over what to do for Thursday 2 January. The road accident toll of fatalities that Christmas was high, 120 deaths in four days. Seasonal drinking was a factor. When would Britain introduce legislation, as other countries had, to criminalise, punish and deter drunken drivers? I decided to see what we could do in a week. I had fine collaborators: reporter Desmond Wilcox and director Anthony Isaacs (no relation).

We set out to shock, tabloid fashion. I had recollections of Tim Hewat's *Searchlight*, 'Slaughter on the Avenue', with corpses cluttering the roadway. But those bodies were anonymous. We could be specific, and hit harder. We would name the victims; family snaps in close-up would fill the frame. Tony Isaacs had an idea to start the programme. He went to Lambeth Fire Station and climbed the training tower, placing the camera there. On the square below he collected 120 volunteers and lined them up to form the words Xmas 1963. On his cue, they lifted their heads and looked straight up towards him, their faces pale on a dark ground. These were the dead, we said in commentary; not statistics, but people. We cut to the first snapshot, described the accident scene and, with heavy brush strokes, crossed off the image. This brutal device recurred throughout the programme.

Desmond Wilcox went to Sweden for the weekend. There, laws were in place to forbid drinking and driving, and punish those who did both. On the Saturday night in Stockholm he talked to partygoers, asking how they would get home. 'We take turns; one of us drinks, the other drives.'

And you? 'We take a taxi. We don't drive ourselves.'

In London, on New Year's Eve, Wilcox went to Jack Straw's Castle, the Hampstead public house. The car park was full. He filmed inside the pub.

'How much will you drink tonight?'

'Oh, about ten pints I suppose; whiskies towards midnight; brandies to bring in the New Year.'

'How will you get home?'

'Drive, of course. The car is in the car park.'

Others said roughly the same.

Later, at the car-park exit, Wilcox interviewed the revellers leaving.

'Are you all right to drive?'

'Shertainly.'

'And you?'

'I could white as walk a line as anyone in the house.'

We came straight from the film to the Minister for Transport, Ernest Marples.

'Minister,' Wilcox asked, 'will you introduce legislation to make it illegal to drive with alcohol in the blood system?'

'No,' he replied, 'public opinion would not stand for it.' At this point he changed gear, engaged the brain, and added: 'Of course, they might, if you made more programmes like this one.'

Unusually, the Chairman of A-R, Sir John Spencer Wills, was in the studio that night. He was there because BET – British Electric Traction, which owned Rediffusion – had interests in transport, owning bus companies at home and abroad. 'I didn't know we made programmes like this,' he told me. I could not imagine Sidney Bernstein saying the same. Dennis Potter wrote TV criticism for the *Daily Herald*. He praised the programme's 'ferocious, well-documented, relentlessly detailed anger'. We had performed, he thought, 'a genuine public service'. It was Barbara Castle, not Marples, who introduced drink and drive legislation – a change of government, and several more 'shock' programmes, later.

Desmond always delivered. He walked a fine line between current affairs journalism on topics that mattered and sob stuff for its own sake. On one occasion – it was one of the hard-pressed mothers in Liverpool – a woman he was interviewing, near breakdown, after a pause started to cry. We looked at the film together, trying to decide whether to leave the scene in. In the pause Desmond, long silent, had prompted: 'Yes?' I took the tell-tale monosyllable out, and kept the tears. On another, I sent him to report on the heart-wrenching journey of a group of British mothers who had gone out to Corsica taking their children, who were dying of leukaemia; unconventional medico Gaston Naessens had promised he had a dietary cure. Was our intent exploitative, or were we right to sound a warning? Desmond rang me from Corsica before recording a statement to camera; I dictated the text he should use down the line. We filmed the sad group of pilgrims posing as if for a family snap. The television critic for the *Daily Herald* again thought the image shocking but, somehow, salutary.

Desmond welcomed help; when I queried just one phrase in Robert Kee's text for a piece on Northern Ireland, he bit my head off. I learned from that. But my role as producer, as I saw it, was first to decide what the programme would do, and then, after others had done the hard work, to fuss and nag over every frame and every syllable to ensure that what we broadcast was accurate, fair, clear, intelligible and as compelling as it could be. That meant winning arguments, often against the clock. I was not myself a film-maker. I worked with those who were. They travelled the world. I, mostly, stayed behind my desk. It was on the run-in to transmission that I could effectively make an impact; insisting on tiny changes between rough-cut and show-print was the skill I honed at *This Week*. I saw film as something I could shape and control. I never felt that about the studio; what might happen there was unpredictable – and that was precisely its virtue. I could cast a debate and marshal arguments for the line a political interview should take. But all was finally in the hands of the protagonists; how it went, broadcast live, might totally depend on a mysterious 'chemistry' between those taking part.

The economy dominated Britain's political agenda in the early sixties: how to achieve steady growth, avoiding boom and bust. I felt an obligation to tackle this topic, if only to educate myself, believing that if, at the end of the day, I understood more of the matter, viewers might also. Later I asked Alastair Burnet, then Editor of the *Economist*, to do a piece to camera, all of fifteen minutes long, in an extended *This Week*. It was a tour de force, and provoked a serious response. We might have tried that more often. But film gave us our best chance to hold the audience, telling them what they needed to know. Sexual titillation we left to the *News of the World*; the cult of celebrity had not been invented; consumerism was for colour magazines. Current affairs dealt with objective reality, even in the so-called silly season. In the summer of 1964 a *This Week* team went to South America to make three films, in Brazil, Bolivia and Chile.

I had never been to South America; I thought it infinitely alluring, and seriously under-reported. I yearned to know more. It would widen our scope and add to our stature if we filmed there. James Cameron would bring a fresh eye to a subcontinent of which he knew little. Anthony Isaacs, glutton for hard work, would direct all three films. A key role would be played by a recent recruit to the *This Week* team: Jo Menell, who spoke fluent Spanish and would certainly get by in Portuguese.

Jo Menell arrived unheralded in my office, and in my life, one day like a sunburst. He was South African. His father, Slip, had been an aide of Monty's during the war and now owned half of a mining corporation, Anglo-Vaal, second in size to Anglo-American. Jo had been to Cambridge, and before that to school at Rugby, where a friend of his father's had kept an eye on him. This friend was Harley Drayton, the prime figure in BET, owner of Rediffusion. Jo never mentioned any of this; he had come to me because he wanted work. After Cambridge he'd got a job on *The*

Times, and since then he'd been in Vietnam for *Newsweek*. I thought we could use him. He was young, active, full of fun and bounce, like Tigger. He could open doors, write, talk; he knew a lot, and had the nose to find out more. He was uncowed by authority, always on the underdog's side. If anyone could set up, in short order, three films in three countries in South America, he could.

This Week's normal style was not to make films 'about' countries, but to travel only in pursuit of a particular story. But this trip had to be different. It was too far, and too expensive, to send a unit to do just one film. We were not, like visiting firemen, responding to a crisis or catastrophe. I wanted an air of discovery in what we did. The theme, if you like, was these countries' extremes of wealth and poverty, and the politics of that discrepancy. But we'd go with open eyes and minds to visit, with the curiosity of travellers, cities and villages, mountains and valleys, that we'd never seen before. I had to explain this to senior colleagues and win their approval. Rediffusion had interests in South America; I consulted those responsible, including George Bolton, Chairman of the Bank of London and South America, and a splendid fellow called Rickatson-Hatt who, travelling from Buenos Aires to La Paz, had once taken a train which had run off the rails; he waited two days in his compartment, reading, until he was picked up. I'd been going to meetings at Chatham House to brief myself, and just managed to sound informed, at least some of the time. David Windlesham thought the enterprise a worthwhile one, and wished me well with it. The location would last six weeks only; a fortnight, less travel, for each film. In London, I awaited the rushes.

Brazil was first on the itinerary; we could easily have made three films and more in that vast territory alone. Our film contrasted the poverty of the arid north-east with the dazzling modernism of the capital, Brasilia; the *favelas*, the slums of Rio, with the wealth and business bustle of São Paulo. The most striking character in the film was a young priest, Father Rudolf de Melo from the village of Cabo, near the city of Recife, in the province of Pernambuco. He marched with his parishioners as they paraded through the village street, demanding change. Father de Melo was eloquent and persuasive. Following in our footsteps, other TV crews sought him out in Cabo. His answers grew more fluent, and his waistline thicker, down the years.

Bolivia brought us to La Paz – city life at 13,000 feet – and to tin mines nearly as high, near Potosi, where the Spaniards mined silver. The Indian women wore bowler hats. The pictures were spectacular. Juan Lechin, the miners' leader, was the dominant political figure; would he be President? Breathless, in the thin air, *This Week* reported on the politics of tin.

Then across the Andes, perilously by air, to Chile. Jo Menell had friends there from Cambridge, and indeed was half in love with the country. We saw the mountains, and the copper mines, and walked with the poet Pablo Neruda at his home on Isla Negra. More slums, here called *callampas*, mushrooms, sur- rounded Santiago de Chile. There was an empowered middle class. The story here was clearer: a general election loomed which just might freely and democratically bring a very nearly commu- nist government to power; a first in history if it happened, as James Cameron pointed out. 'Allende! Allende!' the crowds were shouting. But his opponent Eduardo Frei, an upright Christian Democrat, was victorious at the polls. Salvador Allende's turn to be President came six years later, before Pinochet did for him.

Exhausted, James Cameron came up the Pacific shore to San Francisco, where he and I met. We were there, George Ffitch reporting, to cover the Republican convention that would nomi- nate Barry Goldwater for President. The Republicans met in the Cow Palace. The convention, lurching to the right, nominated Goldwater, throwing away any chance, however slim, of defeat- ing the incumbent LBJ. 'The lunatics have taken over the asylum,' said Ffitch. We hired a crew from CBS the night before the vote and went on a trawl of the candidates' hotels. The cameraman, drunk, kept the lens hood on throughout. The film we sent by jet to London had nothing on it.

At base again, as the South American films came together, I watched David Gill cut Brazil. No point in crossing the globe to shoot interviews in close-up; the scenes Tony Isaacs had captured were ravishing. We saw a peasant family, frail figures in a harsh landscape, burying their child. Over this, David Gill laid the soprano lament from Villa-Lobos' *Bachianas Brasileiras*. Commentary was sparse. Fine film images which tell their own story should not be smothered, our eyes distracted by inadequate words. Such pictures cry out for music. David Gill and I would work together again.

'Are you a candidate for the leadership of the Conservative Party?' At the Tory party conference at Blackpool in October 1963, with Harold Macmillan away ill, Robin Day, for the BBC, put the question to Lord Home. He put it again and again, and got no answer, either way. Alec Douglas-Home's refusal to say no was itself a yes and, as soon became clear, an emphatic one. To the indignation of the *Daily Mirror*, a belted earl became Prime Minister of the United Kingdom.

Would he prove an effective leader of the Tories as they approached a general election against a Labour Party led by Harold Wilson? Home, like a dozen other members of Macmillan's Cabinet, had been to Eton. Wilson had been to Huddersfield Grammar School before taking a degree in economics at Oxford. He was the younger man, a shrewd debater in the House of Commons and, with his trademark pipe and quiet, homely manner, very much at ease in the new medium of television where, it began to be said, future elections might be fought and won. Economics was not Alec Douglas-Home's strong suit, and his reserved manner and gaunt appearance – a make-up lady told him he had 'a head like a skull' – could count against him on the box.

There would be no US-style 'presidential' debate in Britain. There was no likelihood of one party agreeing to its leader taking part; also, Jo Grimond, the Liberal leader, would have to be fitted into one discussion, and might well have been a match for either of the other two. But the party leaders could not stay off television altogether. Believing it was important that *This Week* interview them in advance of the election, I submitted a formal invitation to the new Prime Minister to appear after a visit he was paying to Washington in January 1964. The invitation was accepted; for a while I thought we had an exclusive. But it turned out that Douglas-Home would also be interviewed on *Panorama* on the Monday, three days before *This Week*. His advisers had decided to take the plunge. On *Panorama* he acquitted himself reasonably well. Robin Day asked him forty questions in twenty minutes. All was brisk and lively. The PM's performance won praise.

No one then saw such an interview as a gladiatorial contest, even if it were one to one. Robin Day, putting, on our behalf, a battery of questions, skilfully assembled and courteously delivered, did not claim equality with his subject; it was the Prime Minister's views that mattered. Such was our attitude also. Of course, his answers and his manner might affect his electoral fate; but there was no intention to harass, only a wish to test competence. The following Thursday, *This Week* awaited him. We fielded three interviewers, each covering a different area of subject matter. George Ffitch would deal with foreign policy; Bryan Magee would handle social policy – health and education; William Rees-Mogg, from *The Times*, would tackle the economy. They had eight minutes each. Rees-Mogg went first.

The Prime Minister did not provide convincing answers on the economy or on social policy. He was hesitant, unsure of himself, imprecise in his statements. The questions were searching but also open-ended. They did not come thin and fast, as they had on *Panorama*, allowing the PM to give a brief answer and Robin Day to pass on to the next. Rees-Mogg and Magee took their time, waiting for answers. That was the Prime Minister's problem; there was nothing to stop him answering fully, or to help him if he couldn't. When George Ffitch turned to foreign affairs, the tenor of the programme altered. Douglas-Home now appeared the master of his subject: firm, decisive in tone, wholly constructive in attitude. Asked about the Middle East – no one then talked of 'Palestine' – he offered suggestions for solutions, and spoke of the part the UK might play in achieving them. He was almost a different man.

Afterwards, relaxed, the Prime Minister stayed on chatting over a drink. He had done his best, and to all appearances was perfectly happy with it. I don't think he thought a television broadcast mattered all that much. But the programme as a whole did make clear his strength, and laid bare his weaknesses. The questioning had been completely without venom. Viewers may well have thought the questions difficult, and the answers competent.

In the green room, apologising for my impertinence, I put a point to Alec Douglas-Home, known to use matchsticks to help him grasp economic issues. 'Prime Minister,' I said, 'you were quoted the other day as saying that "political problems were bad enough, they were insoluble; but that economic problems were worse, they were incomprehensible". Given the importance everyone attaches to the economy today, can you really say that sort of thing as Prime Minister?'

'Why not?' he said. 'It's true, isn't it?'

We ought to have put the question on air.

I never think of politicians as dishonest, but I never met another quite like Alec Douglas-Home. When, in the autumn, he called the general election, I went to Downing Street to brief him for the short interview he would grant that evening; we would talk to the other party leaders also. The Prime Minister, just back from the Palace, was taken up with the constitutional import of what he had set in train; the Queen had agreed to his request to dissolve

Parliament. This, irrespective of any political consideration whatsoever, was what he thought he was to talk about. There was not
an adviser in sight. The interview he gave was scarcely a call to
arms. I suspect that, however much the media sought to person-
alise the contest, he still saw the general election as one in which
men and women voted for the candidates of their choice in the
constituencies where they lived, rather than for a party leader
pulling the rest along on his coat-tails.

If we could not stage debates between Prime Minister and
opposition leader, I thought *This Week* should arrange instead for
ministers and their shadows to discuss specific issues in three
programmes on the successive Thursday evenings preceding the
poll on the fourth Thursday. This had not been done before; no
one else seemed keen it should be done at all. With little help
from either party headquarters, I set out to see what could be
achieved. In fact Labour stood to gain from confrontation; the
Conservatives, perhaps realising this, put obstacles in my way.
They made it clear I was on my own; they would not deliver their
spokesmen to the studio. I proposed housing as the first topic; the
Labour shadow was Michael Stewart, a headmasterly figure, later
to be Foreign Secretary. He accepted. The Conservative Minister
for Housing was Sir Keith Joseph, of high intellect, volatile temperament – and Jewish faith, which came into the equation:
Conservative Central Office took pleasure in pointing out to me
that the programme I planned would take place on the Day of
Atonement, Yom Kippur: the holiest date in the Jewish calendar.
Keith Joseph was an orthodox Jew; he would spend the day in
prayer and in synagogue. He had made it clear he would accept
no engagements.

I thought it over; the Jewish Sabbath, any Jewish Holy Day,
including Yom Kippur, actually begins on the previous evening
and runs from sunset to sunset. Thursday, certainly, was Yom
Kippur, but the fast would end, and the service be over, early that
evening. I had childhood memories of staggering home from

synagogue, a little light-headed, to break my day's fast with a glass of milk and a slice of soft bread, before the meal that followed. Keith Joseph's presence was not needed in the studio till Yom Kippur was over. I explained this to Tory Central Office, and asked them to put my request. They refused point-blank; it was unthinkable. I said I would put the invitation to him myself. We were running out of time; it was now late Wednesday afternoon, and Joseph would already be on his way to synagogue. Yom Kippur had begun. I would have to wait till he was home and catch him before he left the following morning. But really orthodox Jews don't answer the telephone on the Sabbath or on Holy Days. This was Catch-22 – except that if he did answer the telephone, that might put the whole matter in another light. Gingerly, I dialled Joseph's home number. He answered at once. I apologised for the intrusion, and explained what I wanted. 'What did you say your name was?' he asked. 'You should be ashamed of yourself; you know what day this is.' I said yes, and again I was sorry, but by the evening Yom Kippur would be over. What about it? He said at once he'd do it. With housing supply near the top of the policy agenda, the programme worked well. It did not surprise me that Keith Joseph, rational as well as emotional, agreed to take part. He did surprise me, though, when in the studio he insisted that we photograph him from – he pointed – 'my better side'.

The Nuffield study of the British general election of 1964 noted this one programme as a modest breakthrough, 'the only time during the entire campaign that a Minister and his Labour shadow met on TV'. But the triptych I had hoped for did not materialise. To achieve it, I would have needed wholehearted agreement in principle from both main parties. Labour, with the press against them, looked on the proposal favourably; the Conservatives were against. They were guaranteed by law a series of election broadcasts, over whose style and content they had total control. Get those right, and otherwise expose their people as little as possible, was perhaps the thing for them to do. In any case, forty years ago the public meeting was still a popular feature of an election campaign. One reason why I had difficulty matching heavyweight spokesmen in studio debate is that they had long since been assigned to speaking engagements across the country. The following Thursday, the Conservatives vetoed a planned confrontation between Denis Healey and Peter Thorneycroft on the nuclear deterrent. All the same, that evening, and again a week later, we managed other studio debates. But they had not the symmetry of Joseph versus Stewart. On the last Thursday, a week before the poll, when we had to have three party spokesmen involved, our efforts produced a lively final pro-gramme, and a comic opera behind the scenes.

I went for controversialists, known for their debating skills, rather than for status and expertise in a particular ministerial portfolio. The contributors would range freely, rather than stick to one issue. I asked the Labour Party to supply Richard Marsh, a rising star in parliamentary debate with a quick mind and a common touch. They'd have liked to help, they said, but he was speaking miles away from London that night, in Harwich or Lowestoft. He could not be released. The Conservatives at Central Office were not helpful, so I approached a backbencher unpopu-lar with headquarters, Gerald Nabarro – a bumptious fellow with a big moustache, blunt of speech. The Liberal spokesman would be Nancy, Baroness Sear. For Labour, in Marsh's absence, I invited Woodrow Wyatt, contesting Bosworth. Wyatt was no more the Labour Party's favourite backbencher than Nabarro was the Tories'; of independent mind and bullish disposition, he was to come out against the re-nationalisation of iron and steel in 1965. Once a conspicuous *Panorama* reporter, he was an effective com-municator. He accepted, and sent round to Television House the suit he would wear that evening.

At this point, enter the Representation of the People Act. Voters cast their ballots in individual constituencies to elect a single

Member of Parliament. Broadcasting authorities, when a parliamentary candidate appears on television at election times, ask themselves anxiously whether he gains electoral advantage in doing so; if he does, then, whether presenting a gardening programme or chairing a quiz, he is banned from the screen. No one questions the right of frontbenchers to speak to the issues of the day, but they are not allowed to canvass votes in their constituency, to the disadvantage of the other candidates. We indicated to our guests they were to address the nation. They were happy to oblige.

Not everyone was content, though. At Labour Party headquarters, Transport House, Woodrow Wyatt was regarded with loathing as a backbencher not to be trusted, who would not toe the line. They telephoned, and urged me to de-book him. I said I could not. I had asked for Dick Marsh in the first place; since he was unavailable, I had invited Wyatt and now, with a programme to get on the air, must stick with him. Some hours passed. The Labour Party rang again. They had news for me. 'Foolishly,' they said, 'the Bosworth Labour Party, in spite of warnings, has sent a loudspeaker van round the constituency telling all who would listen that their Labour candidate, Woodrow Wyatt, will appear on ITV's *This Week* this evening at eight-thirty.' That, said the man at Transport House, would never do. If Wyatt now appeared on *This Week*, the loudspeaker van's activity would constitute a clear breach of the Act. If he were elected, there was a serious risk he could be unseated. They had had the painful task of advising him he must withdraw from his engagement. He had agreed. They would not want to leave me in the lurch; happily, Richard Marsh could after all be released from his speaking engagement on the North Sea, and would come to Television House. He did well; indeed, he was a class above the other two participants.

Surely Woodrow Wyatt had not really been so foolish as to queer his own pitch? It was Transport House that sent van and loudspeaker to breach the Act, deliver one in the eye to Woodrow, and take full party advantage of a television opportunity. John Harris, later Lord Harris, was the man responsible. In his memoirs Woodrow Wyatt confirms my guess – though, depressingly from *This Week*'s point of view, he writes that the invitation to him was from the BBC.

David Butler and Antony King's survey of the 1964 election picked out for notice BBC TV's *Gallery*, the *Ten O'Clock News* on radio, and *This Week*, praising us 'for maintaining a high level of vigorous, informative popular television journalism'. After thirteen years of Conservative rule, Alec Douglas-Home narrowly lost. It was those thirteen years that beat the Tories, not Home's appearances on television. Some believe, though, that with Rab Butler as leader the Tories might have won.

At Granada, I'd produced a short interview with Sir John Wolfenden when he published his report on the law affecting homosexuals. Wolfenden recommended that 'behaviour between consenting adults in private' should be legalised. It took time for public opinion to come round to this sensible, humane and practical view, and time too for Parliament to legislate. I thought this was an issue we should address. Bryan Magee proposed to interview male (and, later, female) homosexuals who lived in fear of the law. We would learn things we needed to know, and let homosexual viewers know they were not alone. None, talking to us, would agree to face the camera in plain view; all were filmed in silhouette. They were afraid to be identified, to reveal to families, friends, workmates, their true natures. Their voices, though, were not distorted. Simply, calmly, movingly, they spoke of how they lived.

To put these programmes on the air, in peak time, required permissions. The Authority, reassured that sensationalism was not our objective, gave consent. We did film men dancing together in a dimly lit club in Amsterdam, but it looked respectable enough. If we had misjudged the mood, a public outcry might follow. The day after transmission, I took a telephone call from a furious viewer. The programme, he said, had been disgracefully in error; in commentary, we had described Amsterdam as capital of the Netherlands, but the capital of the Netherlands was The Hague.

The day the programme on lesbians was to be shown, the *Daily Express* had a cartoon by Osbert Lancaster.

POCKET CARTOON
By OSBERT LANCASTER

" But darling, whatever makes you think that Aunt Winifred is likely to be on the air tonight ? "

We had managed not to frighten the horses; our supposed revelations came as no surprise to many. Television is accused of aiding Roy Jenkins' liberal revolution. It did. By putting into words what families are too shy, embarrassed and inhibited to say, but need to be able to discuss together, TV did us all a service.

My uncle Danny, my mother's younger brother, was a sensitive soul who wanted to be an actor. He was cast in a BBC radio play on a Friday night; his father, a minister of religion, forbade him to appear. Danny graduated in medicine at Glasgow University, and

later became County Psychiatrist of Cornwall, and then of
Cheshire. He and Ethel sent their daughter Susie to A. S. Neill's
Summerhill School, where she flourished. Danny was the most
gentle of men. He lived for the birth of a more tolerant society, and
saw small sign of its approach. Several times, after a *This Week* on
some theme of interest to him, he wrote me a line of appreciation.
He rejoiced that views for which he fought to win acceptance
could now find expression on so public a medium, and be
received and understood by millions.

I produced *This Week* for two years. The work cycle, with transmission on Thursdays, was near-perfect: Friday to recover, the
weekend off, with family. No one ever mentioned ratings to me as
a measure of success. All the same, in the first year *This Week* was
in the national top twenty rated programmes twenty times; in the
second, forty times. Once we were even top of the top twenty, the
top-rated programme of the week. An exposé of Soho strip-joints,
or an interview with a royal? Neither: a report on Turkish immi-
grant workers in Germany, the *Gastarbeiter*. There was no star
reporter, just a Tony Isaacs film. BBC1 was also broadcasting in
German at the time: Mozart's *Zauberflöte* from Glyndebourne, in
its entirety, preceded by a lengthy introduction by Peter Ebert, in
heavily accented English: 'In Act Two, Scene Two, we are coming
to the Temple of Isis and Osiris,' etc. BBC2 was new, and not
widely available. There was nowhere else for the viewer to go. In
such favourable circumstances did I practise my trade.

What we did was noticed; comparisons with *Panorama* were
drawn, to our advantage. In May 1965 the Queen went to Berlin,
her first, hugely symbolic, visit. *Panorama* sent Richard
Dimbleby to cover it in an outside broadcast which appeared
over-reverential, and had technical trouble. For us, Robert Kee
went to Germany; he showed us division in Berlin; he interviewed irredentists looking forward to eventual German
re-unification, to some a deeply worrying, and to many an

unpopular, notion. On the loose rein allowed him, he went back to the site – then in East Germany, now in Poland – of the POW camp in which he had been imprisoned, and to Stalag Luft III, from which fifty, having escaped, were recaptured and shot. This film said that, for all the Queen's visit and the ceremony attendant on it, old scars had not yet healed; old wounds ached still, and would go on doing so for a long time. T. C. Worsley, the *Financial Times*' television critic, praised *This Week*, and pointed to the contrast. *Panorama*'s 'bittiness and lack of immediacy was shown up sharply by ITV's pungent, informative, and slightly disturbing report on German re-unification. This, in the first place, revealed a far better news sense on the other channel; it was the perfect subject for the evening of the Queen's visit to Berlin. Then they allowed themselves their full time for exploring it, where *Panorama*, on present form, would have huddled it into a quarter of an hour.'

Worsley wrote this in the knowledge, by now public, that the producer of *This Week* was on his way to edit *Panorama*.

5

PANORAMA

The first suggestion I should move to *Panorama* came in 1963 when, still at Granada, I was deciding whether to go to A-R to produce *This Week*. The approach from the BBC's Paul Fox, Head of Current Affairs Group Television, was flattering, but half-hearted. He made no offer, but urged me to apply for the editorship of the BBC's flagship programme, then vacant. I agreed, and at the interview was quizzed haughtily and disdain-fully by the formidable Grace Wyndham Goldie, doyenne and mastermind of BBC current affairs. What would I do, she wanted to know, if, preparing to film, say, in one of the Gulf states, when the programme budget was stretched, I was offered free flights, free freight for the equipment, free hotel accommodation? I explained that in ITV we too knew how many beans made five; we accepted no freebies for news, current affairs or, I might have added, any other programme. The job went to the internal candi-date, David Wheeler. The BBC did offer me, though, a post within the Current Affairs Group. I opted for *This Week*.

It was encouraging to have been thought of; no current affairs producer had previously gone from ITV to BBC. Paul Fox was sticking his neck out in suggesting I might. One ITV programme executive only had made the move and made a triumphant success of it: Sydney Newman, lured by Howard Thomas away from his work in Canada to run ABC's *Armchair Theatre*. At ABC Newman showed so clear a vision of contemporary drama, and was so forceful in realising it, that the BBC had to have him; once they did, *The Wednesday Play*, *Z Cars* and *Dr Who* were on their way to our screens. My move, when it came, led to no such glory. But in 1965 Paul Fox asked me again – and this time he meant it.

This Week had continued to win golden opinions, and an SFTA award – the masked statuette which, one eye open, one closed, propped open many a door. And *This Week*, comfortably hammocked in the schedule at eight-thirty on Thursday evenings, was more often in the top twenty than not. *Panorama*'s ratings, on the other hand, were down; its greatest days, it was clear, were behind it. The superb team of reporters Paul Fox had deployed when he was editor – Kee, Kennedy, Day, Morgan, Mossman – was half dispersed, and their replacements were lesser men; there was not, to our shame, a woman in sight, either on *Panorama* or on *This Week*. Richard Dimbleby, a vastly popular figure, still presided, but was now drawing criticism for his old-fashioned courtesy and avuncular manner. Most important of all, *Panorama*'s role was being called into question by other outlets on BBC1. *Tonight*, its old rival, had gone, about to be replaced in the early evening by *Nationwide*, a part-political construct that gave the BBC's regions a national showing. Significantly, a new nightly current affairs programme, *24 Hours*, had been brought in after the news. Of the rationale for these shifts at Lime Grove I knew little.

Nor did I know then how fiercely the argument for changing *Panorama*, and redefining its role, had been put by practitioners inside the BBC. Certainly, over lunch at the Gay Hussar, Paul Fox made no mention of the single subject as an alternative way forward. *Panorama* was a magazine; Paul liked it like that. He wanted a programme that was watched and admired, that would always deliver the lead story of the week. He thought I could raise its ratings, and restore its past glory. He wanted a better *Panorama*, not a different one. He offered me the job, on one condition: Richard Dimbleby would stay as presenter; there was to be no question of moving him. He told me a secret – Richard Dimbleby had cancer. For years he had succeeded in concealing the pain he suffered, and the effects of the treatment he underwent. Paul Fox would not countenance any act or gesture that might set him back. I agreed at once, and accepted on those terms, leaving much unresolved. If Richard stayed, the magazine format stayed; without it, as *This Week* had discovered, there was little for a presenter to do. I hoped Richard Dimbleby's health would mend, or at least that his formidable spirit would keep him going for years more. I arrived at *Panorama* resigned to tinkering with the status quo rather than committed to change.

I told Rediffusion – A-R had restructured and changed its name – I was going, and where. The news leaked. This in itself was awkward, for Paul Fox had not told David Wheeler that I was coming. Worse, I agreed to talk to a journalist following up the story. This was Paul Foot, writing for the *Sunday Telegraph*. He knew that I had run *This Week* without a presenter, waving goodbye to Brian Connell. He put it to me that Dimbleby, criticised for obsequiousness, was an obstacle between the programme's subject matter and the audiences I would want to attract. Surely I would want a change? On that I held the line. But Foot was able to quote me, unhelpfully: *Panorama* was 'a class programme, with very little contact with ordinary people'. I did think film could reach out to viewers more effectively than staid studio presenters, but this stuff about 'ordinary' people was condescending tosh. Foot noted: 'his determination to produce longer items and film reports will have the interesting consequence of considerably lessening the role of the eternal linkman, Mr Richard Dimbleby'.

Paul Fox asked me to lunch at Lime Grove to meet Richard. As I entered the grim, dark-panelled hospitality room a large figure, silhouetted at the window, came forward, smiling, to greet me: 'So you're the young man who wants to get rid of me,' he said. It was impossible not to like him.

The first *This Week* after the news broke that I was coming was likely to attract particular scrutiny at the BBC. I was lucky.

I had a team in the United States which had finished its task and did not want to come home. Was there anything else director Peter Robinson and reporter Russell Spurr could do? In the Dominican Republic, the other half of an island shared with Papa Doc's Haiti, came rumours of a coup, backed perhaps by Castro, to restore the exiled leftist President, Juan Bosch. Lyndon Johnson, acting to quell trouble in the United States' backyard, sent in the marines. Surely, the telexes from Pittsburgh pleaded, they could cover that? To save expense, they could hire a news crew from a US network, ABC. The result was a gem.

We saw their film for the first time on the Wednesday for transmission the following evening. Robinson, a former Cambridge blue at cricket, and Spurr, an experienced Canadian, never knowingly under-lunched, had done an outstanding job. They had hitched a lift with the marines to the Dominican capital, San Domingo, and hit the ground running. Moving across the island, their cameraman started shooting from the truck. All this picture showed was a continuous shot of empty roadway. I had an idea. There was no link man, yet we had to put our story in context, tell viewers where the Dominican Republic was and, in potted form, its history. I thought we could compile a background piece on 35mm film and run it on a second telecine machine, inlaid on the roadway unspooling on the first, the past superimposed on the present. Like tourists, we'd be learning on the way in from the airport. This device worked.

The high point came when Spurr, delivering a statement to camera in the middle of a street, came under fire. He dropped his hand-mike and ran to take cover. The camera kept filming. After a while the firing stopped; Spurr stepped out into the road and started his statement again. I knew we should neither scrub the first attempt nor start the second halfway through. We ran both. To round it all off, Spurr had also secured an interview with Bosch in his Haitian refuge.

Rushes were logged through Wednesday night; editing proceeded frantically through Thursday. So tight up against the deadline were we that the first reel of dubbed film had already been put on its telecine machine and was rolling on air before dubbing had finished on the second reel, several floors above in the theatre. It too was rushed by lift to telecine and inserted, in time to follow on – but not quite perfectly; we saw a second or two of black between the reels. Paul Fox congratulated me. I said, 'But Paul, you must have seen the black between the reels?' He said: 'That's my boy.' I realised that response to the news, however rough and ready, would always appeal to Paul Fox.

The party on the Friday I left *This Week* was one of the happiest nights of my life, capping two good, fulfilling years. I worked with good people; we got on well; we delivered more than was expected of us. A cool researcher, Stacy Waddy, had sussed out my liking for art, and colleagues gave me a maquette by the sculptor Peter Peri of an old man on a bench, feeding birds. I take pleasure in it still.

Joining *Panorama* in July, through the summer I made contact with my new colleagues, among them key figures in BBC Television's daily programming: Derrick Amoore, ex-*Tonight* and now in charge of bringing on *Nationwide*, and Tony Whitby, his deputy, responsible for the new nightly current affairs magazine *24 Hours*. They deprecated recent silly-billy rivalries between *Tonight* and *Panorama* and hoped we could work together without resorting to school-playground tricks such as hijacking each other's interviewees. To us three, it seemed sensible that a proactive *Panorama*'s approach should differ from their reactive responses to the news. I hoped they spoke for others.

Panorama would need, I thought, a new title sequence. A bright BBC TV graphics artist, Alan Jeapes, designed one: images of people – our subject and our audience – cut to music. I asked a colleague at Rediffusion, David Hodgson, to find me a theme tune as lively as *Karelia*, but grander. He came up with the opening of the last movement of Rachmaninov's First Symphony. The melody is stunning – bold, attention-catching, rhythmically exciting. The tune, however, was long, running more than a minute. We succeeded in cutting it down to forty-three seconds. It was still too long.

The sun shone on Lime Grove as I waited, chewing on the summer's events. In early September the Prime Minister of Southern Rhodesia, Ian Smith, came to London to negotiate independence for his country (now Zimbabwe). He sought a settlement that would leave the vast majority of the population, black Africans, firmly under the control of the white land-owning minority. Smith was a decorated RAF fighter pilot who had fought in the Battle of Britain. The British Prime Minister, Harold Wilson, did not want this war hero appealing, on television, over the heads of negotiators at Lancaster House, directly to the British people. Downing Street moved to prevent it.

At Rediffusion Cyril Bennett, having oversight of *This Week* again following my departure, went to the Rhodesian delegation's hotel, on his way to work on Monday morning and asked if Smith would be interviewed live on *This Week* on Thursday. He would.

On the Thursday afternoon at Television House, the interviewer–presenter George Ffitch was plotting the line of questioning when the telephone rang; the Prime Minister's press officer, Trevor Lloyd-Hughes, was on the line.

'George, we understand that you are proposing to interview Ian Smith on *This Week* tonight.'

'Yes, Trevor, that is correct.'

'But didn't you get the message?'

'No, Trevor. What message?'

'That we didn't want him interviewed while negotiations are going on. We particularly asked that he should not be. The other side got the message, and have complied.'

'Well, Trevor, I know of no message, and we are preparing the interview now.'

'George, if you won't agree to pull back from this, I shall have to speak again to Bert Aylestone [Chairman of the ITA]. I don't understand why they didn't pass this on. I'm sure you will hear from Brompton Road.'

'Trevor, if, after this, I hear anything at all from Brompton Road, a full account of our conversation will appear in Sunday's papers. I am sitting here with Colin Legum [of the *Observer*] and Perry Worsthorne [of the *Sunday Telegraph*]; they are both extremely interested by it.'

No more was heard from No. 10, or from the ITA. *This Week*'s interview with Smith went ahead.

But BBC Television, it turned out, had got the message. In the absence of the Director-General, Hugh Carleton Greene, someone at Downing Street had spoken to the Chairman of the Governors, Lord Normanbrook, a former Cabinet Secretary. Finding that the Current Affairs Group had already extended an invitation to Smith, he instructed them to withdraw it. Very reluctantly, they did so. Following *This Week*'s transmission, on the Friday, as Ian Smith departed for Salisbury, *24 Hours* rushed a unit to Heathrow to record a conversation with him before he left.

On this incident I based what I call the doctrine of two telephone calls: the absolute need in a free society for plurality in broadcasting, if truths are not to be suppressed by the state. In totalitarian societies one call suffices. In ours, on this occasion, two calls were made: one was acted on; the other did not get through. The ITA, regulating a less centralised system, simply ignored what was pressed on them.

Grace Wyndham Goldie, Head of Talks and Current Affairs, Television, wrote a detailed account of the BBC's role in the ecology of British political life, spelling out its responsibilities, urging its continued independence. Not a word of this transaction sullies its pages. But there were red and angry faces at Lime Grove.

Waiting, I sniffed the air, and mulled over options for a start to the season. In the drawer of my desk I found a pamphlet by the previous BBC Chairman, Sir Arthur fforde, a former headmaster of Rugby, defining the moral principles on which a broadcaster should base his work. Whether it had been placed there specially for me, or simply left behind by the last occupant, I never discovered. More mundanely, the first internal memo I opened was from Personnel; it instructed that heads of department, when reporting annually on colleagues' performance, should avoid the practice of referring to them by their Christian names alone.

Events decided the subject matter of my first *Panorama*. In late August, India and Pakistan went to war over Kashmir. We were due on air on 27 September. This war did not pose a global threat as Korea had done. Nor did it presage a bloodbath. But it was a shooting war between two major Commonwealth nations; we must cover it. If we could get film reports from each side back in time, there must be enough material for a one-subject programme. Leonard Parkin was despatched to Pakistan, Michael Charlton to India; both were reliable reporters, but neither film report was remarkable. Richard Dimbleby acted as link man. Instead of an eye-opening debut, this was a non-event. I was used to the tight-crammed twenty-five minutes of *This Week*, an egg packed with meat; in *Panorama*'s fifty minutes our material was stretched thin. I ought to have added a studio element. It never occurred to me, though, to add another item on a different topic. It mattered much to me to be seen to succeed; after a sleepless night, I rose at 5 a.m. and set out in search of a newsagent open early, walking from Chiswick to Hammersmith before I found one. The critics confirmed my guess: nothing to set the Thames on fire.

The following Monday, 4 October, the Pope, for the first time ever, was to address the United Nations in New York. The event was remarkable not so much for what the pontiff might say as for the active engagement with the world that the journey from the Vatican to the Americas demonstrated. The address to the United

Nations was scheduled for just after 3 p.m. Eastern Standard Time, when *Panorama* would be on the air. This was Paul Fox's lead story of the day if ever there was one, though it was not easy to stand back from the event itself, and add to it. Richard Dimbleby very readily went to New York to lead our coverage, providing a translation of the Pope's Italian as he spoke. We struggled to get the sound balance right: to hear the Pope, and nothing of Richard, meant few would understand what was said; to let Richard over-ride the other meant not hearing the Pope's voice at all. Messily, we heard both. Next day Richard caught a flight home. The plane stopped at Shannon, and was delayed there. Richard spent the night on a bench at the airport.

At *Panorama*, I proposed to use the longer running time to tackle worthy themes; surely, here at the BBC, ratings were not the prime objective? Modernising British industry was a lively current issue, London's docks a case in point. Containers were on their way and could transform dock practice, sweeping away inefficiencies, and some jobs with them. London's dockers were adamant that not a job should be lost. Among their unofficial leaders one caught the eye: a lively, almost charismatic East Ender, Jack Dash; a communist, a thorn in the flesh of the TGWU as well as the employers. I thought it would be interesting to confront him with a possible future. The reporter Trevor Philpot, a prickly veteran of *Picture Post* and *Tonight* whom I'd inherited, went with him to Rotterdam. The Dutch had introduced technology that transformed their method of working; the workforce pointed confidently to the benefits of change. Dash was adamant this transformation would not wash in London. We saw the future, and it worked, but the dockers would have none of it. Containerisation never came to the London docks but moved downstream, and finally to a new installation at Felixstowe. Thousands of London dockers lost their jobs as a result. I live today at Dockhead, in Bermondsey, and can testify to it; they drive minicabs. The TGWU protested to the BBC that it was Jack

Dash, not any of their officials, who had been the nay-sayer. The BBC rebuffed the TGWU's complaint. The Director-General had liked the *Panorama* item, and wrote to me to say so.

The following week we were still on an industrial theme, reporting from Detroit on the US car industry. Bright, combative and Welsh, John Morgan had been a star on *Tonight*, and sparkled for *Panorama* also. He had a keen mind and a political explanation for nearly everything; among his enthusiasms, rugby and opera were high on the list. He had struck up a partnership in film-making with another Welshman, Bob Rowland, and it was this duo that went to Detroit. Morgan interviewed Lee Iacocca of Ford and the trade unionist Walter Reuther and, at the wreckers' yard, offered a variation on Henry Ford's verdict: 'History', he said, 'is junk!' The film report ended with a spectacular commercial for a new Chevrolet lifted by helicopter to a mountain top. Richard Dimbleby commented: 'I should still be very cross if I'd got my brand new car on top of that mountain.'

The next *Panorama* was introduced by Robin Day: 'Richard Dimbleby, I'm sorry to say, is not well enough to be in his usual place this evening. So the fort will be held for him.'

In this autumn of 1965, with Richard Dimbleby ill and unlikely to return, a critical question was posed earlier than I had expected: who would succeed him as presenter? For so long as it went unanswered, this question would bedevil the running of the programme. There were two principal candidates. One, Robin Day, was certain he should take the job, and fought for it every inch of the way and by every means he knew. The other, Ian Trethowan, believed he could do it too. Trethowan had been lobby correspondent of the *Yorkshire Post* and deputy editor of ITN. Robin had made his reputation as a political interviewer; like Trethowan's, his was principally a Westminster agenda. There's a well-attested story of his remarking to his producer, years later on a reporting assignment for *Panorama* in Vietnam, that he would interrupt a stay in Saigon for the front only 'if you instruct me to do so'; and then, confronted with the headman of a contested village, complaining that 'I should not be interviewing anyone of less than Cabinet rank.' I thought Robin a fine political interviewer, but pompous with it. I thought Ian Trethowan professional, but colourless. I knew Richard Dimbleby believed neither of them should come to personify *Panorama*; James Mossman, a reporter of flair and attitude, might. The issue could not come to a head while Richard lived. But *Panorama* was never principally a political programme.

As the year ended, Richard's life ebbed away. In December he broke precedent and let it be publicly known that he had cancer. This bold, honest gesture made a rare impact. In those days people didn't use the word, let alone admit to suffering from the disease. Doctors avoided telling patients they had cancer; family members avoided admitting it to each other. Richard Dimbleby's last public act, remarkable in someone who normally observed ceremony's usage and valued decorum, was to break a taboo. Paul Fox visited him in hospital, and signalled that there were only days left. In the last *Panorama* before Christmas I asked Jim Mossman to bid him a public farewell, from us, and from *Panorama*'s audience. We knew he would be watching. Mossman praised his professionalism and his courage. He passed on Dimbleby's thanks for viewers' good wishes, and conveyed our own. Richard Dimbleby died two days later.

There was one more *Panorama* before the year's end. This had traditionally been a grand review and retrospective of the year, the studio filled with grandees reflecting on the past, predicting trends for the future. I proposed something different: a film portrait of the year, using film and stills, mostly of *Panorama* stories; no presenter in vision; no commentator. The film's soundtracks, married to those images, would tell the year's story and, by juxtaposition, jolt us into seeing connections we might have missed before. Bob Rowland made it with a fine film editor, Ian Callaway. Two sequences stay with me. At the State Opening of Parliament, which Richard Dimbleby had covered for many years, the voice we heard, as Black Rod banged on the closed door of the Commons chamber, was Ian Trethowan's, standing in for him in his illness. We cut from that to Richard himself; earlier in the year, on the twentieth anniversary of its liberation, he had revisited Bergen-Belsen. Reporting this event in 1945, when he had looked calmly at the worst scenes he had seen in his life and said quietly, clearly, precisely what he saw, Richard Dimbleby had delivered one of the most memorable radio broadcasts of the Second World War. Twenty years later he had gone back to Belsen with Bob Rowland and a film crew. In terrible weather conditions and, as we now know, himself fighting illness, he made his report. We reran part of it, and marvelled at the talent that was lost to us.

Early in the New Year I received a letter from Mrs Mary Whitehouse, complaining forcefully that the scenes of starving, emaciated survivors, of naked corpses piled higgledy-piggledy high, shovelled into makeshift burial pits, were wholly disgusting and ought never to have been seen on television, let alone in a supposedly responsible programme like *Panorama*. I was never able to take Mary Whitehouse seriously thereafter.

For the *Panorama* review of 1965 Bob Rowland did something else remarkable. The actress Patricia Neal, star of *Hud*, married to the writer Roald Dahl, had suffered a brain tumour for which she had had surgery. Convalescing, she was now hesitantly feeling her way back to normal life and, she hoped, to acting again. Rowland asked to interview her. The camera rolling, he handed her a paperback of poems by D. H. Lawrence and invited her to read. Roald Dahl and he had conferred; the book was open at a poem on rebirth. Hesitantly, Patricia Neal read. Miraculously, as she did so, you could see her dawning realisation that she would be well again.

They waited for me in my office, sometimes on Sunday evenings, always on Monday mornings, like dogs waiting for a bone. Robin

Day and Ian Trethowan wanted to know what each was to do in that week's *Panorama*; each wondered who might get to say the two words, 'Good evening', that would mean he was the presenter. I refused to decide between them; I preferred James Mossman to either, and used him when I could. But Mossman was our starriest reporter. He ought not to be confined to West London every Monday evening. To others, the choice seemed simple. Huw Wheldon, Managing Director of BBC Television, was clear: Robin Day was a star, and should have the presenter's chair. (It would not, however, be Richard Dimbleby's own chair. Robin seized hold of it at the first opportunity. The senior floor manager, Joan Marsden, known as 'Mother', who had looked after Richard for a decade, was determined he should not sit in it, and removed it from his grasp.) But Huw Wheldon would not have to work with Robin; I would, and I knew that his appetite for studio interview and political debate could never be adequately fed by the programmes I would bring into being. I did not relish disputing *Panorama*'s contents with him week by week. What I should have done was tell him so at once, and go on, if necessary, without him. But I did not do so, and lived to regret it.

Most found it understandable that I prevaricated, with Richard not yet cold in his grave. Meanwhile, I wanted to salute his memory. He had broken a taboo; *Panorama* should follow his lead. At the end of January 1966 we mounted a programme that surveyed the cancer scene, eclectically, referring to progress in attacking several types of the disease and reviewing treatments then available. We heard of the scientific importance of Burkitt's lymphoma, met a patient undergoing radiotherapy, saw children with leukaemia and learned how chemotherapy could help them; stressed the importance of smear tests in forestalling cervical cancer; collected expert opinion in Sweden and America; talked to a GP and to patients in a cancer ward who were told plainly they had the disease. We realised how ignorant we were about it. The programme began on a golf tee as a former patient, Mrs Norfolk, drove off. She had had a breast removed, a mastectomy, and opened her shirt to show the neat scar. Mrs Norfolk's matter-of-factness, and her swing, helped dispel some of the darkness that shrouded the subject – as did the programme as a whole. I asked David Dimbleby to introduce it, to hold his father's torch. 'If my father had come out of hospital,' he told us, 'this would have been one of the first *Panorama*s he would have wanted to do.' Ten and a half million viewers watched this *Panorama*; the Reaction Index, RI, was the programme's highest ever at 84.

There had been internal reactions before the event. Aubrey Singer, Head of Science Features, wrote a sharp memo to Paul Fox protesting that science was his territory and no business of current affairs; we should withdraw. He was told where to go. At lunchtime in the Lime Grove club I met Huw Wheldon. 'What are you up to?' he asked.

'Tonight we're doing a programme on cancer,' I told him, 'because of Richard.'

'Yes indeed,' he said. 'You remember how Norman Mailer writes about it, "Cancer Gulch"? There's just one thing you need to know.'

'What's that, Huw?'

'Cancer', he boomed, 'equals death.'

Years later, Tamara had a mastectomy; years after that, although hope had sustained us both, the secondaries killed her.

Later in the year, in Mental Illness Week, we made a single-subject *Panorama* on varieties of mental illness – another subject too little understood or talked about – principally the cruel puzzle of schizophrenia and the ups and deep downs of manic depression. Jim Mossman, who knew more than most do of those mysteries, wrote and presented that effectively.

I discussed subject matter with Paul Fox only rarely, and less than he would have wished; but he was kept informed of our plans. General guidance and editorial direction came round weekly in the form of minutes of meetings chaired by Editor, News and Current Affairs. Informally, I enjoyed my infrequent contacts with ENCA and his colleagues; they wished *Panorama* well. We and television news had common interests and co-operation seemed in order. But they warned me off poaching a news reporter I admired, Martin Bell. 'He is good, isn't he?' I was told, 'but please leave him to us.' ENCA meeting minutes were seen, I believe, by governors as well as by editors. They served as a conduit through which influence could be exerted or directives passed on. It was minuted that, in looking forward to the tenth anniversary of the Hungarian uprising in October 1966, one governor, a former ambassador, had conveyed the Foreign Office's wish that programmes should pay due attention to developments in Hungary since, and particularly to the country's growing prosperity. Months later I watched with admiration a film by Christopher Ralling on the rising and the re-imposition of Soviet rule, wincing as the Hungarian puppet government stood to attention at the memorial to Soviet dead. After the bloody anguish of Budapest, the film ended with scenes of well-filled shop windows and holidaymakers on Lake Balaton. I remembered then the item in the ENCA minutes and mentioned it to Chris Ralling. He assured me there was no connection.

One touchstone of a decent current affairs programme is whether it can find interesting ways of tackling issues of government and political decision-making: the economy, industrial efficiency, health, education, transport. I felt this obligation more incumbent on me at *Panorama* than at *This Week*. Others hoped for higher ratings instead. Week in, week out, we did our bit. Looking back through old scripts, I find items on the mobility of labour, and what it meant to those who moved; on regional policy – a new car factory in Midlothian – and on housing. The minister responsible, Dick Crossman, was criticised by the private-sector building industry for disadvantaging them. He wanted to explain. We invited him to meet their representatives in the studio on Monday, Robin Day to preside. Crossman jumped the gun by inviting the builders to see him at the ministry beforehand, and battered them into accepting what he was up to. On his way to Lime Grove he realised that unless the builders he'd browbeaten put up a fight, he might not get a chance to make his case. 'For God's sake,' he said to me in the studio, 'tell Robin that if he's going to bully anybody, he is to bully me.'

Ian Trethowan reviewed the issue of defence expenditure, and gave an account of sterling's travails. We dealt with pensions and prices and incomes, and, over and over again, with Rhodesia. Ian Smith's bid for independence, UDI, dominated my eighteen months in the job; there were eight programmes, or major items, on the subject. Reporters went to India and to the Middle East, to the United States and to the Commonwealth, more often than to Europe. We looked through a window on to considerable portions of the globe.

The dominant issue in the United States at this time was Vietnam. We kept a check on American opinion, and showed excerpts from the televised hearings of the Senate's Foreign Relations Committee. Diplomat and historian George F. Kennan gave evidence: 'The first point I would like to make is that if we were not already involved – as we are today in Vietnam – I would think of no reason why we should wish to become so involved, and I could think of several reasons why we should not wish to.' We picked up, too, on LBJ's rueful greeting: 'Old friends, and members of the Foreign Relations Committee.'

The best film made in my time at *Panorama* was 'Vietnam: People and War'. The reporter was Michael Charlton, the producer Jo Menell, the cameraman – the only other member of the crew – Erik Durschmied. The film was seen by the White House in Washington DC as an attack on the US posture in Vietnam, partly because it showed, graphically, what the war was costing the Vietnamese people, and partly because it cast doubt – as Americans, including GIs, were beginning themselves to doubt – on whether the American endeavour could prevail, the Vietcong and the North be defeated, the South eventually be saved. Joseph

Califano, an aide to President Lyndon Johnson, wrote to me to criticise it. The White House also wrote to the Chairman of the Governors, Lord Normanbrook. Hugh Greene saw the programme as it went out and wrote a line to me immediately, to say he liked it: 'If it is criticised, I shall certainly defend it.' This is exactly the support an editor needs.

The programme was shot as a film, each sequence carefully composed, almost an item complete in itself. Durschmied's camerawork was superb. What really caused the ruckus in Washington was a simple juxtaposition. On board an aircraft carrier, Durschmied, low on the deck with a wide-angle lens, shot fighter-bombers as they launched, close up to and then past him. Still at sea after their mission, the pilots told of how their bombing had gone that day. Next to this, Menell put harrowing scenes of mutilated children having artificial limbs fitted; air power is a two-edged sword. Cause and effect? We were satisfied that it was American bombs – clusters, daisy-cutters, napalm – that had maimed the children, rather than North Vietnamese weaponry. The White House didn't like it. This was before reports of the massacres of civilians at My Lai, but after Morley Safer's pictures for CBS News of US marines torching thatched roofs that might or might nor have sheltered Vietcong. In the film, as on other occasions, we pointed out that 'scenes like this aren't pretty, but the Americans don't try to hide them. The Vietcong and their methods, behind their lines, are not open to scrutiny.'

The film's final sequence – low-key – was of an old woman in a field loading goods on to a rickety cart, pulled by a buffalo. A US helicopter comes over low; the buffalo, frightened, moves off; the load scatters; the peasant catches up with the buffalo, stops it, collects her goods and starts to load the cart again; again the helicopter, and again the goods spill. 'The Vietcong have been here ten years, the Americans three hours. The war in Vietnam at the last is the war for the heart and mind of this woman.'

The film, retitled *The Face of War*, was chosen to represent the

BBC in Europe's most prestigious competition for television excellence, the Prix Italia.

In mid-May, the National Union of Seamen declared a strike, nationwide, for better pay and conditions. This threatened dislocation and real hardship to a country dependent on imports. The Prime Minister, Harold Wilson, announced that the seamen's union was in the control of 'a small group of politically motivated men'. With Paul Fox insisting on urgent response to the news, we mounted a special on the day the strike began. With fifty minutes at our disposal, we could certainly add to coverage – debate the consequences for employers, the government, the nation; test the temperature; look ahead. The studio would come into its own and there would be an outside broadcast from the docks – Hull was chosen; we would question both parties, and put matters to government in conclusion. I approved the running order; the *Panorama* machine took over. Industrial correspondents like Harold Webb and *24 Hours* reporters like Michael Parkinson took part. All went smoothly. In the *Sunday Telegraph*, Philip Purser thought this showed the new *Panorama* could provide full-scale treatment when it needed to without patient preparation. 'The news of the day will still be able to assert itself when it's big enough.'

There were peaks in *Panorama*'s first six months of 1966, but the general level was unexceptional. The peaks for me were all single-subject; the magazine programmes I thought less successful. I had refused to settle on a presenter, and that uncertainty was compounded by the greater indecision: one subject, or several? We had to decide. I urged that, with *24 Hours* now succeeding as a news magazine, *Panorama* should go the single-subject route. I did not know then that others before me in BBC Current Affairs, concerned to redefine *Panorama*'s role, had urged precisely that, even suggesting a length of only thirty minutes. *World in Action* and *This Week* were clearly setting the pace in current affairs.

Paul Fox took me to see Michael Peacock, Controller BBC1,

himself a successful, pioneering *Panorama* editor. Fairly quickly –
I guess preparatory work had been done – he accepted the argument and authorised the change. *Panorama* would move to after
the *Nine O'Clock News*, in itself an improvement; it would drop in
length to forty minutes, which also helped; and it would redefine
itself as a single-subject current affairs programme. I would do my
best to deliver. Should there be, as we went along, serious doubts
or possible changes of mind, I asked that I be given an opportunity to argue my corner. What was I doing that summer? I was
thinking of going to Peru with Jim Mossman. Really? Did South
America matter?

Paul Fox spelled out what had been agreed, and what he
wanted, in a note to 'Editor, *Panorama*, ONLY':

I want to get a couple of things absolutely clear about the new
Panorama season before we set out on it:

1.   Neither I nor Controller BBC-1 nor others up on the Sixth
Floor will be happy with the continuing drop in *Panorama* audiences. They must be improved.

2.   Now that we are embarked on a season of single subjecters,
you must be fully aware of what's wanted: it is NOT stock-
piled, sociological Documentaries. Mental Health was *Panorama*
only because of Mental Health week; Cancer was *Panorama* only
because of Richard. We are not in the Documentary business.
Particularly with forty minutes, we remain very much in the
Current Affairs business.

The new *Panorama* must remain topical, current; all-embracing
the topic of the week. It can mean – and will mean – scrapping
the prepared programme and starting anew on a fresh programme of urgency. This is a firm directive – laid down by
C.BBC-1 – and one I agree with very much.

This memo lays down the law in clear terms. It is typical of its author's gifts and character. Yet it was never going to be easy to lift *Panorama*'s ratings, and the memo still begs the central question: can you both deliver thorough, well-researched work, and react instantly to big news breaking? Must not these two ends sometimes clash? I was by temperament reluctant to spike, and throw the product of hard labour away; others seemed to regard such willingness as a mark of virility. The gap between Paul and me was yet wider. I thought one subject meant just that; Paul that one could morph into two or three for topicality's sake. I made the single subject my aim; he saw it as only one of several possibilities this side of a magazine. Two or three topics, he seemed to say, did not add up to multi-subject; four or five did. Yet the course was now set; we would see where it led us. To hard work, certainly. With Monday transmissions, the weekend was spent at Lime Grove; *Panorama* was a seven-days-a-week job.

In the summer I went to Peru. I am fascinated by how societies deal with deep divisions between rich and poor, and the trio of films on South America we had produced for *This Week* had shown some extreme examples. The extra twist in Peru, as elsewhere in that subcontinent, was the role of the Roman Catholic Church. (And there were the mountains.) In Europe, the Church cared for souls but, in Italy or Spain, say, also propped up the social order. In South America, where conquering Christianity had superimposed itself on Indian culture, the rich were richer and the poor poorer. Some priests began to see it as their Christian duty to side with the poor. A theology of liberation was being born. We would look at this phenomenon through the experience of English-speaking missionaries: Irish priests in the slums of Lima; Maryknoll fathers from upstate New York, high on the altiplano. Jim Mossman, hard to please, searching, cynical, agreed there was a story there. Jim enjoyed telling how, in Rio de Janeiro, he asked the city's PR man what the vast enfolding statue of Jesus Christ, high on the Sugarloaf, was saying to us; without hesitation the man replied: 'He is saying, "Welcome to Rio, have a good time".' Neither Fox nor Peacock was keen, but to Peru we went.

Lima lay under a scarf of mist, the *garua,* that it wore in winter. From the airport we skirted the *barriadas,* the slums that ringed the city. Indian women from the mountains, in thick woven cloth and bowler hat, pissed at the roadside. We spent a day and many US dollars getting camera gear out of customs. The churchmen we talked to in our city-centre hotel told us, as we ate *cebiche* of fish and tender steak, that some tourists thought this was how the Indians lived. In the *barriadas,* it was clear they did not. I had never seen such poverty. Yet the movement from country to city never ceased. Here, there was work; on the altiplano, nothing but thin air.

The *barriada*s themselves were conical jumbles of buildings, piled high in heaps around the city, on steep slopes part soil, part domestic rubbish, the detritus of living; narrow ravines ran between, carrying filth and effluent and, occasionally, a baby's corpse. The church and the priest's quarters were in the little square at the top, clean, orderly, prim with whitewash. The young Irishman who worked there made no attempt to stamp out the rites and symbols of the native religion. The figure of the Virgin, dressed in spotless finery, was borne in revelry around the crowded square; beside it cavorted, to their own shrill trumpets and brittle drums, wild men in animal skins, shaking foxes' heads and cockerels' plumes, in ritual dances born long before the Spaniards came. The Irish priest welcomed them all, and urged on the authorities the need for clean water.

I marvelled at Durschmied. Hand-holding the camera always, he was never in one place for more than half a minute – walking backwards on the road in front of the procession; down in the gutter, shooting boots and knees; in the square's centre, and at its edge; high on the roof for a top shot; closing in on faces and the details of clothing; ending every shot on a tight cutting point; editing in his head. Later, in Puno, we filmed the Maryknoll fathers saying Sunday mass in an open market, the light falling on the altar rigged among the stalls. Durschmied's footage was an editor's dream.

Grit got into Durschmied's camera and stopped it working. For a day he sulked, promising doom. Mossman told him to get on with it. The camera was stripped and ready to roll again. As we filmed the Maryknoll fathers, a newcomer arrived. Durschmied tapped his glasses knowingly: 'CIA.' I couldn't take that seriously. Back to Lima. Jim would go up the coast to the vast US-owned fish-packing plant at Chibote and film more interviews; I would go home.

We got the politics of Peru quite wrong, speculating on the likelihood of an army coup from the right; the coup came, but it was left of centre. But the film Jim made there was one of his finest. 'Unlike the communist, the Christian reformer is pulled in two directions,' he stated. 'He's committed both to the eternal world, and to the here and now.' And he put it to the priest: 'When you give people ideas, you give them a sense of history, and that makes them take risks. You are inviting your people to take risks with their lives, are you?'

'True.'

'Could the Church,' Jim wondered, 'resolve the contradiction between the demands of social reform and the standards of divine justice? Can she do so without eroding the centre of her faith?'

Years later, a ruthless Marxist band, the Sendero Luminoso, Shining Path, terrorised Peru's countryside, murdering peasants by the thousand. No church could support that. But in other Central and South American countries, in the United States' backyard, liberation theology moved men and women to speak and act. Radical voices in the Catholic Church took front stage in politics, and paid the price: in El Salvador in March 1980 Archbishop Romero was murdered in his own cathedral of San Salvador while saying mass. And three Maryknoll nuns were raped, shot and buried at the roadside by the militia because they sided with the poor. In Peru, we were a little ahead of a story that mattered. For me, that was the point of *Panorama*.

After the holidays we would launch a new season of *Panorama*, running after the news at 9 p.m., for forty minutes only. There would be sixteen programmes in all before Christmas. I crossed my fingers.

In September 1966 a new bridge was to open across the Severn, bringing England nearer to Wales, relieving heavy traffic of the need to cross higher up the river and head south again before turning westward to Cardiff and Swansea. To mark this occasion John Morgan and Bob Rowland proposed a film on Wales, and a fine one they made, too: the valleys, ravaged by years of mining; honoured Welshmen at the Eistedfodd, clothed in bardic robes, white samite, mystic, wonderful, looking dark, brooding and full of fire – the Labour politician Jim Griffiths, the baritone Geraint Evans, the actor/playwright Emlyn Williams. Morgan talked to Richard Burton, Glamorgan Welsh, and his bride, Elizabeth Taylor. 'Had you heard of Wales when you met Richard?' he asked. With an eye to Welsh susceptibilities, Huw Wheldon himself came to Lime Grove to view a rough-cut.

In the week before the Welsh programme was to be transmitted, the Prime Minister of South Africa, Hendrik Verwoerd, the ideologue of apartheid, was assassinated in the parliament building in Cape Town. Jo Menell caught a plane out and was back by the weekend with a brief film report. A test was now upon me. I viewed the film; Jo had got as close to the event as he could, interviewing two Members of Parliament, one from the United Party, one Nationalist. If *Panorama* had still been a magazine, there would have been no problem; the ten minutes from Cape Town would have been included. But we were now committed to one subject only, and a film on Wales of higher than average quality, with a peg to hang it on, was ready.

I was against hacking ten minutes out of Bob Rowland's

carefully researched and edited movie, and also against mounting
a rush job on South Africa; Jo's fragment offered a description of
the event, nothing more. The Nationalist parliamentarian gave
this testimony:

> I was sitting in my seat in the Chamber and looking across the
> aisle, as I often did, at our beloved leader, Hendrik Verwoerd,
> and I was gazing at his firm broad brow and his clear blue eyes
> and was thinking how fortunate we were to have such a man to
> lead us, when suddenly I saw a figure come between me and
> our beloved leader, Hendrik Verwoerd, and I saw an arm rise
> and fall, and in the hand I saw a knife, and I saw the knife
> strike Hendrik Verwoerd, and instinctively, instinctively, I knew
> that something was wrong.

Hmmm. You could not parody that.

Verwoerd's assassin, Demetrio Tsafendas, was not a militant
opponent of apartheid but a crazed parliamentary attendant of
Greek origin. The assassination would bring to the fore a new, and
just as hardline, Nationalist Party leader, Balthazar Johannes
Vorster. It would have no other political consequence. The vote-
less millions who grieved for the victims of Sharpeville, and
suffered the daily indignities of 'little' apartheid, would notice
no difference in their lives. I offered Jo's film report to BBC1's
nightly news magazine *24 Hours*. 'Welsh Wales' went out, uncut.
Paul Fox flatly disagreed with my decision. The right thing to
have done, he noted later, was to have split the programme: Wales
twenty-five minutes, South Africa fifteen.

When I looked back, writing this, at the range of programmes
Panorama broadcast that autumn, I was pleasantly surprised. I
remember vividly only favourite films, and wince still at error,
or the clunk of the bog-ordinary. Individual films catch the critical eye, and some go on to win awards, but current affairs is
principally a utilitarian practice; the object is to inform, not

dazzle. *Panorama*'s list of titles to the end of the year was rather impressive.

That season we offered a far-flung report on the Commonwealth, in crisis over Rhodesia, in the course of which a bright young Australian, Rupert Murdoch, expressed the view that prime ministerial conferences 'lead only to clashes over issues which they have no power to resolve anyway'. There were two editions, on consecutive Mondays, on Smith's UDI and the world's reaction. Another examined industrial regional policy. Roderick McFarquar, an expert, presented an edition on China. The landline broke when we went to the Labour conference in Brighton; briefly – though it seemed ages to me – we lost the signal. There were films on Nasser's Egypt – with a rare and exclusive interview – and on the US at mid-term ('Half the Way with LBJ'). We also returned to the territory visited by *What the Papers Say* a few years earlier: the case of James Hanratty, hanged for the A6 murder. Prompted by someone at Buckingham Palace, we made a *Panorama* on the monarchy. Michael Charlton was permitted to film the Queen at work, but not to overhear or talk to her. The palace, still aloof from the media, was dipping its toe in the water.

The last programme before Christmas was a report on Robert Kennedy, commencing his run for the highest office in the United States. Phillip Whitehead, who also produced the film on Nasser's Egypt, did a fine job, with interviewees including Arthur Schlesinger, Daniel Patrick Moynihan and Sammy Davis Junior. 'If he wins,' reporter Richard Kershaw concluded, 'it will seem to millions of Americans like a Restoration. For them Bobby Kennedy enshrines the promises that Jack died too early to keep.'

For its next regular edition, *Panorama* had a new editor.

From the reporters' room, word had reached me that Robin Day, taking a break from ongoing correspondence with Artists' Contracts on the terms of his remuneration, was writing to the Governors and to Huw Wheldon, demanding I be fired and

Panorama's ruinous change of course halted. I shrugged this off, but needed friends more than I knew. In spite of mishaps, I thought the one-subject, forty-minute formula looked promising. I was blind to other moves against me; 'obtuse', someone has since frankly put it. I was not happy in my work, though; others were unhappy with it, and their unhappiness stirred them to action.

Our run proceeded through November, to moderate applause. The mines that now exploded had been laid, surreptitiously, weeks before. The Governors, I gathered, would discuss *Panorama*'s new format at some point; there was no suggestion I should be present. They did so rather percipiently. In his book *Panorama: Fifty Years of Pride and Paranoia*, Richard Lindley quotes Lord Normanbrook in the minutes: 'The single-subject programme seemed often to achieve length rather than depth. It seemed to him possible that the programme was attempting to be *too topical* [my italics]. Immediate comment on the news was the appropriate function of *24 Hours*.' Right on all counts. But, Lindley notes, 'this was not what the BBC management wanted to hear, and indeed, despite his pleas, Isaacs had been refused permission to sing his siren song directly to the Governors'. Hugh Greene, treading warily, said that 'in his view *Panorama* ought to meet both requirements', treatment in depth and topicality. The minutes, says Lindley, 'suggest that the Director-General did not reveal to the Board that the decision *had already been taken* [his italics] to relieve Isaacs of his command'. That decision bore little relation to the programmes we had made in that supposedly experimental autumn.

The one thing about which the Governors were quite clear in their minds, when they discussed the format on Thursday 1 December, was that *Panorama* should be a one-subject programme, treating its chosen topic in depth. They were not sure I always achieved that; but, from the minutes, it is plain that that is what they wanted. The point was made at several meetings that autumn – *Panorama* was discussed five times in all – and most articulately by a beady-eyed trades unionist, Dame Anne Godwin. Bizarrely, as Lindley spotted, the decision to make the U-turn had already been taken; Paul Fox had confronted me with it two days before. The day after the Board of Governors met, that news broke.

When the Governors next met on 15 December, Dame Anne asked what was going on. The press was full of the return to the multi-subject formula: the Director General had some explaining to do. The minutes record:

> Dame Anne Godwin said that the Board had understood at the time of their last discussion that the future basis of *Panorama* would continue to be the single subject, treated in depth, but it appeared to her that the issue had already been decided in a different sense by the time the Board had come to consider it. She regretted that the outcome of the discussions at the production level appeared not to include any positive requirement to deal with subjects in depth. DG [Hugh Greene, Director General] assured Dame Anne that this was not the case.

A fortnight earlier, on 29 November, Paul Fox had told me the decision was irreversible; *Panorama* would return to the multi-subject formula, and to fifty minutes in length. I must either accept that, or leave the programme. I said I'd go. Paul Fox had a circumspect habit of not saying what he thought of *Panorama* on a Monday evening; he waited till after Programme Review on Wednesdays before commenting. But at least he laid it on the line. I cannot say the same for his deputy, John Grist.

This tall, gangling, supple West Countryman, with a rural burr to his voice, always greeted me in friendly fashion, suggesting that he agreed with the line I was pursuing. In fact, behind the scenes, as Lindley's account makes clear, he had been working hard to bring me down. 'Though the single-subject programmes so far had been widely admired,' he wrote in a private and confidential note to Paul Fox, 'the ratings had shifted into a lower bracket since the death of Richard Dimbleby.' At some length he traduced my character and abilities – justly, perhaps: 'It is difficult to have an exchange of ideas with him without him getting fairly rapidly to fever pitch.' Yet, when we met, he smiled. A smiler with a knife.

When I came out of Paul Fox's office and returned to my own, shaken, Grist came to me, and said: 'We hope very much you'll stay at the BBC. Why not do some programmes on your own, on education, say? We'd welcome that. You must need a holiday; you could take one at our expense, perhaps in Malta?' In Grist's note of this meeting, which I have now seen, he reports that he offered me a month's holiday 'somewhere in the sterling area, technically to be covered as a recce for *Panorama*, wife and children at his cost, but major expenses guaranteed'. They did, it seems, want to keep me there somehow, or at least keep me quiet. In his note, Grist added: 'I would be only too glad for him to work for me. However, I did not think it tactful to suggest this at the moment.' Grist was to be the new editor of *Panorama*.

A taxi was waiting. David Webster, kind-hearted and generous, accompanied me to lunch in Knightsbridge. In the cab, I cried. At the other end, red-eyed, I accepted a drink from the European Commission's man in London.

Michael Peacock sent a note: 'We are sorry to be losing you. You have given us some wonderful programmes.' It was not till I read Lindley's book that I learned of Grist's memoranda denouncing me – correctly using my surname – nestling on the file like poison in a well. Happily I was not a BBC staff member, dependent on a superior's assessment. I was free to seek work elsewhere.

Next day I rang Cyril Bennett at Rediffusion. We agreed to meet.

6

SWEETE THEMMES

It felt like failure, but perhaps it was something slightly different: defeat. I knew I was right about *Panorama*, and would be seen to be so. The BBC's premature U-turn postponed necessary change for a decade. It is in the single-subject form that *Panorama* survives today, when both *This Week* and *World in Action* have fallen by the wayside. In the Haymarket magazine *Man About Town*, I put my case:

> I believed *Panorama* should have a sharply defined identity. Its best chance of that was a specific role; one long look each week at things that mattered . . . The BBC gave me a chance, albeit a brief one – ten years for the old *Panorama*, ten weeks for mine. They didn't like what they saw. I was beginning to. So were the viewers. The BBC changed its mind. It's their prerogative . . . 'Auntie' is not quite sure where she is going. She knows where I was headed though; too fast in a new direction.

Hugh Carleton Greene, when I asked to see him, received me courteously in his office in Broadcasting House, though I heard

my calling the BBC 'Auntie' had annoyed him. Conceding nothing, he regretted what had happened, thanked me, wished me
well; perhaps we would work together again.

Like Fred Astaire in the movie, I picked myself up and prepared to start all over again. Football managers get the sack, and
are inured to it. 'When one door closes,' said Tommy Docherty, of
Manchester United and Scotland, 'another one smashes you in the
face.' I was fortunate; Rediffusion welcomed me back with open
arms. Over a drink with Cyril Bennett, all was fixed up. I would
return to Television House as Head of Features, including oversight of *This Week* and – did I mind? – children's programmes
also. In three years I had had three employers. Now, I told
Tamara, it was time to settle down, and take a long view. Less
than eighteen months later Rediffusion lost its franchise.

There was unfinished business at Lime Grove which mattered
to me. At the end of 1965 I had produced with Bob Rowland a
Panorama of the year, a montage of film stories, no studio, no narrator; images and soundtrack told the story. For 1966, Barbara
Pegna and I had done the same thing again. That year had seen
two very different disasters – one aesthetic, in Italy; the other
tragic, involving massive loss of life, closer to home. In November
in Florence, after a cloudburst, the River Arno had broken its
banks; the flood deposited layers of mud and slime on monu-
ments, courtyards, churches throughout the city. It would cost a
fortune to clean up. Appealing to the world for assistance, Franco
Zeffirelli took Richard Burton with him. In his melodious Welsh
voice Burton told us: 'Franco Zeffirelli and I have come here to
Florence to ask for your help.' In October, at Lime Grove one
lunchtime, I had become aware of something much worse. At
Aberfan, in the Welsh valleys, a huge waste tip, the spoil of
decades of mining, undermined from below by torrential rain,
slipped downhill and buried a primary school. One hundred and
forty children lost their lives. The hopes of a village were obliter-
ated, families maimed.

Putting together the *Panorama* review, I found myself in the cutting room juxtaposing these two scenes. Music linked them. Film showed the church in Florence which houses Rossini's tomb; vergers in cassocks were pushing squeegees, sweeping the mud-tide towards the doors. The camera zoomed in to close up on the slurry. Over this, from *Messiah*, I put a chorus: 'And He shall live for ever and ever.' We were still looking at slurry. Another camera pulled back; mud covered the school at Aberfan in which the children were buried. Handel's music still asserted God's love for the world. The programme was transmitted at New Year. My postbag congratulated me on a promising new form. The notes that gave most pleasure were from Robert Kee, who understands film, and from the writer Len Deighton.

Tamara and I took a British Airways 'winter sunshine' holiday in the Mediterranean. In Athens, more winter than sunshine, it snowed; the pass to Delphi was closed. In Cyprus we stayed in Kyrenia, still in Greek hands. In the hills above the town, in Lapithos and Bellapais, we trod in the footsteps of Sir Harry Luke and Lawrence Durrell; at Bellapais the fig tree in the abbey ruins still stood. London tracked me down. My Granada mentor, Tim Hewat, sent a telegram: the commercial television franchises were coming up for renewal. Henceforth there were to be five major companies, not four. Granada's northern fiefdom would be split, diminished – 'a monstrous cantle out' – and confined to the north-west. The Yorkshire franchise was up for grabs, and he was bidding; would I join him? I would not. Rediffusion had been good to me, and I had contracted to be with them. I went to the Post Office to reply, wrote the telegram out in red pen, and handed it across the counter. It was handed back. On Cyprus only one man was allowed to write in red – the President, Archbishop Makarios. I wrote it out again.

The Rediffusion I had returned to was steaming ahead, scarcely a cloud on the horizon. Brownrigg had gone; John McMillan had taken over as general manager, Cyril Bennett had charge of programmes. Paul Adorian, on the main board, an engineer and something of a visionary, had pushed through, just ahead of the BBC, British television's first programmes for schools – a feather in Rediffusion's cap. Enid Love came from the BBC to oversee them.

Rediffusion was hugely profitable; its programmes secured vast audiences and advertising flowed in. *No Hiding Place*, with Raymond Francis, was very popular. John McMillan had splashed out and varied the background to crime with *Riviera Police*; someone suggested that *Underwater Rabbi* could not be far behind. Drama, the single play, came under Peter Willes, who scored a triumph with Harold Pinter's *The Lover*, directed by Joan Kemp-Welch. Pinter's wife, Vivien Merchant, played the lead; *The Lover* won the Prix Italia. Stella Richman, then in the script department, had spotted the talent of a young Scottish scene designer, Alan Clarke, who would later direct *Scum* for BBC TV, and much else of merit. Joan Kemp-Welch excelled in the studio gallery of *Cool for Cats*, a jazz-dance show – a rare reassurance that television was a visual medium after all. The ITA, while broadly approving the companies' populist stance, also looked for some awareness in the schedule of higher things. Rediffusion's responses were few, but spectacular; Joan Kemp-Welch directed Sophocles' *Elektra*, in Greek, and in Latin, *Laudes Evangelii*, a sort of ecclesiastical ballet spectacular set to medieval church music. Someone had the bright idea of doing *Midsummer Night's Dream* with Benny Hill as Bottom.

Entertainment was a less strong suit. Eric Maschwitz was a congenial presence at programme meetings; he had written 'A Nightingale Sang in Berkeley Square', which entertained more than any of us ever did, but I cannot say what memorable programmes he caused to be made.

Late on Friday afternoons, leaving for home, I would pass through a reception area thronged with avid fans of Cathy McGowan, awaiting admission to *Ready Steady Go*. Elkan Allan invented and helped run this hit, aware, as I was not, that for the young, lifestyle was all. Most ITV programmes were aimed principally at working-class housewives. *Ready Steady Go* was not.

It was Rediffusion's staple entertaining shows that were to cause it trouble. Two hugely popular quiz games – Hughie Green's *Double Your Money* and Michael Miles's *Take Your Pick* – were high in the ratings week after week. The ITA, setting aside its previous insistence that ITV's prime duty was to satisfy audiences, now dropped hints that two weekly quiz games was one too many. Rediffusion ignored them, and pressed on. It would cost them.

Current affairs – we called it Features – were in my charge. *This Week* had been in good hands in my absence, but would do better. When I left, Cyril Bennett himself had taken over, asking my advice on possible successors. Desmond Wilcox and Bill Morton put themselves forward jointly to do the job. They made a strong combination. I could see what sort of programmes they would do well: human interest. But I doubted their ability to tackle domestic politics, or hard foreign stories, with authority and conviction. I counselled against. They left to go to BBC2, where they delivered *Man Alive*, the first regular human-interest documentary series. I thought that rather proved my point.

Considering other names, Cyril thought laterally. For one stint he hired the BBC's high-flyer Alasdair Milne, who had abruptly left the Corporation when Donald Baverstock was railroaded out of BBC1 to make way for Michael Peacock. *This Week* was a doddle for him, and a temporary boost for Rediffusion's current affairs. And there came Cliff Morgan, Wales's and the British Lions' great fly-half, who had begun to make a career in broadcasting. Cliff had judgement, enthusiasm, wit and the capacity to inspire. *This Week* flourished; the production team enjoyed their work. But I would need to recruit.

Apart from a few strong documentaries, there wasn't much else to point to with pride in Rediffusion's factual output. The company had supplied no daily news magazine to serve London's viewers locally, as all the regional companies did. But with a quota of local origination to fulfil and a gap at six o'clock, Cyril, in a hurry one day I suppose, had come up with the simple idea of intelligent conversation; *Three after Six*, three lively talkers conversing, caught on. It was cheap, and just about acceptable. Dee Wells and Alan Brien, among other regulars, could not believe their luck; they paid the mortgage with fees received for chatting in the studio, as they might otherwise have done at just that hour in pub, garden or cocktail party.

Also in the schedule was *The Frost Report*. John McMillan indicated that oversight of this fell to me. I wanted none of it. David Frost was then riding high, *That Was The Week That Was* and its BBC successors now behind him. David had an entourage, a bodyguard of gag-writers and ideas men, who sat around the table and obsequiously offered suggestions. No one ever told him he was talking nonsense, that tonight's topic might be mistaken, or that last night's show was crap. I took my place at the table and realised at once that nothing I said would have any effect at all; the show was a law unto itself. David took guidance on the telephone from unseen, highly paid mentors, just before he went on air – Tony Jay was the most respected of these. Crossing my fingers, I let him get on with it. *The Frost Report*, never to my taste, always caused a stir. (Later, for the night of the 1970 general election, he and I were put to work together to make an hour for the network, between the polls closing and the first results. I said, let's do past winners and losers: Adlai Stevenson, 'It hurts too much to laugh, and I'm too old to cry'; Richard Nixon, losing in California, to the press: 'You won't have Dick Nixon to kick around any more.' I could not persuade David Frost to introduce this clip. A few weeks later, he was off to the White House to interview President Nixon.

This Week, and the rest of our output, were strengthened by an exodus from the BBC. In my wake from *Panorama* there followed a group of programme-makers who enjoyed working with me, and had supported what I was trying to do. They were ready to up sticks and chance their luck. Phillip Whitehead, one of the best producers *This Week* ever had, and certainly the best editor *Panorama* missed, took the view I had been badly treated by the BBC; the new *Panorama* worked, he believed, and I should have been allowed time to prove my point. When I invited him to produce *This Week*, he accepted like a shot. The reporter John Morgan, not a natural place-man anywhere, came next; director Jolyon Wimhurst also moved across to work with Morgan. Later came two more, exceptionally bright, junior figures: Udi Eichler and, a mere trainee in the *Panorama* ambit, David Elstein. They added up to a formidable infusion of talent, each imbued with the notion that public service broadcasting had the duty to tell audiences what they needed to know.

The ITV companies' franchises extended only to mid-1968. Those who had them must re-apply a year ahead; those who had not now had their chance. The ITA had a new chairman: the BBC's *Family Doctor*, former Tory MP and Minister of Information, Dr Charles Hill. Would he steer the Authority towards consolidation, or change?

The ITA added to the pattern of four majors a separate franchise for Yorkshire that would bring into being what was almost, but never quite, a fifth major company. The Authority also offered an improved franchise for London at the weekend (hitherto held by ATV, which broadcast to the Midlands during the week), adding Friday evening to deliver a fairer split of the seven days with the London weekday contractor. A cluster of television talent bid for it. Among the key figures were Aidan Crawley, a former Tory MP who had been the first editor of ITN, and who as a cricketer once drove a ball over the pavilion at Lord's; Tom Margerison, science journalist and technocrat; and Michael Peacock, then Controller BBC1. Importantly, the Director of Programmes Designate – in confidence, as the rules allowed –

was Cyril Bennett, his name put forward in a sealed envelope. Rediffusion was not in on the secret.

John Morgan, meanwhile, was making mischief in Wales. There the franchise was held by TWW, Television Wales and West, with bases in Bristol and in Cardiff. TWW's record was unremarkable, and Morgan and others took the view that they were vulnerable; it would be fun to try to unseat them and, if they succeeded, lucrative too. John Morgan had taken it on himself, he told me one summer evening outside a Kensington pub, to organise the Welsh component; the exuberant creativity his countrymen possessed would count for much. There was talent to spare in Wales – not just broadcaster and raconteur Wynford Vaughan-Thomas and Welsh-speaker, poet and novelist Aled Vaughan, but world-renowned stars: actor and film producer Stanley Baker; baritone Geraint Evans, the Falstaff, Figaro and Papageno of his day; and, shining more brightly than any, Richard Burton himself, with Elizabeth Taylor thrown in. Morgan had just flown back from chatting to the Burtons in the South of France. They were up for it; would lend their names, invest, perform. It was nearly in the bag. Would I go to Covent Garden with him the next evening, hear Le Nozze di Figaro and beard Geraint in his dressing room?

Geraint wore only a towel when we were admitted after the performance. 'Now boy,' he asked, 'what do you want of me?'

'It's simple, Geraint,' John replied. 'All you have to do is put up five thousand pounds of your own money, agree to serve as a director, allow us to use your name on the letterhead, and give one performance a year on the telly. That's it.'

'Done,' said Geraint. 'Pasta?'

The rest of the evening went cheerfully. The Welsh stars and Bristol suits came together under David Harlech, and took their title from him for the bid – Harlech.

The process of application and selection went forward. At its end, all the bidding companies were invited for interview at Brompton Road. The four previous major companies had entered bids, alongside the contenders for the new Yorkshire contract. If the talent-rich London Weekend consortium were to be accommodated, the ITA would have to squeeze elsewhere; six into five won't go.

No one at Rediffusion saw it coming; certainly not the chairman, Sir John Spencer Wills. He had, he believed, secure grounds for confidence that Rediffusion's franchise would be renewed; he was aware of no complaints from the regulator, formal or informal, that Rediffusion's service was below standard; the bus-company licences he operated were granted on the basis that, unless the service was demonstrably unsatisfactory, they would be renewed. Besides, the ITA owed Rediffusion and Sir John personally a particular debt. Associated-Rediffusion had got ITV off to a cracking start, but had incurred heavy losses. Then, when Associated Newspapers panicked and sold out, Spencer Wills had personally persuaded Rediffusion's backers, BET, to take up the whole of Associated's holding. Grateful for this, he reckoned, the Authority must renew Rediffusion's franchise. No one thought him complacent at the time, except at Brompton Road. Wills was not used to being interrogated; under questioning, he gave the impression that the Authority had no right to call him to critical account.

On the fatal Sunday morning the results of the ITA's deliberations were given to the applicants, and immediately afterwards to the press. The first words Hill uttered as he made the public announcement revealed his mind: 'If the intention of the Act was that franchises were never to change, there would be no point in this process.' My telephone in Chiswick rang merrily: LWT's application had succeeded. John Morgan, over the moon, erupted down the phone with his news: TWW was out, and would be replaced by Harlech. Corks were popping; joy was unconfined. But had I heard about Rediffusion? I soon did. Rediffusion had lost their sole ownership and control of the London weekday franchise, and had been offered, instead, a half-share in it together with ABC, which had served the Midlands and the North at weekends. The franchise was still estimated to be the most lucrative, but ownership would be split: 49.9 per cent Rediffusion, 50.1 per cent ABC. An unforeseen step up for ABC; for Rediffusion, humiliation.

Two viable companies, two programme staffs, would merge into one. There would have to be serious job losses. In the next days, the separate boards would consider the legal position; did they have to accept what was being done to them? For the two workforces, anxieties bred. People had thought they had secure futures; now they had not. Trade unions prepared to defend everything that moved. Individuals, as two at least competed for each available post, guessed at the odds, and puzzled over the future. Charles Hill, it appeared, had opened a Pandora's Box of discontents.

Given control of the new company, ABC's managing director Howard Thomas took charge of what would be Thames, with his colleague Brian Tesler as Director of Programmes. Cyril Bennett had gone to LWT. The Authority's wish was that ABC should provide the core of new departments for drama and entertainment; Lloyd Shirley, therefore, became Controller of Drama, and Philip Jones Controller of Light Entertainment. From Rediffusion, there would go forward into Thames myself (Features and Children's Programmes), Guthrie Moir (Education and Religion) and Graham Turner (Outside Broadcasts and Sport). Simple enough to state, far harder and harsher to bring into being. The fall of the dice was rough on Peter Willes, Rediffusion's excellent Controller of Drama. In service departments there was gloom and anger. How to choose between two perfectly competent programme managers, accountants, engineers? The official history of ITV records:

Senior executives from ABC Television sent to interview staff at Rediffusion's Television House were refused access to files containing details of employment. One, on a mission to recruit the best from both companies for the new Thames programme department, was asked by Rediffusion's Director of Personnel to leave the building. The staff of both the doomed companies [ABC, of course, would close down also] were anxious and bewildered.

I cannot pretend that, following the ITA's announcement, I foresaw how agonising the outcome would be for many. But I did think I should do what I could to secure my colleagues' continued employment. I lived in Chiswick, and so did Brian Tesler. I had seen him walking with his children in Chiswick Park on Sunday mornings, as I did with mine. In midweek I rang him and suggested that the following Sunday we met there.

It was a brief conversation. I told him the people I worked with did a pretty good job, and worked well together. If he would undertake that *This Week* would hold its place; if he would agree to my bringing into being for Thames what Rediffusion lacked, a daily local news magazine; and if he could guarantee also a monthly documentary, I would bring my department over, in its entirety, into the new company. He agreed at once. We parted, and went home to lunch. The following day I gathered everyone together and told them that their jobs were secure; the programmes we would make for Thames would be programmes we believed in. Meantime, we could get on with our work. I hate to think how things might have turned out if Brian Tesler had lived in Mill Hill.

Brian Tesler had the finest mind of any ITV executive I knew; his memoranda and papers submitted to the network, diligently drafted on Sundays, were immaculately clear. Expert in entertainment, ruthlessly objective in decisions he took about talent, and about programmes, he was the most skilled programme scheduler of his day. A quiet, private man, he preferred to eat a slimmer's lunch in his office. He and Howard Thomas were colleagues, not friends. Tesler was not an intellectual; his tastes in music and film were consistently middlebrow. I never heard him mention a book he was reading. With only a very few jarring moments, we worked well together.

With a year to go before the new company first broadcast it was still in search of a name; my suggestion, Shotgun Television, its onscreen image a cowboy levelling both barrels, was not taken seriously. When LWT, who had thought they might call themselves Thames, dropped the idea, Howard Thomas snapped the title up.

Howard Thomas had put ABC Television together as a convincing working entity almost single-handedly and, as Managing Director, had led it with distinction. He had made his name during the war in radio as the inventor of *The Brains Trust*, the popular 'highbrow' question-and-answer programme which made Julian Huxley and C. E. M. Joad household names. Then he was Editor-in-Chief of Pathé News, famously delivering to ABC cinemas, within twenty-four hours of the event, a fine film record of the Coronation. It was a short step from there to ABC Television. A film-maker I worked with, Peter Bradford, told me he once had a visit from Thomas, who looked at his shelves in surprise and remarked, 'You've got books here,' as if this was unusual in circles he moved in. But Howard Thomas's programming instincts were right for ITV; he moved ABC on and up. He knew the value of grand, eye-catching projects; to that I would owe a great deal. Politically, though, he was feebly deferential to the opinions of members of the ABC board who, like some at BET, were keen at all times to ensure fair play for white South Africa.

ABC's chairman, Sir Philip Warter, a wealthy man and a former director of Great Western Railways, was something else again.

'This is Jeremy Isaacs, Chairman. He's in charge of our current affairs programmes.'

'Good to meet you, Isaacs. About South Africa, you must remember one thing; it is jolly hard to keep the blacks in their place.'

His opening gambit over lunch was on domestic politics: 'I can't think what they've done, having this fellow Heath as leader. I hear he never even went to public school.' The Tory party, and the world, were moving on too fast for Philip Warter. A peak of self-parody was reached some weeks later. Sir Philip was making a goodwill tour of the building to meet the staff. Would I stand by, please, to introduce him to my colleagues? The first office door I opened housed a director and his PA. 'Sir Philip,' I said, 'may I introduce Jolyon Wimhurst and Mary Horwood? They worked on those two *This Week*s on South Africa you so disliked.'

'Ah,' said Warter, 'good to meet you. It is hard to get blacks and whites together, almost as hard as bringing employers and labour together in this country.'

This may have been meant as a joke, but I doubt it. Not a well man, he died a couple of years later.

In any case, to the ITA's horror, in June 1969 ABPC, parent company of ABC TV, was taken over by another show-business conglomerate, EMI. Control of the London weekday franchise, awarded after serious deliberation to ABC, passed in a flash to a richer stock exchange high-flyer. The ITA was embarrassed, but there was nothing it could do. EMI's coup displeased BET and Rediffusion. Sir John Spencer Wills asked Sir Robert Fraser, the ITA's Director General, whether, by a change involving only voting shares, control might not now be handed back to Rediffusion. Fraser refused, preferring EMI's entertainment prowess – dicey as that was – to BET's buses. The EMI accession did, however, lead to the appointment of one of their non-executive directors, Sir Hartley Shawcross, as independent Chairman of Thames.

The twelve months from August 1967 to July 1968 turned out to be happy and productive ones for us programme-makers, and for two good reasons: Thames wanted to get on air with a bang, while Rediffusion wanted to go down with all flags flying. Whatever the fury and dismay in the boardroom, John McMillan saw that the right thing to do was to keep up the standard of programming; staff morale depended on it, as did Rediffusion's last year of advertising revenue.

Since I had returned to Television House from *Panorama*, John McMillan had been putting to me occasional proposals for programmes that would embellish the company's output. He instructed me to commission the historian Alan Clark, later an MP and bestselling diarist, to write a television treatment of his book *Barbarossa*, Hitler's invasion of Russia in June 1941. I did so, and went out to Zermatt to discuss it with him. Clark met me at the station. The views were glorious. But the programme never got made; researching film for it, the Soviet Union being what it was, was too daunting a prospect.

In autumn 1967 McMillan asked me to go to Moscow when *This Week* was filming there. I was to sign an agreement with the Soviet news agency, Novosti, to cover the making of two programmes then in hand, and to explore originating more. David Frost was to go with me, or I with him. He was keen to present *Frost over Moscow*, with a participating audience supplied by the Anglo-Soviet Friendship Society. What this was likely to contribute to genuine discussion or understanding of life in the Soviet Union, I never grasped.

In Moscow, John Morgan was waiting for me. With Jolyon Wimhurst, a Rediffusion crew and the usual accompaniment of an Intourist, KGB-connected guide, he was to make one programme for *This Week* on the Lenin Hills University in Moscow, and another in Estonia, one of the Baltic republics swallowed by the Soviet Union at the outset of the Second World War. This would be the first occasion since then on which a Western crew had been allowed to film in Estonia. To obtain permission for this I had to sign the Novosti agreement. Clause one said that this was a 'Treaty of Friendship' between our two nations; clause two that nothing should be filmed that was not conducive to that end; clause three that the agreement specified a list of subjects to be covered, and that nothing not on that list should be filmed. Morgan had news for me. Phillip Whitehead, *This Week*'s producer, had sent on ahead to Moscow a freelance researcher, Royston Bull, who had lived there for a year when a student and spoke fluent Russian. Novosti knew that, eluding their watchers, he was able to converse with Russians he sought out or met; they objected to Bull's presence, and would insist that I should send him home. I braced myself for meetings to come, and set out to see something of Moscow – Red Square, the Kremlin, the Tretyakov Gallery. Then, with a day to spare on the Sunday before the Novosti meeting, I decided I must see Leningrad. 'Impossible'; no permission had been sought, no arrangements made. In any case, at this notice, no guide would be available to escort me. I persisted; it could be done.

The evening before I went, John Morgan had exciting news for me: Royston Bull had found two artists, highly critical of the regime, who were bravely willing to talk to us, face to camera. They had already been filmed. We would thus be able to present, uniquely, a dissident view of the Soviet Union. This was a journalistic coup of the first order, he thought. Since it would be necessary to get the film to London secretly, I, who was to go back first, would have the privilege of taking it with me.

Very early the next morning I went to the airport to catch a 5 a.m. flight to Leningrad on a day trip, returning by air that evening. In the hotel bar, John Morgan was waiting for me, his face this time grim. There had been an accident. They had been working that day on the Lenin Hills University programme, filming hand-picked Komsomol students relaxing in Gorki Park, picnicking under the trees, playing the balalaika, riding horses. The pictures would be idyllic. However, in an interval, our hero, the admired leader of the Komsomol, picked out for future greatness, had, owing to a fool-hardy act on the part of the controversial Bull, come to grief.

'You know,' said the university's prize student, 'I've never driven a car. Could I drive yours?'

'Why not?' said Bull. It was a rented Zim. 'I'll come with you. We won't go out of the park.' Komsomol, with Bull in the passenger seat, drove into a tree, breaking ankles and ribs, wrecking the car. Both were now in hospital. Novosti would want to discuss this sequence with me tomorrow.

Next day, alone – not a good idea – and shaking a little in my shoes, I set out to the appointed place in the outer Kremlin. The building's scale was intimidating. Novosti's deputy head of international relations met me, acknowledged there were serious matters to talk about. He stopped outside a high double door. 'Now,' he said, 'we will have a *corrida*' – perhaps he had fought in Spain – 'and we will try your Mr Bull, and sentence him to death—' smile, pause, '—unless, of course, he commits suicide first.' He opened the door to a vast empty Hall of the People, capable of seating thousands. At the far end, a hundred yards away and more, was a table with my interlocutors seated behind it. I walked towards them, steeling myself for reproof. In any case, I had dreaded signing the Treaty of Friendship between our two nations. Now there was this. Actually, on Bull, there was not much they could say; the tree had done their work for them. He was out of action, before Estonia. I asked that someone from the British Embassy should be allowed to visit him in hospital. It was the formal agreement that stuck in my craw; for Novosti there was a financial consideration, and for us the *This Week* films. But, signing it, I was party to a lie. They knew nothing of the dissident interviews. Honesty and honour surely required me either to confess what we had done, or suppress the material. I did neither. Journalistic imperatives, my colleagues had assured me – free speech, a blow against tyranny – required that I shut up and sign. Shamefaced but concealing it, I did so. The saga had chapters yet to run. I would leave next day.

Next morning at five I woke to knocking on my bedroom door. It was Valentin, my interpreter, come to take me to the airport. He brought me crab apples from his garden. Had I biros or razor blades to spare? I had not packed. On the floor a suitcase lay open, beside it a cardboard box containing film of the dissidents. I checked out. A burly chauffeur put my luggage in the boot. On the way to the airport I seemed to see policemen everywhere. Rushes for despatch to London were usually formally documented, the contents listed, the package consigned as freight to British European Airways. What I carried had gone through no such process. 'Valentin,' I said in the car, 'I have film with me for which we haven't done the paperwork. Is it all right today, to take it out without?' He gestured, doubtfully; maybe, maybe not. 'OK,' I said, 'when we get to the airport, I'll put it in my suitcase and take it as personal luggage.'

'At the airport? Are you mad?'

'Well then, let's stop now for a pee, and put it in my suitcase here.'

We stopped in the woods, opened the boot, opened the suitcase, put the cans of film inside, threw away the cardboard box. I moved to get back into the car. Holding the door, Valentin said, 'And now we have nothing to fear but the driver.'

I was never so glad to drink a cup of milky tea as when I boarded the BEA plane, homeward bound. On arrival at Heathrow, ITN's agent met the flight. He carried a cable from the crew in Moscow: 'Isaacs arriving hand-carrying 640 feet of exposed negative. Please meet.'

Later, the interviews were translated; late at night, they were broadcast. All hell broke loose.

The Russians sent furious cables, denouncing Rediffusion for its explicit breach of the Treaty of Friendship. There was no answer to that. The crew was home by then, from Moscow and Estonia. John Morgan was stripped bare at Moscow airport; hidden under his shirt he had icons he'd purchased at a street corner. John McMillan stirred himself to destroy the film of the dissidents, personally visiting the cutting room to remove it. Believing by now that, not least for the risk they'd taken, the writers' texts should be published, I offered them to *Encounter*. Thus the dissidents appeared in print; but they made no stir.

I have been bothered over this business ever since; partly I wondered if anything happened to the dissidents, who may not have been identified; partly out of real concern for Valentin, the interpreter, surely endangered. I was never in touch again, and I shudder now at how I treated him, recalling the 'gifts reserved for age' in Eliot's *Little Gidding*: 'the awareness of things ill done and done to others' harm/which once you took for exercise of virtue.'

In the spring of 1967 I had admired an edition of ITN's *Roving Report* on a coming famine in the Indian state of Bihar, reported by John Edwards. Since then the famine had worsened ominously, and I thought another film could be made there. Later that spring, the telephone rang. It was Jack Gold, an ex-*Tonight* film-maker of high distinction. He was free for six weeks; could he do anything for me? He proposed a topic: New Orleans jazz. I doubted he'd do the subject justice in the time he had and suggested he go to Bihar instead.

Jack had taken a first in law at the LSE before turning to film editing. In the cutting room he had learned what makes a film and, crucially, what to leave out. A week before the unit was due home, Jack rang to say he was finished: he knew exactly what he'd got, and that he had no need to expose another roll. The film was shot by a superb cameraman whom Jo Menell had spotted at the BBC, Mike Fash. Jack had him enter the darkness of the hovels in which the peasants lay; in the gloom, as the lens adjusted to the light, human forms appeared, spotted with illness, and spoke. Years of drought and failed harvests were taking a terrible toll.

Jack cut the film over a strange, sunny weekend in London, the streets round Television House deserted on a Sunday. War had broken out in the Middle East. My sister-in-law, Rena Weinreich, was trying to get on a plane to Tel Aviv; Israel appeared in peril. In fact, Israel won a dramatic victory, capturing vast swathes of

Arab territory with consequences that plague Israel, and Palestine, today.

Bihar's parched earth, cracked in ferocious heat, stretched for miles, not a blade of grass visible. Jack had started the cut I saw, two minutes over-length, with the river's broad flood surging along; then wreaths of flowers on the surface; then the realisation that the river carried corpses too. A strong start, but the parched earth was stronger.

'Jack,' I suggested, bracing myself for argument, 'the river is a great idea; but do you need it? Why not go straight to the cracked earth, and the bare feet over it?'

'OK,' said Jack, and it was done. It is the mark of a master to retain objectivity over his own work; Jack got to essentials and stuck to them in everything he ever did. Some of that work, happily, was made for me. All his films were a delight; one of them, *The Naked Civil Servant*, a masterpiece.

As the year went on, the goodies we dedicated to Rediffusion's swansong ran, without interruption, into provision for Thames's launch; it was an opportunity to give talent its head. Stephen Frears made *St Ann's*, a picture of life in the poor district of Nottingham where his father was a general practitioner. It contained one extraordinary shot: a long, long hold on a wideshot in a Victorian wash-house, still in use, a 'steamie'; the longer the shot held, the more the vanished world came alive to us.

Ian Martin, who had produced for BBC2 *Six Sides of a Square* in Gibson Square, Islington, came over to us and took charge of documentary output. He brought Richard Broad, the director, with him. Looking for a subject to be shown on Thames's opening night, we chose sex education. *What Shall We Tell the Children?* by a fine journalist, Sally Vincent, revealed a startling state of affairs: children were taught about sex neither at home nor at school, because adults were too embarrassed to talk to them about it. It was a devastating report. Alas, industrial action kept it off the air that night.

Another temporary victim of union power was Ross Devenish's film on the American Indian, *Now That the Buffalo's Gone*. This was shot in colour – Thames's first colour documentary. The title song was by Buffy Sainte-Marie. The narrator was Marlon Brando.

One Sunday morning, Ian Martin locked his front door behind him. His wife and the children were already in the car; he was taking them to lunch with grandparents. The telephone rang inside, and kept ringing. Ian went back in, and lifted the receiver. It was Security at Television House: a Mr Brando had telephoned; he was at the Hilton, and would like to be called back. For months we had been pursuing Brando, whose support for the American Indian was well known; he had said that he would narrate our film, without fee – but we could not track him down. He was either in Los Angeles, or Hawaii, or on location in North Africa; he was never where we called him. But now he was in London.

A few hours later, Ian and I greeted Marlon Brando at Preview One, a comfortable viewing theatre in Fauconberg Court behind Tottenham Court Road tube. Outside, the refuse bins ponged like nothing else in London. Brando liked the film. It was in three parts: a sketched history of the white man's arrival and acquisition of American Indian land by treaty and by force (the Indians did not believe anyone 'owned' land, and so lost it all); Indian families today, fishing and hunting, in well-watered forest in Washington State; the desolation of life on the reservation, with its staggeringly high suicide rate. In the afternoon we went to his room at the Hilton.

Brando said he would do the commentary – 'Great,' we said – but he wanted us to know for sure what we'd be getting. 'I don't do commentator's or announcer's commentary,' he said. 'I do it naturally.'

'Fine,' I said.

'I'm not sure you know what I mean,' he said.

'It doesn't matter,' I said. 'You do it as you like. We'll be very happy with that.'

'No,' he said, 'I do it naturally, and I want you to know exactly what that means.'

He picked up a piece of paper off the bedside table, and began to read to us some mundane information the hotel provided. Up to then he had been talking quite normally. Now he adopted a strange, hesitant speech, inserting – arbitrarily, it seemed to me – long pauses between words, and sometimes within words, between syllables, to dubious effect. The sense was wholly garbled.

'See,' he said, normal again, 'naturally, not like an announcer. That's how I do it. OK?'

I thought fast; we could cut the pauses out.

'OK,' I said.

The girls in the office were agog when he came in to do the commentary, and found all sorts of excuses to visit the dubbing theatre. But you could hardly see him in the recording booth: he was shorter than expected. He read. Later we cut out the pauses. He asked for no fee, as agreed, just expenses, a room at the Hilton for a week. This turned out to be two rooms, one, on another floor, for his London girlfriend. Charges were incurred for flowers and for jewellery. It might have been cheaper to settle on a fee. But we were not complaining.

Now That the Buffalo's Gone did not go out, as intended, in colour; a dispute with electricians over additional payments meant that it was seen, first time round, in monochrome. It registered all the same.

The big change in my life, back at Rediffusion and then at Thames, was that I no longer spent my week making programmes but had charge of others who did. I ran a department: Features. Current affairs and documentaries were familiar territory; children's programmes involved not just a different audience but different categories of programming, including drama and entertainment. They came under the close scrutiny of the ITA, and were planned by a Network Children's Committee. In this new territory I was fortunate to have as a colleague Lewis Rudd, who had been my deputy on *This Week*. In spite of his real strengths in that area, he was enjoying a new role in children's programming, including drama. Thames produced *Shadows*, single plays about the supernatural; *Warrior Queen*, with Siân Phillips as Boudicca; and a very popular science-fiction serial, *The Tomorrow People*. Lewis worked with Sue Turner to invent *Magpie*, a long-awaited ITV equivalent of the BBC's *Blue Peter*. Thames had the clout to command two slots a week for an informative and entertaining children's magazine; *Magpie* was a huge, lasting success. 'One for sorrow, two for joy, three for a girl, four for a boy, MAGPIE!' Ever since, I have counted magpies.

Lewis's great coup, though, was in light entertainment. Why should we not, he and I discussed in Rediffusion's last year, offer children comedy? Lewis undertook to find a proposal, and the talent to deliver it. He came back excited. The funniest comedy he'd hit on, a possible source of talent for us, was on BBC radio, *I'm Sorry, I'll Read That Again*. The producer was Humphrey Barclay, who responded to an instant opportunity to make television comedy. David Frost's company had already made *At Last the 1948 Show* for Rediffusion. For us, Humphrey Barclay devised and produced *Do Not Adjust Your Set*, surreal scripted anarchy. It was an immediate hit. It starred, though we did not know it then, half the *Monty Python* team: Eric Idle, Terry Jones and Michael

Palin. *Do Not Adjust Your Set* became must-see television, and not just for children; adults left their work early to watch it. I suggested to Philip Jones we should transfer the programme to his care for peak-time viewing. The performers were keen; but Philip's pipeline of situation comedy hits was chock-full. When Idle, Jones and Palin surfaced it was on BBC2.

Rediffusion had never had a daily weekday programme; Tesler and I had agreed that Thames would. At Teddington Lock, where ABC had studios that Thames would inherit, I climbed aboard the MV *Iris*, one of 'the little ships' that went to Dunkirk. There, I was introduced to Eamonn Andrews. Brian Tesler attached a condition to our undertaking a daily magazine: Eamonn must introduce it. I needed no persuasion, though Eamonn, a stranger to current affairs, would need tender loving care, and guidance in his earpiece. But he was a name, and a talent, and, if a stick-in-the-mud at times, an easy man to work with.

For Thames, I now engaged producers to make our daily magazine *Today*. This, in a way, would be Thames's signature – the pledge of what was promised; the first new Thames show to be seen on air. Eamonn presented it behind glass, in full view of the public passing, in Kingsway. After its first week, the critic Francis Hope, a poet and Fellow of All Souls, wrote of it in the *New Statesman*: 'There is nothing wrong with this programme that firing the production team would not put right.' Changes, after an interval, followed.

The producer who, first in double harness, then single-handed, turned *Today* round and made it a telling success was Andy Allan, a Geordie with a first-class degree in philosophy who came to us from ITN. Andy Allan would go far. He revelled in *Today*, mixing reactive reportage with the performer's scripted column. Kenneth Robinson, with an extraordinary tic in one eye that vanished as soon as he was on camera, contributed droll observations on the byways and oddities of London life. Monty Modlyn, an unstoppable intruder, barged his way into privacies that were no business of his. The audience, or a desensitised part of it, loved him. In a doctor's waiting room, at first sitting *stumm* as if he were just another patient, he startled his neighbour by asking, 'What are you in for today, dear?' Monty made Michael Winner look well-mannered. His worst excess – worst in that he came nearest to causing death by heart attack – was played out in Madame Tussaud's. Still as a waxwork, Monty posed, microphone in hand. Visitors trouped past; some gawped, 'He's so real.' One group were mesmerised. Monty broke the spell. 'Are you enjoying yourselves, ladies?' Shrieks of terror, fainting fits, convulsions. No one sued. Monty also doorstepped the Queen, stepping forward, without notice or permission, to talk to her when she arrived one day at the Festival Hall. He called a book he wrote *Pardon My Cheek*. We did.

I thought that *Today*, in responsible mode, would report London government, at that time opaque. It was hard to know who was accountable for what – borough, Greater London Council or Whitehall. There was no elected mayor. It was never easy to make GLC proceedings palatable, let alone compellingly viewable. I did my best to get on terms with the leaders, but eye-opening announcements from them were few. One encounter stuck in my mind. In a taxi one afternoon, between St James's and Westminster, a star GLC member, Jeffrey Archer, explained to me that all was going well at County Hall: 'We've installed a bar for the press. That helps, if you follow my logic,' he said.

Today was held together, year on year, by Eamonn. Brian Tesler knew that *The Eamonn Andrews Show*, halting chat with celebrities on ABC's Sunday nights, would not work for Thames. Instead, Tesler had the bright idea of buying rights to *This Is Your Life*, which had been a hit for the BBC. With Eamonn holding the commemorative and intrusive red book, Wednesday evening became Thames's most watched and lucrative: *This Is Your Life*, before *Coronation Street*, followed by sitcoms back to back, or Benny Hill, or both, delivered the audiences advertisers demanded, without fail. But the fees for *This Is Your Life* did not match Eamonn's contractual expectations; so on three or four evenings Eamonn introduced *Today*, coping, sometimes convincingly, with a liquorice allsorts bag of mixed subject matter. He managed most of it – human interest, showbusiness, crime, humour, even GLC politics. One item, though, wholly defeated him: an interview with Andy Warhol. Warhol, testifying to the power of his image – like Mao or Marilyn or a tin of Campbell's soup – was content simply to be. Whatever Eamonn asked, he said nothing. The long silences, and the cruelty of it, were excruciating. The sweat poured off Eamonn's brow, rivulets ruining his make-up. Somehow the agony ended. Years later, when Eamonn died of a sudden heart attack, I thought of the stress he must always have been under.

When Eamonn had a night off, Bill Grundy took over. His most famous encounter, alas, came much later, with the Sex Pistols, determined to shock. Bill, unshockable, appeared to encourage them to use language never heard before in early peak time. Much fuss resulted.

This Week was the lead element in Thames's networked current affairs output. The programme prospered under Phillip Whitehead for three good years. In Northern Ireland his work, though it dug deep, escaped any taint of bias. Before 1968 very few had probed beneath the surface of Ulster's political scene. *This Week* sent reporters to Northern Ireland. Phillip had had difficulties reporting there for the BBC; now again he found it hard going. Ulster Television resented visiting cowboys reporting on their patch. To do them justice, Brum Henderson, UTV's genial, hospitable MD, a giant bear of a man, by his white hair more polar than grizzly, was too well aware that he, his staff and his people would have to live with the consequences of reporting that inflamed passions, as we in London never would. In the last resort, UTV could refuse to screen our networked offering. The Authority did not relish this opting out; neither did we.

In 1965 the Wilson government had succeeded in instructing

the BBC not to interview Rhodesia's Prime Minister, Ian Smith. I thought the ITA, whether by nifty footwork or a tactfully deaf ear, came out of that rather well. Early in Thames's tenure, *This Week*, under Phillip Whitehead, reported on misconduct by Members of Parliament. Three MPs had been paid by a public relations firm, in cash and kind, to make the case for the Colonels' nasty regime in Greece. In raising parliamentary questions, hosting receptions, even speaking on the floor of the House of Commons, the MPs had failed to declare an interest. *This Week* was very sure of its facts. On the night of transmission, unusually, Howard Thomas, Managing Director, looking a little embarrassed, appeared at Television House. He had the ITA's Director General, Sir Robert Fraser, with him. This was no casual visit; Fraser had come to stop our transmission, if he could, or at least soften its impact. 'Why pick on these three?' he asked. 'It's unfair. You could make similar allegations against any Member of Parliament.' If that were true, it more than justified our report. But he came too late. Before midnight, one of the MPs – Gordon Bagier, Member for Sunderland – went on his local television to own up and apologise. Phillip Whitehead's *This Week* won an SFTA award.

On 21 August 1968 my telephone rang at six in the morning. It was Robert Kee. 'The Russians have invaded Czechoslovakia. I'm on my way to Prague. Durschmied has left Paris. We'll meet up on the border, and get in somehow.' They did, though not that day. Robert and Phillip Whitehead both had good contacts there. The footage from Prague, shot by TV crews from different countries, was sensational: tanks in the streets, people beating on their sides with bare hands; Czechs remonstrating with Soviet conscripts, 'What are you doing here?' – they had been told they were to fight the Americans – 'Leave us alone. Go home.' The Prague Spring was over, crushed by military might. Robert's interviews were authoritative and heart-rending. The film we got back was good as any, better than most.

Later Phillip Whitehead, who knew Czechoslovakia well, made a documentary in the *Report* series – *Remember Czechoslovakia*. It dealt with crises in the new democracy's affairs: in 1938, betrayal by the West at Munich, leading to Nazi occupation; in 1948, under the Soviets, the crushing of parliamentary government, replaced by one-party communist rule; in 1968, Dubček ousted, the Prague Spring aborted, Soviet rule reaffirmed. On each occasion the West did nothing. The ironies of these repeated betrayals made tragic viewing. ITV entered *Remember Czechoslovakia*, as the BBC had done my *Panorama* on Vietnam, for the Prix Italia. But at Mantua in 1970 the Czechoslovak representatives protested, as perhaps they had to. They tried to stop the screening, saying it would spoil 'the friendly atmosphere'. The Italian secretariat ensured that the film was screened, but afterwards rebuked ITV for its entry, reminding it of Article Six, Appendix Three: 'In the choice of entries, broadcasting organisations should bear in mind the suitability of the works for being broadcast by all the organisations participating.' For the *Listener*, I wrote an open letter to the Secretary General, Dr Gian Franco Zaffrani, protesting in return. The crowning irony was that the film showed the role played by Czech Television in defending freedom in 1968.

Later, when I had become Director of Programmes at Thames, I was asked to talk to a London meeting of the programme committee of the European Broadcasting Union, the happy folk who bring us the Eurovision Song Contest, on freedom of expression in broadcasting. I had no quarrel with the broadcaster's obligation to be impartial and accurate in factual reporting. I argued, however, that playwrights critical of society should be able to express their views at the public's, or the state's, expense. I was arguing for *Cathy Come Home*, for Jim Allen and Gordon Newman, for Howard Brenton and David Hare. To this European audience, I cited ancient Athens. Aeschylus' *Persians* deals with the greatest military victory in Greek history entirely from the viewpoint of the defeated. Sophocles' Antigone is torn between her loving duty to her family and the state's iron law; she chooses, against Creon's decree, to bury her brother's corpse. Euripides' *Trojan Women* shows humanity suffering in defeat, but the example is Trojan, not Greek. And Aristophanes' comedies, also paid for in part by public funding, mercilessly lampoon, year after year, the leading political figures of the day, rather as did the BBC's *That Was The Week That Was*. It was right, I suggested, in democratic, pluralistic societies, that this should happen.

Some of my listeners were having none of it. In France, ORTF was state-owned, state-run. A formidable Frenchman got straight to the point. Free speech was all very well, he said, but in the end, after all, broadcasters owed their first duty to the state. 'During the *évênements* of 1968,' he told us, 'I looked out of my office window at the young and rebellious demonstrators parading along the avenue. I looked at the TV screen in my room. On it, I saw the same pictures I could see from the window. I gave orders at once for the cameras to be switched off, and the coverage abandoned. I did my duty.'

Thames, its prosperity and pre-eminence among ITV companies increasingly apparent, began to raise its sights. Two documentary series that counted came along. The first, drums beating, colours flying, was *Mountbatten: The Life and Times of Earl Mountbatten of Burma*. There were thirteen hours, and it was all complete: Peter Morley had made it for Rediffusion, intended for use in their new franchise period. The executive producer was Mountbatten's son-in-law, John Brabourne. Morley's principal collaborator on *Mountbatten* was the historian John Terraine, who, with Correlli Barnett, had guaranteed the accuracy, rigour and authority of the BBC's epic of 1964, *The Great War*. The star of *Mountbatten* was Mountbatten himself. The programmes were sumptuously made; archive film was skilfully interwoven with interview and original shooting on locations worldwide. The signature tune of the Russian Imperial Guard stirringly recalled

Mountbatten's ancestry and set the mood for each triumphant episode.

The programme-makers, although rigorous in their factual narrative, had found a style of proceeding very much to Lord Louis' taste, a sort of triple whammy of praise: the commentator would say how wisely and bravely Mountbatten had conducted himself in this instance; carefully chosen interviewees, some of them, like the archivist Alan Campbell-Johnson, on Mountbatten's payroll, would testify to the same effect; modestly, Mountbatten would confirm that they had got it right, and detail again his achievement. (I know this was Mountbatten's preferred method because when I prepared to interview him a few years later for *The World at War*, sitting beside him on a blue silk bedcover in his Kinnerton Street apartment, he particularly commended it to me.) To mark the series' appearance on Thames' screen, it was arranged that we interview its hero on *Today*. I found him in make-up.

'What do you want to ask me?'

'Well, sir,' I said, 'what viewers will want to know is whether in your whole life you have ever once made a mistake.'

'No,' was the confident response.

Mountbatten, the series, demonstrated that documentary of this order could work in ITV's schedule, in near-peak time.

Phillip Whitehead made *The Day Before Yesterday*, a six-part political history of Britain from 1945 to 1959. He had excellent historical consultants on hand: John Barnes, for the right, biographer of Baldwin; for the left, Bernard Donoughue, biographer of Herbert Morrison. Robert Kee wrote the commentary and narrated. More than any other series, this one showed me how effective the combination of newsreel and interview could be. Archive footage pictured living protagonists; interviews cued newsreel of the event. The material was more vivid and plentiful than that for battles of the First World War. Those interviewed were younger, in the flesh more like their own images on film. The cut from one mode, archive, to the other, original shooting, seemed to lend a continuing ripple of tension, like little jolts of electricity, to the film's surface.

Phillip Whitehead has many virtues as a programme-maker; finishing ahead of time, or well within it, is not one of them. As the air-date neared, there was crisis in the cutting rooms; night after night, Robert Kee was furiously scrambling – he was right to be furious – from one steenbeck to the next, readying commentary for each of six films. The problem was not transmission, but the preview before transmission. Thames knew they had something decent to hand, and counting up the politicians of influence who figured in the series, they had decided to screen *The Day Before Yesterday* to an audience of bigwigs in St Ermin's Hotel, within the purlieus of Westminster. Invitations went out; acceptances came in. A projector was installed and a screen rigged up in an awkward, darkened room. But would there be a film to show?

When a film is fine-cut, and the fine-cut signed off as final, the cutting copy goes to the lab for neg-cutting. From the joined-together complete negative, an answer print is struck. It has no joins, but it is ungraded and less than perfect. But for a preview, the answer print will serve. One more night's work might have done it, though I have my doubts, but the episode of *The Day Before Yesterday* chosen for the preview was not completed in time to be sent for neg-cutting. There would be no answer print; instead, the cutting-copy would be shown. To make sure it didn't break, the editors worked all night to reinforce the joins, held together with sticky tape, with more sticky tape. The joins jolted in the projector, throwing it out of kilter; the heat of the projector melted the joins. To the bewilderment of the high-powered audience, and the dismay of Thames's public relations staff, the screening was a shambles. Every time the film broke, I said I was sorry, and hoped the fault would not recur. Every time it did. On air, the series was fine.

When Thames took its name from the river, I proposed a title film – a collage of sound and pictures of the River Thames. We would start at the source and go down to the sea, seeking out incident that was lively and amusing, dawdling in reaches that were tranquil. The film, making its own logic, would catch the river at a cusp in its history; the last flicker of life for old watermen's customs; the coming threat of containerisation and the death of London's docks. It would feature swan-upping and the Boat Race; a rude Max Miller look-alike in an East End pub, and Trafalgar Night in the Painted Hall at Greenwich. It would have no commentary.

David Gill filmed for a year in gaps between other projects, picking up ceremonies he could be sure of, responding rapidly to the unforeseen. On the dark side, we wanted a body fished out of the river. The news that there was one came to me in Chiswick on a Saturday afternoon. As luck would have it, it was way upstream in Gloucestershire, near the source. By the time the film store was unlocked and the camera crew racing west down the M4, the corpse had been retrieved, and all was quiet again.

We made much use of music; Vaughan Williams' *Fantasia on a Theme by Thomas Tallis* followed the young stream as it swelled into fullness; brown cows in a meadow chewed the cud to the yodelling song from Walton's *Façade Suite*; sailing barges cut their way across the broad river at Rotherhithe to Britten and Rossini; for containerisation at Tilbury, shot on a fish-eye lens for futuristic effect, the editor, Mike Taylor, found Milhaud's jazzy *La Création du Monde*; *Rule Britannia*, sung by all, blared out over Trafalgar Night at Greenwich.

What I most wanted was a wedding, and one happy couple agreed to our filming them as they went by water from riverside church to riverside pub – green lawns sloping down to a jetty – for the reception. The bride wore white, as did the swans she met on the way. Over the river journey, Michael Jayston read stanzas from Edmund Spenser's *Prothalamion*:

Ye gentle Birdes! The world's faire ornament,
And heavens glorie . . .
Let endless Peace your steadfast hearts accord,
And blessed Plentie wait upon your bord;
And let your bed with pleasures chaste abound,
That fruitful issue may to you afford,
Which may your foes confound
And make your joys redound
Upon your brydale day, which is not long;
Sweete Themmes! Runne softlie, till I end my Song!

Chris Dunkley, in the *Financial Times*, thought it at times more 'audio-visual poem than a common or garden film', one of the first programmes he'd seen he'd 'willingly buy as a video-cassette'. The cameraman was Ron Osborne.

Sweete Themmes seemed a bit obvious for the title, and *Runne Softlie* a tad optimistic. We called it *Till I End My Song*.

7

THE WORLD AT WAR

Making *The World at War* was – at least until Channel Four came along – the defining experience of my working life; having the opportunity to do it, my greatest good fortune.

In 1964, BBC2 had married the skills of programme-makers to the disciplines of history in *The Great War*: a history of the First World War – they called it the Great War, though the next was greater – in twenty-six forty-minute episodes. Gordon Watkins, a gentle stickler for truth, and Tony Essex, the powerhouse, had charge of the production. Two historians, John Terraine and Correlli Barnett, provided backbone. Imagery and touching eye-witness memories pulled one way; Barnett's and Terraine's commentaries, insisting on harsh military necessity, tugged against pathos. The combination was compelling. Michael Redgrave narrated; Wilfred Josephs wrote memorable music; there was a haunting title sequence. It was television to stay in for.

The Imperial War Museum was a prime source of film material; its director, Dr Noble Frankland, and his staff advised on its use and vouched for its authenticity. Noble Frankland was driven to despair by the last-minute opportunity Tony Essex allowed him to view and comment on each episode. He was further outraged by the re-use of sequences to represent different battles in succeeding years, and by the mix of authentic footage with staged reconstruction. Frankland protested in the press, and to the Director General direct. When the series was repeated on BBC1, a disclaimer acknowledging that some material was reconstructed was carried on each episode. Infantry leaving the trenches, stumbling through barbed wire towards machine guns, is that war's recurring and enduring image. In spite of blemishes that only purists noted, the BBC's *The Great War* remains a major achievement. The question was when might they get round to doing the Second World War.

The BBC had documentary-makers on staff, yet three years after showing me the door, post-*Panorama*, they enquired if I'd be interested in making a series on the Second World War for them. The emissary was Derrick Amoore, a brilliant but self-destructive senior figure in Current Affairs. I was indeed interested, though not convinced he was serious and, in any case, happy at my work for Thames. I then discovered I was not the sole candidate; others were in the frame. When I asked, Why the delay? Amoore told me that 'the computer had fouled up; the funds were not available'. I thought, Could we do it here at Thames?

Four factors prodded this notion towards reality. Two were series Thames had already made, *Mountbatten* and *The Day Before Yesterday*; one was an excellent programme-maker's proposal; the clincher was a change in company taxation.

Peter Batty, documentary-maker, wrote to Thames suggesting a military history of the Second World War. As Controller Features, it was my shout. I did not want to commit to Batty's treatment. It was fine as far as it went, but for me it was too narrowly, too single-mindedly a military history. War-history buffs might have enjoyed every frame, but I thought the risk was monotony; to most viewers one gun firing, tank manoeuvring, plane diving, bomb exploding, looks and sounds very much like another. I wanted instead to display, over twenty-six episodes, the total experience of the combatant nations. The Second World War was total war; civilians suffered more losses than did fighting men and women. I put Batty's proposal aside.

Then, in mid-February 1971, the Minister for Posts and Telecommunications (former middle-distance runner Christopher Chataway) stood up in the House of Commons and announced that the special tax levied on ITV would be reduced, and that a review would consider whether its basis should alter from revenue – the companies being taxed at source – to profit, the surplus left after expenditures. He attached a condition: if the change were made, the money thus made available must be spent on programmes.

I went at once to my boss at Thames, Brian Tesler, and he to his, Howard Thomas, and suggested a history of the Second World War. We needed to take the decision and announce it immediately, in case a somnolent BBC should scent danger, recover itself and get in first. They instantly agreed. I asked Noble Frankland for the IWM's collaboration, and for his own services as adviser. He assented. On 1 April we started work. Noble Frankland was to be our sole adviser. I saw no need for conflicting advice, and the IWM would be a principal archive source – though the considerable advantage of that was partially vitiated by the UK's agreement that royalties for the worldwide use of German war footage, captured by us and held in London, should nevertheless be paid in Germany to Transit Films.

My account of early consultations goes something like this:

I asked our historical adviser, Noble Frankland, to let me have, on one sheet of paper, or the back of an envelope, 15 military subjects, the decisive campaigns, which I would not be forgiven if I left out. This he did.

Here is Frankland's account, set out in his book *History at War*.

'Look me in the belly-button.' Lord Reith towers over the prize-winners, 30 June 1950. (Glasgow Academy)

Twenty years on, Controller of Features, Thames TV. (Thames Television)

Sidney Bernstein, inspiring, interfering: 'There's no one else you would want to work for, Jeremy.' (Granada Television)

Denis Forman, heir-apparent; the jewel in Granada's crown. (Granada Television)

Tim Hewat invented a language for television journalism: clear, terse, urgent.
(Granada Television)

Daily Mirror

3d. Friday, February 21, 1964 ✦ No. 18,715

'This is how I'll beat the jitters'

NO ELECTION BEFORE JUNE, SAYS SIR ALEC

By VICTOR KNIGHT

THE General Election will not be held before June. It may even be put off until October.

This was made clear last night by Premier Sir Alec Douglas-Home.

Sir Alec was being interviewed in the ITV programme "This Week." When the great Election Question was put, the Premier chuckled.

"I don't think I'm going to answer this," he said, "because it's really another way of getting me to confirm either a date in June or a date in October.

"I think those are the really practical possibilities now we are getting nearer the time when it is difficult to have one in March."

The Premier added: "I shall decide when I think it is in the interests of my party, and in the interests of my country, too."

Sir Alec admitted, in effect, that the Tories would lose the election if it were to be held now.

He said many people were getting "jitters" about a Labour Government.

And he hoped that from now on, the country would begin to decide that a Labour victory was "out."

Sir Alec went on: "I'm doing everything I can to help the country to see that the continuance of a Conservative Government is good for the country — whereas Socialism would be bad.

Vague

"I hope I succeed, and the jitters stop."

The Prime Minister gave a fairly impressive performance. But it was not as good as his appearance on TV last Monday.

When the questioning became a little too hot, he took refuge in vague phrases.

But Sir Alec stuck firmly to his guns by repeating his statements earlier this week about the strength of the British economy — despite the bad January trade figures.

He said the Government had evidence to show that last month's fall in exports was unlikely to continue.

A prime minister strips for action. Alec Douglas-Home in Studio 9, Television House, February 1964.

(Mirrorpix)

This Week in Brazil: a peasant in the market at Cabo in the parched north-east. (Jo Menell)

Richard Dimbleby in the chair at *Panorama*: 'So you are the young man who wants to get rid of me.' (BBC Photo Library)

Sunday at Lime Grove studios: JI at the steenbeck; producer Jo Menell; and, back to camera, film-editor Ken Bilton. (BBC Photo Library)

James Mossman, my preferred *Panorama* presenter, cool, elegant, acerbic. (BBC Photo Library)

Robin Day, a 'star', wedded to the political interview. (BBC Photo Library)

Ian Trethowan, informed, authoritative, unexciting. A future Director-General. (BBC Photo Library)

Back to Rediffusion: 'Come home, all is forgiven'; with Cyril Bennett in a Windmill Street salt-beef bar. (Matthews News and Photo Agency)

The Earl Mountbatten of Burma prepares to shine, discussing his TV series on *Today*. Eamonn Andrews looks on. (Thames Television)

Getting noticed. The Desmond Davis Award at BAFTA, March 1972: Mike Wooller hands the statuette to Princess Alexandra. (Thames Television)

David Attenborough read the citation, making my day. (Thames Television)

Prix Italia prize winners: John Hurt in *The Naked Civil Servant* and ...

... Norfolk farmer Geoffrey Morton, with two of the family.
(FremantleMedia)

Bologna, for the ceremony: Jack Gold, JI (with moustache), Verity Lambert (Controller Drama), Frank Cvitanovich and John Edwards (Controller Features).
(Thames Television)

Even before we had reached the necessary formal agreements, Isaacs and I had begun to map out the structure of the series. My first contribution was to observe that the original outline was far too much Europe-orientated and far too little directed towards the problems of the war in the Far East.

I urged too that we should break away from received British prejudices about the war and that, for example, the series should make it clear that the civilians who suffered most were not Londoners nor the people of Coventry, but the Germans from bombing, the Russians from siege and occupation, and the Japanese from both conventional and atomic bombing. I also wanted it to be made clear that the land operations which decisively exhausted the German army were not in Africa, Italy or France, but in Russia.

Frankland also refers to the overriding architectural problems confronting the producer of a series on a conflict lasting several years: how to combine, in one continuous narrative, battles that are fought and won in a comparatively brief timespan – events like El Alamein, say, or D-Day – with campaigns that last for years – protracted bombing offensives, or the enduring struggle to keep Atlantic sea-lanes open; how to combine accounts of successive campaigns with themes – the strategic conduct of the war, the effectiveness of a war economy, the choices open to those living under occupation – that have relevance over the entire period. How do you complete a treatment of any one of them without anticipating the conclusion and so spoiling the story? If you opt for twenty-six event-based episodes, the viewer will never see the wood for the trees. If you choose twenty-six themes, each over-arching, you end up with stasis, with no sense of forward movement in time, no beginning, no middles, no progress to an end; no narrative, no eager anticipation of next week's episode. In *The World at War*, and later in *Cold War*, getting that arrangement right was the first task I set myself.

As soon as the series was announced, I heard from Major John Macdonald. 'Mr Isaacs,' he wrote, 'I hope you will take this opportunity to do justice at last to the 10,000 men of the 51st Highland Division who fought on, after the retreat from Dunkirk, at St Valéry en Caux.'

'Alas', I wrote back, 'there would not be space.'

A very great deal must be omitted; not only Major Macdonald's Highlanders, but much, much more. I was making a television series, not compiling an encyclopaedia. Making history for TV is different from writing history. Robert Kee, who has done both (and with whom I was later to work on *Ireland: A Television history*), points to the differences. 'Not only,' he writes of television history,

does the story get rather arbitrarily broken up into the number of programme sections, but the television need to prevent the viewer from switching off, or at least going off to make a cup of tea and losing the narrative thread, often drives narrative on at a pace that would not be natural in a normal book. Bold things get done. Swathes are cut through history; qualifications and reservations that should be made get left out; many fascinating details get left out too, while some achieve a dimension to which they are hardly entitled. Then there are the weekly gaps between programmes down which may be dropped much superfluous chronology too difficult to be dealt with otherwise. In other words, a professional discipline other than that of history itself is at work. Which does not mean, of course, that in both film and book standard historical discipline is not at work too as far as possible.

But 'as far as possible', Kee adds, 'is not the sort of qualification an academic historian much likes'.

'The weekly gaps between programmes' as a repository into which to drop what you leave out is a notion I have found helpful. I am not a historian. Throughout my time in television I have set out not to tell viewers what I already know, but to find out, with others' help, just enough about any complex subject to inform them; my hope has been that, if I understood the result, they would also.

Noble Frankland suggested fifteen military topics; here is what I had in mind for the other eleven programmes.

To begin with, there plainly had to be a background, an introduction to the war, an explanation of its causes. To this we devoted one programme, calling it 'A New Germany'. Like all first programmes introducing longish series, it crammed a great deal into a little space. We concentrated on the German people's reaction to Versailles; the ravages of unemployment and hyperinflation; Adolf Hitler, and the Nazis' rise to power.

We needed also to examine the home front – not only in Britain, but in all five principal combatant nations – Britain, Russia, the United States, Germany and Japan. How efficient were the wartime economies? How was morale maintained? In the First World War, A. J. P. Taylor pointed out, the news that a loved one had been killed came to the home from the front; in the Second, the grim news often went the other way – fighting men might learn that a parent or a wife and child had died in the bombing of their homes.

Peter Batty, who himself made six of our twenty-six programmes and imparted to each of them an energy that drove the story forward, tackled the US entry to the war in 'On Our Way'. It was Russian manpower and America's industrial might that in the end brought victory for the Allies. The sight of US production lines gearing up to make guns and tanks and ships exuded and engendered optimism.

Phillip Whitehead, working with writers Angus Calder and Neal Ascherson on 'Home Fires' and 'Inside the Reich', offered contrasting accounts of how Britain and Germany mobilised their war efforts. Britain came well out of the comparison. The British people excelled themselves in the Second World War. Women played their full part – to a greater extent than in any other nation. Democracy actually worked; the British war machine was more efficient than that of the despotic Third Reich. Far from being a centrally controlled command society, Germany under Hitler was a collection of satrapies which jarred with each other. German women's place was in church, in the kitchen and with their children; they were not mobilised for war production, though slave labourers were, by the million.

In the 1970s, every film-maker dealing with the Soviet Union had a hard task; state censorship closed all doors. We wanted to show the full brunt and horror of Germany's Eastern Front battles on Soviet soil, where truly massive forces were deployed, millions were killed, captured in battle or starved to death, and more than 20 million civilians lost their lives. To do that, properly, we needed to talk freely to Soviet veterans and civilian eye witnesses, and we needed access to archives. We asked the Russians to cooperate; for eighteen months, they refused. We made a tactical error whose honesty cost us. We sent the film archive in East Berlin a treatment that made reference both to Stalin's decimation of the army's officer corps in the purge of 1937 and to his wilful, near-fatal, refusal to attend to the many warnings he received of Hitler's imminent invasion in June 1941. Stalin had been dead eighteen years when this document was written and despatched; Khruschchev had come, criticised Stalin, and gone. Yet we met silence and denial. The British Foreign Secretary, Sir Alec Douglas-Home, made matters worse; exasperated, he sent home 130 spies – low-grade espionage agents, part of the 'trade mission' in an extensive compound on Highgate Hill. Moscow retaliated. The doors we knocked on remained closed.

I shuffled the order of making, hoped, and pressed on. 'Barbarossa' went ahead early under Peter Batty – the story could be told largely from the German point of view. Jerry Kuehl made a fine job of 'Stalingrad' – all film, no interviews. The movie sequence showing Russian troops rushing across the snow to link hands as they closed the circle around the Sixth Army had, we noted, been staged for the cameras. Like Nazi Germany, Soviet Russia excelled in film as propaganda; 'Red Star', Martin Smith's account of the Soviet war economy, made full use of it. It took Soviet bureaucrats a long time to realise that *The World at War* would give full credit for the key role their country had played in defeating Hitler. When they finally woke up to this, interviewees were made available late in the day. I welcomed that, though we would have to slot them into virtually completed programmes. The Soviet witnesses, dressed in uniform, hung with row on row of medals, spoke to us with less spontaneity and frankness than did others. The Second World War was over; the Cold War was not.

Reg Courtney-Browne, a colleague from Rediffusion days, had lived for years in Japan, married there, spoke Japanese. He was our entry to the Japanese cult of dedication to the Emperor; for him, soldiers fought to the death, and kamikaze pilots set out on suicide missions. Here the images were fresh. To win, Japan needed quick conquest. In protracted struggle with the United States, it could not hope for victory. Firestorms consumed Japan's cities, killing tens of thousands in a night.

What could we, the British, have done if we had been invaded and occupied by the Wehrmacht? Would we, heads down, have simply got on with our lives? Perhaps resisted? Collaborated even? *Dad's Army* makes me laugh every time. But I feel uncomfortable with *'Allo 'Allo*, a similar comedy series set in the German-occupied Channel Islands. The handful of Jewish refugees found there, on British soil, were handed over and deported to the gas chambers. For Britain as a whole, the issues were hypothetical; it did not happen here.

In choosing to touch on the issues Nazi occupation raised, I decided not to come to grips with the anguish of Poland where, counting Jews in, a third of the population died, or with the twists of conscience in a France defeated and divided, which Marcel Ophuls addressed with masterly skill in *Le Chagrin et la pitié*. I chose to film in the Netherlands. Michael Darlow, a gifted film-maker whose work I knew well, and a dear South African – Afrikaans-speaking – friend, the journalist Charles Bloomberg, worked together on 'Occupation', and later on 'Genocide', a film on racism, the Holocaust and the experience of Auschwitz. The Netherlands lay close to us, just across the North Sea. The story of Dutch fascism, of collaboration, of Christian and communist resistance, was containable in one fifty-minute span. Poland's experience, or that of Yugoslavia, where 1.5 million died in civil war, would have demanded more space. In the Netherlands we found witnesses who spoke English. R. M. Van der Veen, a member of a resistance group, told of his experience.

> I came there on the platform and there was twenty-four people, young and old, ladies, children, men – chained together in an iron chain. And they were, of course, transported to Germany to be gassed. Four Germans were there – three on one side with tommy guns and one on the other side of the group. I was alone. It was twelve o'clock. You were in the midst of a city on a railway platform – what could you do? If I could by surprise shoot down the three, the other man was there; with my pistol – I was helpless. But even when you got all four, what can you do with twenty-four people who are all linked together in the midst of the day after a shooting party in a place that's crowded with Germans? So you walk away, and that is absolutely terri-ble. And if you have that experience you have a new stimulus to risk yourself for the few possibilities we had.

Out of Holland's 140,000 Jews, 105,000 perished. 'Occupation' was one of the first two films to be completed; the other was 'France Falls'. Howard Thomas was concerned that there should be action, i.e. fighting, in every episode. He questioned whether we needed even one programme preliminary to the war itself; but eleven of our twenty-six programmes would deal with subject matter other than combat. I needed this to be understood. I put 'Occupation' in front of him and awaited his reaction. He was taken aback, even disappointed, and said so. However, he showed it, and 'France Falls', to Clyde Packer, owner of Australia's Nine Network, taking Muir Sutherland, in charge of overseas sales, with him to the Savoy. Clyde Packer, Kerry's father, said 'yes' at once. 'For heaven's sake, don't tell Jeremy what he'll pay for it,' Thomas told Muir on the way back to the office. 'He'll only want an increase in the budget.'

Hitler's genocide against the Jews and gypsies, and the mass murder of others, is not a military subject. But I could not leave it out; not just because I'm Jewish, though that counted, but because I could not separate the evil of Nazi racial doctrine – Aryan supremacy, *Untermensch* subjection – from the Allied cause. Most people in Britain did not realise what Nazi racism in practice meant until the gates of concentration camps at Belsen and Buchenwald were opened by British troops in 1945. Auschwitz, Sobibor, Treblinka – death camps – were worse. I wanted a programme that showed the camps in which millions perished, before the series came to the Reich's nemesis in Berlin. Darlow and Bloomberg's 'Genocide', clear, restrained, compassionate, tackled an almost impossible subject. The IBA, after deliberation, agreed that 'Genocide' could be shown at 9 p.m. There was no commercial break.

Two non-narrative programmes on the aftermath of the war finished the series. Jerry Kuehl's 'Reckoning' made good use of harrowing colour film to show the desolation of cities laid waste, vast numbers of refugees on the move. The historian Steven

Ambrose summed up: 'The most important single result of World War Two is that the Nazis were crushed, the militants in Japan were crushed, the Fascists in Italy were crushed – and surely justice has never been better served.' The very last programme, 'Remember', which I produced myself, was an opportunity to reflect on individuals' experience, and to count the millions of dead.

In the bar at Lime Grove, editing *Panorama* in 1965–6, I had bumped into Tony Essex, who made the BBC's *The Great War*, and asked how he did it. 'At all costs, make your mind up what you are going to do, and stick with it. If you change your mind halfway, the result will be chaos.' I remembered his counsel; but, halfway through our production cycle, reluctantly, I dropped one film on which we'd started work, and diverted energies to another. My original list proposed a film on the overall direction of the Allied war effort, 'The Big Three' – Churchill, Roosevelt, Stalin. I did not go through with it. We had no difficulty putting on record those close to Churchill and Roosevelt; but we had no chance of finding anyone close to Stalin able to speak. A writing historian might not have been put off by this; informed analysis would fill the gap. But I had set my face against using commentators on screen, except in 'Reckoning'. Looking back, I'm sure I was right; the programme I was rejecting belonged in another series. We had no film on the Italian campaign scheduled. Italy, Churchill thought, was a soft target; victorious there, turning north-east to Munich and Vienna, Western troops might enter Germany before the Russians. He was wrong. Produced by Ben Shephard, 'Tough Old Gut' took us, via Monte Cassino and Anzio, to Rome. The series gained a strong film. As others have pointed out since, the bigger omission was China.

Noble Frankland and I agreed on our structure, and got on well as we went along. He had plenty of time to read outlines, view rough-cuts and remonstrate with me if he had critical points to make. When, on one occasion, he pointed out an error, I took the point and made the correction. Meanwhile, individual writers and producers tackled, within limited airtime, the complex historical issues an episode might throw up. Here's David Elstein, student of history turned TV producer, on 'The Battle for Britain':

Television history is essentially narrative: it has to tell a story which is clear and to the point. Most historians, on the other hand, present the evidence they have accumulated, weigh it, and reach conclusions based on it. Television history is simply unable to handle material in that way, because the audience cannot be expected to keep several conflicting pieces of evidence in mind while waiting for the programme to reach its conclusion.

A typical example of 'filleting' concerns the Luftwaffe's decision to bomb London on September 7, 1940, instead of the RAF fighter bases. Some historians have suggested that the main reason for this change in tactics was that Berlin had been bombed in August, much to Hitler's anger. The scriptwriter, Laurence Thompson, and I agreed that a more likely reason was that the Luftwaffe assumed the fighter bases had been put out of action and that, in bombing London, they would either have a clear run, or would force the remaining fighters to defend the capital, and so expose themselves to German gunpower. In the end, we neither mentioned the retaliation idea, nor why we had excluded it: which was poor history in one sense, but 'good' television in another.

Elstein wrote that in 1974,* when television had no recourse except straight linear narrative. Today it is possible, on a set of DVDs, or making use of a dedicated website, to direct the viewer as student immediately to other explanations, alternative narratives. However, in Phillip Whitehead's 'Inside the Reich' we find,

*Journal of the Society of Film and Television Arts, 1974.

juxtaposed, three witnesses saying what they knew of the Nazi genocide against the Jews, with differing tales to tell:

Christabel Bielenberg: One day a friend of ours who used to collect food cards for these Jews came to me and with – she came with another woman with dyed blonde hair – I can see her sitting there now, twisting her wedding ring and telling me it wouldn't be for long, that she would help me in the house and her husband need never go out, he could live in the cellar or wherever.

Narrator: But Christabel Bielenberg's husband was away and he was involved in a plot to overthrow Hitler. She consulted her trusted neighbour and friend, Carl Langbehn, another conspirator. Langbehn told her compassionately but firmly that the risks to herself and her family and to the conspiracy were too great.

Christabel Bielenberg: I was astonished, overcome really at the response that I got from my neighbour who told that under no circumstances whatsoever could I house these people. That housing of Jews meant concentration camp not only for myself, but for my husband, possibly also for my children. I can remember going through and out into the road and out of the darkness came a voice – I knew there was somebody there – came a voice saying, *'Frau Doktor, Frau Bielenberg, haben Sie einen Schluss gefasst?'*, which means 'Have you decided?' And I simply couldn't say no; I just said, 'Well, I can't for longer than two days.' And I let him into the cellar.

They stayed for two days and after, on the second day, or rather in the evening they must have left because in the morning she was gone, the cellar was empty, the bed – the little bed I'd put up all tidily arranged and they had gone.

I know – knew later that they were caught buying a ticket at a railway station and were transported to Auschwitz.

And why I say this is the most painful and terrible story for me to have to tell was because after they left I realised that Hitler had turned me into a murderer.

Albert Speer: One day, in 'forty-four, Gauleiter Hänke came in my office and told me that he was visiting a concentration camp in Upper Silesia and warned me never to go in a concentration camp there because horrible things would happen. This, together with other hints I got, should have made – should have made my decision to go to Hitler immediately, or to Himmler, and to ask them what is going on and to take my own steps, but I didn't do it, and not doing it was, so I think nowadays, the biggest fault in my life.

Emmi Bonhoeffer: We felt that people should know what was going on and maybe typical is this little experience which I had one day standing in the line for vegetables or something like that. I told my neighbours standing around me that now they start to kill the Jews in the concentration camps and that it is not true that they only are brought there and can live there as they live here as it was told them. They are killed and they even make soap out of them – I know that. And they said, 'Frau Bonhoeffer, if you don't stop telling such horror stories you will end in a concentration camp, too, and nobody of us can help you. It's not true what you're telling. You shouldn't believe these things. You have them from the foreign broadcasts or so and they tell these things to make enemies against Germany.'

And I said, 'No, that's not from broadcasts. I know that directly from first-hand. You can be sure it is that way.' And coming home I told that my husband in the evening and he was not at all applauding to me; in the very contrary. He said, 'My dear, sorry to say, but you are absolutely idiotic what you are doing. Please understand a dictatorship is like a snake. If you put your foot on its tail, as you do it, it will just bite you and nobody will be helped. You have to strike the head.'

Christabel Bielenberg twisted her knuckles as she spoke. Emmi Bonhoeffer's husband paid with his life for his part in the plot against Hitler. Albert Speer, surely, was economical with the truth.

John Pett was not known to me when we started work; he made three of the series' best films, on D-Day, Burma and the Pacific. Working on all three with the same film editor, Jeff Harvey, he evolved a style of his own. He made less use of inter-view to camera, more use of montage on the soundtrack, skilfully sneaking in very short clips of voiceover at just the right moment. A GI, parachuting into France the night before D-Day, simply says, 'I was afraid. I was nineteen, and I was afraid . . .' 'Morning', Pett's film on D-Day, is almost my favourite of the series.

After the beach landings, a Frenchwoman, liberated, Madame Theresa Broher, tells of her feelings: '. . . the biggest joy in our life. And we admired those courageous soldiers, they came from so far away to liberate us and we gave to them everything we could give them – cider also, calvados also – and our friendship. It was very emotional – and we feel – we became free.' It's the pause before she brings out the calvados that I notice every time.

Ted Childs produced 'Wolf Pack', the battle of the Atlantic, the war against the U-boat – a formidable challenge, because there is very little film of war at sea; Ted made bricks without straw. But at its end I actually understood how we defeated the U-boats. Ted Childs later produced *Morse* for ITV, and has been properly wreathed with laurel ever since.

I made Jerry Kuehl associate producer of the series at an early stage.* He contributed also as writer and producer – both 'Stalingrad' and 'Reckoning' are his – but as associate producer he

---

*In the official history of ITV Jerry Kuehl is wrongly described as my co-producer; he was not.

had a different role: to check facts, keep an eye open for script errors, and spot, challenge and correct misuse of film. Noble Frankland and the IWM staff would also validate; Jerry was our own in-house watchdog. He barked often. This is how he categorises producers' contrasting attitudes to archive film:

The first is that since everything is what it is and not another thing, and every piece of film shot was shot at a particular time and a particular place and not somewhere else and at a different time, no scenes which have not been positively identified can ever legitimately be used ... The second is the notion that if you've seen one Stuka, you've seen them all. For such producers there is nothing except stock shots. If what is needed is a Panzer MK IV travelling from camera left to camera right through snowfields during the battle for Demyansk in 1942, it really doesn't matter if the tank and the snowfield were filmed in Pomerania in 1944.

Most producers, Kuehl notes, are neither frauds nor idiots. They are 'obliged to exercise practical judgement in each case where film is used. Explanation of the techniques of the RAF pathfinder squadrons in 1942 need not be illustrated by film from any particular raid, but clearly must not show aircraft which did not enter service until 1943.' In the end, Kuehl thought, 'The *World at War* producers have generally worked to a higher standard than is current in the industry, and some of them have worked to a very high standard indeed.' If we did, Jerry Kuehl had much to do with it.

A series dealing with the twentieth century must have verifiably sourced film and credible witnesses. Finding both of these is down to the researcher, the key figure on whom the integrity of completed programmes chiefly depends. On *The World at War* (and again on *Cold War*) I was fortunate to work with superb researchers. Their contribution is unremarked by the outside world, and undervalued in the industry. Yet it is crucial.

To draw on experience in Hamburg and Berlin, as well as London and Coventry,we needed researchers who spoke German. Susan McConachy, blonde and blue-eyed, was our star. She found Traudl Junge, Hitler's secretary. After a long while, Junge grew to trust Sue, and was interviewed. Sue's hardest task was to track down members of the SS, and persuade them to talk, on the record. Her worst moment came when Karl Wolff, Himmler's adjutant, put his hand on her knee and confided: 'My dear, you are just the type from whom we liked to breed.' Here is how she found, and dealt with, him:

My first clue was from a personal contact made by a colleague outside Germany. I had an address near Munich . . . Many phone calls, a letter through a third party, and nearly a year later, I finally met the old man. Not in his home, I still didn't know where it was, but in a hotel in Berlin. He was most charming – quite unlike the fantastic figure we had imagined in Munich. Again the long process of establishing trust began. I visited his home several times. He agreed to talk about the subjects where he claimed he had first-hand knowledge. He wanted to explain the ideology of the SS to us. A contract was drawn up which gave him the option to read a transcript of the entire interview to check the factual accuracy of what he had said. The interview was long and tricky. It went on all day. After lunch I asked him to repeat the story he had told me one evening over supper about an incident at Minsk at which he had been present, when a hundred people were shot into an open grave as a demonstration for Himmler. He looked a bit surprised. He had forgotten that he had ever mentioned that. Then the film ran out. I wondered if, with time to think, he would actually tell the story again. When we were ready to go he did in fact tell it. I was relieved, not just because I'd got the story, but because he'd had the time to reflect on what the consequences of telling it might be and I could feel less responsible if he did in fact end up in court again when the programme was shown. Twenty rolls and a lifetime later we left to rush to catch the last plane back to London.

When Sue told someone in the Teddington canteen she was working on a series about the Second World War, he asked, 'Who's playing Hitler?' Sue McConachy still had nightmares about her work long after it was finished.

The World at War's film researchers were John Rowe and Raye Farr. They divided between them attendance on the archives of the world – London, Koblenz, Washington, Tokyo. They looked for specific sequences necessary for the programme outline, but they also looked at everything the archive held that might be useful or relevant. They had the time, and put in the hours, to do so. They sought, Raye Farr tells us, to get behind the newsreels, back to the original negative, which offered the chance of uncut film, 'so that editors might have some freedom to create effective visual sequences, without being hamstrung by the clipped newsreel style of the past, and the heavy hand of wartime censors'. The newsreels of the Second World War, like some wartime TV footage today, were issued for propaganda purposes, to lift morale at home and lower it abroad. You see what the censor wants you to see: armies on the advance, not on the retreat; weapons dealing death, very little dying. There are very few dead and wounded in newsreels of the Second World War; the censors cut them out. Farr points to a way round the difficulty: 'Soldiers know that men die, sometimes hideously, on the battlefield. Films made for the instruction of the army medical corps will contain more realistic elements than newsreels which aim to encourage civilian commitment to a government's war aims.'

The two researchers arrived at the doors of the archive before they opened, and stayed late. Farr again:

Not until you have made a nuisance of yourself do the staff throw up their hands in exasperation and say, 'See for yourself' – which is what you've been waiting for. Or, better yet, they realise you're still not going and say, 'You've already seen every foot of film we know of on the war, you may as well look at this – we don't know what's in these cans because we've never had time to go through them.' And they reveal a vault of unopened treasures. We are greatly indebted to Herr Homan at the Bundesarchiv in Koblenz for just such an offering.

What Raye Farr showed me, when I joined her in Koblenz, was material shot behind the German lines on the Eastern Front by a gifted documentary cameraman. He appears not to have been shooting for the newsreel. Some of his footage was almost idyllic, showing soldiers at rest and leisure. Other sequences were more menacing. He filmed three German soldiers gently, almost reluctantly, but, in the end, firmly clearing a village of its people, sending the men in one direction, the women and children in another. Somehow, we know they will never see each other again.

Making *The World at War* was a feat of logistics. Liz Sutherland, production manager, sent researchers, producers, camera crews all over the world and brought them back again. The supervisory film editor, Alan Afriat, set up the systems that made it all happen; when literally millions of feet of film are selected for viewing or shot for the series, it is crucial that every shot is logged, numbered and held where it can be found for use, and matched to the negative from which the show-print will be struck. Get any of that wrong, and you are in trouble. Alan's system, and Roger Chinery who worked with him, got it right.

Each film for *The World at War* was made by an individual producer, sometimes working with a writer, sometimes writing it himself. The key relationship was between editor and producer. Afriat explains:

Some producers will supply a very detailed pre-production script with what could almost be a final commentary, while at the other extreme the editor may just get a list of sequence headings with a bundle of marked up transcripts of interviews to be slotted in somehow. I think the ideal lies somewhere in between. A too rigid commentary line restricts the story and flow which the pictures dictate and the editor has to be careful not to tie himself too closely to the words or throw out good and useful material because the commentary doesn't call for it.

On the other hand, he adds, editors are not historians, and need guidance. I wholly share Alan Afriat's view that commentary comes last, not first. He kept in his mind throughout what sounds would accompany, but not dominate, the pictures.

In current affairs, I had been used to a weekly turnaround. Now research alone took ages; months after we started, we still did not have a single finished film. Assemblies of eight hours' length came down to six, to three, to one and a bit. At each stage, editor and producer would consult; then the editor would bar the cutting-room door, hoping not to see the producer for a week. 'Producers who hover in the cutting room', Afriat reckons, 'are seldom popular, and in any case I think a producer who becomes too familiar with the details of a programme has his judgement impaired when he sees the programme as a whole.' Afriat's practice in shortening, surely right, was not to lose sight of good stuff too early; it's easier to lose it later if you must, than cut it, forget it and find no way back to it. As the assembly gets shorter, scrutiny of each sequence, every interviewee's contribution, grows more intense; much gets trimmed, some is now omitted altogether, and for good.

At seventy minutes' length, there is another viewing. Maps, stills, some music have been added. It's still loose, but beginning to look a bit like a film. Now it's the series producer's turn to be involved. 'This time,' Afriat writes, 'Jeremy Isaacs will be there as well as the producer and writer, and we will probably run the film in the theatre first and then move on to a viewing machine for a closer analysis. For the editor, this is the most critical viewing – either it will be a smooth run to a fine cut or perhaps there will be a sharp change in tack involving radical restructuring.' How vividly I recall the thrill of entering the viewing theatre with Alan, eager to see how this next episode is coming on. Then come decisions: the truly brutal business of getting the film down to thirty seconds either side of fifty-two minutes.

Afriat was expert at finessing the final omissions with the least possible damage to the whole. 'The more you see a shot, the more you undervalue it and the quicker you absorb its information. It needs a lot of discipline to remind yourself, "I thought it was fantastic the first time I saw it." Often as I fish through the trims, I stop and wonder why I chose one shot in preference to another: the truth is that the shot I chose is now familiar while the one I rejected looks fresh – the first choice is usually the right one.' And the viewer, on air, has only one viewing; it will be fresh to him.

Now the film is down to length, the writer arrives to fit his narration to the picture, and the composer to discuss with producer and editor where his music will be needed, and precisely how much of it there will be. Afriat confides: 'The editor hopes there will be plenty of commentary over some sequences where effects will be difficult, but for others he will be battling to keep the commentary to a minimum, and always will be imagining the soundtrack so that enough pauses are left to allow music and effects to establish.' A common fault with compilation films – and you could say the same of football commentaries – is a tendency to bombard the viewer with aural and visual information at the same time. Max Hastings told me once that, lying ill in bed for a week, he had watched *The World at War*, and – as welcome a compliment as I've ever been paid – had clearly heard every syllable of speech in it. It was because of the skill of our editors and the dubbing mixer that he could say that.

We never put a script in the narrator's hand until we had ourselves fitted the text to a rough mix on the track. One of us would record the commentary, and we would try it for size, cue by cue, noting exactly the fractions of seconds each space measured. Then, after the commentary proper is recorded, a final review. Alan Afriat again: 'Jeremy Isaacs will go through the film with a toothcomb; one or two picture changes here, a change of commentary there, lose a sentence in this sequence and drop this piece of music . . .' Others did the work; in every film, I wielded the tweezers. Since the producers and the editors knew their business, there was little to do.

Every series needs signatures: a title that trips off the tongue; a title sequence that sticks in the mind's eye; a theme tune you remember. *The World at War* had all three, made for each other.

The name had to convey the scale of the conflict; it was not to be triumphalist, for we were going to see the conflict from conflicting points of view; it could not be just *The Second World War*, for fear of imitators. The words *The World at War* just came. Our main title was of metal. I briefed the designer John Stamp, but nothing prepared me for the magic he wrought. I approved the typeface he proposed, and asked that the faces he chose to mix through be both compelling and anonymous; the effect we wanted was of courage and endurance. I could not have bettered his choice. Isobel Hinshelwood found the pictures, and cleared them for transmission worldwide. The flames through which all moved were John Stamp's invention, and bound the whole together. The faces inspired the composer and all of us.

In the entrance lobby of a British Film Institute building in Soho, I bumped one day into Jonathan Miller, whom I knew slightly. Jonathan had succeeded Huw Wheldon in editing and presenting *Monitor*, and had made for the BBC a marvellous version of *Alice in Wonderland*. I told him what I was up to, and that I was looking for a composer. 'Have Carl Davis,' he said immediately. 'Jack Gold tells me he's very good.' I met Carl, and we hit it off at once. In a flat in Battersea, with a small baby, Hannah, and a rather larger spaniel, and his wife, the actress Jean Boht, in the background, he played me a possible theme. It was too tumty-tum four-square. 'Uncooked,' he now calls it. The theme needed to convey both immense suffering and the will to survive. It would introduce battles we would win, and crushing defeats; it must not have too upbeat an ending, but should tail off, leaving the mood up in the air, to be resolved in the film that followed. Afriat played Carl some Martinů: an elegy for Lidice, the Czech town the Germans razed to the ground in retaliation for the assassination of Heydrich. He wrote again. The piano could only hint at the orchestral sound, but this time we both knew he had got it right.

Inviting Carl Davis to do the music for *The World at War* was one of the best decisions of my life. The studio session at which he conducted the title theme was exhilarating; the musicians knew, I sensed, they were playing something that would last. Thereafter Carl wrote separately for each episode, using a smaller chamber group in which the horns and the clarinet of Alan Hacker stood out. 'Genocide' used no music. Various editors turned, for period atmosphere or martial effect, to disc, lending variety. 'France Falls' concluded with the German victory parade up the Champs Elysée; their boots crashed in step to *Preussens Gloria*, off disc, replacing the actual recording on the newsreel soundtrack. I put a 'Dona Nobis Pacem' by Haydn over the end of 'Remember'. But Carl's incidental music, both particular and unifying, was a triumph for which he has my undying gratitude. It is impossible now to envisage the series without it. When *The World at War* was first seen in New York on WORTV, Channel 9, and their commercials came in too soon, his father would ring the station to complain: 'That's my son's music you are cutting into. Don't do it.'

The main title would carry, superimposed, as well as the names of writer, producer and narrator, the episode title and the timespan it covered, telling the viewer where we were starting and how far we were going. That helped settle demarcation disputes between producers when one was angling to include an event, and the juicy footage that went with it, which rightly belonged elsewhere.

I did not at first want an actor to narrate the series. I did not want Laurence Olivier. I had had good experiences using a different sort of narrator who would both write his own words and also know exactly what he was talking about. Robert Kee, who had done a fine job of both on *The Day Before Yesterday*, knew about the war. Ludovic Kennedy was an expert on naval warfare. I toyed with the notion of getting four such writer/performers to join the team and do half a dozen episodes each. That would have been an error; a coherent series should observe unities. Perhaps Robert Kee could have done them all, if his patience would have stood it, and other commitments allowed; he has one of the great distinctive voices of our day. But it was not on. Michael Redgrave had served *The Great War* well; Olivier, surely, was the apposite choice for us. His name, Thames's sales departments thought, was bound to help them. The ITV network had a right to be consulted over the proposal, unprecedented, to carry twenty-six episodes of documentary in peak time; and they wanted Olivier. Granada's Director of Programmes was David Plowright, brother of Joan, Larry's wife. He volunteered himself as an intermediary.

I found Sir Laurence in the temporary premises of the National Theatre, The Huts, a collection of wartime shacks and Nissen huts on Upper Ground, SE1. It was lunchtime. He was in shirtsleeves, eating an apple and sipping a glass of champagne. I hardly knew what to say to such a star. He had no inhibitions. 'We have a little commerce to discuss,' he said, putting my project in its place. I described what we wanted him to do; told him how many days it would take, over what period. We allowed one day for each episode, and a safety margin. We parted, promising to meet again when I had films complete and commentaries ready for recording.

Months later, 'France Falls' and 'Occupation' were ready. We sent the scripts off to Olivier; he could glance at them in the train up from Brighton.

I was tense and anxious as I walked, for the first time, down the Tottenham Court Road from Thames's Euston Road HQ to the sound studio we were using, one floor up on the south side of Oxford Street. A purple London cab, chauffeur-driven, delivered Sir Laurence at the unprepossessing door. The atmosphere as we greeted each other was pleasant on the surface, edgy beneath. Liz Sutherland, who did everything exactly right, had provided for him English apples and English cheese. Peter Batty was quietly sure of himself; I wasn't, not at all. The preliminaries over, recording began.

Actors need direction, and expect to get it. 'How would you like me to do this?' is a standard request. Our answer was, in effect, 'Not too like yourself; hold yourself in; don't overdo it.' The narrative style we wanted was understated. The colour was in what other voices had to say; the drama, sound and fury, lay in the action, not the narration. By convention, the producer would direct the recording; 'France Falls' was Peter Batty's film. I was there, though, at every episode. Hesitantly, we recorded 'France Falls'. Olivier bade us farewell. We would meet next day to record 'Occupation'.

As soon as he'd gone, Peter Batty spoke his mind. 'It's no good; he's a disaster. It is too quiet; his voice keeps fading away at the end of the line. We can hardly hear him. He'll have to do it again. But really,' he said, looking at me, 'you must get rid of him.' I spent a bad night. How does a current affairs producer, dealing for the first time in his life with a great actor, find words to tell him that he isn't good enough? I decided to play the programme back to him, and let that speak. I explained that we had a problem, and we watched the film together. After half an hour he stopped me. 'I see what you mean,' he said. 'It's tired. I'm tired. It comes right just about there. I'll do it again.' He did, and it was better. He recorded commentary for 'Occupation', also satisfactory. I was relieved.

A few days later, I heard from his agent, Laurence Evans. 'Trouble, I'm afraid,' he said. 'Larry wants out. Will you come and see me?'

I went round to his office. He was reassuring.

'We have a contract,' he said, 'and will perform it. All the same, there is a problem; Larry is tired, very tired. He's done *Sleuth;* that was meant to be an eight-week shoot and took sixteen. And he's had three weeks, with matinées, of *Long Day's Journey into Night.'* He did not say Olivier had been, before those taxing assignments, very ill. He did not need to. Everyone knew he'd had cancer.

We discussed how to play it from here. 'Have you told him he's wonderful?' he asked.

'Surely,' I stammered, 'he doesn't need me to tell him that?'

'Oh my dear boy,' he said, giving me a long look. 'Of course he does.'

Every morning from then on, as I walked to a recording, I would prepare an anecdote or a joke to relax him a little, lighten his mood. He might, or might not, have studied the script; he always watched the film before going into the commentary box. At first we tried to record his commentary directly to picture, but this was not essential, and we soon abandoned the attempt. After viewing, we recorded to the stopwatch, rather than to the film. We sat around chatting before we got to work. Once or twice he muttered something that suggested he thought he knew more than we did about the war. He did not, and he very soon gave that up. He revelled in pronouncing foreign-language personal names and place names just as they should be; his French, German, Russian were impeccable. He said Soviét, not Soviet; Stalín, not Stahlin. Given a chance at Americanese, he seized it. A Yank, he assured us at one point, would never have said, 'He didn't give a damn,' but 'He didn't give a good goddam.' We made the change. What he yearned for, and didn't find, was fine language, purple patches verging on oratory, rather than the clipped prose style we affected. We saw commentary as cement, not stained glass.

In the autumn of 1972 I flew to Bordeaux, drove east and north past Bergerac and Périgueux to Limoges. There in the Limousin, I went to the village of Oradour-sur-Glâne, or what is left of it.

In spring 1944 the SS Division Das Reich came this way, despatched from the Eastern Front to shore up German defences in the west. Men of the French resistance shot at one of their patrols and killed a couple of their men. The Germans went straight to the nearby village of Oradour and exacted a terrible revenge. There was nothing unusual about this procedure; Das Reich had performed it many times before out east. It was rare, though, in Western Europe. The French preserved the ruins of Oradour just as the Germans left it. The local cemetery held the graves of those who died, their names and photographs set in stone. I walked the length of the village, deserted, and knew I had found the sequence that would start the series. I sent Thames's best cameraman, Mike Fash, and the director Hugh Raggett, to see what they could do. Raggett hired a helicopter to skim over and along what had been the main street; Fash and he filmed the square, the ruined church, and a house or two, with a painter's eye, against the skyline, and in light that froze them in time. It cut together marvellously well. Neal Ascherson wrote words that would give the sense of universal experience I wanted, and justify our title:

Down this road on a summer day in 1944 the soldiers came.
Nobody lives here now.
They stayed only a few hours.
When they had gone, a community which had lived for a
    thousand years was dead.
This is Oradour-sur-Glâne, in France.
The day the soldiers came, the people were gathered together.
The men were taken to garages and barns. The women and
    children were led down this road.
And they were driven into this church.
Here they heard the firing as their men were shot.
Then they were killed, too.
A few weeks later many of those who had done the killing were
    themselves dead – in battle.

They never rebuilt Oradour.

Its ruins are a memorial.

Its martyrdom stands for thousand upon thousand of other
*   martyrdoms in Poland, in Russia, in Burma, in China – in a*
*   World at War.*

When the day came to record this, Olivier did it very well. Finished, he stood up in the recording booth, resplendent in red braces, and reached for an elegant brown tweed jacket. I joined him in the booth and remarked, pointedly, 'You do realise, don't you, that those words at the start of this are, out of the whole twenty-six hours, the very first words the viewer will hear?'

'Ah,' he said, and put the jacket down. 'I'll do it again.'

This time we got perfection – with the letter 'a' in the phrase 'garages and barns' pronounced more ways than you might think possible, and the 'a' in 'Glâne' unlike any other 'a' you ever heard.

When I listen again to Laurence Olivier's narration, the voice I hear is deft, subtle, strong, compelling. I do not believe it could have been better done.

With music, effects, voice-tracks mixed and laid, and now final commentary ready to be added, we are off to the dubbing theatre, where another unsung hero, the dubbing mixer Freddie Slade, will put the icing on the cake. On his fingers depend the final audio balance of the film, and the articulation of each sound element in its own right. We may ask for music to cross-fade to effects just here, or vice versa, but we never – and I mean *never* – want to have two tracks clash, voiceovers compete with music, commentary with effects. We want clarity, audibility and sometimes even silence, for a split second or two, to emphasise a point. With Freddie Slade, we get it. Alan Afriat has yet more to do, supervising the laboratories as they grade the print and develop the different versions needed for overseas sales. I can leave the theatre a happy man.

It took fifty of us three years to make *The World at War*. We started on 1 April 1971; 'A New Germany', the first episode, went to air on 21 October 1973; the last, 'Remember', was shown in May 1974. All went out at 9 p.m. on Wednesdays, with a repeat on Sunday afternoons at 5 p.m. Audiences averaged 7 or 8 million, rising on occasion to 10 million. *The World at War* was an ITV achievement; but I doubt the BBC could have bettered it. Its making, at a time of high prosperity for ITV, demonstrated what a commercial system of public service broadcasting could do. In the United States in 1974 *Variety* magazine, the showbiz bible, reviewing that year's television, opined that a measure of its home-grown quality was that the best action series on offer was the import *The World at War*. It duly won an Emmy. Huw Wheldon told me he had become used to being congratulated on its success, 'a typical high-quality BBC product'. He would graciously accept the compliment.

No one threw money at *The World at War*, but there was no penny-pinching either. There was a budget for the series, of course, but since none of us had any idea at the outset what the cost of anything so massive might be, we far exceeded it. In practice, we were allowed to spend whatever was needed in staff time to get it right. The cash budget was set at £440,000; we spent £880,000. But that was not the real cost. Neither Thames nor any other ITV company then applied total costing: all overheads, including staff salaries, were available, without charge, to the programme budget. The exception was overtime; unquantified in advance, that counted as cash. Everything else – research, filming, cutting, dubbing – was free. The real cost of *The World at War* was far, far higher than the cash cost. So far as I know, no one ever worked it out. Thames's income from advertising was so much greater than it could ever spend that no one needed to. And eventually the sales of the series recouped its cost many times over.

In one respect, though, Thames was ferociously determined on economy; mean, even. No one, except Olivier, and Carl Davis (through PRS, like all composers), got a royalty, though one or two producer-directors, after industry-wide negotiations, did receive something for the overseas sales of their work. We were all servants, working for hire. That included me. *The World at War* has sold worldwide, in a hundred countries; it has never been off the air in the United States. VHSs sold by the hundreds of thousands; so now do DVDs. I meet people who think I'm rich as a result. I'm not. While the series was making, I acted also as Thames's Controller of Features, and some of the time as Executive Producer, Documentaries; my salary was less than £20,000 a year. When the series was seen to be a success, Howard Thomas decided a bonus was in order, and awarded me one of £5,000. The cheque was made out for £1,600; income tax bit off the rest.

The premiere was at the Imperial War Museum; we showed 'Alone', David Elstein's film on the Battle of Britain. It was well received, and it needed to be; Hugh Dundas, Rediffusion's Chairman and then on Thames's board, was present. Well over six feet tall, Hugh, known as 'Cocky' Dundas, had flown Spitfires. My father and mother were my guests that night, hobnobbing with Lord Mountbatten and enjoying it. I was proud of them. Olivier did not put in an appearance. After a little research, and to his huge delight, we gave him a model Blackburn Skua, for a shelf somewhere; he'd flown one in the Fleet Air Arm. Years later a note came from him in a spindly hand, saying how glad he was he'd done it, thanking me for it. Apart from all else, it worked having him as narrator; newspapers worldwide, on their TV preview page, would use his picture to bill that night's episode.

The World at War is still seen today. It is by no means perfect, or complete. It is well known that there is no explicit mention in it of Enigma or Ultra, only references to an ability 'to crack enemy codes'. We finished work in May 1974; the papers revealing just what happened at Bletchley Park were published two months later, in July. Neal Ascherson, the series' most distinguished writer, has pointed to our neglect of Poland in 1939; the Battle of the River Bug, he states correctly, mattered more than the Battle of the River Plate. That episode, the second of the series, was titled 'Distant War', betraying at once the British perspective of the makers; war was not distant from Warsaw in September 1939. And, although we tried to show the crucial importance of the Eastern Front, and the massive contribution the Soviet Union made to the Nazis' defeat, we didn't do it as effectively as we might have done if the Russians had not for two years refused us their co-operation.

The historian Richard Overy, in a new introduction to Mark Arnold-Foster's fine book which accompanied the series, reckons that today we would take a harsher view of the Wehrmacht's general behaviour. We now know that German armies, not just the SS, were deeply and widely implicated in murderous repression against civilian populations, particularly, but not exclusively, on the Eastern Front. Furthermore, Overy told a conference at London University's Queen Mary that it was now time to take account of new information on foul behaviour, low morale and desertion among Allied troops in various theatres. Tellingly, he pointed to China, the long-lasting and bloody Sino-Japanese war, as the single most neglected aspect of a global conflict. But Overy also believes that the scope of *The World at War*'s ambition gave writing historians, who might otherwise have preferred to cherry-pick, the courage to embrace in their work the war's whole panoramic sweep. That had never occurred to me.

The World at War – and later *Cold War* – showed how terrible events affect ordinary lives. That is its greatest strength. The best thing said to me about it came on a visit to an Open University summer school. A middle-aged Glasgow woman, studying history, told me: 'I did'nae fancy history at all, until I saw your series.' She was the viewer John Reith thought broadcasting should serve.

8

SOMETHING TO SAY

The best political dialogue I ever had responsibility for bringing about in a television studio took place off-screen. It was the moment I realised Margaret Thatcher, then Secretary of State for Education, was a leader with a future. She was taking part in a half-hour local programme for Thames Television, broadcast live early on a Friday evening; we made space, after the news, for a senior political figure to answer questions from an informed studio audience – that evening mostly teachers. Already controversial, Thatcher had proposed to abolish a staple prop of the welfare state, free milk in schools, and as a result was being labelled 'Margaret Thatcher, Milk-Snatcher'. Her office, absurdly protective of her, did not want a shouting match. The Secretary of State, they warned, 'will want to know the areas of questioning in advance'. Looking handsome and not at all nervous, she took her seat on a platform next to the presenter, and faced her interrogators. Everyone behaved, put their hands up, took their turn, didn't interrupt. Thatcher was calm, almost anodyne; the mood flat, the half-hour unexceptional. As the credits rolled, her escorts looked relieved: no harm done. The TV lights went out, she came down from the dais on to the studio floor, the audience left their seats and surrounded her. Then what should have been the real programme began.

The teachers had never had the chance to put questions to any Secretary of State before. Now they hurled them at her, with zest – exactly the interrogation her entourage had sought to prevent. Each wanted not just to ask but to listen, both to the other questions and to her answers. Points came thick and fast. Completely in command, Thatcher began to enjoy herself, after a time playing off one against the other. 'Look, he said he wanted a higher priority for infant schools. You are asking me to spend much more on higher education. I can't do both; there's not enough money for it. Do you see that? What would you do?' You could see some of them trying to work it out.

The image the press office wanted to avoid – minister surrounded by angry protesters – was in front of us, and it was fresh, spontaneous, appealing, convincing, the give and take of argument. The audience participated; the politician seized the chance to make her case.

This episode displayed to perfection, it seemed to me, an ideal use of television (except that it wasn't televised) in democratic practice. It made contact between government and the governed. The minister expounded her view; the teachers made their point; eyeball to eyeball, each was aware of the other's reaction. Yet it was no mere shouting match.

I never took the view, as John Birt and Peter Jay have argued, that television journalism had an inbuilt bias against understanding, nor do I believe it ever need have. It is not the medium that determines what we see, but the use to which we choose to put it. And we are free to make that choice. Television current affairs, I always thought, should aim to generate light, not heat. It must also convey, somehow, the real feeling that issues and harsh experience provoke. Government must weigh the effects of what it proposes. The citizen should have the opportunity to put a grievance, and also to hear the answer. If it falls to the TV presenter to put the citizen's case, then he must listen to the answer also.

How to combine even-handedness with liveliness is a recurring problem in current affairs. In the late fifties, Granada's *Under Fire* got there almost in one. This confronted one or two protagonists with an audience of potential dissenters, invoking an us–them, north–south divide by keeping the speakers in London and the questioners in Manchester. It worked, for a while, pretty well; but the crowd in the studio was a crowd, and soon behaved like one. Speakers were shouted down. *Under Fire* generated more heat than light, and lapsed. David Frost, in his work for Rediffusion, *The Frost Report*, prosecuting the swindler Dr Emil Savundra or the dope-dealing medical practitioner Dr Peto, launched his well-prepared interrogations in front of aggrieved victims who amounted almost to a lynch mob, baying for blood. But trials on television are exceptional, and undesirable. For the most part, in the sixties, TV studios were more sparsely populated. They could be used for interview, for discussion or, theoretically, for a statement to camera, uninterrupted, undisputed, as when Alastair Burnet held forth on the economy for *This Week*.

A first requisite for intelligible political utterance on television is adequate time. The dreaded words, 'I'm sorry, that's all we've got time for,' ring always as a death knell in my ears. I once heard a noted interviewer ask a Secretary of State for Northern Ireland, 'What is the solution there?' adding, 'We've only got a minute and a half.' The time needed is a reflection both of an issue's complexity and of the number of participants. All too often producers, fearful that talk will dry up or tension flag, invite far too many; six people in a thirty-minute discussion means five minutes each, so they lay on a dozen instead. Or a studio audience makes points or asks questions, but not necessarily in logical order. For me Robin Day's or David Dimbleby's *Question Time* was a better programme before the audience was given a role – beyond asking the main question, that is. The simpler format was less touchy-feely, but provoked a better platform discussion. Nowadays, access is all.

In news, responses to large issues reduced to a soundbite are the curse of political discourse. When *Channel Four News*, running an hour, was about to start, ITN briefed Whitehall's press officers, who then still had authority to decide whether to advise the minister to appear on the screen or not; 'then' being before Bernard Ingham for Thatcher, and later Alastair Campbell for Blair, sought to decide everything from the centre. ITN explained that on this new programme ministers would normally have two or three times as long as they were used to having to reply to questions, explain their intentions, respond to events. Every pencil took note.

I hate it when argument becomes a shouting match, or debate a punch-up. The press often describes such occasions as 'poor politics, but good television'. I disagree; it is bad television, the medium abused, the audience ill served. Good programmes offer parties to an argument adequate opportunity to state a case. LWT's *Weekend World*, the product of John Birt's and Peter Jay's attack on TV's 'bias against understanding', aimed at clarity always; the clarity, however, was always precisely that perceived by the production team.

At *Panorama* we had interviewed Harold Wilson half a dozen times, on Rhodesia or the economy. I was back at Rediffusion to greet the Prime Minister after Labour's devaluation of sterling in 1967. On the Sunday the deed was done, he'd gone on television to address the nation, and famously remarked, 'The pound in your pocket is not devalued,'* raising a storm against himself. By the time he came to us on the Thursday for *This Week*, he looked under the weather. He'd been to the dentist that day, he told me. I commiserated. 'It wasn't', he said, 'anything like as painful as

---

*What he actually said was: 'It does not mean, of course, that the pound here in Britain, in your pocket or purse or in your bank, has been devalued.'

the tooth I had pulled at the weekend.' Wilson was at his ease on television.

Ted Heath was the Conservative Party's choice to succeed Alec Douglas-Home. A stolid speaker, lacking a light touch, he had to learn to use the medium. I spotted him once in a corner, watching a recording of his own performance on a monitor. I wanted to say to him, as to Alec Douglas-Home, be yourself; what matters most is that you know what you want to say, and can find a way of saying it clearly.

For the general election in 1970, by which time Harold Wilson and his kitchen cabinet had had a major falling-out with the BBC, we interviewed Heath for an election *This Week* in Glasgow. When I opened the door of his dressing room at STV's studios, used by the female cast of the soap opera *Take the High Road*, the bachelor Tory leader was in his underpants, changing his trousers. Heath thought he wouldn't win that election; coming with a late run, he did. Wilson, interviewed at Thames in the Euston Road, was pretty sure he'd win, and lost.

Douglas Hurd, acting as Heath's aide at No. 10, took a sharp and quizzical view of the television people he had to deal with. He might, on Heath's behalf, on occasion stipulate a particular interviewer. That was hard for us to concede but, in the end, why not? It was the answers that mattered most, not who put the questions. There were no spites, resentments and shouting matches, as between Wilson and the BBC. Heath, I think, had learned from Harold Macmillan, whom he had served as Chief Whip, not to pay too much attention to press and broadcasting, but simply to get on with the job. I called on Ted Heath in Downing Street once, to prepare him for an interview next day – the terrier-like Jonathan Dimbleby was our choice to do it, a first time for him – and found the problem was not so much to calm the Prime Minister down as to wake him up. The mention of key topics for discussion – the economy, Europe, the trades unions – provoked not a flicker of interest. Then I remembered a review of a Festival Hall concert I knew he had attended; what about that Schubert, then? At once his face lit up, and the conversation became animated.

In 1974 Heath lost control – a three-day week, the lights out, the miners threatening and rampant. Earlier in the year Jim Prior, then Lord President of the Council, and Arthur Scargill of the mine workers' union were interviewed on *This Week*. Scargill came accompanied by two minders, big men both, who stood behind him as we spoke. 'Mr Scargill,' I said, 'you say you'd like the Britain you live in to be the sort of state East Germany is. Is that right?' 'Certainly,' said Scargill. Behind him, the minders turned their eyes up, grimaced disagreement, shook their heads in exasperation; no GDR for them. Heath chose to call an election on the issue of who runs the country, expecting to win, and lost. Harold Wilson, I thought, expected to lose, and didn't very much want to govern again, but won. His wife, Mary Wilson, was miserable about it.

When James Callaghan was Chancellor of the Exchequer, I'd had a run-in with him at a perilous moment of the economy's equilibrium when 'confidence' was low. We were interviewing him for *This Week*, and made the mistake of running for him the film report that would be seen before him. The reporter, and an excellent one, was Godfrey Hodgson; on the confidence point, he'd spoken to some City men in a bar, well away, who were personally scathing about the Chancellor. Callaghan was furious, and refused to go on with the interview unless we cut them out; I declined to do it. Stalemate. Summoned to the studio, my superiors gave in – no doubt prudently – to his demand. 'I wouldn't like to have that young man', he said of me, 'on the end of a hotline to Moscow.' But we never clashed again. I was Thames's Director of Programmes by the time he was PM, and out of the immediate firing line. In autumn 1978 everyone expected an election. Callaghan postponed it, and endured the chaos and fury of a winter of discontent. The next Prime Minister was Thatcher.

Margaret Thatcher sought to dominate the media, as she did

her Cabinet colleagues and the House of Commons. She wasn't fearful of it, or pernickety, or tetchy about trifles. She may have shared her husband Denis's view of the BBC's *Today* programme – 'Marxist radio', he thought – but she wasn't constantly on the telephone to complain. Bernard Ingham, her press officer, worked hard to establish Downing Street's version of events in the press and in the public mind. But I never had the impression that the Prime Minister lost sleep over media criticism. She got on with her job. There were, though, occasions when she exploded in fury over television coverage of current affairs. Ireland was always a sore point with her; her friend and campaign manager for the leadership contest, Airey Neave, was killed by an IRA bomb at Westminster, and later her parliamentary private secretary, Ian Gow, was murdered also, at his home in Sussex. When the BBC's *Panorama* recorded, but did not transmit, film of an IRA road-block set up at Carrickmore, she angrily sent Whitelaw out of a Cabinet meeting to complain to the BBC's Chairman. On another occasion she denounced Thames Television for a *This Week* inves-tigation into the killing by security forces of three IRA bombers at Gibraltar, 'Death on the Rock'. Thames's Chairman, Ian Trethowan, set up a heavyweight independent inquiry into his programme-makers' actions. They were found to have behaved impeccably. She was scarcely pacified. And in the 1983 general election she was not pleased when, in a *Nationwide* election spe-cial, a formidably bright viewer, Mrs Diana Gould, asked a series of pertinent questions about the sinking, in the Falklands War, of the Argentinian battleship *Belgrano* – the only time a television interviewer disconcerted her.

There wasn't a single incident in my years at Channel Four that provoked a hostile assault from the Iron Lady, though I often wondered what might have transpired if, in our vulnerable early days, we had reported and commented on the Falklands War. As it was, that conflict was won before we came on air. But the long miners' dispute, the strike and the government's crushing response, did fall to us to cover; we showed some programmes outspokenly in the miners' favour – including one film by Ken Loach that Melvyn Bragg commissioned for LWT and did not use. Under Liz Forgan's eagle eye *Channel Four News* held the ring for accurate reporting, and we came through unscathed.

At a seminar on broadcasting at 10 Downing Street in September 1987, when I was known to be moving to the Royal Opera House, Mrs Thatcher laid into ITV as 'the last bastion of restrictive practices in Britain'. Seeing me sitting there, she also attacked me for restrictive practices at Covent Garden. I said I was used to taking responsibility for what I'd done, but I'd never yet had to do so in respect of things for which I was not yet responsible. The discussion was supposed to be devoted to the merits of a free market, set out in a keynote speech by Alan Peacock. The Prime Minister, however, demanded to know what control she would have over satellite signals beamed into this country. Could messages from Gaddafi be prevented from reaching British screens? I said that I was not in the least concerned that Libyan propaganda might be seen here, but was very glad to be living at last in a world in which the Soviet Union could no longer block signals from the West. I guess her real concern was hardcore pornography.

Later, at the Opera House, I met her more than once. At *Il Trovatore* – not my finest hour – she asked, 'Why an Italian producer, Mr Isaacs?' A good question, as it happened. Another time, she told me she'd seen a *Carmen* at Earls Court. 'Rupert tells me he's going to broadcast it on Sky. Do we really need a BBC?' It was hard to take this seriously. At a party at Kenneth Baker's house – I knew his wife Mary from my days at Thames; she was a director – my host brought me up to his principal guest. She turned to the circle round her, jabbed me in the chest and stated: 'This man is the devil. Nine and a half years of doing absolutely everything right, and he doesn't believe a word of it.'

At Thames, we invented a discussion programme of ideas

which aimed always at clarity. *Something to Say* lasted an hour, and was broadcast at 11 p.m. It was produced by Udi Eichler, who, by his choice of participant, elevated the project to the intellectual stratosphere; he booked Nobel Prize winners, and above. The subjects were scientific, artistic, political, ethical, philosophical. There were only ever two participants, plus the chairman, Bryan Magee.

Magee was good, thoughtful, searching, but what made the programme was the format. Each protagonist was invited to state his argument separately for twelve minutes or so, proceeding by question and answer with the chairman, but uninterrupted by the other. Commercial break. Magee then invited each to comment on the other's presentation, and debate was joined. The result was an intellectual treat. I once went into a pub when *Something to Say* was on, and was gratified to notice that the argument was heard out in silence. Ratings were low; but the 'wow' factor was considerable. Later at Channel Four, Udi Eichler produced *Voices*, in which the level of cerebral speech was at least as high.

Could there be a *Something to Say* in the UK dealing with politics, with large issues that affect our lives? I see no reason why not; you can see the formula work, in miniature, on *Channel Four News*, BBC2's *Newsnight* or on Jonathan Dimbleby's weekend programme. But political debate on mainstream TV is too often patchy, hurried, unsatisfactory. Calm exposition is a rare event. I am for more of it.

My oldest friend in politics – oddly, for we disagree – is Michael Heseltine, practical, liberal, humane; for him, though, self-interest is the dominant motivation in human affairs, a fact he keeps inviting me to face up to. Our friendship goes back to the Oxford Union, where he preceded me as President – running for office, some of us thought, on his record as Treasurer, on the slogan, 'Three course lunches 2/6d, four course dinners 3/6d'. Our friendship, which lasts, has survived a bump or two on the way. One little item occurred when, at Thames, I had oversight of *This Week*, produced by David Elstein. The programme dealt with Concorde; Michael was Minister for Aerospace at the time, and the question at issue was whether the supersonic marvel would ever be economically viable. Michael gave the programme an interview; David Elstein decided to use none of it. Apprised of this, I rang Michael, to alert him to that and to apologise. It was a bit odd, he thought; he had given up time to do it. But he didn't seem at all angry. Elstein told me his reason for not using a single answer was that it was all gobblydegook. Years later I put this to Michael. 'Quite right,' he said. 'There was nothing else I could say.' Lesson: when you have nothing to say, keep quiet.

9

BEAUTY, BONNY . . .

A large man, wearing a grey top hat, tails and a cherubic smile, is riding a horse on a fairground carousel. Round and round he goes, and doffs his hat to us. It is Charlie Squires, ex-stoker in the Royal Navy, ex-film editor at Rediffusion, now a director. We are at Epsom, and this is the end of his marvellous film, *Derby Day*, celebrating, as did William Frith in the Victorian painting, a day out for toffs and Cockney barrow boys alike. Charlie, a film editor of genius, may well have owed his job at Rediffusion to his being a stoker in the navy, but he owed his advancement to his talent alone. He was a documentary-maker to remember. When Rediffusion was compelled to merge with ABC in 1968 I met Charlie, bald on top but with dark curls, wearing his hair sur-prisingly long down the back of his neck. 'Why are you wearing your hair like that, Charlie?' I asked. 'So as they don't cut my fucking head off, mate,' he told me. *Derby Day* was his best film.

In my years at Thames, documentaries were my particular pride: series and singles, especially singles. They said more of the individual's talent, allowed more play to the imagination, than series could. And they too had something to say. Thames's documentaries varied widely. So did the makers. Michael Darlow had worked at Granada. He proposed to us to film *Johnny Cash at San Quentin*, jail-rock. Before he had signed, a note arrived for me from Howard Thomas: 'Do not hire this man, I hear he is a trouble-maker.' I replied at once, untruthfully, that the deed was done. Darlow had been an actor and a theatre director, and would one day write a biography of Terence Rattigan. He was also a persistent campaigner for independent programme-makers, in ITV, in Channel Four, and in broadcasting at large. For Thames he made, apart from two exceptional episodes of *The World at War*, fine part-dramatised biographies of artists, with Michael Jayston as Charles Dickens in *The Hero of Our Life*, Leo McKern as J. M. W. Turner in *The Sun is God*, and Roy Dotrice in *Hazlitt in Love*. They atoned a little, I hope, for the glaring absence of a strong regular arts strand in Thames's output.

'Climb the highest mountain . . .' John Edwards, a reporter who relished the outdoor life, got wind of an expedition to climb Annapurna in the Himalayas by the ferociously difficult South Face. ITN were contracting with the climbing party to carry regular short reports of the expedition's progress, and asked us to split the cost with them and make a full-length documentary for Thames. The expedition was led by Chris Bonington, who had assembled a strong team of climbers, including Dougal Haston and the already legendary, beer-swilling, hard-smoking Don Whillans. John Edwards went out with ITN's camera crew as our producer and to help out with the logistics; 140 porters carried the baggage on the first leg.

Annapurna – the Hardest Way Up made a spectacularly thrilling film: beautiful because mountains are beautiful; thrilling because when, at five o'clock on the afternoon of 27 May 1970, Chris Bonington opened up the radio at Camp IV, Dougal Haston, high above him, came on the air:

'Hello, Dougal, this is Chris at Camp IV. Did you manage to get out today?'

'Aye, we've just climbed Annapurna.'

Haston and Whillans had reached the summit – 26,545 feet above sea level. Two days later another pairing made the attempt, but missed. The day after that – tragedy. Ian Clough, coming down the mountain, was killed by an ice avalanche below Camp IV. Our camera was turning as Mike Thompson brought the news that he was dead.

Part of the interest in all this was the difficulty of filming at altitude, the main problem being to get cameras high enough. On this peak, only a great climber could get one anywhere near the top. Two years later we accompanied another Bonington-led expedition to Everest itself. One of the climbers, Mick Burke, was himself a fine cameraman who took remarkable pictures as they attempted, unsuccessfully, to climb the South-West face. Later he too was killed, climbing high and filming. Death is a high price to pay for sport; mountaineers, for reasons I think only they understand, risk it.

My hope for single documentaries was that each one should be, distinctively, different.

Richard Broad had worked with Ian Martin at the BBC on *Six Sides of a Square*, and followed him to Thames. He had a good mind, clear convictions and a strong sense of structure in his film-making. He tackled complex subjects with zest and determination: human misuse of the earth's resources in *Limits to Growth*; agriculture in the third world in *Black Man's Burden*. This last was a tract showing grim toil for poor reward in Tanzania, and how we, white consumers, benefited, according to Richard, at the black producers' expense. Richard filmed poverty at and below the subsistence level. Thames's ACTT crew refused to live in anything like such conditions, preferring the nearest Hilton 50 miles away. The film was strong, if a trifle heavy-handed. Normally a documentary would have been shown at 10.30 p.m. I persuaded Brian Tesler, against his better judgement, to screen this one at 9 p.m. instead. The ratings graph shows audience numbers minute by minute; five minutes into *Black Man's Burden*, 90 per cent of the audience had gone, the line on the page plunging vertically. Tesler never fell for such an argument again. Broad went on to make other good films, including a period costume account of a nineteenth-century coal strike in the North Country, and series on Irish history, *The Troubles*, and *Palestine*.

Ken Ashton was a swaggering rough diamond who mined seams of gold in London's East End. Ken proposed to film in Bermondsey, asking what high-rise building and the death of the docks had done to the old community spirit: Had it really existed? Was it still alive? His camera trawled the streets; Ken knocked on doors, and chatted in pubs. A researcher dug out pre-war newsreel of 'hopping' in Kent, when whole streets took holidays together, harvesting the hops. In the local, grandmothers reminisced over hardship shared. In those days, they said, 'We was all one . . .' I was on a selection panel to choose ITV's documentary entry for the 1972 Prix Italia. We met at the ITCA's offices in Mortimer Street. It was an unsatisfactory morning; nothing we saw seemed a likely prizewinner. During lunch I offered, since Thames was just up the road, to have another couple of possibles sent down. Among them was *We Was All One*. I had thought the subject too local for the Italia. Not at all, said James Bredin, our chairman: they like themes; 'community' is all the rage this year, this could win. As *Eramo tutti insieme*, it did. The Prix Italia counted for much, and this was Thames's first. Ken Ashton went out to collect it.

The jury had praised the film's truths, the revelation of what community was. 'Of course it's all bollocks,' said Ken. 'Lies from beginning to end, not a word of truth in it. It's all nostalgia for a world that never was. Now, I've got another film that needs making, that really will tell it as it is. But we've got to get a move on.' Ken got the go-ahead for his next, *Harry's Out*. Harry was a villain, coming to the end of a prison term, due for release next week. Harry, we gathered, was a character; lots of patter, the gift of the gab. Ken would meet him at the prison gates and tour the neighbourhood as he greeted old mates. A riotous tour it was. However, we also had to listen to Harry's thoughts on life in Britain today. 'They're all on the take,' he reckoned, 'everyone's on the fiddle. Top to bottom, it's riddled with it.' Harry particularly had it in for Edward Heath – 'He's setting the example, he's encouraging everyone to line their pockets, isn't he? Course, we're all going to do the same.' It was all capitalism's fault. We were in the saloon bar, jammed in the corner, Harry was holding forth, we could not get away. Not my favourite film.

But Ken had a way with him; besides, he was a member of the cricket team, a dashing bat who had made at least one hundred.

'What's next, Ken? We know all about the East End now.'

'No, no, no, you don't. Harry's just a loudmouth. It won't be easy, but if you really want the truth, I can make you a film that will give you goose-pimples. Real villainy. There's things going on down there you wouldn't believe, knives, guns, bombs, war.'

It was gang war he was talking about, the Krays and the Richardsons. Peeling another layer of skin off the onion, Ken fearlessly went to work again. Months later he emerged with material that was incoherent in form, riveting in detail: a young mother confronted with the barrels of a shotgun poking through her letter-box. The film seemed to be saying that violent gangs were terrorising the East End, and that the police were doing little about it. Chief Superintendent Bert Wickstead, known to the tabloids as 'the Grey Fox', working out of Stepney Police Station, was on the case. He asked to see the film. I watched it with him and his colleagues. We knew their task was not easy; shotguns intimidate witnesses. They said nothing throughout, and little at the end. 'Interesting stuff there,' said Wickstead quietly. 'I've been trying to put these villains away for quite a time. I tell you, if you put this film out now, you will maybe spoil everything. This is a tricky time. I am about to act. I must ask you to hold off.' And, jovially: 'There are things in that film, by the way, some might say reflect on my reputation. Well, I'm always looking for ways to augment my pension. Good afternoon, gentlemen.' Not really sure on what ground we stood, we postponed transmission.

For weeks nothing happened. Was Wickstead bluffing? Then the placards shrieked, EAST END SENSATION. In dawn raids on homes in the East End, the police had made dozens of arrests; the result of months of painstaking police work under the direction of Chief Superintendent Bert Wickstead, 'the Grey Fox'; a blow had been struck against the gangs who were terrorising London; they might never recover. 'Ah . . .' we breathed a sigh of relief. 'We did do the right thing.' All was now *sub judice*. We hoped we had something that would be worth transmitting when the cases had been tried, the guilty convicted and Wickstead congratulated by the judge on a job well done.

After months of silence, the case came to court. In a crowded courtroom, prosecuting counsel rose to his feet. Another sensation: for lack of evidence, he was forced to abandon his case. Witnesses would not testify. All charges were withdrawn. How this happened, or what Wickstead achieved by this, we never knew. But one way or another, we'd been led up the garden path. Some people in our film had left court, not without a stain on their characters, but without anything proved against them. We never got to know the 'real' East End.

For his master's degree in film at the Royal College of Art, a young Italo-Argentinian, Carlos Pasini, made a version of Kafka's *Metamorphosis*, in which a young man wakes up one morning and finds he has turned into an insect. It was wonderfully realised. I hired Carlos instantly, and asked him, as a sort of test, to film on a Wandsworth housing estate: de-personalised living space, much inferior to the back-to-back rows of small terraced houses, each with its own garden, that the high-rise blocks had replaced. The result was *Where the Houses Used to Be*. Carlos Pasini was a natural film-maker. He went back to Argentina to make a film on Eva Perón. As well as the presidential palace in Buenos Aires, we saw the small up-country town she came from, and the theatre she acted in. An actress who knew her well in her young days stood in the theatre aisle wearing a hat and gloves, as was proper, and told us of Eva Duarte, of her acting, her nature, her astonishing career. At its peak, they called her 'Reina del Corazón' – *Queen of Hearts*. Carlos's film was a gem. Tim Rice and Andrew Lloyd Webber asked to see it when they were working on the musical *Evita*. They watched it often. Carlos Pasini got little thanks, acknowledgement or reward. His film, to my mind, got closer to Eva Perón than either the musical *Evita* or Alan Parker's big, brash movie of it.

Film-makers wanted to stay at Thames and work with us. We kept on as many as we could keep busy. Jolyon Wimhurst worked with John Morgan on films on Covent Garden and on Munich – opera in two cities – before Munich hosted the 1972 Olympic Games. He showed us the Cuvilliés Theatre, where Mozart's *Idomeneo* was premièred; the fairy castle of Neuchwanstein and Wagner's mad King Ludwig; Richard Strauss's *Salome*, and its curse – which, Morgan would suggest, haunted the city; the failed revolution of 1919, the beerhalls and the Nazis' first show of strength. Jolyon shot *Hurricane*, a snapshot of Alex 'Hurricane' Higgins, snooker star, in his whirlwind early days. Higgins, the fastest cue in snooker, could rattle off a century break in less time than it took to expose a roll of film. One shot told all. And Jolyon collaborated with the critic Philip Purser on *The One and Only Phyllis Dixey*, the best-known stripper of the Windmill era. Philip had met Phyllis in her forties with her husband, and his girlfriend, a member of Phyllis's troupe. He wrote a book about her, and a screenplay for us. Nude, yes, but as English as a pot of tea, Phyllis Dixey died early of cancer. There was an embarrassing fracas when Jolyon cast his actress girlfriend in the lead. The crew objected. Filming ground to a halt. Mike Wooller, who performed a marvellous stint in charge of documentaries, revived it and saw *Phyllis Dixey* through to a good conclusion. He brought in Mike

Tuchner to direct, and upped the budget. Lesley-Anne Down played Phyllis. Philip Purser, in *Done Viewing*, complains I stripped off a voiceover stream of consciousness narration he was particularly proud of. 'High-handed,' he says. Cack-handed also, perhaps.

Udi Eichler now seems to me among the most remarkable people I have worked with. The son of an Austrian aristocratic father who had had several wives, he was distinguished by both sweetness of personality and seriousness of intellect. He was commended to the BBC by a famous broadcaster, Lance Sieveking, and obtained a general traineeship. Sieveking and he kept in touch. Udi and I had worked on *Panorama* together. Living the Reithian ethos as much as anyone I knew, he came after me to Rediffusion and to Thames. He had a keen mind, and an open one. When Channel Four was thought of, Udi kept in touch with Keith Joseph, on the right of Margaret Thatcher's Tory party. He lived with his wife Diana and children in a commune in Kew, where several houses had been knocked through into one another. Each family had privacy, but the community shared the tasks of supervising and feeding children; members could go to work without having to worry about making lunch, or having tea ready when the children came home from school. They took turns helping each other. Every Sunday evening they gathered in one large room to discuss the week, share their difficulties and problems, speak their minds. I attended one such session. Udi had proposed to me three films on closed communities: a monastic institution, an Israeli kibbutz, and his own home. Wild horses would not have persuaded me to live there; but what is documentary for, if not to gain understanding of others? The three films were modestly revelatory.

Udi was more open about himself than the rest of us. Charles Bloomberg once found him on the telephone talking a colloquial Viennese. Udi gestured him to take a seat and chattered on, talking and listening. After a while, he put his hand over the

mouthpiece and said, 'I won't be long. I'm just talking to my analyst.' Telephone time was costly; yet at Thames no one monitored
it. During *The World at War* a colleague, Rosemary Winkley, a PA,
asked my help. Rosemary was a balletomane, and spent every
lunchtime, and many other hours, photographing ballet dancers.
(Her sister was married to Clive Barnes, the theatre and dance
critic, then in New York.) She was concerned for the fate of Valery
Panov, a soloist with the Kirov in Leningrad. Panov was Jewish;
because of this, he thought, he was held back in the Kirov, yet he
was not allowed to leave the Soviet Union. Rosemary was trying
to get him out, and to support him until he could. She had a short
film clip showing him whirling round the Mariinsky stage. Would
I show it to Laurence Olivier, and get him to send Panov a message? I did show it to Olivier. He composed a short telegram of
excessive praise – 'You are the greatest dancer in the world,' etc. –
and urged Panov to keep his spirits up. Rosemary was delighted;
Panov, we hoped, sustained. Years later, when Panov did get out,
the Israeli Embassy hosted a reception for him; I stood in line to be
introduced. When he heard my name, Panov embraced me and
thanked me warmly for all I had done to help him. I was surprised, and a little embarrassed; I had done very little. When he
published the story of his life, *To Dance*, I received a signed copy.
I found my name in the index, and looked up the reference:
during long years of frustration and loneliness, he had been
cheered by weekly telephone calls from a dear friend, Rosemary
Winkley, made from the offices of Thames Television by permission of her generous boss Jeremy Isaacs. I suppose Thames could
afford it.

Udi Eichler made other good programmes in the features
department. He produced several series of *Something to Say*, and
one that caused much hoo-hah, *Sex in our Time*. This was typical
Udi. In it, he proposed to speak frankly about sex. The seven programmes, intended for late-night transmission, consisted mostly
of studio talk, and aimed to inform. They never made it to the air.

I was in West Wales, walking the Pembrokeshire Coastal Path, when I was told that the IBA's officers were adamant the series could not be shown. They had the right to see any programme in advance of transmission, had done so in this case, and were now inviting Thames's board to withdraw it from the schedule. The programmes were utterly harmless; it was an index of the regulator's timidity that they were not aired. The Broadcasting Act prohibited programmes which might cause offence; the IBA always interpreted this to mean causing any offence at all, to anyone, ignoring both the interests of those who actively wanted to see what they objected to, and the indifference, a sort of tacit approval, of the great majority.

There was no intention to shock, or even to titillate, in *Sex in our Time*. The series calmly, even clinically, set out to inform, satisfying the sort of curiosity that a dictionary might. Of course, adolescents search dictionaries out of a prurient curiosity rather than an etymological one. But that does not mean the entry is pornographic. I had doubts about just one programme, a report on the Soho sex industry; sleazy shop windows and strip-club exteriors. Whatever the intention, such scenes risk appearing prurient. I would cheerfully have lost this; but it was not that which had caused offence in Brompton Road. One programme was devoted to female sexuality; with the aid of mirrors, members of a women's group inspected their vaginas, to learn which bit does what. Viewers were to see only diagrams, broad lines drawn on card, formalistically, in black ink; not a hint of pink. Today, billed as education, this would seem too dull to deserve a mention; then, it was beyond the pale. The Thames board, on which some liberal souls sat, was divided, but inclined not to trouble the Authority further. Nor was I. They would never have relented. I did regret, though, not being able to show a scene in a sex shop in Croydon. The owner demonstrated a vibrator by applying it to the table top where it rattled away merrily. The customer was impressed, but wanted to know if it would interfere with the television . . . *Sex in our Time* was patently well before its time. Today, Channel Four screens *Sex Tips for Girls*, *Designer Vaginas*, *More Sex Tips for Girls* and *The Sex Inspectors*, all as graphic as you please. I caught, the other day, five fleshy minutes of tits and bums in a film called *Porn with Attitude*. But porn, with or without attitude, demeans. On the stages of the world, *The Vagina Monologues* grind, revealingly, on.

One future Prix Italia winner repeatedly knocked on our door and complained she was not admitted. This was Mira Hamermesh, who had escaped from Poland in 1939 after hair-raising adventures, arrived in Israel, come to London, married, had a son. She was a painter, but went back to Poland to study at the Film School at Lodz. She showed me her graduate film, *Lesson Two*, a short, chilling tale. Prisoners, in German hands, are lined up for selection: 'Can you write? Read?' Those who can get a cross marked on their backs in whitewash. Others struggle to get it also, by rubbing backs on backs, garment on garment. Those with the mark are marched off, fast – to their deaths. The story could only have been told on film. Anyone could see how good a film-maker Mira was. We had few slots, and many claimants. Mira was sure it was because she was a woman that she was not hired. Eventually, she was given the chance, and seized it; in *Two Women* we saw a Coventry shop steward exchange places with a Hungarian doctor, cutting across role and class.

Mira's best films were to come. For Channel Four she made the first of a trilogy of masterpieces, *Maids and Madams* – apartheid seen through the lives of African servants and white mistresses, bound together yet separate; and *Talking to the Enemy*, in which a Palestinian woman in exile goes back to find her home in Israel, and meets the Israeli mother who lives there now, having lost her son in war. *Caste at Birth*, on the caste system in India, was made for the BBC. For *Loving the Dead*, Mira Hamermesh went back to Poland in search of family no longer living. Mira thinks her painterly skills contribute to her film-making. They do. But it's her mind that counts, and our minds that her films take over by their power.

What I find enriching about the single documentary is its capacity to tell us, visually, what we don't yet know. British television is rich in film-makers; if only the formats schedulers prefer would move over and make room for them. Nick Fraser's *Storyville* on BBC4 shows what can be done, though it consists for the most part of foreign buy-ins.

It was Michael Parkinson who suggested I should see a film-maker new to me, with a project dear to his heart. Tall, grizzled, quietly spoken, looking like the trusty marshal in a John Ford movie, Frank Cvitanovich came into the room. He was married then to the film-maker Midge Mackenzie. They had a severely handicapped child, Bunny, and Frank wanted to make a film about him. Frank and Midge refused to accept that Bunny's condition could never improve. They had come to believe in the work of a Philadelphia-based specialist, Glen Doman. Doman preached that constant exercise would one day free cramped and twisted limbs for movement, and that constant talk would unlock the child's mind and empower him to speak. Friends took turns, in relays, to be with Bunny, work his limbs, subject him to speech, day after day, striving to bring about a miracle. Frank, at this point, did not want to make any other movie; he wanted to film Bunny's treatment, and show us its effects.

I warned Frank that we could not give *carte blanche* to any doctor to propagandise for a cure, unfairly arousing parents' hopes; but I agreed to his making the film. In *Bunny*, Dr Doman got to explain his method, but viewers were left to make up their minds on the theory he proposed. Theory it remained; in spite of tiny changes in his condition, perceived or imagined, Bunny faltered and later died.

But what a film-maker! As soon as I saw a cut, I knew that Frank Cvitanovich was a seriously talented director. He shot in long, loose takes, and left them long in the cutting room. Frank's art was to conceal art. From then on, he parlayed his way into making one film for Thames after another. Not interested in big budgets, he put forward simple subjects. Frank used to inveigh against journalists in documentary who wanted to tell you things; he was particularly hard on journalists who told you things to camera. He thought that, in the right hands, the camera alone told a story.

One day, chatting, he poured scorn on an elaborate project we had for the environment. He could find a way to do it better, his way. He wanted to make a film about Shire horses. The legend is that he made the pitch when we were standing next to each other at the urinals; we could have passed each other in the corridor, and sealed it there; it is possible we talked in my office. In any case, the conversation did not last longer than two minutes. He told me he had a subject for his next film; what did I think of Shire horses, big farm horses working the fields, in Norfolk, say? That would say more about the environment than any United Nations tract. During the war I had been evacuated to Kirkcudbrightshire, to a farm that had bred Clydesdales. There were high barns full of empty horse boxes, lined with the fading coloured cards of prizes won, red, blue, yellow, green. I said, 'Yes. Do it.'

That is the right way, I think, to commission a film from a film-maker whose worth you know; you don't need a treatment or a shooting script. Today, by contrast, the commissioning editor will insist on what he wants. The film-maker's fancy must fit the format, the stylebook's line, the marketing department's brief. How many people will tell you they want to see a film about Shire horses? Not many. *Beauty, Bonny, Daisy, Violet, Grace and Geoffrey Morton* won the BAFTA award, and was ITV's entry for the Prix Italia.

Frank's is a very simple film; all it shows is a year, and a bit more, in the lives of Grace and Geoffrey Morton, farmers, and their Shire horses. At one point, a stallion serves the mare. Eleven months later a foal is born. We see all this in loving detail. Meeting in the lavatories one day – this I do remember – I asked Frank what sort of music he would be using. 'Brass band, I suppose?' I said, thinking of clumping great hooves and oom-pah-pah. 'No,' said Frank. When the foal, freed from the milky silk membrane that had protected it in the womb, struggled to its feet, it began to step delicately about, and then danced for the sheer joy of living to Beethoven's 'Spring' sonata. Magic!

10

PUSHING THE BOAT OUT

Why not me? Thames needed a new Director of Programmes. The search had lasted some weeks now; no one had spoken to me. The ITV companies prided themselves on short lines of communication at the top. In charge was the Managing Director; beside him, a Programme Controller; since a seat on the Board came with it, the post was entitled Director of Programmes.

The four major ITV companies, to which Yorkshire Television (YTV) had been added in 1968, shared network production, and were capitalised, equipped and staffed to do so. The schedule was compiled by five people meeting weekly on Mondays: the programme controllers of the major companies. So the post at Thames was an important one. But why the vacancy?

Howard Thomas, who uniquely in ITV had put together two successful major programme companies in succession, ABC and Thames, had now, early in 1974, followed Hartley Shawcross as Thames's Chairman. Thomas's choice to succeed himself as Managing Director of Thames lay between his Director of Programmes, Brian Tesler, flawlessly in charge of Thames's programme output, and George Cooper, prim, efficient, ABC's and

Thames's Sales Director. Cooper too had a track record of consistent success. A martinet, he kept a tight grip of his department: Thames's salesmen wore suits to the office; their shoes shone and their hair was trimmed. Thomas, as expected, chose Tesler – and then failed to agree terms with him. Tesler's contract with ABC, and with Thames, had been arrived at through a private company which leased his services. EMI, who now held the controlling stake in Thames, said they would have none of that. With a rigidity uncharacteristic of a showbusiness empire, EMI insisted that such a procedure was against its practice. But Tesler refused to alter his tax status, pointing out that other EMI executives had similar arrangements. Instead of fighting his corner, Thomas retreated. The offer to Tesler was withdrawn; George Cooper was appointed over him instead. As ITV's official historian puts it: 'Thomas and Tesler were locked in a state of mutual astonishment at each other's behaviour in allowing the most important appointment in the largest ITV company to fail for such a trivial reason.' Tesler soon resigned to join Thames's rival, LWT.

Whatever Howard Thomas's strengths in management – and he made some brilliant decisions, not least hiring Sydney Newman to create *Armchair Theatre* – getting on well with colleagues was not one of them. Tesler was a loss. Now Thomas and Cooper set out to fill the gaping hole, though Cooper knew nothing of programmes or programme-makers. Thomas wooed first Bill Cotton, a light entertainment star at the BBC, and then Stella Richman, who had been, briefly, programme controller at LWT. Both turned him down. Though aware of my limitations, I knew I could do the job. I asked to see George Cooper and Howard Thomas. 'You know me', I said, 'as a current affairs man, and a documentary maker. It is true I have little experience of drama or of entertainment, but I know what I don't know, and will willingly work with experienced colleagues.' Tesler had been meticulous in showing board reports to his senior colleagues; I was aware what our priorities were. I got the job.

Thomas had looked outside, not in. But actually we were seeing a changing of the guard; the ITV companies were throwing up programme executives qualified to lead from within their own ranks. Some of us at least were journalists. At the programme controllers' table I would join Cyril Bennett (LWT), my old boss at Rediffusion; Paul Fox (YTV), my boss at the BBC; and, for Granada, succeeding Denis Forman, David Plowright, who had been news editor when I joined Granada in 1958. Now, with a long, successful stint at *World in Action* behind him, David revelled in wider responsibilities, and had charge of major drama. He brought negotiating clout to the table: two episodes a week of *Coronation Street*. 'Wash your mouth out,' David would say if anyone suggested moving *Coronation Street*, just once, for whatever reason, to another slot. The fifth controller was Bill Ward, representing ATV. We all liked Bill. He had directed *Sunday Night at the London Palladium* when it started. On the first ever run-through, Lew Grade had panicked at the realisation that the scene change into 'Beat the Clock', which the crew were struggling to achieve in thirty minutes, would shortly have to be completed, live, in three, during the commercial break. It was; Lew packed Bill off for a couple of nights in Paris, no expense spared, no questions asked. Bill had also directed ATV's *Golden Hour*, from the Royal Opera House, capturing for posterity Maria Callas and Tito Gobbi in Act Two of *Tosca*. The recording vanished into the archive's mustiest corner until retrieved and re-shown on Channel Four. Looking at it today, I marvel at the rightness of Bill Ward's direction. As a colleague at controllers' meetings, Bill had one drawback: to any controversial proposal he could make no meaningful response; promising an answer next week, he would depart to Great Cumberland Place to consult Lew. No one ever remarked on this. We just waited.

Programme controllers' meetings, taking up most of Mondays, varied the week's routine; the company was fine, the mood mostly amiable, the hospitality rituals we observed pampering and luxurious. Each company took it in turn as host; we met usually in a boardroom with a dining room next door. Enormous meals were served, and fine wines offered. A box of large cigars lay on the table.

Too many cooks? ITV's schedule in those days benefited from plurality; within an understood framework, different minds contributed differing programmes. It was the general practice not to criticise what other companies put forward, within their quota, for the schedule. I found a welcome for Thames's output; we had all-round strength in depth. The principal discord arose from LWT's position, fighting more severe BBC competition at the weekends. LWT did not have the benefit of Thames's drama or situation comedies, or *This Is Your Life*, all shown in our airtime. They had no *Coronation Street* or *Emmerdale Farm* either, both of which played in the week. LWT could not close out the weekend itself; it had to take programmes from others, and was rarely satisfied with them. Granada's taste in comedy dismayed LWT: *The Wheeltappers and Shunters Club* was not just from, but for the North; could they please be spared it? Granada's David Plowright, representing 'The House of Hits', was adamant; another series of *Wheeltappers* was on its way. Only LWT suggested it should play in London on weekdays instead. At the heart of this bickering lay a serious and complex disagreement between Thames and LWT over 'the London split' – how much each company should contribute to the network.

The solvent, if disagreement grated at Controllers, was humour, much of it Jewish; all his life Cyril Bennett told Yiddish jokes. John Birt, and then Michael Grade, succeeded him. Paul Fox, not used to hearing Yiddish at BBC Programme Review, relaxed and savoured his cigar. If you consider that Bill Ward reported to Lew Grade, and David Plowright to the Bernsteins, and add me, Jeremy Israel Isaacs, you might conclude that Jews ran a significant chunk of the British media. Such an appearance was deceptive. Jewish humour there may have been; control in

Jewry's interest, never. Successive *This Week* reports on the Middle East incurred criticism from Israel's supporters to a far greater extent than from the Arab world. At the preview of a Thames series on *Palestine*, we had the Israeli ambassador in one viewing room, six Arab ambassadors in another. Both sides had points to put; the Arabs insisted that, from their viewpoint, the Holocaust was an irrelevance.

I only ever half-enjoyed the horse-trading on Mondays at Controllers. Content to leave the niceties of the schedule to others, I was glad when a subcommittee was set up to whom we could delegate. The job that mattered to me I did solo: commissioning Thames's programmes, and shielding the talent that delivered them.

How good was Thames then? Pretty good; the IBA's awkwardly melded new creation was a success. Its children's programmes, current affairs, documentaries were all rated highly; so were both drama and light entertainment. In 1974 the IBA published appraisals of all the companies' performance, six years into their franchises. The verdict on Thames was warmly approving. Yet the IBA, its programme staff suggested, had hoped for, and now expected, just that little bit more. Drama and entertainment were praised for their reliability, their popularity; but could they not take more risks? Thames was making high profits; it could afford to splash out. The company's management, it was hinted, should ensure that 'shareholders were not too grasping'. The IBA was telling us something. This was a chance to push the boat out that might not come again.

Thames Television studios at Teddington Lock were run as a factory, with an efficient production line. There were three studios: the smallest for *Magpie,* and other lesser-scale work; the middle-sized one for situation comedy, with modest sets, recorded in front of an audience (their response bulked out later, with a laughter and applause track); the largest for drama, and the occasional entertainment spectacular. It all fitted together neatly, provided no one over-ran. How, though, within tight constraints of time and space, could we aspire to excellence? 'Promise me one thing, Jeremy,' said the chief engineer Stuart Sansom, when I got the job. 'Don't ever give us drama that takes more than two days in Studio One.' With Stella Richman's *Jennie*, Stuart Sansom had seen the writing on the wall. I gave no such promise.

Except for a major special, for Christmas perhaps, entertainment was unlikely to make heavy demands on studio space. *Opportunity Knocks* had its own straightforward routine; situation comedies were, by definition almost, peas from one production pod, half a day's filming and one easy day in the studio. (Benny Hill stretched that a bit). Thames made about eighty sitcoms for the network a year, easily fulfilling our quota. Philip Jones, controller of entertainment, a lovely man, would have liked to do more; he had writers and subjects queuing up. But there was a limit to what the network would take from us.

More of the same? A severe analysis might have reached another conclusion. Rarely, if ever, did any ITV situation comedy match the quality of the BBC's best work. There was no *Hancock*, no *Steptoe*, no *Till Death Do Us Part*, no *Dad's Army*, no *Likely Lads*, no *Porridge*. *Bootsie and Snudge* (Granada) and *Rising Damp* (YTV) came near; I am not sure that any of Thames's, hugely popular as they were, did the same. Regularly, Philip had four or five shows in the top twenty, among them *Bless This House*, *Never Mind the Quality*, *Feel the Width*, *Love Thy Neighbour* and *Mother Makes Three*. Unless one fell out, nothing new could squeeze in. Vince Powell and Harry Driver were Philip's most regular writers. Johnny Mortimer and Brian Cooke were into their stride. John Esmond and Bob Larbey were banging on the door.

Philip Jones was ITV's most consistently successful entertainment executive. He knew that good writing was the essence of success; radio served the BBC well, he thought, as a writing school for television comedy. The centre and end commercial breaks, eating precious minutes from the running time, deprived the writer of room to paint character; you can say more in twenty-nine minutes than in twenty-four. I asked Philip to move, at his own pace, towards new themes, new talent, new writing. In his peak-time slots, no one had licence to fail. I regretted Thames had not picked up on *Do Not Adjust Your Set* and given itself the chance of its own *Monty Python*, before the BBC; but *Python*, after all, started on BBC2, where experiment was encouraged. You could argue that a notion of what appealed to an unsophisticated sense of humour was determining our choice of themes and writing, and holding us back. Comedy, too, needs to take some risk.

Later, I did stiffen Philip's resolve to dispense with Hughie Green's *Opportunity Knocks*, an inexpensive, very popular talent show that had been on the air for fourteen years. For this, search teams auditioned nationwide for hopeful talent. Write-in campaigns, not always innocent, helped determine the result. Hughie Green, in his dealings with us, was always a pain and got steadily worse. He displayed, annually, discontent with his studio berth at Teddington, and argued at each budget round that one show at least, at extra cost, should be done as an outside broadcast. His preferred locations were a nuclear submarine or a NATO airbase. He enjoyed wrapping himself in the Union Jack. He was allowed to try it once, and that was enough. The mixture of patriotism and propaganda – he expected the audience to rise and sing a specially composed number, 'Stand Up for England' – was excruciating and inappropriate. Philip bore the brunt of Hughie's pressure at the weekend, and protected me from most it. On one difficult Sunday he rang to say that Hughie was insisting that a pubescent wannabe pop-singer, Lena Zavaroni, then about twelve, sing 'Help me Make it Through the Night'. Philip had vetoed that. Hughie Green never forgave me for killing off *Opportunity Knocks*, denouncing me to anyone who would listen as a communist. It still had, it is true, a following; but not a God-given right to the slot.

With fingers crossed, aiming at younger viewers, Philip

replaced it with *The Kenny Everett Video Show*, naughty bits and all. The young, and the young at heart, enjoyed it – my son John fell off the sofa laughing; some older viewers may have been less keen. At the best of times, it is hard to predict what will succeed in comedy. Cyril Bennett used to tell of Frank Muir and Denis Norden, after their writing heyday, at a party in LA, being asked what they did for a living. 'We're consultants on comedy to the BBC.'

'Consultants?' – an expression of incredulity – 'You mean you know?'

Thames's drama output, as the IBA acknowledged, was also a success story. Yet here there was more real chance of change. Lloyd Shirley was Controller. A Canadian, he'd had charge of ABC's features, including the arts programme *Tempo*, before succeeding Sydney Newman at drama when Newman went to the BBC. He'd been an actor, and had a nose for writing and a way with him that took others, admiringly, along. He had a cultural chip on his shoulder, but little to be chippy about; his track record spoke for him. As Thames's Controller, Drama, he had delivered series that consistently drew high audiences. *Public Eye* with Alfred Burke, and *Callan* with Edward Woodward, are among the best remembered. Kenneth Haigh played Joe Lampton in John Braine's *Man at the Top*. And there were six Restoration comedies by Congreve, Vanbrugh, Shadwell and Sedley, *The Way of the World*. Lloyd's wife, Virginia, was a scholar, and advised. Boldly, Lloyd Shirley had commissioned two films by Mike Hodges which pointed in an important new direction. *Rumour* and *Suspect*, thrillers shot in 16mm on location in dark cityscapes, were fast-moving and exciting. For Hodges they led to *Get Carter*, and Hollywood; for Thames, they led to *The Sweeney*.

The more ambitious drama, to meet the need the IBA had identified, and for whose prestige Howard Thomas and the Board yearned, was in fact already in the making. *Jennie, Lady Randolph Churchill* was a seven-part portrait of Winston Churchill's

American mother. Lee Remick gave a fetching performance in the lead. *Jennie* went on to wow American viewers on PBS. Accidentally, it also helped precipitate a change in the controllership. Lloyd visited the unit on location at Blenheim. In the evening, tired, emotional, smitten with sexual jealousy, he gave vent to his feelings, publicly, among cast and crew, at the Bear in Woodstock. The incident was noticed; management, above my head, took a dim view. Perhaps it should all have been smoothed over, covered up, forgotten. But Lloyd had now done a demanding job for nearly a decade; he too sensed it was time for a change. Besides, there was the new departure to which *Rumour* and *Suspect* pointed. If Thames set up a separate company to make film series for television, Lloyd could have charge of that. It did; Euston Films. There was an opportunity to appoint a new Controller, Drama. I arranged to meet Verity Lambert for a drink at the Café Royal. As we talked, it became clear to me that she could succeed Lloyd. That was very much her view too.

Verity had started in television as a junior secretary in Howard Thomas's outer office at ABC. She became a drama PA, learning the ropes of rehearsal and studio, coping with crises and the tensions of live transmission. She followed Sydney Newman to the BBC. He gave her the chance to produce a series for children; it is still with us, *Doctor Who*. Sydney, she told me, watched the completed first recording, liked it, told her to get rid of the theme tune which he hated, and left her to get on with it. The theme tune stayed. Verity was bright as they come, tough, and utterly fearless. Working with Midge Mackenzie and Georgia Brown, she had just finished making *Shoulder to Shoulder*, a vivid telling of the suffragettes' story. I thought her credentials were ideal, and would appeal to Howard Thomas. They did.

Verity had as clear an understanding as I did that high ratings were a prerequisite. But, like me, she relished the chance to widen the range of our offerings. There had been, there was then, there is still too great a preoccupation in TV drama with crime and detection. I understand that; I read crime thrillers myself. But enough is enough. I asked Cyril Bennett once why TV drama did not venture into the worlds of politics or, nearer to home, show-business. 'My boy,' said the old master, 'there are two subjects which are poison at the box office; politics and showbusiness. You and I may be interested; the public could not care less.' After a few weeks, I asked the new Controller, Drama what she had for me. She had found, she said, two marvellous ideas for series; one was about an idealistic left-wing Labour MP, too radical for his party, antagonistic to the compromises of power; the other about an all-female rock group. Thames made both *Bill Brand* and *Rock Follies*.

Trevor Griffiths devised and wrote *Bill Brand*. Trevor was a proudly combative, ideologically committed writer. His father, a chemical worker, had died slowly of an industrial illness. Laurence Olivier, opening himself to new work with an edge, put on Griffiths' *The Party* at the National, and played in it. One day, recording commentary for *The World at War*, he showed me the printed text, a study of a revolutionary group to whose cause people gave their lives (the Workers Revolutionary Party, I guess). He turned page after page after page: 'Look at this,' he said with relish, 'this is the longest speech in the history of British drama.' He was using audio tapes to learn the authentic Glaswegian in which he would deliver it.

Now, with only the treatment for *Bill Brand* to go on, Trevor Griffiths insisted on explaining to me why the scene in part eight, still to be written, would depict a particular sex act between man and woman in the way it would. This was vital, not just to the human relationship but to the politics; I must guarantee now that we would show what he wrote, close up, in explicit detail. I said it was impossible for me to give any such guarantee. He must write it honestly, we should shoot it as we thought proper and as frankly as we dared; together, we would find out if it was trans-mittable or not. Grumbling, he set off to write. Jack Shepherd played the main role, intensely. Stella Richman was executive producer. Stuart Burge, a quiet, lovely man, aware, expert, with a light touch, produced. Two major talents shared the direction: Roland Joffé and Mike Newell both went on to eyecatching careers in film. *Bill Brand* was strong meat, the argument too close, the mood too bleak for some – there were very few jokes. Thames put it out at nine o'clock, after much soul-searching on my part, and kept it there. Network colleagues shifted it to after *News at Ten*, replacing it at nine with *Streets of San Francisco*, or some such.

My scheduling decision may have been a sort of watershed. Now I had *Bill Brand* at 9 p.m. on Mondays, a documentary series, *Destination America*, in the same slot on Tuesdays, and *Clayhanger*, a twenty-six-part blockbuster from ATV, based on Arnold Bennett's novels, on Wednesdays. The network moved *Clayhanger*, too, out of peak. We lost share at 9 p.m. on all three evenings to the BBC. On Thursdays, at 8.30 p.m., we played *This Week*. Thames's ratings dropped a little; its revenues soared. The only effect of low ratings as far as the sales department was concerned was that advertisers, to make more impact, bought more time, pushing up the price in doing so. Such were the benefits of monopoly. But plainly I was not the most ratings-oriented Director of Programmes that ever was.

If *Bill Brand* was sombre, the other newcomer, *Rock Follies*, was a cocktail of colours screaming 'watch me'; a combination of rock concert and seaside fairground. It had a soundtrack to match, by Roxy Music. The scripts were by Howard Schuman; in them we met an all-female rock group in a wicked, cut-throat world. Schuman, up to the minute if not ahead of it, wrote with tart wit, in a slangy shorthand; dialogue crackled. Andrew Brown, hip, witty, indomitably optimistic, ruthlessly intolerant of error, was the producer. Three very different actresses – Charlotte Cornwell, Julie Covington, Rula Lenska – brought the group energetically to life. *Rock Follies* set the screen alight. It was not a ratings winner, but I commissioned the second series.

We pushed the boat out also for Alan Ayckbourn's *The Norman*

Conquests, across three evenings, with Penelope Keith, Richard Briers and Tom Conti, and for Leo McKern in *Rumpole of the Bailey.* And the brass-band signature tune went oompah, oompah as Barry Foster's *Van der Valk,* based on Nicholas Freeling's detective, set out to counter crime in Amsterdam. At Euston Films, Lloyd Shirley and George Taylor made *The Sweeney;* later Verity Lambert and Linda Agran came up with *Minder.* Thames drama had the best of both worlds.

I never could watch, let alone enjoy, violence on the screen, and used to hide behind a newspaper whenever frightening images threatened. At Channel Four we would show markedly fewer acts of violence than did any rival. But at Thames I valued and defended *The Sweeney.* It was not just that John Thaw as Regan, and Dennis Waterman as his sidekick Carter, gave engaging performances, and worked well together; or that Leon Griffiths, Troy Kennedy Martin and others wrote taut scripts. What mattered was the pace film brought, and the sense of being in the streets. *The Sweeney* was hugely popular. I once teetered a little at an episode which portrayed a psychopathic killer, but when Mary Whitehouse complained was ready with a rebuttal. The real issue *The Sweeney* posed was not violence – there was not so very much of that – but the depiction of a police force that cut corners to catch criminals. There's some evidence that real policemen imitated *The Sweeney* rather than *Dixon of Dock Green.*

It was an article of faith among broadcasters, applauded by the critics and by the IBA, that single plays mattered; the writer's inventive voice counted for something valuable. Format drama should not swamp the schedule. The single play was a touchstone of our responsibility to writing and to audiences, and we should keep the form alive.

Verity gave me a script to read by Philip Mackie, my insouciant, dear colleague of Granada days. Economy marked his style always. Denis Mitchell, for Granada, made short documentary profiles of Soho characters he knew; one of them was the homosexual Quentin Crisp, who had earned a crust by modelling, nude, at state-run art schools. Philip's *The Naked Civil Servant* told his story. I thought it the best script I had ever read, and that we must make it. Arranged in a sequence of short scenes, it was terse and lucid and touching. Stylised caption cards punctuated the narrative, lending it an attractive, laid-back, uninvolving air. Yet the climax, when Crisp defended himself on a trumped-up charge of importuning by telling us who he was, and how it felt to live as he did, was overwhelming. The play ended with Crisp still dreaming of the ideal love he would never find.

I warned George Cooper he should read something that might cause offence, though actually I thought the script so innocently direct, so tactful in its restraint, as to escape criticism. He was supportive. Jack Gold directed, utterly in the spirit of the piece; Barry Hanson was the producer. They filmed it in four short weeks – twenty days and one day over – for a direct cost of £75,000. There was, in the end, nothing sensational about *The Naked Civil Servant*; it was just sensationally good.

The IBA, too, was supportive – until the film was finished. Then the Director General himself, Brian Young, took exception to a brief scene of anal examination (for the army), and to a caption card in a bathroom scene in which Crisp rationalised his loneliness by noting sadly that 'Sex is no substitute for masturbation'. I suppose the ex-headmaster of Charterhouse had spent so much time warning against self-abuse that he could not bring himself to appear to advocate it. Verity saw him with Philip Mackie to plead our cause, advising Philip to leave it to her. Philip, however, launched an immediate attack on the schoolmasterly figure before him. They could not change his mind; the caption, one of a series, must be cut. We changed it, abysmally, against Jack Gold's protest, to 'Wasn't it fun in the bath tonight?' (Years later, on the film's third showing on Channel Four, I got the IBA – at a full meeting of the Authority – to reverse its decision.) *The Naked Civil Servant*, more than any other single programme of my time, did set the

Thames on fire. In his performance as Crisp John Hurt surpassed himself, finding voice and manner to carry the whole off wondrously well. He won BAFTA's Best Actor of the Year award; the role, decisively, helped make him. At a party at my home in Chiswick, he, playfully, squeezed my bum.

The programme which persistently raised problems for the Authority was, inevitably, *This Week*, because *This Week* on occasion saw its role as disclosing material powerful institutions sought to suppress. In clashes with the IBA, *This Week* regularly pointed to a fundamental divide between those motivated to publish, and those who, in case of difficulty or doubt, were inclined against publication. The IBA was concerned not to risk breaching the provisions of the Broadcasting Act. It was also concerned, though less overtly, not to fall foul of government.

Most ITV boards saw it as their duty to guard against threat to the interests of their shareholders, i.e. the tenure of their franchise, and were over-cautious as a result. Yet the franchise was granted to broadcast responsibly, not to maximise profits. Granada, too, sought to operate within the Act, but would broadcast if it could. Agonisedly, but also, I thought, admirably, Sidney Bernstein refused to screen a *World in Action* report on Freemasonry; his brother Cecil was a mason, and pledged to secrecy. For Cecil, to broadcast masonic ritual was to break his word, and would cause him untold anguish. Sidney could not let that happen. Granada's journalists were furious and frustrated. But a brother's trust was respected, as it should have been. Blood is thicker than ink. And, in any case, Freemasonry in the UK is more of a curiosity than a political force. Apart from this lapse, Granada staunchly backed its journalists all the way, defending their work against the IBA's criticism and, on one occasion, handing over to the BBC material from a *World in Action* on defence costs which the IBA would not pass. Paul Fox broadcast it on *Panorama*. In the chair at LWT John Freeman, himself a former journalist, was supportive when he needed to be of John Birt's carefully controlled programme output. I never felt confident of quite such determined support at Thames; there was an unwillingness to accept journalistic imperatives, and a wobbliness under pressure. It was always possible for me to argue a case; but the instinct of others sometimes gave the game away.

Sir Philip Warter, whose first conversational gambits I found disconcerting, appeared feeble as well as risible, and was not around long enough to make a difference. His successor, Lord Shawcross, Hartley Shawcross, was of a different stamp. As Attorney General he had been Chief Prosecutor at Nuremberg, and a Cabinet presence in Attlee's government. Then the City claimed him. He moved to the right. He was outstandingly able, calm, authoritative. It was hard not to admire, and harder not to take kindly to a Chairman of the Board who urged we find ways of spending more money on programmes. But he had fierce political views. I found him once in his office gazing in horror at the centre-spread of the *Sunday Times*. 'Look at this,' he said, 'intolerable!' What roused his ire was a piece about the My Lai massacre in Vietnam, questioning how long, if much else like this was happening, the United States could claim moral authority for the war, and carry on fighting it. It was the question, not the massacre, that disgusted him. I pointed out that the author, the much-respected Ronald Butt, was the solidly right-wing former political columnist of the *Financial Times*. Shawcross was not assuaged.

On 30 January 1972, 'Bloody Sunday', British paratroopers shot dead thirteen Irish civilians in Londonderry. We failed to send a crew to cover the march that led to the massacre. We had planned to send more than one but the union, ACTT, demanded such excessive terms for working in Londonderry that weekend that I refused to let them go. By next day, however, two *This Week* reporters were on the scene. The government at once appointed Lord Widgery to enquire into what had happened, thus rendering large issues of responsibility and guilt *sub judice*. When Shawcross learned that *This Week* would cover the aftermath for the following Thursday, he forbade us at first to do anything at all. I resisted. His concern was not just that eyewitness interviews we obtained might taint the well of justice. It was more root and branch. He did not trust us, or any journalist, to edit material honestly, and without intention to distort. You might ask how, in that case, he had ever agreed to chair a company whose ethos must be, at least in part, journalistic; but no matter. I argued on. We compromised. He would not be swayed into allowing editing; I refused not to report on the killings. In the end, with the IBA's approval, we ran two uncut reels of film, clapper-board to clapper-board; on one, Peter Williams talked, in their barracks, to members of the Parachute Regiment; on the other, Peter Taylor talked to an inhabitant of the Bogside, Jack Chapman, who happened to be a former British soldier. What Chapman told us of what he saw has stood the test of time. Taylor also interviewed the commander of the Provisional IRA's Derry Brigade, but the interview, because of the restricted nature of the programme, never saw the light of day – till now, that is, at a screening in January 2006.

In the published diaries of Cecil King, publisher of the *Daily Mirror*, there is an extraordinary entry for Friday, 26 October 1973. It is quoted in Jeremy Potter's volume 4 of *Independent Television in Britain*. King wrote:

> On Wednesday Hartley Shawcross had lunch with me. He is Chairman of Thames Television and has been disturbed at the volume of left-wing propaganda put out by the commentators from his station. He had up the man responsible, and questioned him about the bias shown by his department. The man said he was a left-winger himself, as were most of his staff. He would not brook any interference with his work, though of course the directors could dismiss him. If they did so there would be a strike and the station would close down.

I wish I knew precisely what encounter, and with whom, Hartley Shawcross had in mind in making this staggering allegation. He had up, he says, 'the man responsible'. But that was me, and I had no such conversation with him; nor would I ever have talked the nonsense he said was told him. Cecil King, of course, was an egotistical political fantasist who plotted, with one or two others, to depose Harold Wilson and put in power a businessman's government, with leading roles for Mountbatten and himself. Fantasy? Paranoia? Maybe, but that diary entry carried weight with some; in 1977, Anglia and Southern used it to argue for a new network company of the political right to combat bias and bad taste. But I never heard a whiff of the complaint Shawcross – if King hadn't imagined it – was making.

The difficulty for ITV's programme-makers was that publication was never just a question of what a company, its management or board, decided. The company was not the publisher. In the ultimate failsafe device, that role was given by the Act to the IBA. Their first instinct was not to publish at all, but to regulate. This contradiction burned up energy for years. Instead of operating as newspaper owners, book publishers and theatre managers were obliged to do – publish and take the consequences at law – broadcasters in ITV could only submit themselves to the regulator. The IBA, if in doubt, would consult its solicitors, a cautious firm without the least innate sympathy for utterance, who would reinforce the doubts expressed to them, rendering lack of assurance doubly sure. All the same, at Thames, programme-makers fought their corner all the way.

For a decade from 1968 *This Week* was preoccupied with the troubles in Northern Ireland. Early on, the programme reported the issues as seen by either side – the Protestant/unionist/loyalist majority, the Catholic/nationalist/republican minority – on consecutive Thursday evenings. The programmes were well balanced, the contributors evenly matched, but forceful and outspoken. Ulster Television, the Authority acquiescing, broadcast neither; they claimed that local opinion might be dangerously inflamed in the interval between the two. I would guess myself that UTV were more concerned about broadcasting trenchant republican opinion than the loyalist view; but in any case they, not we, would have to live with the consequences. Subsequently *This Week* reported on the role of the British army; sectarian polarisation of housing in Belfast; the disabling Protestant strike; the sceptical and unenthusiastic nationalist attitude to a visit by the Queen in her Jubilee year; the status and treatment of Maze prisoners. *This Week* marked, in 1974, five years of the Troubles, and in 1976, the anniversary of the Easter Rising in Dublin.

In 1973 David Elstein had become producer of *This Week*. Elstein was a superb producer; he has a steely intellect, is logical and decisive. In internal debate at Thames, he was almost too clever for his own good. As a union spokesman, he was a thorn in management's side; as a manager (he later became Thames's Director of Programmes), a hammer of the union. Under him, *This Week* dug deeper, and hit harder. Among the programme's assets was Peter Taylor, a reporter who had read Classics at Cambridge and started out with Thames as a researcher. Patently honest, like all the best researchers, Peter won the trust of those he talked to. Today, his lengthy, revelatory reports on Northern Ireland and on security matters have become touchstones by which others are judged.

In May 1975 the IBA insisted on postponing an edition of *This Week* about IRA fundraising in the USA; it would have been aired when the polls were still open in an election for the Northern Ireland Convention. Thames staff made public protest, tetchily. Another programme was substituted. The IBA rapped Thames's knuckles, complaining of 'a continuous attempt to evade, or even defy, the Authority's clearly expressed wishes'. They had the ultimate say, of course, but they wanted to exercise their power covertly, condemning all attempts to interest newspapers in the process of censorship. Management was asked to see to it that such behaviour was discontinued. But why should journalists, who take trouble to deliver timely reporting, keep silent when a regulator interferes?

In 1976 Labour's Secretary of State for Northern Ireland was a pugnacious ex-miner, Roy Mason. Over dinner at the Culloden Hotel, Belfast, in November, Mason heatedly berated the BBC Board of Governors for 'giving the IRA a platform for propaganda, and bringing comfort and aid to the enemies of the State'. The dinner came to be known as the second battle of Culloden. How to report the conflict in Northern Ireland posed a constant dilemma for television, and for other journalists. Should one hear from terrorists, or not? Dare one report malpractice by those countering terror or not? My view was always that we had to report on the terrorist campaign, and the political motivation for it; to do so was not to promote or glorify evil men committing evil acts. My view was also that, whatever our abhorrence of murder, and our sympathy with those in the RUC and the army who risked their lives to counter and prevent it, they too must face reporting, not whitewash. If their task was to uphold the rule of law, they themselves must observe the law.

In spite of all the difficulties, *This Week* devoted six editions to Northern Ireland in 1977. In most of them Peter Taylor was the reporter. One programme, on conditions inside the Maze prison following the government's abolition of special category status, contained a lengthy interview with the Chief Officer of the Prison Officers' Federation in Northern Ireland. He wrote to *This Week* praising the programme for its 'superb handling of a delicate topic' and noting that it was 'an accurate description of life at the Maze'. A few days later he was murdered by the IRA. Shortly afterwards, Taylor investigated allegations of ill-treatment by police officers at the Castlereagh detention centre in Belfast.

Roy Mason then wrote to the IBA Chairman, protesting about *This Week*'s 'tendentious language', accusing the programmes of giving 'incalculable assistance to those who are interested in building up a case against the RUC'. The IBA, in turn, protested to Thames, and demanded assurances that future reporting would present the situation 'in the round'. But although that should certainly be a responsible journalist's endeavour, it is easier said than done. We did our best. Once or twice we found good reason to report something that united warring communities. But we could not falsify facts. Is it really credible that current affairs television should, with sanitised selectivity, portray amity where there is discord; calm where there is violence; discipline and dedication, when corners are cut and rules abused? The IRA's and the loyalist gangs' worst cruelties, and the British security forces' calculated responses, were more lethally brutal than journalists reported them.

Early in the seventies Bill Hardcastle, the former *Daily Mail* editor, now presenting Radio 4's *The World at One*, sent a cub reporter, Jonathan Dimbleby, to see me, looking for advancement. Jonathan had made a promising start on radio; he was a natural for television too. A *This Week* interview he did with 'Tiny' Rowland, denounced by Ted Heath as 'the unacceptable face of capitalism', caught the eye for its tenacity. But his report on Ethiopia, 'The Unknown Famine', was as good as *This Week* ever got. 'Its impact', says ITV's history, 'was without precedent, in terms of public response and subsequent action by governments and international agencies. It raised £1.5 million for famine relief. Jonathan received the Richard Dimbleby Award for the best factual programme of 1973.' What I best remember of 'The Unknown Famine' is the work of Thames's cameraman, Ray Sieman. Ray was fairly tall; the people he was filming were sitting or lying on the ground, starving for nourishment or waiting to die. Ray held the camera below his knees, and walked among them.

In 1975, with Martin Smith directing, Peter Taylor made 'Dying for a Fag'?, a shattering report for *This Week* on the effects of tobacco on health, and followed it up with further programmes dealing with the responsibilities of government, manufacturers and advertisers. An estimated 200,000 people gave up smoking after seeing 'Dying for a Fag?' The industry was then still in denial, contesting at every point the notion that smoking could damage your health. Philip Morris, makers of Marlboro, then agreed to co-operate in the making of a further programme; they wanted a chance to put their case. From panoramic billboards and cinema commercials, we know what 'Marlboro Country' looks like: great rolling plains, mountains behind; cowboys riding the range, breathing God's fresh air and, we assume, off-camera, smoking Marlboros. Elstein, Smith and Taylor put this proposition to the test. *This Week* made use of the Marlboro TV and cinema commercials, as seen in the United States (at the time they were banned in the UK); Philip Morris's public relations department had been happy to let us have them. The film contained, edited with meticulous fairness, the responses of one of the tobacco giant's senior executives to the questions Peter Taylor put. It could not be faulted on that ground. Indeed, Philip Morris had suggested the programme precisely in order to put their spokesman in front of the camera – cigarette in hand. But sight of it complete, on air, provoked an earthquake. Martin Smith had filmed *This Week*'s own mini-commercials, featuring six 'cowboys' on horses, and interviews with their respective physicians. The oldest cowboy was propped up in the saddle. He had been a heavy smoker, and was dying of emphysema. The contrast between the actors in the commercials and real cowboys coughing their lives away was devastating. We called it 'Death in the West'.

Philip Morris launched a legal onslaught to prevent further showing, seeking to have the negative handed over to them. Their principal thrust did not go to the truth of what the film contained, but was against our method in making it. They claimed that they had been deceived, that the right to include their commercial had been obtained by false pretences, and that our use breached their copyright. This last point gave Philip Morris a purchase. Initially, in spite of the potential cost of fighting the case, and the vaster cost of losing it, Thames resisted bravely. In the end our insurers, the Prudential, helped force a settlement. Above all else, Philip Morris wished to prevent 'Death in the West' being screened in the United States. It never made it on to network screens, not even PBS. But it did circulate as a sort of *samizdat* bulletin in the anti-smoking cause. The sick cowboy on the horse died, a telling icon in a battle won; the other five followed him shortly afterwards. Before long, tobacco companies, in the US at least, were owning up: cigarettes cause disease, and too many may kill. Tobacco manufacturers have since faced a series of product liability suits with damages running into billions of dollars.

There were three current affairs programmes a week on ITV in those good days: *This Week, World in Action, Weekend World.* Viewers were well served.

Other factual programmes, from different departments, made their mark – David Bellamy's *Botanic Man* (his TV debut) for one. The Thames sales department, although eager to hear our plans, was forbidden to lobby for specific programmes; it was none of their business. But exceptions could be made. They had difficulty in reaching male viewers; would I consider a magazine, late evening, for motorists? I would; the outside-broadcast department would enjoy making it. And holidays? To that too I agreed. *Wish You Were Here*, with Judith Chalmers, was a continuing success. Now, an extension of afternoon hours offered new opportunities. We might, I thought, have a magazine for women, which would not, repeat not, deal with 'women's subjects' – make-up, cooking, embroidery – but would be presented wholly by women. Before we committed to *Good Afternoon*, it was put to me that we should conduct market research. How many viewers would look favourably on an all-women show? The percentage reported was 'zero'. We went ahead anyway. Under Catherine Freeman, *Good Afternoon* quickly prospered; the presenter Mavis Nicholson, sharp, earthy, Welsh, was a particular star. The audience grew. I never used market research, in advance of transmission, again.

There are three categories in the Prix Italia: drama, documentary, music. A network may enter only two categories in any one year, and must supply a juror in the third. In 1976 ITV's entries in documentary and drama were both from Thames – *Beauty, Bonny, Daisy, Violet, Grace and Geoffrey Morton* and *The Naked Civil Servant*. Both won. This was unprecedented; the BBC had never done that. I had given the nod to two ideas, seen each realised, and now saw the makers wreathed with laurel. Verity Lambert and I went out to Bologna with Frank Cvitanovich and Jack Gold for the presentation ceremony. Frank wore a black velvet suit for the occasion, a change from his usual bomber jacket. I was wearing a moustache, before wife, daughter and secretary united in urging me to remove it. There are pictures, regrettably.

It is customary for Italia prizewinners to host a party. In Bologna, not having foreseen the need, we had made no preparations. 'Ah well,' we said, 'we'll give the party next year, in Venice.' That year, as it turned out, Thames again represented ITV. We had an entry in the music category.

For a fire practice one summer day in Euston Road we had to leave our place of work and assemble outside. Reluctantly, I joined the parade and looked around for something to do. I spotted Francis Coleman and Margery Baker from Adult Education, responsible for what few ventures we made into arts programming, and also for Religion. Something had been stirring in my head, and now popped on to my tongue. In Vienna that Easter with Tamara, I had heard Haydn's St Nicholas Mass at the Hofburgkapelle. With a small orchestra, soloists and the Vienna Boys' Choir, it was bliss. We know St Nicholas as Santa Claus. I went across to Francis and Margery and asked them to do it for me, please, as a Christmas special. They were delighted. However, believing they could make more of it, and without telling me, they did Benjamin Britten's St Nicholas Cantata instead. Margery Baker shot a performance in St Albans Cathedral, and married visuals to it. ITV, pushed for an entry, put it in for the Prix Italia. Thames went in full force to Venice. We would host a proper party to celebrate our success in Bologna.

On the chosen evening we assembled to await our guests. Trays of drinks and canapés made their appearance, in readiness. Then came startling news: the St Nicholas Cantata had won the music category. Hat trick! It was quite a party.

Thames had made its mark in Europe; but could we do so across the Atlantic? The US networks were the hardest market of all to crack. Americans equated British excellence in television with the BBC; Thames wanted to bang its own drum. So we bought out five evenings on New York's Channel 9, WORTV, the old RKO station. (It was Channel 9, not a major, which had played *The World at War*. When it opened with an episode on Hitler's rise to power, WOR's commercials were boasting: German Beer is the Best Beer.) We programmed WOR Monday to Friday, from 5 p.m. to closedown. Advertisements were sold at a higher rate than WOR's $4000 for a sixty-second spot. It was not a straight-forward process; WORTV's compliance officers raised problems over language and decency, both in *Beauty, Bonny* – the stallion – and in *The Naked Civil Servant*. I said: We're programming this; if those don't go, we don't go. WOR, and the FCC, Federal Communications Commission, to which it answered, relented. Offence was taken, however, at Benny Hill's 'barefaced cheek' in dropping his trousers, and the manic zest with which, like Harpo Marx, he chased the girls. And they pointed to an element of racial stereotyping in his work: Chinamen were chinks, and looked it. Political correctness raised its head and prepared to cross the Atlantic.

WOR's transmission centre and its offices were in a corner of the then sleazy Times Square. I would go there late and, in presentation control, take calls from viewers wishing us well. 'Who are you guys? Stick around, we need you.' I toured the networks, hoping to interest them in some at least of our wares, and was greeted warmly by the vice-presidents who took commissioning and scheduling decisions. Typically, they'd be Phi Beta Kappa graduates from Harvard, but each, it seemed to me, had left part of his brain at home. The Nielsen ratings were all that mattered; predict those accurately, take no chances, rely always on test marketing – the focus group approach – and the job was done. No exceptions. 'Your programmes are too good for us, Jeremy,' one explained, a little embarrassed.

'Even *The Naked Civil Servant*?' I asked. 'Surely there's a market for that in San Francisco or here in Manhattan?'

'But not in Mississippi or Alabama,' was the answer. 'We're a network. We have to keep the affiliates happy.' They went at the pace of the slowest. Initial over-reaction to Benny Hill, though, was misleading; recycled, chopped up into convenient mini-packages for late-night transmission, *The Benny Hill Show* ran and ran and ran.

US television pays lavish lip-service to British and other foreign television, dishing out International Emmys and crowning big players with 'lifetime achievement' awards – 'gravestones', Laurence Olivier called them.

But while American tributes to the Brits are heartfelt, they arise more from wonderment that such things should be, rather than from any intention to emulate.

Someone once called the US grandees' bluff. Granada showed off Olivier's *King Lear*. For Larry, for Sidney Bernstein, the cream of Manhattan showbiz society showed up, the network bosses among them. This was not, after all, any old Lear, but Olivier's. Lauren Bacall, an old friend of Sidney's, was there too. The select audience could not have been more admiring; on all sides, praise gushed. Lauren Bacall had had a drink or two, and gave it to them straight. 'You are fucking hypocrites, all of you. You say it's marvellous. But not one of you would ever fucking show it, would you?'

To mark the fortieth anniversary of Edward VIII's abdication in 1978, Verity Lambert came up with *Edward and Mrs Simpson*. This, we hoped, would appease the pangs of Thames's Chairman and board for the big event. (*Bill Brand* and *Rock Follies* did not count.) Verity bought rights in *Edward VIII* by Frances Donaldson, a sharp-eyed author it was a pleasure to know. To my surprise she asked Andrew Brown, who had produced *Rock Follies*, to take charge of this constitutional, regal drama; a king gives up his throne for love of an ambitious woman. It was an excellent choice. Simon Raven wrote dry, insightful scripts. Waris Hussein would direct.

Wallis Simpson, plainly, must be played by an American actress. We cast Cynthia Harris. She had some difficulties when she first saw the scripts; Wallis did not come over as the irresistibly glamorous, fairy-tale princess she fancied playing. Mrs Simpson, rather, of shady origins, having trustingly been asked to look after the Prince of Wales for a few weeks by another of his lady friends, had ruthlessly swept her rivals aside, left her second husband, and so insinuated herself into the Prince's affections – she knew how to please him – as to grip him to her for life. Attractive, yes; glamorous, perhaps; determined, certainly; in love, maybe; loved, absolutely; romantic, not very. Cynthia Harris would have to take it, or leave it. She took it, and well too.

'I danced with a man who danced with a girl who danced with the Prince of Wales.' Edward was handsome and debonair enough, admired, fancied; he escaped as often as he could from the severities of King George V's and Queen Mary's court. A lightweight, a flibbertigibbet, even a playboy, he briefly won deeper popularity when, in the dark thirties, to government ministers' disapproval, he expressed sympathy with the unemployed in South Wales. Forced to choose between the throne and marriage to a twice-divorced woman – a marriage of which the Church of England could never then approve – he chose Wallis, and an empty exile. Edward Fox would play Edward Windsor.

With some excitement, I attended the first read-through in the spacious Serbian community centre in Notting Hill. We sat at long trestle tables. The cast read; the author, Simon Raven, listened. When we broke, Edward Fox seized me by the arm and walked me round the room. 'Mr Isaacs, a word, please.' He was disappointed in the scripts. He was not convinced they showed clearly enough what a handsome, winning fellow the Prince of Wales had been, a man with whom any woman could fall in love. 'He was more charming than this,' he said. I said I thought Simon Raven's scripts were fine. He was not persuaded. 'Mr Isaacs,' he said, beating himself over the heart with the knuckles of a clenched right hand, 'I am an actor, and' – thump, thump – 'I feel it here!' We left it at that.

The production team did an outstanding job. The story gripped. The abdication speech, superbly delivered, crowned the series. *Edward and Mrs Simpson* would be the talked-of success of 1978.

But by now I was not happy in my work. I need space to breathe; and I did not have it.

On a Monday evening in July 1977 I went to bed at ten o'clock, early but not unusually so for me. The telephone rang. It was Peter Fiddick of the *Guardian* wanting a word. Tamara took the call. I said it was late; I would not speak to him. Next morning, from the *Guardian*'s front page, I learned that Bryan Cowgill, a combative Controller of BBC1, was leaving the BBC to come to Thames as Managing Director. This was seen as a great coup for ITV. Some months before the expiry of George Cooper's four-year contract, Howard Thomas had moved to replace him with a programmer and scheduler. The evening Fiddick rang me there had been a Granada Guildhall lecture, at which he had picked up news of an upheaval at the BBC, where Cowgill had been due to move to a new post of Director, News and Current Affairs. Now the BBC, furious, insisted he clear his desk and leave the building immediately. George Cooper must have been shattered. He had certainly been shafted. And it came out of the blue. Thames was riding high; its results for 1977/8 were better than ever. Thomas would have claimed, no doubt, that the company, whose future prosperity must determine his course, needed stronger leadership; that he was only fulfilling his duty to board and shareholders. But he had now frozen out one managing director and, three and a half years later, dropped his successor.

On the Tuesday I was at a grandiose conference called 'London Looks Forward' which Thames had organised at the Royal Festival Hall; it was opened by the Duke of Edinburgh. There, Howard Thomas half apologised to me for giving no forewarning of a change that must affect my function and future; he knew Cowgill's arrival was bad news for me. He had recently been urging more grand projects on me, among them a series based on Samuel Pepys's diaries (of which he particularly relished the naughty bits). It was a good idea, but one which, at that point, neither Verity nor I could easily see us tackling. The truth is, Thomas liked to divide and rule.

Bryan Cowgill was intelligent, forthright, down-to-earth, above all competitive, and had a ferocious temper – his nickname was 'Ginger'. I rang him up on the Wednesday, and suggested we meet. Early the next evening we dined together at the Brasserie St Quentin on the Brompton Road. It was empty. We sat by the window. I said, 'Bryan, I am looking forward to working with you. But I want to make one thing clear; I am Director of Programmes at Thames, responsible for the programme department, for all our programmes and for the schedule. I need to know that you accept that.'

'That's right,' he said, 'that's agreed.'

'In that case,' I enquired, 'what will you do?'

There was a long, long pause. I waited.

Eventually he said, 'I see my job as looking after the welfare of fifteen hundred people.'

I said, 'That's all right then. They deserve that, and will welcome it.' But the silence spoke louder.

There were only mild differences between us over programme policy. The point for him was not policy; he just wanted to do the job. He was determined to introduce a midweek sports programme, and to spend much more money, upping the ante to buy Morecambe and Wise, and the Miss World competition, away from the BBC. He lost his temper with me once, erupting in sudden fury over some boxing match or other that the Programme Controllers Group had failed to snap up and stick in the schedule. This was in character. When it happened, the best advice was to let it blow over; his wife Jenny, we gathered, knew how to handle his rages, and could be consulted in emergencies. What I found difficult to bear was not the exceptional outburst, but daily routine.

Every evening, after six o'clock, the summons came: would I come up? There he was in his office, alone with a bottle of gin, wanting to talk. All he talked of was programmes. He was shrewd and fair in his assessments. But any business we had to transact was soon dealt with; then what? We sat and sat. I did not drink gin. At seven o'clock, if I could, or seven-thirty, I would look at my watch, make my excuses, drive home. This went on for months.

His commitment to sport did stoke up tension between us. Cowgill had been in charge of BBC's 1966 World Cup coverage, when England won (his account of Harold Wilson trying to squeeze into the picture with the winners was worth listening to), and again in Mexico in 1970. He was very good at it. He wanted to increase Thames's investment, and improve – he didn't rate it at all – the standard of our sports coverage. He wanted change, fast.

But there was a difficulty; our Controller of Outside Broadcasts, Graham Turner, had charge of sport, and had cancer.

I visited him in King's College Hospital, and winced myself at the pain he bore bravely. I did not tell him that Cowgill wanted him out. I did tell Cowgill that I would say nothing to Graham if I thought it would lower his morale, weaken his resistance, hasten his death. Cowgill accepted that, but after a delay, leaving Turner in charge of outside broadcasts, he moved to put sport at Thames in other hands.

I suspect now that it was not just Cowgill's constant presence at my shoulder that was bugging me; nor was it the constant hassle with the IBA over Northern Ireland – in that, Cowgill was unfailingly supportive. Something was telling me that I had achieved at Thames all I ever could. At any rate, I made up my mind to go; I would tell Cowgill that I wanted out.

The opportunity came on a Film Purchase Group trip to Los Angeles. On the whole, these expeditions were enjoyable enough. We would stay in expensive hotels, eat large American breakfasts, arrive at viewing theatres to find platters loaded with pastries, sample a film series or two, lunch at the studio commissary, view some more, do something pleasant in the evenings. This time, Bryan Cowgill and I flew out together on an Air New Zealand flight, first class, and checked into the Beverly Wilshire. He was contracting Morecambe and Wise at the time, awaiting confirmation from London that the deal was done – something to celebrate when it was. He was happy. The next night we dined at Palm, where they serve 'surf and turf – great seafood, great steaks'. We ordered both. We ate. I told Bryan Cowgill what was on my mind.

'Bryan, you don't leave me space to work in. I want to leave Thames. I've made up my mind.'

'No.' He was aghast. 'Please don't do that to me. Please.' As emotion overcame him, so too did some ghastly stomach upset: a long stream of semi-solid surf and turf arched up out of his mouth, and poured over the table. Next day it was clear something – perhaps a bug caught on the plane – had upset his digestive system. Back in London, we got on with our jobs for some weeks. I let him know I had not changed my mind. It was arranged I should see him and Howard Thomas together on a Friday morning in June.

That week another minor crisis imploded over coverage of Northern Ireland. The IBA had hoped *This Week* would stop reporting critically on the conduct of the struggle in Northern Ireland by the RUC and the security forces and would instead present an 'all-round picture'. According to Jeremy Potter in *Independent Television in Britain*, volume 4, the IBA was under pressure from the Secretary of State, Roy Mason. The Authority in turn expressed concern to Thames about the cumulative effect of its programmes, all of which appeared to have a common starting-point which was critical of, if not actively hostile to, majority opinion in Ulster. But at the same time the IBA's own officers cautioned members that

> no service would be done either to the population of Northern Ireland or to the rest of the UK if Independent Television were to refrain from coverage of the more difficult and controversial issues current in Northern Ireland. It has been our experience, all too sadly, that reactions to many network programmes about Northern Ireland have done little more than reflect the existing deep divisions within the community. Until those divisions show real signs of reconciliation it is not to be expected that our programmes will receive general approval and commendation, least of all from ministers and others who have the unenviable responsibility for trying to achieve reconciliation and genuine progress.

This Week notified the Authority's officers that it proposed to deal with a forthcoming report by Amnesty International which made allegations about ill-treatment of suspects held for questioning by the RUC at Castlereagh detention centre; the findings vindicated *This Week*'s investigation of the previous year. The Authority indicated that the programme, which would be unwelcome in any case, should not be broadcast until the report was public, and the Secretary of State had had an opportunity to comment on it in Parliament. This last stipulation was an odd one; it appeared to be a throwback to the fifties, when 'the fourteen-day rule' prevented broadcasters from treating controversial matter until fourteen days after discussion in Parliament had taken place. The rule was a blatantly illiberal piece of nonsense which had no place in a democracy. Coaches and horses were driven through it; it lapsed. Was it now to be revived? On the Monday, the *Guardian* published extracts from the report; the matter was now in the public domain. Had *Newsnight* been in business then, it would have dealt with it that night. Thames urged the IBA, through its officers, to think again, and permit *This Week* to present its report, independently researched and verified, in its normal Thursday evening slot. The IBA still refused.

On the Thursday afternoon the Secretary of State for Northern Ireland, Roy Mason, released to the House of Commons the government's formal statement in response to the Amnesty report. Marooned at Teddington, I rang the IBA and asked to speak to the Director General, Brian Young. I was not put through. Bryan Cowgill also rang, urging that surely now, since the Secretary of State had uttered, the Authority would change its mind. 'No. The decision must stand.' He and I were equally angry. I told *This Week*, and instructed that a standby programme be broadcast. It was not. ACTT members at Euston and throughout the system carried out their threat to take action; ITV's screens went blank for twenty-seven minutes. A caption read: 'The advertised programme at this time has been cancelled.' Light music was played. The blank screen was the nightmare any television producer feared most; now it was upon us, calling attention both to censorship and to unaccountable union power.

I had thought I was arguing with the IBA's highly intelligent Director General. But he was merely the servant of the Authority, and the Members had spoken. They did so against the advice of their own programme staff; David Glencross, Deputy Director of Television, wrote a note criticising their decision. But the Members were the Authority, and could not be gainsaid.

So a mixed body of non-broadcasters took a simple editorial decision, and one of timing at that, instead of leaving it to the judgement of the programme company it franchised, stuffed to the brim with able journalists and garlanded executive talent. The root of this ridiculous state of affairs lay in a simple mistake: the Authority, not the programme company, was the publisher by law, and could do as it liked. This dispensation, which represented not the will to publish, but the will to control publishing, lasted a while longer: the law was not finally altered for a decade.

Next day I went to work, angry with the IBA and with the union; dismayed at the blank screen that had mooned, insultingly, at the viewers. The BBC asked if it could see the material we had been barred from screening. I said, 'Give it to them; let them use it if they choose.' This later raised eyebrows. But why? They too were pursuing the story, in the public interest. The object of journalism is to disclose, not secrete. Why collect information people have a right to know, and then bin it?

I went upstairs to the meeting with Cowgill and Thomas. I told them what I had done. Thomas disapproved; could I get the material back? I enquired; it had gone over to Lime Grove. I left it at that.

The other issue was soon settled, and without heat. I explained to Thomas my decision to go. My contract had a year to run. Not long ahead, another franchise round was coming up. They must surely either have a commitment from me well into the next franchise period, or let me go before it. Both said they wanted me to stay, and asked that I reconsider. I doubt they meant it. I said no, I preferred to leave.

I did not say, 'OK, I will stay. If you want me to go, fire me.' They did not say, 'We don't want you anyway; you're fired.' That might have been expensive. I left the room, and wrote confirming I would go. For the third time in my life – 'career' does not seem the right word in this context – I was leaving good employment of my own volition.

Ben Marr, the kindly Scot who served as Thames's Company Secretary, looked at me with astonishment, and some concern. 'Whatever you do, Jeremy, keep up the payments on your pension and health insurance.' Thames made me a reasonable settlement, the board gave a farewell lunch. Howard Thomas asked me to choose a leaving present; Pepys's *Diaries* and Byron's *Letters* now fill a shelf.

It was partly Howard Thomas's doing. He must have known Cowgill and I would be as oil and water. It was certainly what Cowgill wanted; under pressure, after I left, to appoint a new Director of Programmes – a post requiring IBA approval – it took him eighteen months to do so. He wanted badly to do the job himself. Jimmy Jewel understood. 'I know how you feel, lad. It were just like me and that Hilda Baker in *Nearest and Dearest*. There was no room for the two of us.'

I I

HOLLYWOOD

Jeremy Isaacs Productions, JIP, was slow to find orders. Our earliest days were comically rudimentary. In 1978 there was no British market for independent productions. With no capital, and no cashflow, we had no separate premises. When telephone lines to my home in Chiswick failed one morning, I was reduced to making calls from the phone box on Duke's Avenue, stuffing florins into the slot. I needed work. A few weeks after leaving Thames, I found myself back at Teddington, in a cutting room.

Kevin Brownlow and David Gill were making *Hollywood*, a thirteen-part series on the early 'silent' years of the film industry in California. I was helping fit commentary. It was disconcerting, a little odd, to be back there with them, perched on a stool, peering over their shoulders at the steenbeck's small screen. Into that half-unreal world came word that, earlier that day in Hove, my mother had suffered the stroke that killed her. The message did not say she was dead, only that there was no time to be lost. By the time I got to the hospital to which she'd been taken, it was indeed over for her.

My father was calm, numbed, as together, mechanically, we

went the rounds of what needed to be done. I did not view Sally's corpse; I had had a preview of it not long before, when she and Isidore had celebrated their golden wedding, surrounded by family – the more, as far as Sally was concerned, the merrier. Through a half-open door in the flat on Palmeira Avenue, close to the synagogue and the county cricket ground, I saw her resting. She lay, stretched out on a bed in repose, like a statue recumbent on a catafalque, at peace. Her life, I guessed then, was almost over. With age, her judgements had grown more severe; of a performance by Sybil Thorndike she wrote: 'a wonderful actress, whom I never hope to see again'. At the cinema she might enjoy the film she'd come to see, but took a dim view of virtually all coming attractions, booming out during the trailer, 'I shall not be there.' She would have wanted to be there, though, for *Hollywood*.

Towards the end of making *The World at War*, in the summer of 1973, I held a party. I gave everyone on the production team a copy of Kevin Brownlow's oral history of the early years of Hollywood, *The Parade's Gone By*. It was hard not to think of *The World at War* as a military operation; not quite an army fighting a battle, more a unit seeing through a campaign. I thought we should keep together if we could – and *Hollywood* might be our next posting. For the book Kevin Brownlow had conducted 120 interviews, detailed, graphic, hilarious, moving. Capture those on film, marry them to clips of the movies, add music, which always accompanied the mis-called 'silent' cinema, and the result could be history that entertained.

I always championed the single documentary, the individual one-off. But the success of *The World at War* and its wide international distribution whetted Thames's appetite for series, and shifted our priorities.

I first met Kevin Brownlow in 1959, in a cutting room at World Wide Pictures in Cursitor Street, off Chancery Lane. I was there editing a documentary for Granada, *The General Strike*. Kevin was next door. The cutting rooms were unusually long and narrow, and ran at right angles to a corridor along which a railing enclosed the building's central well. A boyish figure, singing and laughing as he worked, kept dancing backwards out of the cutting room into the corridor, holding a strip of film up to the light and, without pausing, dancing back in again to make the cut. Kevin later made, with Andrew Mollo, two singular movies anyone would be proud of: *It Happened Here*, on the hypothetical Nazi occupation of Britain, and *Winstanley*, on the English Civil War's attractive revolutionary. Each was made on the thread of a shoe-string, a day at a time, stretched out over years. The films were authentic in detail, the cinematography exceptional; the column of helmeted stormtroopers passing through a deserted Parliament Square, Big Ben behind them at dawn's early light, sticks in the mind. I was serious about using *The Parade's Gone By* as the basis of a documentary series. I might have initiated it anyway; it helped that in 1974 I became Thames's Director of Programmes.

I invited Kevin to come to see me, and put the suggestion. He was dumbfounded, and wary; a cineaste, he was not sure that television was a serious medium, or that its cramped screen could do justice to the cinematographic qualities he loved. (It can't, of course.) I warned him, he reminds me, that 'television is an ulcer-producing activity'. All the same, he left the building exhilarated. Sod's law struck. Outside Thames, a sudden violent pain over-came him, and he collapsed on the pavement. He thought, 'This isn't fair, I haven't even said Yes yet.' Acute peritonitis put him out of action for weeks. When he recovered and made contact again, time had been lost. The men and women he had talked to for the book – actors and actresses, producers, directors, art directors, editors, cameramen, stunt men, property men – were getting older every day; we must get on. I put Kevin in touch with Thames's Jolyon Wimhurst, who started their conversation by saying, 'You're mainly interested in silent films, aren't you?'

'Yes.'

'Well, I ought to tell you that I can't stand silent films.'

Wimhurst later made way for John Edwards as Head of Documentaries. John was enthusiastic. Other colleagues thought of 'silent' cinema as jerky, flickering images in black and white, with performances, archaic in style, rendered grotesque by over-acting, the whole punctuated by slightly comical captions – inter-titles telling the story: precisely the view Kevin was committed to sweeping away.

The original idea, however hubristic it now seems, was to do a history of Hollywood from the beginning up to the moving present. But it soon became apparent that the studios wouldn't co-operate. In 1974 MGM made *That's Entertainment*, a smash hit compilation, and Fox launched its own history, a TV series entitled *That's Hollywood*. John Edwards wondered whether there was a series for us in the silents alone. Kevin thought there was, and 'It's never been done.' With the success of *That's Entertainment*, the studios were more determined than ever to hang on to their own, and deny others access to their archives. All the same, we decided to proceed with our own history of their silent cinema.

Kevin Brownlow needed to feel himself wholly at ease with us. He needed – shades of my crash at *Panorama* – a partner he could trust, who would help get things done within Thames's system, and could also keep a close eye on any tendencies to splash out in Hollywood style. John Edwards and I discussed who this paragon might be, and he proposed David Gill. David had been a ballet dancer; dance, like film, moves in time. He was an ex-editor, a colleague on *This Week* and my collaborator on *Till I End My Song*. This marriage, made in the Euston Road, might have been made in heaven, but the proof of that lay far in the future. Kevin Brownlow's diary for the early months of 1976 describes our first steps together.

Jan 9: Over to Thames, where I showed them 'Hollywood – The Golden Years', and our Ben Lyon interview which was a model of what such interviews should be – compulsive viewing, charming, informative and often hilarious. John Edwards said he was much encouraged. We had a splendid lunch in the Thames canteen – three courses for 65p!

Jan 14: Today I bought a carpet sweeper – and a television set! It was a black and white portable model and cost £68. V was very much against one which dominated a room. This could be parked on a shelf.

Jan 15: David Gill came round for a discussion about the Thames series. It was a bit hard to keep a conversation going because he always had a second thought coming as you're answering his first, and he cut through you. But he seemed very nice.

Several things were going on here. Kevin and David were getting to know each other; John and David were finding out what they liked and disliked in the films Kevin knew and loved; Thames was finding out how difficult it would be to prise out of the major studios clips from old movies they owned. The studios thought the old films would never again find an audience; if they did, they were determined that they alone should exploit them.

Kevin's diary again through February shows how he wooed his colleagues. On 16 February he showed David a programme ranging from the incredibly primitive – *Bank Robbery* (1909) – to the highly sophisticated – *Smouldering Fires* (1924). 'He hasn't clicked on yet, but we're getting there.' On 19 February he showed Murnau's *Sunrise*. 'John Edwards said, "I can't stand German Expressionism!" The others were very impressed.' For the showing on 24 February, Brownlow played safe. He ran *Kid Brother* (1927) with Harold Lloyd and *The Crowd* (1928). 'This time the reaction was unanimous.'

On 1 March this:

David Gill and I took Bessie Love [the actress] to a restaurant and came to the conclusion that he should ask the questions, because Bessie knew that I was aware of all the answers. This proved a mixed blessing. Bessie was full of pep, but also full of subordinate clauses which would make the narrative move in a series of jerks. And she giggled (nervously) too much. However, every mag had something very good and she was an excellent mimic. John Edwards was reasonably pleased and fixed our US trip afterwards.

The big decision had been taken, and it was mine. We had no permissions from the studios to use excerpts from their movies; without them we had no series. What we had was a galaxy of interviewees we could, expensively, film. Their talking heads, however eloquent, would hardly suffice on their own. Yet, if we delayed filming till the studios were won over – and who knew how long that would be? – many of our cast might be dead, or too infirm to talk. Several weeks on location in the States would cost a substantial sum. I decided to risk it, reckoning that in any case it was a duty to capture these pioneering memories for posterity. Thus all the interviews were recorded before the right to use excerpts was – expensively – granted. John Edwards made a start. The long-haul task of winning over the studios was seen through by Mike Wooller. He secured us what we wanted in the end.

By the point at which I left Thames, *Hollywood* was in the cutting room. Mike Wooller must have realised I needed something to do. At Kevin's and David's prompting, he asked me to return as a consultant, to help with commentary and assist in editing. Bryan Cowgill did not object.

In the cutting room I was bowled over, though unsurprised, by the excellence of what I saw. The interviews were riveting, touching and amusing in turn, the images generated by great film-makers stunning, and the two skilfully combined to make points that were always specific: this is how this stunt was done, how this director worked, how we achieved precisely this effect, what she was like to act opposite. Ignoring chronology, *Hollywood* began with a dazzling montage of contents: an elegantly extended title sequence, accompanied by Carl Davis's swooping melody; then some of 'silent' cinema's high achievements, set in vivid context. What I saw at Teddington, enriched by Carl Davis's music, was mouthwatering, as are the episode titles: 'Pioneers'; 'Single Beds and Double Standards'; 'Hollywood Goes to War'; 'Hazards of the Game'; 'Swanson and Valentino'; 'Out West'; 'Trick of the Light', cameramen and special effects; and 'End of an Era', the coming of sound.

In episode 10, 'Man with the Megaphone', the director Allan Dwan tells how he got started. His employers in Chicago had lost a crew, and sent him to look for it and get it back to work:

So I came to California, there was no Hollywood then, Hollywood was a little district that had some orange groves and lemon groves and a few cottages, but by asking questions I learned there was a company in San Juan Capistrano that nobody knew about much and I went down there and found these people of ours in a little hotel and all idle, the director was away on a binge, he was an alcoholic and they were waiting for him to come back and put them to work. They said we're just waiting for our director to come back and then we'll go to work. So I wired the company in Chicago and said you have no director, I suggest you disband the company. And they wired back, you direct. So I told the company, I got them together and I said, 'Now either I'm a director or you're out of work'. And they said, 'You're the best damn director we ever saw.'

Dwan was a damn fine director too.

All *Hollywood*'s virtues stem from Kevin's deep and detailed knowledge and love of early cinema – in which, however, David came almost to emulate him – and from their common skills as film-makers. What could I contribute? Well, a little thing perhaps. It was fiendishly difficult to fit the commentary. Kevin was to write it, and Kevin knew too much. Not more than a tiny percentage of what he had to say could be squeezed on to the soundtrack. My watchword, learned from Robert Kee, was that commentary should complement picture and be kept to a minimum. The eye cannot be receptive if the ear is assaulted. Kevin defended every necessary syllable, but his innate reasonableness, and his own eye for the image, won out. He knew the picture was the thing.

The first choice as narrator was Laurence Olivier. He agreed to do it. Indeed, at a preview in Los Angeles in June 1979, it was his voice that was on the track. Thames was repeating in LA its New York experiment of 1976, buying out a week of time on KEJ Channel 9 to showcase its programmes. An episode of *Hollywood – the Silent Years* was screened; Sean Day-Lewis reported in the *Daily Telegraph* that this 'finely crafted hour-long episode in the Thames and Jeremy Isaacs tradition of historical compilation was praised by the local critics and won seven percent share when the other twelve LA channels were offering their most competitive peak-time programming'. At the launch party for the series, *Hollywood* met a different fate. Day-Lewis was there:

> Despite the gallant efforts of the British Consul-General, Mr Tom Aston, demanding silence in rising tones of fury before storming out into the petrol scented evening air, the cocktail chat did not diminish. When the volume of the surrounding television monitors was increased to a roar, the talking swelled to shouting. It would have been a good launch for *Hollywood – the Deafening Years*. Olivier was shouted down.

But Olivier did not narrate the series in the end. After recording a couple of episodes, he wanted out, and this time could not be persuaded to stay. Mike Wooller asked me to try to hold him. We talked quietly at Thames's Euston Road offices. He was regretful, but adamant. He relished the subject matter, had looked forward to hobnobbing, vicariously, with great figures of the past, liked the people he was working with. The reason he gave for quitting was hard to answer, and, for the producer of *The World at War*, something of a snub. 'You must understand,' he said, 'when I perform, I do so with my whole body, not just with part of it. I never feel happy or fulfilled using my voice alone. I can't act that way. It's not me.'

Kevin Brownlow has a totally different recollection of this episode. He says he and David Gill wanted to get rid of Olivier – 'too theatrical . . . refused to take direction' – and that I was called in as executioner, or at least to approve the death warrant. There may in fact have been a sad and angry stand-off which I could not resolve. I can testify, however, that Larry was relieved to be leaving. Kevin Brownlow, after what he calls 'the grim decision', wrote down the comment Olivier made. 'I know it's their baby, but I'm the fucking milk, and I don't like their bony gums on my tits.' In any case, Olivier and I parted friends. James Mason took over the role, and brought it off admirably.

Hollywood began transmission on ITV in January 1980 to wide acclaim. Critics agreed that the series should banish for ever the notion that 'silent' films meant poor projection, jerky and flickering images – or, indeed, silence. 'Suddenly', wrote Peter Fiddick in the *Guardian*, 'it becomes possible to guess what it was like to be in one of those picture palaces, watching miracles of dramatic entertainment – and with a 100-piece symphony orchestra, for heaven's sake, to fuse audience and image.' For S. S. Prawer in the *TLS*, the highpoint of the first episode was

> an excerpt from Victor Sjöström's *The Wind*, in a print of miraculous clarity, which enables us to see Lillian Gish demonstrate once and for all the range of emotions that could be conveyed in a silent film, with the subtlest, least melodramatic means, by a

great actress who had gone through the Griffith School. The effect of this electrifying sequence, which needed hardly any intertitles, was heightened rather than diminished by its juxtaposition with a filmed interview given by Lillian Gish in the 1970s, in which – beautiful in a new and different way – she spoke about her experiences while making *The Wind* in the 1920s.

Satisfied customers are rarely so explicit; the production team could take pride. Kevin, of course, had a wonderful time saying I told you so; the early film-makers knew exactly what they were doing. He insisted on describing me as 'the team's Irving Thalberg', the legendary Hollywood producer. I thought this way over the top but, since Tamara always claimed that Thalberg was a distant cousin of the Weinreichs, I had to live with it.

For Brownlow and Gill, and for Carl Davis, *Hollywood*, though years in the making, marked not the end but the beginning of a journey they would take together. If a television company makes a series demonstrating that silent films are masterpieces, the logical next step is to present them in their entirety. Thames, flush with funds and conscious of the prestige such a move could bring, now set out to do this. They would restore great movies of the silent era, and give them a cinema screening. In November 1980 they began with a showing at the London Film Festival of Abel Gance's *Napoleon*, first seen in 1927. The BFI and the National Film Archive helped.

For years, on top of all else he did, Kevin Brownlow was obsessively occupied in searching out, retrieving, restoring lost and missing reels of Gance's youthful masterwork and, in the end, piecing the whole together – well, not quite the end, and not quite the whole, because it seems there's always the possibility that another sequence or two will turn up – the last time I saw *Napoleon* it was forty minutes longer than on the first occasion. But the first occasion for me was sensational enough.

Gance took the camera off its fixed tripod, and hurled it into the midst of the action. 'He put it on wings', is Brownlow's phrase. But the high point of novelty in Gance's technical armoury was the use of multiple screens, in conjunction, to deliver a triple image to devastating effect. Soon after this was demonstrated, however, the talking picture revolution consigned the innovations of *Napoleon* to the scrapheap.

The version shown to a packed audience on that Sunday in Leicester Square in November 1980 was in four parts, beginning at 10.30 a.m. and ending at 5.15 p.m. Nigel Ryan, Thames's Director of Programmes, tall, elegant, Francophile, escorted Lady Diana Duff Cooper, herself a star of the silent screen. Two linked phenomena were before our eyes and ears: Gance's film, lovingly restored, and Carl Davis's magnificent score, played by the Wren Orchestra, conducted by the composer. Beethoven was the main inspiration (he originally inscribed the 'Eroica' Symphony to Napoleon; later, disillusioned, he removed the inscription), though in the programme, Carl listed more than thirty period works on which he'd drawn. (He jokes sometimes that his favourite composer is 'Borrowed In'.) He quoted from Honegger, who wrote the score for Gance's original showing. The big, recurring romantic themes – for Josephine de Beauharnais, and for Napoleon's Eagle of Destiny – Carl wrote himself.

At the end of the movie, intended to be one of six, the young Napoleon crosses the Alps to take command of the army of Italy. The scene expands across three screens to show the camp spread out, the Alps behind. Destiny beckons; Napoleon's eagle, in giant close-up, fills all three screens. It is a moment never to be forgotten.

Napoleon lived; it had not yet, however, been seen on television. The programme dropped a heavy hint: 'Britain's new Channel 4 begins in 1982 with the express aim of offering viewers a wider choice, and programmes that have not been possible before. Thames believes Gance's *Napoleon* fits these aims, and will offer it to Channel 4 for a new audience to appreciate.' As I passed through the crowded foyer, Sue Summers, a bright journalist, called out; 'Are you going to put this on Channel Four?'

'If *Napoleon* isn't right for Channel Four,' I answered, 'nothing is.'

Easier said than done. I had a problem: the climactic triptych. The effect of two additional screens had been overwhelming; I must achieve that on TV also. But how? The answer seemed simple: persuade two other broadcasters to join the transmission and show the last sequence on three screens simultaneously. Thames in London must surely agree to help. If I could only get BBC2 to co-operate, I'd be home and dry. I rang its Controller, Brian Wenham, shrewd, cultured, on the ball. I explained what I wanted. 'Brian, will you help in this?' A pause.

'Jeremy,' he asked gently, 'how many people do you know who have three TV sets in their living room lined up together?'

Collapse of slightly manic party; I settled to do without the triptych. The eagle, in close-up, still made its effect.

In successive years, up to 1989, Thames and Channel Four funded, and Channel Four showed on television, masterpieces of the silent cinema, 'Thames's Silents': *The Crowd*, *The Wind*, *The Thief of Baghdad*, *The Big Parade*, *Greed*, *The General*, *Ben Hur*, *Intolerance* among them. For each, Carl Davis wrote and conducted a life-enhancing score. From 1990 'Channel Four Silents' took over: *The Chess Player*, *Wings*, *The Phantom of the Opera*, *Sunrise*, *Nosferatu*. In 1999 Michael Jackson, Channel Four's Chief Executive, pulled the plug, one year before the grand project's twentieth anniversary. That year's selection, ending the sequence, was *The Iron Mask*, in which Douglas Fairbanks is stabbed in the back.

A more tragic ending came earlier. In September 1997 David Gill – a lovely man, a fine film-maker – died suddenly. At that year's 'Silents' performance Kevin asked me to say a few words about David, whom I had known so long, and to whom I owed so much. I agreed, but spoke rather of their fruitful, happy collaboration. Theirs was one of the great creative partnerships, I said, fit to be mentioned in the same breath as Rodgers and Hammerstein, Laurel and Hardy, Powell and Pressburger, for the pleasure they had given.

The novelist and playwright Stanley Price tells a story. He had a play on in the West End. After the run, it was shown on television. As the credits rolled, his telephone rang.

'Stanley, your father and I saw the play.'

'Yes, Mother.'

'Stanley, your father and I quite liked it.'

'Yes, Mother.'

'Stanley, your father and I hope it will lead to something.'

Hollywood – the Silent Years led to something. Brownlow and Gill's series sparked a renewed appreciation of the early years of cinema across the world.

12

GLASGOW

The hall porter at Edinburgh's George Hotel found a hire car to
take Tamara and me to Barlinnie. The expensive saloon deposited
us at the prison gates; inside, we waited to be conducted to the
Special Unit, a prison within a prison. A warder from the unit
arrived, and brought us to a new set of high-security barriers. He
unlocked a door in the wall and motioned us through. The prisoner we had come to meet greeted us in his cell. The walls were
lined with books, one shelf stacked with LPs. There were pot
plants. On the low table, lunch was ready. There was fresh brown
crusty bread, home-made; a salad with ham, pineapple in the
salad. Our host was slim, muscular, lively, alert, welcoming. His
short hair was thick and curly. He had an open face and a piercing
stare. This was Jimmy Boyle. In his early thirties, he had spent
most of his life in gaol, months of it in solitary confinement. He
was a violent criminal, a convicted murderer; according to the
Daily Record, 'Scotland's Hardest Man'. In prison, he had written
his story, *A Sense of Freedom*, and in 1977 seen it published. Now, in
1979, I was going to film it.

Jimmy Boyle was born in the Gorbals in Glasgow in 1944. I

was from another world – Jewish middle class and Catholic working class were poles apart; yet the Gorbals linked us. This was where my mother's father, the Reverend David Jacobs, had lived when he served at the synagogue in South Portland Street. The Gorbals then consisted mostly of tenements, three or four storeys high, well built of red sandstone: an attractive, respectable neighbourhood that meant much to the newly arrived Jewish community before it spread north, across the Clyde, to the West End, or south to Cathcart, Giffnock and Newton Mearns. But the Isaacses still knew the Gorbals; we had spinster cousins who kept a liturgical bookshop, and my mother went there to buy soft white cake-bread veined with cinnamon and crisp glazed strudel for Sunday tea. Glasgow's kosher restaurant, Geneens, a haven of solid eating in the austere post-war years, was another draw. Wursht and egg, even made with wartime powdered egg, was a feast of a plateful, sizzling slices of red spicy sausage set in a yellow field of omelette. I once spotted Chico Marx, looking exactly as in the movies, tucking in there, spitting on the floor. The Gorbals housed not just the Jewish Institute Players but also the Citizens' Theatre – not the European landmark it became under the great triumvirate of Giles Havergal, Robert David MacDonald and Philip Prowse, but the theatre of the playwright James Bridie (O. H. Mavor), home to a dazzling cluster of Scotland's acting talent. There I saw the funniest show of my life, a Christmas pantomime called *The Tintock Cup*, boasting two grand dames, Duncan MacRae and Stanley Baxter; the two conversed across the street, 'hinging oot the windae', or were found in the powder room of the Barrowland Palais; 'Here Bella, take my partner, wull ye? Ah'm sweating.'

My mother's surgery was on Glasgow's south side, in Eglinton Street, just a few blocks away. She had patients in the Gorbals, and climbed tenement stairs to visit them, four floors up. The neighbourhood was decaying by then; the sandstone façades remained, looking fine enough, but the stairways were cold, damp and filthy, and the crowded interiors, with shared lavatories on each landing, were in disrepair. The Gorbals was becoming a slum, notorious, too, for the violent behaviour of some who lived there. Eventually Glasgow Corporation, in what now seems an act of vandalism, razed the neighbourhood to the ground, leaving the Citizens' isolated in a flattened desert. The people who had lived there were rehoused in impersonal tower blocks that soon became slums almost as bad as those they replaced. Before demolition, though, the Gorbals saw years of raucous inner-city living, in a world I hardly knew.

On 3 September 1939 I had been evacuated with my brothers from Glasgow to Kirkcudbrightshire in Galloway. We went to the village school at Rhonehouse. Here, under one roof, classes mingled; after an edgy start, when our city accents must have jarred, we got on well. By the time our parents came down to visit, our speech was unintelligible to them: 'I hinna ony'; 'I dinna ken.' Back in Glasgow one day, on the corner of Byres Road, out of the blue I met two former classmates from Rhonehouse, up in the city on a lorry bringing goods. We greeted each other, spoke a little, ran out of things to say; we were worlds apart again. At Glasgow Academy, fee-paying middle-class schoolboys disdained children who went to the city's other schools. There were exceptions – Glasgow High, Hillhead, Kelvinside Academy, Hutchesons and Allan Glens; the rest were beneath our notice, outside our select, narrow world. Somehow, in the village school I had come to know that this was wrong. From 1945 the only Labour supporter in my class at school, I resented this notion of superiority and social exclusion, but could do little about it.

One divide was sport; public schools played rugby and cricket, other Glasgow schools played 'fitba'; the ball was round. On Saturdays, hundreds gathered on the touchline for rugby at New Anniesland; tens of thousands squeezed into Ibrox or Parkhead. At school, like everyone else, I played soccer in the playground with a tennis ball, and on Saturday afternoons I walked from

Hillhead to Firhill to watch Partick Thistle. Quixotic, reliably unre-
liable, Thistle were losers; good to watch, heartbreaking to follow.
Billy Connolly says the club's real name is Partick Thistle Nil. The
Jags had an inside forward called Peter McKennan, a dribbler
known as 'Ma Baw Pete'. He stood once, stationary in front of three
defenders, daring them to make the first move; impatient, I called
out to him to pass, 'Get rid of it!' Pityingly, my neighbour answered
with a question, 'And who would he get rid of it tae?' Watching
Thistle was a weekly agony – as someone noted, it's not the despair
that kills you, it's the hope. At the season's end, stoicism: 'Ah well,
the pies were wonderful, and there's always next season.' Away at
Oxford, I had wanted not to be wholly cut off from fellow
Glaswegians. The HLI helped, but that was twenty years behind
me now. Maybe Jimmy Boyle's Gorbals was a way back.

As soon as I left Thames, Frank Cvitanovich said I should read
A Sense of Freedom; it would make a strong film. I doubted my ability to make a feature film for TV, even if it told a true story. But I
read the book, and was bowled over.

A Sense of Freedom recalls a childhood of thieving and gang
fighting, leading to Approved School and Borstal. It portrays
years of brutal villainy – moneylending, protection rackets, knif-
ing and razor-slashing. It tells of acquittal on two murder charges
and conviction on the third. At the heart of the book are the years
spent in prison, months and months of it in solitary confinement,
and the absolute determination of the prisoner never to give in. In
gaol, sometimes confined in a cage within a cage, Boyle survives,
not by acceptance of his fate but by active, violent resistance to
brutality practised against him, and constant protest at the denial
of his rights. Naked, smeared with his own shit, he defies warders
and governors alike. His anger erupts into explosions of violence;
each one adds to his sentence. In these quarrels his enemies
always deliver the last blow.

Jimmy Boyle doesn't deny the bulk of his crimes. He carried a
knife, sometimes a gun. There's one ghastly description of a street

fight and its aftermath that shows how close to killing he came. In this clash of cutting and stabbing, he receives terrible wounds to head and body, finds himself covered in blood, sees his gut peeking out from the bottom of his trouser leg. His friends patch him up. The other gang are putting it about that he is dead, or near it. He is too battered to retaliate, and in too much pain to walk. He has himself carried to a pub, and just sits there, propped up, pretending to be well, sending out the word that he is not beat, yet. The first two murder charges he got off easily enough. He says he had nothing to do with either killing; the police, evidently, could not produce evidence that would convict. But it was only a matter of time. Eventually the police did get a conviction, though he insists he never killed the man who died, Babs Rooney.

Rooney's been hassling moneylenders who are paying Boyle. He and a friend he's been drinking with, William Wilson, call on Rooney; the door is opened by a pretty girl, Sadie.

> Babs was in bed, but he got up, putting on his trousers, remaining bare-chested . . . We discussed the money situation, about him going at the demand, and he agreed that what they had done was out of order, so we decided to forget it . . . After a while he brought up an old score about a pal of mine who went to his house, or his sister's house, with a revolver, intending to shoot him, and we argued about this very heatedly. His girl Sadie was in the other room attending to the child, so I took my knife out and ran it down his chest and cut him with a slashing motion. Both of us were standing and Babs just stood there, and said nothing. I went into the next room and assured Sadie that Babs wasn't very badly hurt and she should say nothing to anyone and she went along with this. She had been around and knew the score.

Boyle, in his account, leaves, goes downstairs, goes back up again to get William Wilson, finds the door locked and the lights out, goes home. Next morning early, there's a knocking at his door; friends bring the news that Babs Rooney is dead, and that William Wilson has been charged with his murder. 'I was completely stunned,' he writes, 'as I had been so casual about the whole thing, knowing that I had only slashed him.' He hands over his clothes, which are burned, and his knife, and seeks shelter elsewhere.

Wilson, caught in the house with the dead body of Babs, was charged with murder, on his own. The police found Boyle's fingerprints on a beer can; they moved heaven and earth to find Boyle. Two months later they caught up with him in a pub in London's East End and brought him back to Glasgow, where he was charged with murder. If convicted, he would face a life sentence. (A couple of years earlier, it could have been the death penalty.) Sadie gave evidence for him at the trial; his QC, the eccentric Tory MP Nicholas Fairbairn, made great play with the police's claim to have found the bloodstained knife 'under the linoleum at the entrance inside the doorway of my room in the Gorbals house owned by me'. 'Why,' Fairbairn asked, 'should it be hidden in a place where the first flat-footed policeman entering the house would stand on it?' In vain. 'In a courtroom packed with police and civic dignitaries' the jury delivered its verdict: guilty of murder.

Lord Cameron, who had presided over Boyle's first murder trial, sentenced him to life imprisonment, and recommended he serve no less than fifteen years. The police grinned and shook each other's hands; one danced. The knowledge hit Boyle that his life would be spent in prison. 'My whole being was dead, my life was no longer. I was state-owned . . . forever.' For years, fury led him to provoke rather than conciliate; it sustained him in violent resistance to indignity and ill-treatment. Anger and pride kept his spirit alive, but defiance made his situation worse at every turn. After years in Peterhead and Inverness, the violence and counter-violence grew so bad that it seemed certain to end in his, or someone else's, death in custody.

The level of violence in the Scottish prison system could not be allowed to continue. There were fierce riots at Peterhead and brutal assaults on prisoners engaged in protest. An enlightened head of the Scottish Prison Service, Alex Stephens, sought another way. He consulted psychiatric opinion. He had the backing of a free-thinking Conservative minister, Alick Buchanan-Smith, and the co-operation of forward-looking members of the Scottish Prison Officers' Association. They knew something had to be done, before someone was killed.

The Special Unit at Barlinnie, a secure prison within a secure prison, was set up to find new ways of confining dangerous prisoners. It took the risk of trusting them, treated them humanely, encouraged them to take responsibility for their own actions. The unit was governed by regular meetings of staff and inmates; the latter, suspicious at first of every device put forward, were slowly won over to taking a new look at their lives. Before he entered the Special Unit, Jimmy Boyle had come to realise the futility of the course he had taken, but saw no alternative, except submission. Here was an opportunity to change, grow, prepare for a future that had long seemed out of reach. In the Special Unit he kept fit, read, received visitors he could embrace. He learned to sculpt, studied through the Open University, wrote a book; fell in love and married. He hoped for parole, and release.

I had written to Jimmy Boyle in the Special Unit, expressing an interest in filming his book. He would want to meet me before giving a go-ahead; meanwhile his agent, Tim Corrie, was happy to agree modest terms and grant an option. Realising the project would require feature film resources, I knew I needed a partner.

At an early stage I took the idea to Scottish Television, STV, the ITV company based in Glasgow – the source of Roy Thomson's candid remark that an ITV franchise was 'a licence to print money'. STV was now an eminently respectable concern, meeting the regulator's key benchmarks, but never quite setting the Clyde on fire. Its habitual accent was genteel; we didn't often hear the idiom of slum, street, pub or terraces on their screen. STV's franchise would be up for renewal in 1980. It needed to be seen to be spending genuine money on worthwhile programmes. I would try my luck there. I knew that I would get a sympathetic hearing from the Managing Director, Bill Brown.

An unlikely man to be in charge of a commercial TV station, Bill had trained as an accountant. He came from Ayrshire, Rabbie Burns's 'Auld Ayr, wham ne'er a toon surpasses, For honest men and bonnie lasses.' Bill was honest as the day is long, fair-minded and plain-spoken, admired and trusted. I liked him a lot, and quietly applauded the way he had strengthened STV's programme-making, though I had declined his invitation – before the Thames job came up – to return to Glasgow as STV's Programme Controller. Boswell told Dr Johnson that 'Scotland has many fine, noble prospects'. 'Let me tell you, sir,' Johnson replied, 'that the noblest prospect a Scotsman ever sees is the high road that leads him to England.' I stayed south, and waited.

Even at Thames I had had my own difficulties with broad Glasgow speech. Whenever *This Week* reported from that city, my colleagues in the cutting room demanded subtitles. We made one film on gang warfare to which the city fathers took angry exception. 'Don't tell anyone,' they seemed to be saying, 'and it will go away.' But Glasgow could do without the publicity such reports brought. Now I had a Glasgow project that was hugely controversial there; the city divided on sectarian lines, Protestant and Catholic, but united in rejecting the label of gangsterdom. The Scottish tabloids treated Boyle himself as a giant of crime and for the most part were theologically, Calvinistically, unforgiving: he was bad, and could never change; predestination marked us all, for life. The Special Unit's attempt to treat violent prisoners as human beings capable of reform was doomed, therefore, to failure. People like Boyle, given responsibilities and 'encouraged to grow'? Nonsense; we were being conned.

Would Bill Brown bite this bullet? He would, and did. He had support on his board from the writer and theatre director Bill Bryden, but without Bill Brown himself *A Sense of Freedom* would never have been made. Several STV managers were openly opposed; no one else would have seen the project through.

There was good reason to believe we might succeed. Others were setting the example: the BBC had made a stunning film for their *Play for Today* slot in broadest Glaswegian. Revelling in the sectarian divide, *Just Another Saturday* showed a day in the life of a working-class Protestant lad, leading the Orange parade on the Twelfth of July, twirling his long drum-major's stick, tossing it high, celebrating victory at the Battle of the Boyne and claiming manhood. It was written by the west of Scotland Protestant who himself had been that boy, Peter McDougall, and directed by a fearless Edinburgh Catholic, John Mackenzie, rapidly making an international reputation. *Just Another Saturday*, electrifying, revelatory, thrillingly realised, won the Prix Italia. STV needed something like that. I offered Bill Brown and his Programme Controller David Johnstone a package: rights in the book, a script by McDougall, Mackenzie to direct, myself as producer. John Mackenzie would choose a film continuity girl and a lighting cameraman, Chris Menges; for all else, STV would pay. The deal was done. Now all I had to do was deliver.

Peter McDougall went to see Jimmy in the Unit to get his screenplay going. The book, rich in incident, covers twenty years of Boyle's experiences. Peter had to distil ruthlessly. We skipped the scenes of childhood; important as they were, they would have meant casting a boy actor. And we did not explore the new environment of the Special Unit, whose complex relationships deserved, in truth, another film entirely. We concentrated on the years before Barlinnie, showing only, in the first hours there, his dawning realisation that a new beginning was possible. Action on the streets, endurance in prison: this would be the core of our movie. John Mackenzie, also making the thriller *The Long Good Friday*, had to have a script he could direct. It was down to me to cajole, chivvy, bribe Peter – I was paymaster – into handing over precious pages.

Peter McDougall had come to London from Greenock at the age of sixteen, to see life, find himself, make a living, make a name. He worked as a house-painter; when he spoke scornfully of 'watching paint dry', he knew what he was talking about. He lived at the corner of Primrose Hill, just a few yards from the Queen's public house. The Queen's was where I met Peter to discuss progress on the script, or the lack of it. It nearly put me off lager for life. Peter had a stocky, muscular build and an open, determined countenance. He wore his thinning hair in a ponytail. He had few clothes, but was very particular about them; a white T-shirt with Fiorucci on it, and expensive calf-leather boots. He'd bought the T-shirt, he told me, at Harrods, where he had also acquired the heavy notebooks, encased in embossed leather, on which he wrote in a fine italic hand with a broad-nibbed fountain pen. He was proud of his words, and of how they looked on the page.

I admired the economy of his writing. Film needs fewer words than theatre; the Scots understand that. The film actor does it with a look, a change of expression, not a speech. The speech Peter put in men's mouths – there were few women in this story – was salty, laconic, effective. He made every word tell.

While we were getting our project under way, one of Peter's finest scripts, *Just a Boy's Game*, was being filmed on location in Gourock. Gourock's townscape lent itself to filming as suburbia never could. The shipyard showed high cranes, eerie and menacing at night, a spectacular place to set a fight. The crowded pub we drank in, a square, low block in an empty wasteland, rocked with noise. I hoped *A Sense of Freedom* might be half as good as *Just a Boy's Game*. Whatever they might think in Surrey, people in Glasgow would hear their accent in it, recognise characters they knew, understand what we were on about, watch it, and react.

Producer's privilege: I wanted Bill Paterson to play Jimmy Boyle. I thought the intelligent energy of his lead performance in

David Hare's *Licking Hitler* could not be bettered; I did not see how we could pass him over. I did not know what I was talking about. John Mackenzie chose David Hayman, a fine actor and the right shape. Some prison scenes called for Boyle to be near-naked. Paterson was stocky and of solid build; Hayman, slim, wiry, would better look half-starved, yet fighting fit. He was the right choice; he read, thought, willed himself into the character. Other fine actors took key roles; Jake D'Arcy and Alex Norton made an instant impression. I'll not forget watching the first scene shot. Jake D'Arcy, leaving work at the shipyard, is told that Boyle is after him for money he owes; cold, D'Arcy caught the high tension needed on the very first take. The actors understood every nuance. They trusted John Mackenzie completely, too, and that helped. Mackenzie never dictated interpretation; he concentrated on timing. Putting the sequence together in his head as he worked, he insisted on a look half-left to see Boyle enter, and two beats on the close-up, before fear showed in the face. The film, when shot, would be a dream to edit; but shooting it was a nightmare. In the production office we lived from hand to mouth.

We wanted to shoot *A Sense of Freedom* in Glasgow. Glasgow didn't want us to shoot it at all. In the studio the film-maker is king; all is at his disposal. Filming on location is different. The film crew works in the street with police permission, and indoors as paying guests in someone else's house. STV put their full resources behind the Boyle film, but they did not own Glasgow; Glasgow City Council did. Seventy per cent of housing stock belonged to the city. We needed short lets in city-owned premises to get our work done. STV's location manager, hail-fellow-well-met Joe Miller, found a succession of premises in which we could film, and signed contracts to rent them for modest facility fees; £25 a day was the going rate for an empty apartment, or a disused pub. Joe was a fortnight ahead before we started. What we hadn't reckoned with was the Boyle factor; as shooting began, the subject cast a long shadow before us.

The tabloid press – the *Daily Record* was particularly active –

kept up a furore of shrill protest: Why are this lot making this terrible film, glorifying violence, here? They should be stopped. Glasgow's pettier politicians woke up and climbed on the bandwagon; this film, they claimed, would blacken Glasgow's name. Councillors demanded that contracts for letting to us be torn up and, crucially, that no more be issued. Private landlords now jibbed at making us free of space they owned. Glasgow has plenty of pubs; very few would let us over their threshold. Protestant pubs wanted nothing to do with a 'Catholic' film; Catholic pubs wanted no part of this film. It was no use protesting either that it was a true story, or that it was only a film; door after door slammed in our face. The result was that the production office, instead of letting everyone know by 3 p.m. one day the call for the next, simply did not know itself, even at 6 p.m. where we would work tomorrow, until at last Joe Miller, exhausted from running around the city, could report success. Some colleagues seemed unfazed by this nail-biting process; I could scarcely believe what was happening.

Actors and extras have something to eat during the lockout

I decided not to take the City Council's edicts lying down, and asked a friendly councillor, Michael Kelly, later Lord Provost, what I could do about it. He advised me to speak to the Chairman of the Housing Committee. This was Baillie Jean McFadzean, a formidable political force. I telephoned and asked if I could put my case to her committee. This film would do Glasgow no harm; STV, and people working on the film, paid rates too; we had rights which should be respected. Would they not think again? Word came that they'd hear me; I should come to the City Chambers in mid-morning. Joe Miller and I arrived promptly for our appointment in one of Britain's most imposing Victorian buildings, symbolic of the wealth and strength of the Empire's second city. We climbed the wide marble staircase and passed along the corridor to the doors of the committee room. There we waited outside, on a heavy, leather-padded bench. I rehearsed my arguments. The door opened; Councillor Kelly came out. 'Jeremy,' he said, 'Baillie Jean has asked me to tell you that the Labour caucus has met and has voted, by twenty-nine votes to seventeen, to deny your application. She thought you should know that before you came in.' I went in anyway, made my case to blank faces, and left again uncomforted, somewhat staggered at the casual arrogance of one-party rule.

The *Daily Record* kept the heat on. There was a front-page story every day: BOYLE FILM, NEW OUTRAGE. Either we had already given offence, or we were about to do so; residents were up in arms at our intended visit. But the point came when reporters on the news desk assigned to the story could find nothing new to say. Near the bottom of an inside page the *Record* ran the cross-head QUIET DAY ON BOYLE FILM. I knew then we'd make it.

Throughout all this STV kept its nerve, though some wished they'd never heard of us. David Johnstone, Programme Controller, was scrupulous in his dealings with me, never failing to repeat in every letter he wrote that it was a vital condition of the agreement between us that '1. the film should not glorify crime or the criminal; 2. the violence shown should be within limits set by the ITV code; 3. the language used should be consonant with the provisions of the Broadcasting Act'. Since a major point made by the film was that crime led only to misery and suffering, there was little danger of the first proviso being transgressed. On the second – I am, as I have already said, squeamish to a fault – the violence shown would not and did not cross the line; it came nowhere near the explicit relishing of it which makes today's cinematic reputations. Language, however, we argued about. What that came down to was how many 'fucks' – the word, not the act – the finished film should contain. Here there was a difficulty. We aimed at realism. Realistically, we all knew that the characters in the film said 'fuck' often; on the terraces at Firhill I heard little else. Bill Brown urged me to be sparing, and cut. Peter McDougall resisted. Script in hand, I explained to STV's managers that verisimilitude suggested that, here for instance, the indignant intruder would naturally ask, 'What the fuck are you guys doing?'

'No, no, Jeremy,' they told me. 'Quite wrong. What he'd say is, "Listen you fucking fucker you, what the fuck do you think you're fucking doing?"' I cut.

In one key matter STV excelled itself: we managed somehow to replace virtually every location we'd lost. One interior, though, required a public let from the City Council; we had arranged to film the courtroom in which Boyle received his life sentence in the spacious confines of Springburn Public Hall. We had booked the use of part of it. The City Council reneged on the contract it had with us, saying it had changed its mind. STV went to law, to the Court of Session in Edinburgh. The court instructed Glasgow City Council to comply. They agreed, but didn't do it: when we arrived, we found the doors locked against us. A carpenter holding a jemmy looked at me meaningfully. I knew we had the law on our side – I had seen the order. I asked the carpenter to do as little damage as possible. Filming, though late, went well. I was able, just, to get to Kelvin Hall in time to see a great boxing match; lightweight world champion Jim Watt of Glasgow fought Charlie Nash of Belfast. Both were skilled. Jim Watt won.

Much of *A Sense of Freedom* was set in prison, so it was only sensible to film in one rather than build a set. I hoped the Scottish Prison Department would co-operate. It didn't. What then? Inspiration struck.

As well as *A Sense of Freedom*, I was also producing at this time a television history of Ireland for the BBC. For that, we would film in Kilmainham gaol in Dublin, revered in Irish history as the site on which, one by one, the British shot the leaders of the 1916 Sinn Fein Rising. Well preserved, Kilmainham could stand in for Peterhead and Inverness. There were plenty of cells; in this one, Boyle would be kept in isolation for months, in the cage within a cage; in this next, naked, he painted the walls with his own shit; down this corridor he was dragged to see the Governor; in that he ran the warders' punitive gauntlet. Make-up, Irene Wilson, did a fabulous job on cuts, bruises and shit, producing further supplies of a filthy-looking mixture whenever it was needed. David Hayman's performance was all we could have hoped for. We were nearly there.

STV's crew, some of them in Dublin for the first time, worked hard all day and partied all night. They pretty well took over a hotel beside the Liffey, and drank and sang into the small hours. Some of them had made new friends in Dublin; some never went to bed. The night I joined them, one big man, who had played right-half for Celtic, sang Sinatra's 'My Way'. All were convinced that draught Guinness in Dublin tasted better than it did in Glasgow. Had the Liffey been Guinness, they'd have drunk the river dry. Back home, they argued urgently for a pipeline under the Irish Sea.

There was music to add. Frankie Miller wrote and recorded a ballad, 'A Sense of Freedom', which John Mackenzie used over the end credits. I went to the other music recording session at

Wembley with a single musician, the rock guitarist Rory Gallagher. I watched a composer at work. We played him sections of the film; instrument in hand, he improvised, matching the mood, heightening tension, reinforcing tempo. Rory Gallagher fans still remember *A Sense of Freedom* for his music. The film was edited in Glasgow by STV's best editor, Alan MacMillan, now a fine director. The sound mix was too complex for STV's equipment, so we finished off in Wardour Street.

John Mackenzie's film *A Sense of Freedom* made a powerful impact on many who saw it. The feel and rhythm of the piece were cinematic, every scene the right length; the pace carried the viewer along. In it, we saw a man holding himself together against all odds, slowly coming to realise that the evil he had done and the violence he had inflicted had led only to further violence, and got him nowhere. It did not show him repentant or asking forgiveness. It showed him on the brink of a new way of living, and all the possibilities that held.

STV were delighted with it, and made haste to offer it to the network. With no more reluctance than greeted any regional company's offering, it was accepted. The IBA's officers were divided; they hummed, hawed, hesitated, but in the end agreed that so serious a work should be shown, after *News at Ten*. It must be followed, however, the next evening at the same time, by a discussion of issues that it raised. Anna Ford chaired that. It's a tribute to the film, and to the controversy Jimmy Boyle always provoked, that in Scotland anyway the film's audience stayed high and level until it ended. The following night's discussion drew just as large an audience; that held up to the end also.

Not everyone liked it. In the BBC1 programme that reviewed the week's television, *Did You See?*, chaired by Ludovic Kennedy, Tom Mangold claimed, uncorrected, that the prison brutality shown was vastly exaggerated and could never have taken place. In fact it was understated, and was itself the reason for the Special

Unit's existence. The unit had wider lessons to teach; the purpose of prison is rehabilitation as well as punishment. By refusing to treat prisoners as whole human beings, confining them three to a cell in demeaning conditions, we deny ourselves prisons in which the inmates grow a bit and leave confinement less likely to return. I would put prison reform high on the list of subjects to which television should return, year on year.

And Jimmy Boyle? He was in prison, in the Special Unit, throughout our filming and for some time thereafter. When might he be paroled? Not, it was clear, before the fifteen years Lord Cameron had recommended he should serve had expired, and probably not until a couple of years later, given the additional sentences he'd earned in prison and the controversy that would attend his release. But the parole system would take its course in the end, provided Jimmy kept out of trouble. Every year he routinely applied for parole and, refused, was cast into black despair. Then, when it looked as if a future application, though all was still shrouded in secrecy, might succeed, the Scottish Prison Service announced he was to be moved from the unit to a conventional prison. Jimmy was miserable and furious at once; to go back to Inverness or Peterhead did not bear thinking about. He feared the worst. Prison staff would bully, humiliate, provoke him, and the old dilemma would be back: if he was humble, his self-respect would go; if he retaliated, his conduct would count against him, the hope of living again in the outside world be postponed, indefinitely. He wrote to friends, asking them to help fend off this move. But it happened.

They sent him not to any of the hell-holes of his past – which, in any case, were now under new management – but to Saughton in Edinburgh, whose Governor was a thoughtful, level-headed public servant. The move was intended as a test and challenge; had he learned anything? Would he keep his cool? In fact, he did. He did day-release social work from Saughton on a huge tower-block estate outside Edinburgh, Wester Hailes, so crudely planned that at first there were no shops, no pubs and no bus stop. Jimmy by now was embarked on the course to which he was to stick for several years, trying, by offering his lost years as a warning, to help young people stay away from crime. He left Saughton in the early mornings for Wester Hailes. One day he took the bus to the city centre instead, to file a document on a client's behalf at St Andrew's Square. There he spotted, in overcoat and homburg hat, Lord Cameron, who had sentenced him, and whose approval would be needed before he could be paroled. If 'Scotland's Hardest Man', unchanged, still harboured violent resentment, here was an opportunity to wreak physical revenge. Lord Cameron raised his hat and said, 'Good morning, Mr Boyle.' Boyle replied, 'Good morning, Lord Cameron,' and told him he should be aware of the ravages heroin was wreaking in Edinburgh's slums; Edinburgh then had the highest rates of heroin addiction in the UK. A few months later the board granted him parole.

In the Special Unit Jimmy had married Sarah Trevelyan, a visiting psychologist, daughter of the film censor John Trevelyan. Together they set up home in Edinburgh and, more, a centre to help young people in trouble, particularly from drugs. At the Gateway Exchange, behind Calton Hill, they offered advice, counselling, tea and buns, books and music, and the chance to learn to sculpt. They asked friends to help fund what they did. Tamara and I wrote a modest cheque. Some of Jimmy's admirers were wealthier. Alec Horsley, a Quaker industrialist, made donations that helped get the Gateway going. I found it well used and appreciated. When I visited, Jimmy would take me across the road to Pilton, the nearest housing estate to it and the worst slum I ever saw in the UK; every second house was boarded up so that the street frontage looked like a mouth with teeth missing. Drugs, and later Aids, were rife.

Then there was his sculpture: fierce and supple forms, wholly concerned with anger and suffering. Jimmy would never let on who bought it, but I believe he sold entire shows. My guess is that one of his patrons may have been Elton John, and I doubt if he worried too much about the number of zeros on the cheque.

Jimmy visited us in Chiswick; he was good company, hospitable and caring. Living alone in Hove after Sally's death, my father Isidore Isaacs, jealously guarding his independence to the end, slipped in his bath, injured himself, was unable to get up, and lay for hours before he was found. He never recovered. Jimmy was horrified to hear what had happened. Again, in 1986, when Tamara died of the recurrence and spread of the cancer which years before had led to mastectomy, he was at once in touch. Jimmy too suffered personal tragedy when his son died of drugs.

I saw for myself the good works he did, and everyone knew of. After years of it, though, he reckoned he had paid his debt to society, and began to enjoy himself. He drove around Edinburgh in a bright blue Rolls-Royce. In partnership, he imported and sold champagne. He and Sarah bought a fine house with a garden for their own children, and, during Edinburgh Festivals, held happy court there.

Today, it's rather different. His marriage to Sarah broke up. With a new partner, he lives much of the time abroad, in France and Morocco. He writes; a novel has been optioned in Hollywood. I see him only seldom. But I find him one of the most remarkable men I know. His courage and strength give strength to others. The anger in him has burned out; the endurance, and the charm, remain. What kept him going was his sense of freedom.

13

CRETE

The flight to Canea arrived late, and the luggage later. As we waited, into the baggage hall shuffled a little old man with a beret on his head. In his right hand he held a shepherd's crook, a foot taller than himself; in his left, clamped between thumb and forefinger, three flowers, picked that afternoon in his garden, which, with some formality, he presented to my second wife, Gillian. This was George Psychoundakis, shepherd, resistance fighter, author, poet, man of letters. It was April 2000 and George had invited us to his village, Asi Gonia, for the St George's Day ceremony of blessing the sheep before they go up to the high pastures for the summer.

I first went to Crete, which the Greeks call The Great Island, for a week's wander, stopping off on my way to Jerusalem to attend my brother Michael's wedding. This was in 1972. I fell for it at once. Crete is Greek, and more than Greek; a Minoan culture flourished here, uniquely, millennia ago, as Knossos, Phaistos and Aghia Triada demonstrate. After that was destroyed – no one quite knows how – Crete was Greek. But invaders and conquering empires also left their mark. When Venice 'held the gorgeous East in fee', it held Crete; the arsenal at Canea, the walls of Rhethymnon and Heraklion, bear witness. Then came the Turks, with mosque and minaret, and the long Cretan struggle to be free from Ottoman rule. I enjoy places whose history is writ in stone. And the Cretan landscape has that attractive combination of mountain capped with snow and, below, gentler slopes and valleys covered with woods and grasses and spring flowers; everywhere the scent of wild thyme and, on the cheeks, a hot wind from Africa; the whole bathed in light. I ate soft new broad beans cooked in oil, pods and all, on the harbour at Canea; marvelled at Knossos and the archaeological museum at Heraklion. At midnight on the Greek Orthodox Easter Saturday at Ieropetra the town exploded; Judas Iscariot in effigy went up in flames and fireworks, and the streets rang with the cry 'Christos Anesté – 'Christ is Risen'. At Aghia Gallini, no hotel was yet built; there was only the half-finished skeleton of the first one. I had a room on the cliff face. Lying in the sea – to call it swimming would be to exaggerate – I looked up at snow-capped Mount Ida. Then to Jerusalem, longing to know more of Crete.

The invitation came in 1979. Would I make a film on the 1941 battle for Crete, marking its forthcoming fortieth anniversary, for New Zealand Television? The programme controller who made the enquiry, Alan Martin, had once worked at Television House for Rediffusion. The battle for Crete had been close-fought, dramatic and of some military interest; the German assault on the island had been the first ever attempt to seize a land mass from the air. I knew that, with Greece fallen and Rommel advancing on Egypt, Churchill had hoped desperately for victory here; defeat in Crete marked almost the darkest hour of the war. Evelyn Waugh, in *Sword of Honour*, had castigated chaos and cowardice on the retreat south to Sphakia and the navy's ships. And I knew of a heroic Cretan resistance, after the troops were taken off, to German occupation, in which a motley crew of British, some classical scholars, played a key role.

Among those who fought most bravely in the battles to defend the airfields in the north, which turned in the end on a razor's edge, were the New Zealanders. General Freyberg, New Zealander, was commander-in-chief of Allied Forces on Crete. The New Zealand Division, particularly the Maoris, fought well; it held together, just, and was evacuated. Not all New Zealanders got off the island, though – some stayed on for months, sheltered by villagers at risk to their lives, until they too could be taken off by submarine. During their stay, links were forged that lasted; to be a New Zealander in Crete is to be welcome everywhere. *The World at War* omitted completely, as it had to, countless actions in which fighting men from various countries – Australians, South Africans, Indians, Poles – had given their all. Here was an opportunity to make amends to one singular band at least. I quite agreed with Alan Martin's judgement; New Zealand viewers deserved a film on the battle for Crete.

He and I met in a quiet hotel behind Canea; we visited Maleme airfield, whose loss was crucial to the outcome, and stood before the war memorial at Galatas, scene of wild, heroic fighting, where an annual ceremony of commemoration was held. There would be a specially big turn-out for the fortieth anniversary in May 1981, when the film would be screened in New Zealand. We would have to film the parade in 1980. Flags and banners and spring flowers would make a lively contrast to the black and white of combat newsreel. In London, I asked Tom Steel to produce the film; his best work at Thames had been the story of another island, St Kilda, out in the Atlantic, before its people moved to the mainland. We prepared an outline, and a modest budget – a tad too modest as it turned out. Alan Martin duly commissioned JIP to make the film for NZ2. Tom Steel got vigorously to work.

The plan was simple: there would be months of research to find relevant film and identify participants, then two weeks' filming in Crete. On that one trip, Tom would film the battle sites, and

interview those who had fought there and were willing to make
the journey back. Graphics showing tactical dispositions and decisive moves would be made, and editing completed, in London.
Tom had most help from New Zealand, which sent key witnesses.
But he cast his net wide. The twenty-year-old Lieutenant W. B.
Thomas had fought gallantly at Galatas, been wounded and captured there; now Lieutenant-General 'Sandy' Thomas, with years
of service in the Australian army, took the trouble to make the trip.
He had an exceptional ability to voice the fears that every brave
man lives with, and must overcome. From Canada came an ex-
Hussar, tank troop commander Roy Farran. He had led his two
puny Matilda tanks repeatedly into action at Maleme airfield, and
up the main street at Galatas to the square, when the town was in
German hands; 'The place is stiff with Jerries,' he shouted, before
returning to the charge. Farran fought as bravely as anyone could
in Crete. Later, in post-war Palestine, he enjoyed a different fame.
After the execution by the British of two Zionist terrorists, and the
notorious hanging by Zionist terrorists, or freedom fighters, of
two British army sergeants in reprisal, his treatment of a young
Jewish lad who came into his hands led to his fleeing Palestine.
The lad died; his body was never found. Returning, Farran went
unpunished. The last twist in this ghastly cycle came when the
terrorists sent a letter-bomb to London to kill him. It killed his
brother. A handsome figure in 1980, Farran was Commissioner for
Horse-Racing of Saskatchewan. He had good memories of
Galatas.

The most exotic bird to fly in was Kapitän Freiherr von der
Heydte, who dropped on Crete with the 1st Battalion of the 3rd
Parachute Regiment, all volunteers, some of them no more than
seventeen years old. They came down on well-camouflaged New
Zealand positions, and many of them were shot to death as they
fell, or dangled, caught up in their harness, from trees. Von der
Heydte, a hawk-like gnome of sharp gaze and clipped speech, was
a useful witness to his men's ultimate triumph. On the outskirts of

Canea he took prisoner some British officers bathing naked in a swimming pool, unaware of the Parachute Regiment's advance.

Crete was lost by a hair's-breadth; it was 'Touch and Go', Sandy Thomas told us, the title we gave the film. We concentrated on Maleme. Airfields at both Rethymnon and Heraklion were successfully defended, and denied to the Germans. If we had held Maleme airfield also, we could have held the island. Even as the battle for Crete continued, the Messerschmitts and Stukas that gave the Germans total air superiority were pulled back from Greece and sent east to prepare for Operation Barbarossa, Hitler's attack on Russia. Maleme was lost not through lack of bravery, but through poor communications – there were too few wireless sets – and a strange, tired, lack of commitment in command. Anthony Beevor, in his book on the battle, forerunner to his accounts of Stalingrad and Berlin, gives graphic vignettes of ruthless killing: both sides let the Geneva Conventions go unheeded and few prisoners were taken. Beevor's verdicts on the mistakes the Allies made, and those responsible for them, are damning. At Hill 107 above Maleme airfield, we saw for ourselves how fire could be directed at planes landing troops on it. Yet the local commander, who had no radio, remained on the reverse of the hill, and never once went forward to view the most critical site of the battle before, isolated and concerned not to be cut off, he abandoned the position. The Germans were able to land troops at Maleme airfield to secure it; no Allied counter-attack was launched, though reserves were available in plenty.

Ultra signals gave information, obtained by cracking the enemy codes, on German plans for attack. The commander-in-chief, Freyberg, was the sole recipient; for his eyes only. Crucially, Freyberg misinterpreted one message and believed, incorrectly, throughout the engagement, that the main assault would come by sea. To guard against that eventuality, he held in reserve east of Canea 11,000 troops, who saw little or no action. He had five battalions to spare. Placed west of Maleme airfield, and to the south behind and above it, they could have defended it; sent forward when it fell, they might have retaken it. Since Freyberg destroyed the Ultra signal after he'd read it, no other commander had a chance to discuss its implications, and his consequent strategy, with him. In the armchair, the critical mind boggles.

On 25 May 1941 there was fierce fighting for the little village of Galatas. 'Sandy' Thomas led his platoon fast up the main street, through German fire, to the square, where he fell wounded. Forty years on he re-entered the square in procession, marching behind the Greek flag and the flags of Great Britain, Australia and New Zealand, at the ceremony to honour those who died. Each year the band plays. Greek Orthodox clergy and local dignitaries take part; there are music, prayer and speeches. The square is crowded; at the café on the corner, drinks are on the house. The war memorial lists the numbers of Greek, British and Commonwealth troops who died. It also tells of 120 'unrecruited others' who gave their lives. Cretan resistance began on the day of the invasion; one old warrior, a *pallikari,* showed me with pride his knives and pistols. To the island's chagrin, the Cretan division of the Greek army had been sent to the mainland to fight there; it did not return. But the local people, women as well as men, rose on the first day and fought the invaders with any weapons they could lay their hands on: guns, scythes, axes, sticks. An Englishman, Captain Michael Forrester MC, put himself at their head. Beevor quotes a New Zealander: 'Over an open space came running, bounding and yelling like Red Indians, Greeks [i.e. Greek soldiers] and villagers including women and children, led by Michael Forrester, twenty yards ahead. It was too much for the Germans. They turned and ran.' Alas for such Greek passion, the battle for Crete was lost in the end. Cretan resistance, however, had only just begun.

The most striking aspect of the battlefield reunion was the fellow feeling between these two sets of islanders, Cretans and New Zealanders, particularly marked in those New Zealanders who had stayed on in the mountains. We followed one six-foot veteran on an unexpected visit to the remote hamlet that had cared for him. There were no men in the village; they had all gone to work in Germany. The women took over. They were poor, but insisted we all sit down to eat, and foraged for a feast to put in front of us. They found a cockerel, of which every tiny morsel was served – the claws, the comb, everything but the feathers. Our New Zealand friend came back year on year, whenever he could.

Touch and Go was a well-crafted film, and did well in New Zealand. It was £14,000 over budget. Graciously, and pleased with what we had done, Alan Martin agreed that NZTV would pick up the tab. JIP had retained the UK rights in the hope of a sale to BBC TV; but trying to place it there was a daunting, disheartening, instructive experience. Yes, BBC2 would take it, but for a derisory price. Being offered £2,000 for two showings of a film that cost £100,000 to make brought home to me just how tough the life of an independent producer must be in the buyer's market that was UK TV. This dispensation could not last when the fourth channel came.

At the ceremony in the square at Galatas, at the back of those attending, there stood a quiet figure of a man, silent, serious, holding a crooked stick, wearing a medal. You can just see him in our film, in the crowd yet somehow apart from it. This was George Psychoundakis, author of *The Cretan Runner*, a personal account of the Second World War in Crete. The translation is by Patrick Leigh Fermor, a fluent Greek-speaker who spent the war years in Crete for SOE, the Special Operations Executive. Leigh Fermor's most famous exploit there was the capture, in April 1944, and subsequent removal from the island, of the German commander, General Kreipe; high on the white mountains they quoted Horace to each other as dawn rose over Ida. George played no part in that. What he did, for three years of war, was run messages for the resistance that could not be sent by wireless without giving away the operator's position. George carried them from one lonely hideout to another, going at great speed across cruelly hard terrain. In the mountains of Crete, distance means nothing; journeys, uphill and downhill, are measured by time. George ran, and kept running.

Leigh Fermor met him first in July 1942.

He was small in stature, and as fine-boned as an Indian, looking little older than 16 though he was actually 21. His eyes were large and dark, and his face, in repose, thoughtful and stamped by a rather melancholy expression which vanished at once in frequent fits of helpless and infectious laughter that almost anything seemed to provoke.

In Leigh Fermor's hideout, George handed over his messages – letters from agents in western Crete – and waited for the replies, which he hid around his body. They talked, and drank, till it was dark.

It was plain that George was enraptured with the excitement of our secret life, in spite of the appalling trudges which kept him forever on the move in those merciless mountains. When the moon rose, he got up and threw a last swig of raki down his throat with the words 'Another drop of petrol for the engine', and loped towards the gap in the bushes with the furtiveness of a stage Mohican or Groucho Marx. He turned round when he was on all fours at the exit, rolled his eyes, raised a forefinger portentously, whispered 'The Intelligence Service!', and scuttled through like a rabbit. A few minutes later we could see his small figure a mile away, moving through the next moonlit fold of the foothills of the White Mountains, bound for another 50-mile journey.

Leigh Fermor remembers George telling him, through a long day's march, the plot of a novel he'd read about life in the Byzantine Empire, *Kassiani*, and on another occasion reciting, over two hours, an epic poem he had written himself about the war. Even so, some years after it, when George handed to him, in five

George Psychoundakis, drawn by Patrick Leigh Fermor in his young prime. (He is labelled Vlasios Bertodoulakis from his nickname of 'Bertódoulos', the clown Bertoldo in the old Italian comedy which was formerly popular in Greek translation.)

thick exercise books, his account of his war experiences, he was astonished at what he read. 'From the first page,' he tells us, 'I was unable to stop.' Leigh Fermor made up his mind to translate the text into English, and have it published. It was, he thought, 'a completely truthful account of Resistance life' as if 'one of the Rualla Bedouin, by a sudden miracle of literacy, had given us the Arab version of *The Seven Pillars of Wisdom*'. In beguiling prose, Leigh Fermor introduces George Psychoundakis's simple, vivid tale. Without his selfless efforts, *The Cretan Runner* might never have appeared in any language; George would certainly have found it harder to find a Greek publisher than an English one. Happily, John Murray, publishers of Byron, obliged.

The Cretan Runner displays no strategic overview; George writes of what he did, and what he saw. There are no heroics; all is matter of fact. Long, arduous uphill journeys, heavy loads, narrow escapes from capture are all part of the day's work. George is a member not of a fighting band, but of a British-run SOE operation. He carries a pistol, but seldom uses it except to fire a *feu de joie*, crying, 'We'll beat the cuckolds yet.'

His false papers, he tells a German sentry, are 'gut papier, Kamerad'; his boots are stuffed with maps at the time. The nearest he comes to death is when, foolhardy, he braces himself against the side of a bottomless perpendicular cave, and what floor there is gives way beneath him.

A high point in his story, and in his life, is his visit by submarine to Egypt and to the Holy Land. In Cairo, the Cretan irregulars are fêted and feasted. George meets Sophocles Venizelos, son of the Liberator Venizelos and a future Prime Minister. One day he climbs to the top of the pyramid of Cheops, 'knee-over knee-over up those huge steps', and down again. Next day, even George has to stay in bed. In Jerusalem he goes at once to the Church of the Holy Sepulchre, and is proud and happy to find the Greek Orthodox Church in charge.

George Psychoundakis dedicates *The Cretan Runner* 'to

Laurence Olivier
recording commentary
for *The World at War.*
(FremantleMedia)

Anthony Eden,
interviewed at his
home in Wiltshire.
(FremantleMedia)

Traudl Junge;
Hitler's secretary at
Thames TV, Euston.
(FremantleMedia)

As we were:

Top left:
Jerry Kuehl,
associate producer.

Top right:
David Elstein,
producer.

Middle left:
Neal Ascherson,
writer.

Middle right:
Raye Farr,
film researcher.

Bottom left:
Sue McConachy,
researcher.

Bottom right:
Alan Afriat,
supervisory film-editor.

(The Society of Film
and Television Arts)

Rock Follies: Rula Lenska, Charlotte Cornwell, Julie Covington give it their all. (FremantleMedia)

The Sweeney: John Thaw and Dennis Waterman. Real policemen did it their way. (FremantleMedia)

Jack Shepherd in *Bill Brand*; political drama in peak time. (FremantleMedia)

Hollywood led to a revival of 'silent' cinema. Kevin Brownlow, film-editor Trevor Waite, composer Carl Davis and David Gill. (FremantleMedia)

Jimmy Boyle wrote *A Sense of Freedom*. Filming it was never easy.
(*Liverpool Daily Post*)

Robert Kee wrote and presented *Ireland, A Television History*, making every syllable tell.
(Getty Images)

Ian McKellen as Walter on C4's first night. (Channel Four)

Paul Bonner,
Channel Controller.
(Channel Four)

Liz Forgan,
Factual.
(Channel Four)

David Rose,
Fiction.
(Channel Four)

Naomi Sargant,
Education.
(Channel Four)

My father, Isidore Isaacs (left),
with Ora and Isaac Michaelson.

My brother Michael Ben-Yitzak, and his wife Ribbie with Hillel, a few months before the
bomb explosion on 4 July 1975.

At home in Chiswick with Tamara, 1982. She died in March 1986.

Bury St Edmunds Registry Office, April 1988: marriage to Gillian. (Jane Bown)

Ted Turner, visionary founder of CNN: 'We're going to make a history of the Cold War; get me that Jeremy Irons.' (Alpha)

Pat Mitchell, *Cold War* executive producer. Later, President of PBS. (Alpha)

Martin Smith, series producer *Cold War*. He led by example.

brothers-in-arms who fell fighting in 1941, and Cretan and British friends who worked for freedom during the dark years that followed'. I met him first, briefly, while filming in 1980, and again, with Tamara, in 1985. We called on him and his wife in the village of Platanias, and lunched together. In the evening, at the taverna, families took turns to dance together, in a circle. George was employed then as curator of the German war cemetery near Maleme, tending the graves of the young parachutists who had died in May 1941. The British awarded George the British Empire Medal; the Germans found him a job, and an enlightened consul ensured that his son attended *Hochschule* in Berlin. At the cemetery gatehouse, he inscribed to me my copy of *The Cretan Runner*. Then, from under the counter, he produced his latest publication: a translation of *The Odyssey* into Cretan verse, the fifteen-syllable rhyming couplets of the *Erotocritos*, a sixteenth-century romantic epic. This magnum opus was succeeded by a translation of *The Iliad*; each an astonishing feat. For this, Leigh Fermor, seconded by C. A. Trypanis, Professor of Modern Greek at Oxford, recommended to the Academy of Athens that the shepherd from Asi Gonia be awarded a prize. George spans oral and literary cultures. My Greek is utterly inadequate but, somehow, we communicated with each other; a spark was struck.

In 1998, happily married now to Gillian, I went to Crete to start writing a book on my time at Covent Garden. We rented a small apartment at Plakias, on the south coast. On the coach from Canea airport, I noticed we were just in time for the annual ceremony at Galatas. We hired a car to go to it, and arranged to see George, now living in Canea. Again, he was pleased to see me, and invited us to his home. But I had to get back to my writing table.

In the spring of 2000, out of the blue, came a postcard from Canea, in an elegant hand, in English; would we come, as George's guests, to Asi Gonia, for the blessing of the sheep on St George's Day? Gillian said at once, 'Let's go.'

From whom was the postcard? From George, yes; but who had

written it? And what did he mean by 'as his guests'? A little detective work pointed to the artist John Craxton, who lived in Canea. Craxton, reiterating George's eagerness to see us, explained that we would stay, free of charge, at a beach hotel in Georgoupolis, convenient to Asi Gonia, compliments of the proprietor, leaned on perhaps by the local tourism office. George's other guests included a former British ambassador to Greece, Michael Llewellyn-Smith. Passionately interested in Crete since undergraduate days, he had written an excellent guidebook to the island, and had long known George. Indeed, in an emergency, he had once driven George's son to hospital, possibly saving his life.

It was Easter, by the Greek Orthodox calendar. On Saturday night we went to service in Vrysses. Off the pleasant tree-lined street, the church was crowded to the rafters. Socially ambitious fathers-of-families vied to supply tall candles for the altar and its surrounds. Easter Day, beginning at midnight, was for feasting. On Monday, St George's Day, we'd be in Asi Gonia; the saint is the village's patron and protector. We drove the route the day before, and saw in the streets of Asi Gonia carcasses hung under trees, ready for the feast. On the day itself the road up was clear, though folk came from far and wide to join the celebration, but the village itself was packed with sheep, flock after flock after flock. The tiny church was too small to hold more than a few worshippers; for the serious business of the morning, each shepherd brought his flock down a marshalling slope, to be milked in the paddock beside the church. The handsome, bearded priest waited nearby, a bunch of hyssop in one hand, in the other a basin of holy water; vigorously, through several hours, he splashed and sprinkled. Jugs of warm, foaming milk were handed round, with soft white bread, to all. In the village, beer, wine, raki flowed. Scraps and hunks of roast meat were loaded on to platters at the inn, where George had a family interest by marriage. We feasted. Gillian sat beside George as he spooned sheep's brains into his mouth, straight from the skull.

At the end of the day the sheep moved up to the high pastures, where they would stay until St Cyprian's Day in October. The smell of sheep shit was everywhere. More pungent still was the cheese we bought to take home: a hard, cylindrical drum that made its presence felt on our flight, and back in England. In Canea we went to George's home, with modest gifts, to say goodbye. The malt whisky seemed particularly acceptable. He showed us his published books, and the manuscript of his next.

The Cretan Runner begins with 'the drone of many aeroplanes, scattering Death on all sides'. It ends with the liberation of Canea. 'I reached the marketplace, when all at once I heard shouts and music and cheers, and realising the entry had begun, I ran towards the shouting as fast as my legs would carry me.' Still running.

I think often of Crete, and always then of George Psychoundakis.

14

IRELAND

Ireland fascinates, partly because of its history and beauties, mostly because of its closeness and otherness; *John Bull's Other Island*, but not John Bull's at all. I went there first, with my parents, for a family holiday in the summer of 1946, just after the war when food and clothes rationing, austerity, were the order of the day at home. We stayed at Greystones, south of Dublin, and had a great time. We were abroad, yet people spoke English, or a version of English. The Isaacs boys enjoyed the steaks at Jury's, so big they lapped over the edge of the plate; we believed we suffered from wartime meat starvation, and that no portion could be too much for us. These were. Of more interest to my parents was clothing, of which we were all in need. Clothing was rationed in Ireland too; but clothing coupons, we were assured, were easy to obtain. Outside Clery's in Grafton Street a newspaper seller offered them at sixpence each. Inside, too late, the clerk laughed them away: 'Sure we don't bother with these at all.' My mother returned home, through British customs, wearing several corsets beneath her costume.

John F. Kennedy went to Ireland in search of his roots in the summer of 1961. The first Catholic President of the United States was sure of the warmest of welcomes. Granada, which looked to outside broadcasts to fill afternoon airtime, decided to take coverage of the event from RTE – Radio Telefis Eireann. Brian Inglis, a West Briton from Malahide, formerly on the staff of the *Irish Times*, would supply a commentary. I went too. At the Red Bank in D'Olier Street, where the *Irish Times* drank, I met Seamus Kelly, the paper's diarist, also their theatre critic. Kelly had a face like a potato; John Huston cast him as the Fourth Mate in the film *Moby Dick*. 'Not a dry seat in the house,' Seamus would say, and write, of a particularly powerful performance. I got down to New Ross in County Wexford, near which the Kennedy homestead was said to lie. Peering at an insignificant shack in the corner of a field, the foreign press were inclined to take the Irish word for it; of visible signs of a Kennedy connection, there were none. But New Ross was the port the President's forebears were said to have sailed from, and its mayor, Andy Minihan, a livewire, never missed a trick in publicising his town. For me, this was the first of many happy visits to Wexford – to film traces of the rebellion of 1798; to enjoy a Celtic film festival; and later, almost regularly for a while, to revel in the Opera Festival.

The actual business of broadcasting JFK's visit was undemanding, but fraught. Installed in front of monitors in the Post Office in O'Connell Street – occupied by the rebels of 1916 – we concentrated our gaze in keen anticipation of Kennedy's arrival on Irish soil. 'Cue.' We were on the air. The screen remained blank. 'The President's plane has been sighted,' we were told; screen blank. 'It is circling the airport'; blank. 'It is making its approach'; blank. 'The plane has landed'; still blank. 'It is taxi-ing; it has halted'; still no picture, not even a general view. Eventually, just as the door of the plane opened, a split-second before we saw the President, a picture appeared. Brian Inglis and the other commentators waffled away, anticipating what they could not see. Next day Kennedy would be driven to Wexford. RTE had cameras in Dublin, and at New Ross. During the drive they proposed to run a film of the route over which commentators would offer helpful information until we had live pictures of the family cabin and the quayside at New Ross. To put separate sound on picture you need a 'clean feed' of sound, music, speeches, effects, whatever, to which commentary is added. At some point RTE contrived to lose this 'clean feed'. We could see the pictures all right, but they already carried commentary by RTE's excellent Michael O'Hehir. This was all very well, but not what Brian Inglis and I had come for; plainly he could not just talk over O'Hehir. I repeatedly urged the RTE engineer assigned to us to find out what was wrong, and put it right. He could not help me. I could listen in, if I liked, on the control line. 'Hullo there, Paddy,' someone was asking, 'can you hear us in Kildare?' As the hours dragged on, with Brian mute beside me, I expressed myself fairly forcefully. Years later, introduced to RTE's new Director General, George Waters, I met that engineer again; for he it was. Brian Inglis must have been heard at least some of the time, because Brum Henderson, Managing Director of Ulster Television, took us off the air, citing Brian's – and, no doubt, Michael O'Hehir's – dangerously partial commentary. But maybe it was the mere sight of a Catholic US President that worried Brum, who never failed to tell me how many early American Presidents were of Ulster Protestant origin.

The Troubles, which I made for Granada in 1962, was a modest toe in the water of Irish history. Keeping the surface of the film in period, I made use of the newsreel images that helped inflame the nationalist passions of Irishmen and women: the funeral of the old Fenian Jeremiah O'Donovan Rossa in 1915; the coffin of Terence McSwiney, Lord Mayor of Cork, who died of his hunger strike in Wormwood Scrubs in 1920, entering Cork Harbour draped in black, greeted by tens of thousands. For Easter 1916, I had Norman Rodway read Padraic Pearse's Proclamation: 'Ireland summons her children to her flag, and strikes for her freedom';

and we saw the centre of Dublin in ruins, after the Rising. It was
the British executions of the ringleaders that firmly alienated
public opinion, which at first had no notion of what the conspir-
ators were up to, and no liking for them. We saw armed men in
the streets of Dublin in the war years that led to the Treaty, and in
the civil war that followed it. And we saw the massive parades in
the north-east of Ireland back in 1911 and 1912 and 1914, at which
the Protestants of Ulster asserted that they would not be ruled
from Dublin, were loyal to the British throne, and would fight to
keep things as they were. Brian Inglis, fair-minded, was ideally
placed to write the commentary. In Liverpool, Fritz Spiegl and
Bridget Fry, who arranged the theme for *Z Cars*, helped with the
music. Stan Kelly, also from Liverpool, sang 'The Wearing of the
Green':

>*'Tis the most distressful country*
>*That ever yet was seen*
>*For they're hanging men and women*
>*For the wearing of the Green.*

The newsreels that represented Irish history to me, shot silent,
were given added force by music. The film-maker George
Morrison had made two grand newsreel compilations, *Mise Eire*,
I Am Ireland, and *Saorstat, Free State*. He commissioned scores from
the Irish composer Sean O'Riada, who re-worked folk melodies.
The music for *Mise Eire* is recorded by the RTE Symphony
Orchestra; the theme that represents Irish nationhood is as grand
as any film music I know.

At the British general election of 1970 the young Republican
activist Bernadette Devlin carried Mid-Ulster for Sinn Fein.
Surprisingly, against Sinn Fein tradition, she took her seat in the
House of Commons. There, on 31 January 1972, the day after
Bloody Sunday, when the Paras shot dead thirteen civilians, she

darted across to the government benches and slapped the face of the Home Secretary, Reginald Maudling. *The Times* described how, 'arms flailing and fists flying, the diminutive mini-skirted MP threw herself at the Government front bench, sending Maudling's glasses flying'. She called him a liar, and a murdering hypocrite. Later that day she appeared on Thames Television's *Today* programme to explain her behaviour. The other party to the discussion, a Conservative MP, remonstrated with her: 'Nonsense. If Reggie Maudling is anything like as bad a man as you say he is, I'm a Dutchman.'

Quick as a flash, Devlin replied, 'In that case, Sorr, you would not be the first Dutchman who has done my country grievous harm.'

Whom did she mean? She meant the Protestant King William of Orange, whose troops, many of them Catholic, won the Battle of the Boyne in 1690, defeating James II and entrenching Protestant rule in Ireland. That victory is celebrated in parts of north-east Ulster to this day. If there was ever a persisting political problem whose roots lie in history, the relationship between Catholic and Protestant, nationalist and loyalist, in Northern Ireland is it. You have to know that history, and the history of how England and Ireland came to be involved with each other, to understand how things came to the present pass. I never thought I'd have the opportunity to make a longer history of Ireland. But the chance came.

In 1978 we had endured ten bloody years of the renewed Troubles, which began with civil rights protest and confrontation in 1968. I had left my post at Thames and was in search of gainful employment. The telephone rang. Desmond Wilcox, my old Rediffusion colleague, now Head of Features, BBC TV, asked if I would be interested in producing a series on Irish history. Robert Kee was involved and, Wilcox said, was keen to work with me. The idea may have been born, I speculated, in the mind of the then Controller of BBC2, Brian Wenham; if not, it was certainly approved by him. He saw that the story needed to be told on television and that Robert Kee, who had now published all three volumes of his history of Irish nationalism, *The Green Flag*, was the ideal man to do it. The subject fascinated; I enjoyed working with Robert; I leaped at the chance. I read *The Green Flag* and was keener than ever. With other irons in the fire, I agreed terms for less than a full-time commitment, and reported to Kensington House, a long, low building off Shepherd's Bush Green.

An added attraction was that the series – thirteen parts seemed the right length – would be a co-production between BBC TV and RTE. The BBC would put up much of the cost in cash and facilities; RTE's expert staff and support on the ground would be invaluable. So would their archive. BBC Northern Ireland were also to be involved; they would need to be sure that justice was done to Ulster's point of view, and that London and Dublin were not conspiring to sell Belfast down the Lagan, and Londonderry down the Foyle. Our guiding star would be Robert Kee. His reputation went before him; none would dispute his commitment to getting as near the truth as possible. *Ireland: A Television History* was bound to simplify; there are not enough words in a television hour to tell all on any complex topic, and compressing a nation's history to thirteen hours means that a great deal will be omitted. Yet Robert's prose, both in print and on screen, refuses always to make things out to be simpler than they are; again and again he cavils at the obvious, insisting on qualification, spelling out necessary distinctions. We had the advantage that the instances he would cite, the judgements he would offer, the phrases he selected to make his point, had been fructifying in his mind for years. He knew what he wanted to say.

The politics of broadcasting such a series at such a time – blood in the streets of Belfast and of Birmingham; the British Embassy in Dublin burned down – were too complex for us to be left entirely unsupervised. We appointed three historical advisers: John Murphy, Professor of History at Cork University; A. T. Q. Stewart, author of *The Narrow Ground*, from The Queen's University, Belfast; and F. S. L. Lyons, Provost of Trinity College, Dublin, and the much-respected author of *Ireland since the Famine*. They read scripts, and offered advice. Each might have preferred different emphases here and there. All three accepted that Robert knew his stuff; he would say nothing that surprised or affronted any of them. The series, they understood, was not intended to alter informed academic attitudes, but to guide viewers, British and Irish, through a past which was unfamiliar to many and comprehended by few. I have never worked on a programme which better exemplified what broadcasting is for.

Britain's past is closely intertwined with Ireland's, always by geography and proximity – it is 14 miles from County Down to the Wigtonshire coast – and for centuries by history also. Norman knights, descendants of those who had conquered England in 1066, set sail for Ireland in 1170. They landed in County Wexford on 1 May and dug themselves in at Baginbun:

> *On the creek at Baginbun,*
> *Ireland was lost and won.*

It was England's rulers' later attempt to keep a grip on these Normans that first led the English to concern themselves with Ireland. They had not done so before. They have done so ever since. We see 'the Irish problem' as 'Britain's Irish problem'; the Irish see 'the Irish problem' as Britain. Whether Ireland ever had in the distant past been a nation in any modern sense or not, an eighteenth-century ballad expressed what Irishmen and women wanted:

> *A nation once again*
> *A nation once again*
> *That Ireland, long a province,*
> *Be a nation once again.*

But what, Robert asked, if a sizeable minority of Irish people, concentrated in the North, did not want to be part of an Irish nation at all? That question lies at the heart of the present conflict, and of the killing on both sides. For many Irish people, the North is still 'unfinished business'. But for many Irish people the troubles of the North are the last thing they want to see come south.

Robert Kee started the series, and the book he wrote to accompany it, like this:

> Some people think it is dangerous to go into Irish history, because by looking into old troubles you may aggravate new ones. But as a historian of Ireland, Dr A. G. Richey, replied over a hundred years ago to people who made this same charge then: '. . . a knowledge of the truth is never dangerous, though ignorance may be so; and still more so is that half knowledge of history which enables political intriguers to influence the passion of their dupes, misleading them with garbled accounts of the past.'

Robert went on:

> Northern Ireland has had its fair share of political intriguers and their dupes, and more than its fair share of garbled accounts of the past. Ungarbling the past is what this series is about.

The chief technical and stylistic problem we faced concerned the early episodes of the series. Previous series I had been involved in making were based on newsreel film and eyewitness interviews. For *Ireland*, neither would be available to us until we reached the twentieth century, seven episodes in. I distrusted dramatic reconstruction, and would use it as little as possible. Jenny Barraclough, a talented documentary-maker assigned by Desmond Wilcox to work with us, disagreed with me on this. In the 'Famine' episode,

for instance, she was for recreating harrowing scenes on the road-
sides of Connaught and in the workhouses of County Cork,
where thousands starved to death. Robert barred that, preferring
a low-key approach; it is hard, using well-fed actors, to imper-
sonate the starving convincingly. But we did allow some
reconstruction. We had to. We showed Parnell walking at
Avondale in County Wicklow; using only the exact texts, an actor
gave extracts from his speeches, as did another for Gladstone, in
the BBC's film studios at Ealing. For the more distant past,
though, we were confined to landscape, contemporary visual
records and, occasionally, the present as a metaphor for the past.
A hurling match stood in for the seventeenth-century Battle of
the Yellow Ford.

It worked; and perhaps the crucial contribution I made in the
two years of effort was persuading Robert, one gloomy morning
of self-doubt in Chiswick, that it was going to. As any traveller
knows, landscape is history; stones speak the past. From the
chamber graves at New Grange, aligned thousands of years ago
to catch the sun at the winter solstice, to the great burial mounds
of the Irish kings at Tara, where in the 1840s Daniel O'Connell, the
Liberator, addressed crowds numbered in tens, maybe hundreds,
of thousands, in the cause of Catholic emancipation and the suf-
frage, Ireland's landscape afforded us one stunning sequence after
another. Lambay Island, where the Vikings landed; the round
tower at Glendalough, where terrified folk sought refuge from
the Scandinavian invaders; the monasteries at Clonmacnoise,
serene relics of Irish Christianity; and the doorway in Derry of a
townhouse, headquarters of 'The Honourable the Irish Society' –
the City of London body that renamed Derry 'Londonderry' in
the seventeenth-century Protestant plantation of Ulster.

Robert not only knew but did his stuff, leaping ashore at
Lambay with the Vikings, striding the creek at Baginbun as the
Normans dug in, jumping the moat as Cromwell assaulted and
sacked Drogheda. Outdoors, he looked and acted the part; in the

city, or in his study, he was nattily dressed. We filmed out of sequence, all over the place; continuity, in the cinematic sense, was lacking. It did not occur to me to rule what he should wear, so he'd appear in different outfits in the same programme. This was remarked on, but did not matter. What mattered were his words, and those could not have been improved on. 'Of all the rebel leaders who *shine* through Irish history, none was more *effective* than Michael Collins'. This exactly captures the pride Irish men and women feel in this great man's courage and leadership – pride, that is to say, in the life and career of a ruthless terrorist, who ordered the killing of enemies, police or intelligence officers, in their beds. 'We have murder by the throat,' Lloyd George proclaimed in October 1920. A year later he shook Michael Collins by the hand at Downing Street, after Collins signed the treaty which partitioned Ireland and brought the Irish Free State, and later today's Republic, into being. (He believed the treaty would enable Ireland to move towards the ultimate goal of a 32-county republic.) The oath of loyalty to the monarch was to stay; a partitioned Ireland was not the whole loaf. 'I have signed my own death warrant,' Collins told his friends. But he was safe, he thought, in Cork. 'Sure,' he said, 'they'll not kill me in my own country.' They did. We interviewed one of those present at his killing in an ambush in County Cork. Collins was both an effective terrorist leader and a statesman of genius.

I had quite excellent colleagues in the making of *Ireland: A Television History*. Jenny Barraclough and Jenny Cropper directed admirably. The researchers attached were also exceptional. Robert and I lunched an applicant, John O'Beirne Ranelagh, then at Tory Central Office. His father had been 'out', on the rebel side, in 1916. He was acutely intelligent, and very well-informed. Robert kicked me under the table – hire this man; we did. John Ranelagh wrote his own history of Ireland shortly thereafter, and later a long, solidly researched history of the CIA. He followed me to Channel Four. A BBC trainee also joined, Michael Waldman, bright as a button. He was a pleasure to work with, less of a pleasure to be worked over by, as I found years later to my cost when, at the Royal Opera House, I gave him a free hand to bring BBC cameras into Covent Garden – *The House* was much enjoyed by millions in the UK and abroad; not by me. Vicki Wegg-Prosser, utterly reliable, did all the film research. An old stager, Gordon Watkins of *Picture Post*, *Tonight* and *The Great War*, collated scripts and watched out for inconsistencies and errors. Gordon had a home in County Cork. It was reassuring to know he had his eye on us.

The BBC made ample facilities available. I never once had cause to study a programme budget in my time at Kensington House. I was aware how many weeks' filming and editing had been allocated; when, in the accelerated surge to finish ahead of a rival Thames series, *The Troubles*, I asked for an additional cutting room, it was granted at once.

For the music, I toyed with the idea of using the renowned Irish folk group the Chieftains, but could not quite see them, with their crowded schedule, easily delivering the split-second cues we should need for each of thirteen episodes. This may have been a failure of nerve on my part; I could have tried. But I was more than happy with the composer I did choose, Francis Shaw, who provided exactly what was wanted for the main theme. To record it, RTE laid on its symphony orchestra. I told the orchestra manager of my gratitude, and mild surprise, that he had allocated two three-hour sessions to record two minutes of music. 'Well,' he said, 'you have to remember that these are the boys that took two days recently to record the national anthem.' The boys played excellently.

RTE's executives on the project were Jack White, Controller of Programmes until he died of a sudden heart attack, and the Controller RTE1, who succeeded him, Muiris McConghail. Muiris, a bold spirit and a bit of a buccaneer, was also an Irish scholar and a film-maker in his own right; he made a memorable documentary, and wrote a fine book, on the Blasket Islands, following in the steps of Maurice O'Sullivan's masterpiece, *Twenty Years a-Growing*. As Controller of RTE1, he once had the nerve to take the Taoiseach Charles Haughey off the air in his speech to the Fianna Fail Ard Feis before he reached his peroration. Haughey and Fianna Fail never forgave him, particularly as he had worked with Conor Cruise O'Brien when the latter was Minister for Information in a Fine Gael government. I ate Sunday lunch more than once in Rathgar with Muiris, his wife Maire and their children. At their hospitable table, I was the only one who didn't speak Gaelic. I cherish his friendship, and much admire him.

Maire de Paor, steeped in Irish cultures, was the invaluable researcher RTE attached to the team. A feisty redhead, and the wife of the medieval historian Liam de Paor, she and Robert spatted, not always amicably. She was passionately patriotic; Robert was concerned to point out that the nature and course of Irish nationalism were more complicated than patriots might like to believe. In 1916, for example, Pearse had proclaimed that Ireland had already 'struck for her freedom' on five previous occasions. One of those, Robert would point out, was not a national rising at all, but a fracas in the front garden of a small farmhouse in County Tipperary, when one policeman was killed; the 'Battle of the Widow MacCormack's Cabbage Garden'. Directing us to the spot, the locals referred to it as 'the war-house'. You can still see where the cabbages grew – but 'Battle' there never was. In County Wexford, filming the story of the rebellion of United Irishmen in 1798, we looked for the site of the Battle of Oulart Hill. A stone at the roadside bore an inscription in Irish: 'The Men of Cork came this way.' 'Who were they, then?' Robert asked Maire. The rebels, Maire thought. She didn't like it when he pointed out that, Irish language or no, they were militiamen who had served the government in putting the rising down.

Irish farmers, I had read in the paper, were on the march to protest against taxes on them, an unheard-of imposition. While we were looking for the battlefield of Oulart Hill, we met a farmer who, when we stopped the car in a drizzle and wound the window down, asked us where we were from.

'London.'

'That's where I made my pile.'

'On the dogs?' I asked.

'No,' he said, 'building motorways with Cubitt, Fitzpatrick, Shand. I paid no taxes. Look at this,' he said, indicating the farm buildings, 'it's all mine, and they tell me it's worth two hundred thousand today.'

'And,' I said, 'you still don't pay taxes.'

'No,' said he, 'but we're coming under pressure.'

Our researchers found men and women of seventy and over who had vivid memories of the past. Edward McLysaght remembered the 1916 rebels: 'My heart was with them; my head was against them.' Maire Comerford, already ninety when we talked to her, had been a member of Cumann a Bann, the women's movement in the years before 1916. Vincent Flynn killed several under Michael Collins's orders, despatching two British officers in their bedrooms before breakfast on the morning of 21 October 1921, the first Bloody Sunday. 'I put them up against the wall, said "The Lord have mercy on your souls", and plugged them both.'

In 1966 RTE had made a film to commemorate the fiftieth anniversary of the rising, and had interviewed the relatives of the rebel leaders who had visited them in the condemned cells at Kilmainham before their executions, strung out over agonising days. There was nobility as well as pathos in their reported last remarks. RTE's film remains a uniquely valuable source of testimony. What could we have done without it – reconstruct the heartbreaking goodbyes? I think not. Yeats wrote in 'Easter 1916':

And what if excess of love
Bewildered them till they died?

I write it out in a verse—
MacDonagh and MacBride
And Connolly and Pearse
Now and in time to be,
Wherever green is worn,
Are changed, changed utterly:
A terrible beauty is born.

Our story had beginnings, and fascinating middles, but no end. As well as making sense of the past, we were involved in deciphering, too early, the history of the present. The killing in Northern Ireland went on. Both the BBC and RTE had qualms about including any statement from the IRA. It was forbidden. At the BBC, only the Director General had authority to grant dispensation. In the Republic, Conor Cruise O'Brien, totally opposed, with Margaret Thatcher, to allowing the IRA the oxygen of publicity, had put through the Dail a law expressly forbidding any utterance of theirs to be broadcast. With the killing of innocent civilians in full spate, we could not decently show the IRA's then leadership justifying their actions.

After some to-do, we were allowed to interview an IRA activist of an earlier decade, Joe Cahill, recounting his role in the forties and fifties. He had a political agenda, and could now be seen as a witness to the past rather than a hooded killer. To achieve even this, our request went all the way up to Ian Trethowan, BBC Director General, who granted it. In Eire, Muiris McConghail succeeded in having the Dail pass a waiver to Conor Cruise's draconian law, specifically exempting *Ireland: A Television History* from its provisions. The co-production would have looked lopsided, and RTE foolish, if one party had crossed this hurdle and the other fallen at it.

But we did need to convey the intensity of feeling still prevalent, and the current force of violence in Northern Ireland. In the late summer of 1979 I crossed with Tamara by the ferry from

Fishguard to Rosslare. We drove north to Londonderry, where I met a BBC crew, and then on to Belfast. Just for once, I acted as director. My BBC PA, throughout the series and on this trip, was Deirdre Devane from Dingle in County Kerry, herself the very embodiment of England's and Ireland's inseparable closeness. We were to film a Sinn Fein march up West Belfast's Falls Road, ending with speeches at Casement Park. At BBC Northern Ireland, I asked if it would be safe for Deirdre and Tamara to accompany us. 'Better not,' I was told. 'You never know.'

The long march snaked up the Falls. At Casement Park a platform had been erected opposite the stands to film the speeches. A banner stretched across the stand – 'Sassanaigs a bhaile.' Being a Scot, I could just about work out what it meant: 'Sassenachs, go home.' 'How's your Gaelic?' I asked one young lad. He had none. The heavens opened. Drenched, I took the cameraman with me and sought shelter in the stand, in an empty, central, enclosed area that may have been the directors' box. It was reached by a stair up into it, though we'd found our way in, up and over, from the front. From there we filmed the speeches: 'The struggle, the war, will go on.' Sinn Fein wanted to refute a recent claim of Britain's commander in Northern Ireland that, militarily, the IRA was beaten. As the speaker hammered this home, two slim, hooded figures suddenly appeared in the box beside me, brandishing guns. This propaganda coup, the forbidden public appearance of armed terrorists, was wildly applauded. In the slit of the nearer balaclava I looked into the eyes of an IRA killer or potential killer. The hatred I read there shook me; it was a woman's gaze that held mine. She slipped away. Later there was a bit of a riot; stones were thrown at security forces as the marchers retraced their steps. No one was hurt.

The series, Robert's series, was completed successfully and broadcast, to the satisfaction of both co-producers and to the liking of the audiences they served. The BBC, aware that the UK contained 1.5 million citizens of the Irish Republic, and many more of Irish ancestry, commissioned research at a school in Coventry. 'Don't you criticise it,' the children insisted. 'That is our series.' I was particularly glad to hear from Gordon Watkins that working on it had been for him a worthwhile end to a distinguished career.

Ireland: A Television History won the BAFTA award for the best factual series of the year. The award should have gone to Robert, but it was made to me. Robert insisted I deserved it; he had in mind, I guess, my holding things together when despair struck. But, as far as I'm concerned, *Ireland* is one of the finest of authored documentaries, and it was Robert, TV journalist and historian, who made it so. I admire not just his presence on screen, but the way he writes commentary to picture. I see him always, in my mind's eye, rear-view, late in the evenings, hunched over the steenbeck, running the film backward and forward, finding words that will make the point, fit the space, enhance the picture, make speech and image one. I didn't say much of this when I was handed the BAFTA statuette at the London Hippodrome. Anthony Andrews won Best Actor for Sebastian in Granada's *Brideshead Revisited*. 'I thank God', he said, 'for Charles Sturridge' – the director, who had helped him to it.

'Aagh,' I groaned, 'that's the worst ever. Why drag God into it? It can't get lower than that.'

'Don't you believe it,' said the film director Lindsay Anderson, at my table. 'You haven't heard anything yet.'

He was right. Next year Philip Saville won an award for directing, superbly, for the BBC, Alan Bleasdale's *Boys from the Blackstuff*. Philip walked up to receive it, making 'down, pride' downward-pushing gestures with his right hand, and again invoked the deity. 'I thank God,' he said, 'who has placed me in the twentieth century, in the most powerful medium known to man, television.' TV prizewinners must keep God busy, unless he has better things to do.

Ireland: A Television History has not been repeated as often as it might have been on a BBC mainstream channel, partly because there is still no ending; the last episode always needs bringing up to date. Robert's fine one-volume history, written to accompany the series and many times reprinted, has been revised more than once. On the last occasion, puzzling to find a paragraph for the final page, Robert fastened, he told me, on the proceedings of the Northern Ireland Assembly, available on the web, online. He decided that it was significant that old antagonists were sitting down together, talking and working, engaged in the practical business of government. Martin McGuinness of Sinn Fein (and the IRA) was working to better primary-school education; a member of the Democratic Unionists, Ian Paisley's party, was improving roadways. Progress. He wrote this up, and sent it to the publisher. Next day the Assembly was dissolved. He rang an old wise head for advice, and asked, 'What is the future now?'

Long pause.

'I think you could say that the future is indefinite.'

Pause.

'And it could go on longer than that.'

When we started Channel Four, and were looking for audiences to serve, I thought of the millions of Irish in Britain who wanted to stay in touch with home. It occurred to me also that decent programmes made in English might be comparatively cheaply acquired. So I went shopping in Dublin. Knowing RTE's budgets were always stretched, I suggested we make drama series together; in effect, C4 would be putting money into work RTE could not otherwise afford, and we would both show it. In return, I would also have the Gaelic cup finals, football and hurling, commentaries by Michael O'Hehir included and, without cash changing hands, RTE's principal current affairs programme, *This Week Tonight*, to be shown not in peak time, but on Sundays, at midday. Actually, remembering Northern Ireland, I took UTV's *Counterpoint* one week in four. In drama, we co-financed *The Year of the French* and *Lost in a Free State*, and we both bought into, as did UTV, the independently produced *The Irish RM*. For weekday afternoons, I took Gay Byrne's *Late Late Show*.

John Ranelagh had charge, among much else, of Irish affairs. I watched *This Week Tonight* go out occasionally and once commented to Ranelagh that the last I'd seen, a studio discussion on housing, had not been up to much. Actually, I was out of order – the whole point was that we should show, uncut, unmediated, what they showed. Later in the week he came back to me, glowing: 'RTE have got a terrific show for us next Sunday. It will knock you sideways.'

'Yes, John.'

'They have done an investigative job on the Minister for Justice, Sean Doherty.'

'Yes.'

'He has been stepping over the mark. RTE have sworn affidavits from witnesses that he has been browbeating the Gardai in County Roscommon for interfering in a Fianna Fail pub that keeps open after hours. He himself told the local sergeant to lay off it, threatening, if the sergeant went on, to personally ensure that he was posted to Donegal or Sligo.'

'That sounds good,' I said.

John Ranelagh was back next day, with a long face.

'Jeremy dear' – he usually called me 'Jeremy dear' – 'there's a problem. RTE won't let us have the film.'

'Really, why not?'

'They say it's not the sort of film that should be seen in England.'

'You go back to RTE and tell them that is bloody nonsense. We have a contract. I expect to see it on our screen.'

Next day John was back again, with a longer face.

'RTE say you are quite right, but there's a bigger problem. The film is clearly defamatory of Sean Doherty. He is threatening to sue; you wouldn't want that. They'll go ahead, but they won't let us have it.'

'I thought you told me that they had sworn affidavits backing up every charge they make?'

'Yes, that's true; the witnesses will give evidence in an Irish court; but Doherty could sue Channel Four in the UK, and the witnesses would never give evidence in a British court. So, you see . . .'

I told John to tell RTE that we would take the risk. Doherty did not sue.

The bigger villain in Fianna Fail's government was the Taoiseach himself, Charles Haughey. 'Here big man, that's for you,' said one businessman he'd helped, handing him a bundle of banknotes. Before that, two able Irish reporters wrote a book about Haughey, *The Boss*, that exposed some of his tricks. At a very jolly dinner RTE gave us at the grand Berkeley Court Hotel, to thank us for topping up their drama budgets, we discussed our next collaboration. I suggested we should adapt *The Boss*. Consternation. 'Have you read it?' I had not. 'We must get you a copy. We'll try downstairs at the bookshop in the lobby.' We did. Did they have it in stock?

'No,' said the clerk. 'We don't keep that – mind you, there's a great demand for it.'

'What? If there's a demand for it, why don't you stock it?'

'Ah well, you see, yer man comes in here sometimes, and he has asked us not to display it.'

I have never not enjoyed being in Ireland.

15

JERUSALEM

At ten in the morning on Friday 4 July 1975, my brother Michael and his wife Ribbie parked their two young children – Hillel was two years, Boaz ten weeks – with Ribbie's parents, Israel and Margaret Soifer, at 5 Mapu Street in Jerusalem and went on to do the weekend's shopping. Twenty minutes later, at a pedestrian crossing at Zion Square, there was an explosion; a bomb had been attached to the back of an old refrigerator left on the pavement. Fifteen passers-by were killed, Michael and Ribbie among them.

Next day I flew to Tel Aviv and was met by my cousin Raymond Joels, whisked past immigration officers, and driven to Jerusalem, dazed. In Mapu Street, family members and friends were huddled round a table, planning the next day's funeral. A familiar face looked up at me as I entered the room: Ora Michaelson. She had arranged for Michael and Ribbie to be buried at the Sanhedria cemetery, within the city. I did not know one Jerusalem graveyard from another. I knew where I would stay that night, and for the next week of mourning: at 19 Balfour Street, with the Michaelsons.

*

I first went to Israel in 1955, just after leaving Oxford. Eight friends paid all of £50 between us for an old War Department fifteen-hundredweight Bedford truck, Bessie, and drove it down the Dalmatian coast through Yugoslavia to Athens. There, we thought, we might get a boat to Israel; in the two previous years' long vacations, I had made similar expeditions to Greece and to Italy. This was a last chance to travel before I reported to Maryhill Barracks for National Service in the autumn. My parents were pro-Israel, of course; all Jews were. But they were not keen Zionists. Indeed, my father had been a member of the Anglo-Jewish Association, opposed, if not to the Zionist ideal, at least to Zionism in practice. British Jews, AJA members believed, should make their homes in Britain. My father's affiliation to the AJA was the source of a bitter quarrel with his dear friend, the sculptor – later the Queen's sculptor in Scotland – Benno Schotz. Benno was a Zionist; they did not speak for years. I shared my father's views of where my future lay but, in a holiday spirit, set off to Israel to see for myself.

There was no boat from Piraeus to Haifa, or none we could afford. On an impulse, we crowded on to a small steamer going, via Port Said, to Limassol. From there, mistakenly, I thought we might get cheaper passage on a fishing boat to Haifa, rather than on Lloyd-Triestino's finest. We docked in Port Said, though with Israeli visas in our passports only one of us, the American philosopher John Searle, was allowed ashore. A youthful Egyptian athletics team, fresh from a congress in Europe, were fellow passengers. They were good to look at but, absurdly, we didn't talk. A less appealing memory of an Egyptian on board is of a docker at Port Said, meaningfully exhibiting his penis to me in the ship's urinals. At Limassol, there were no fishing boats to Haifa. A shipping agent got us a passage in steerage on the *Lamartine*, which we could have boarded, at greater cost, at Piraeus. The captain allowed us to sleep on deck for the night's crossing, provided we went below when he docked. Thus my first sight of Israelis was through a porthole: trousered legs belonging to dock workers and porters.

Once arrived in Israel, we dispersed to follow our separate paths. At the offices of Zim, the shipping line, I enquired for Isaac Michaelson and his family, and set off up Mount Carmel to find them. They'd moved, another family member told me, to Jerusalem. I hitchhiked a lift first to Tel Aviv. In the blazing heat, the driver bought me a *mitz*, fresh grapefruit juice in a long glass. Accustomed to thimbles of canned fruit juice at the British breakfast, this treat betokened a new world. In Tel Aviv, in Allenby Street, I found a cousin on my mother's side, Batya Israeli, who made me welcome. She'd practised dentistry there since the thirties; now her daughter, Geulah, was studying at the American University in Beirut. There was carp, which I disliked, for supper on Friday night. On to Jerusalem.

The Michaelsons had not yet moved into Balfour, but were preparing to do so. I slept on their temporary floor, and took their daughter Edna, a friend for life, to the cinema. We saw Nicholas Ray's *Johnny Guitar*; its campness escaped me.

Isaac Michaelson had been my father's friend in Glasgow, and was best man at my parents' wedding. He was an eye doctor of renown, who later dedicated himself to the prevention of blindness, worldwide. His younger brother Joe, an ear, nose and throat specialist, married to Malka, a pianist, had followed him to Israel. The youngest Michaelson, Harry, was still in Glasgow, a dentist; my brother Raphael married his daughter Ruth.

Isaac Michaelson, of Glasgow, met and married a *sabra*, a Palestine-born Jew – Ora. Both served in the British army in the Second World War. Ora, looking good in uniform, rose to the rank of captain. Her father was the engineer responsible for the railway line that ran from Kantara, on the Suez Canal, to Haifa, and thence up to Jerusalem. (The same route George Psychoundakis took on his wartime visit from Egypt to the Holy Places.) Isaac and Ora were a fine couple: he supremely intelligent, but the mildest of men; she strong and courageous as a lioness defending her cubs. We met rarely in Scotland, but I came to love Isaac and to honour him. He took a different newspaper each day, he told me, to ensure he sampled a full range of opinion. Did I really think a person's sexual orientation mattered? he quizzed me reprovingly. I never did again. And why so keen on Christopher Fry and the verse drama of the day? Was it really any good? He never laid down the law, but, eyes twinkling, always provoked thought. In May 1948, when the State of Israel was proclaimed and the Arab armies invaded, he and Ora, taking two young children and cases of surgical instruments with them, rushed from Glasgow to London and got on a plane for Rome and then Lydda. Fighting there forced a landing at Haifa. Isaac and Ora would make their home in Israel.

In 1955 in Israel all was optimism and, it seemed to me, idealism; people were building a new state, a new life. The Jordanian army had seized the Old City of Jerusalem, cutting Jews off from the Wailing Wall; grand old Arab houses in West Jerusalem had been vacated by their unwilling owners; yet Jews and Arabs mingled in the streets in safety. The Palestinian refugee camps were far away; no one asked quite how they came to be filled. 'They invaded; we defended ourselves; we won,' was the simple Israeli explanation for everything: no angst, no guilt. The Michaelsons would move to tree-lined Balfour Street, named for the British Prime Minister whose declaration stated that the Jews should have a national home in Palestine, without prejudice to the rights of the native inhabitants. The contradiction has consequences that are still with us. Then, I saw only the bright side. The sun shone; there were falafel and ice-cream in the street. Rucksack on back, I traversed the country: north to Dan and Dafne, close to the Jordan; south to my cousin Raymond at Kfar Mordechai. The bus from Beersheba dropped me in the sand; I trudged across it till I found him at his farm. He'd only ever seen me in city clothes before.

Raymond, once he had made up his mind to go to Israel, followed the regular route: agricultural training with the youth movement Habonim; a camp somewhere in Europe; a boat across the Mediterranean. Like other British young men and women who made *aliyah*, he joined a kibbutz, Kfar Hanassi, where he married Dorothy. But he found communal life restrictive; he wanted his own plot to farm instead, part private, part co-operative, and moved south. I'd never met a Jewish farmer.

In the north, above the Galilee, I stayed a few days on Kibbutz Hulata, a drained swamp. The kibbutz belonged to a political movement, Ahdut Ahvoda, left of Mapai, but not as far left as Mapam. When I asked those I met of my age to explain the precise differences in their various politics, the answers were all about bringing up children – 'We allow parents to be with their children after work in the evening; they only permit it at weekends.' Why teenagers should have definite views on this sort of thing, I never understood. The young people I met were earnest, but pleasingly irreverent. Hiking, they sang: *'Le Ben Gurion yesh Cadillac, Cadillac, Cadillac; Le Ben Gurion yesh Cadillac, ve lanu yesh ka zeh.'* 'Ben Gurion goes in a Cadillac, and we go like this.' One older man threw me; 'Come and live here,' he told me, 'we need educated young people like you from the West.' He flicked a light switch on and off. 'We're going to get black Jews from Africa; some of them won't know how to use electricity.' This was racism, wasn't it? I had not seen it coming, and didn't like it. When others urged me to stay, I refused, though having to serve two years in the British army didn't seem the most convincing of reasons. I could serve in the Israeli army instead, someone pointed out.

At Moshav Habonim, on the coast below Haifa, I fell in with a bunch of South African Jews. (A moshav is a communal settlement somewhat similar to a kibbutz, but more loosely structured.) Beneath the ruins of a crusader castle, the South Africans grew paw-paw in the middle of their banana grove. I played cricket for them against the Iraqi Petroleum Company north of Haifa, where the pipeline – no longer functioning – came to the sea. The moshav's cricketers were a casual lot who managed without a captain – not their style. Much more correctly dressed, and properly led, was the IPC's team, though that day they too were a motley crew. 'We've got the cook and bottle-washer playing today,' a wife explained to me, indicating one or two sallow-complexioned cricketers. 'Everyone else is at the Embassy garden party.' A senior manager from Peterborough, whose juniors seemed terrified of running him out, made fifty runs, and saw them to victory. I liked the moshav folk better but, dutifully, prepared to catch the boat home. Edna and I heard a symphony concert in the open air on Carmel, and said goodbye. I met up with my fellow travellers from the outward trip, and together we retraced our steps. The drive from Athens up the centre of Yugoslavia, over the Alps and into northern Europe, got colder night by night. When I stripped off for the army medical in Maryhill Barracks, a woman corporal gawped at my suntan. It did not last.

It was nearly fifteen years before I went to Israel again; by then, both Suez and, in 1967, the Six-Day War were in the past. My sister-in-law Rena got herself out to Israel for the latter from Heathrow, posing as a nurse. Jack Gold's film on the Bihar famine was in the cutting room as I waved her off and wished her luck. In 1969 the Israeli government invited me on a brief trip. The guided tour they provided was informative enough. I saw the Old City, now open; the view from the Golan Heights, down across the threatened, vulnerable narrow plain, to the sea; security measures in kibbutzim against PLO marauders with deadly intent. But, as ever, it was informal conversation, away from official guidance, that told most.

Access to the old Temple site in East Jerusalem was the precious trophy of Dayan's dazzling military victory, but the West Bank was a poisoned chalice. Wise voices had counselled giving it up, with Sinai and Gaza, immediately, but were ignored. Isaac Michaelson, my barometer of liberal opinion, was concerned. Always known as Mike, Isaac had spent years in African states leading Israeli medical teams in the fight against bilharzia, working to prevent blindness. In Jerusalem, he had operated on Yemeni children, born blind, and given them sight. He thought occupation corrupting.

Israeli television, only recently introduced, was up and running. The BBC's Hugh Greene had advised on its setting up. I had already met the very first Director General of the new service, Elihu Katz – an American-born Israeli citizen, a professor of sociology, expert in media – at a TV festival in Monte Carlo. We talked about government pressure on broadcasters, and how to cope with it. Israeli TV had a weekly interview programme which everyone watched; government leaned hard on it to keep out-of-line speakers off the platform it offered. With only one public broadcaster, and no commercial alternative, Israel's TV was more of a political punch-bag than Britain's. Elihu Katz and his wife Ruth, a musicologist, became firm friends of mine. There was plenty to talk about. *Boomerang*, a discussion programme presented by Amnon Rubinstein, a lawyer who later became a government minister, was unpopular with government; its run was terminated. Dan Ben-Amotz, an entertainer with a satirical bent, had also been banned for poking serious fun. A housing minister was accused of corruption. 'Politics, you see,' said Ben-Amotz, 'is a matter of give and take,' gesturing, 'That one gives. This one takes.' Dayan had instructed the army to bulldoze houses in Qualquilya, suspected of harbouring terrorists. Ben-Amotz told viewers that where he lived they'd had a spate of burglaries and found a cure. 'We knocked down all the houses in the street; now there are no more burglaries. Easy, isn't it?' Dayan's people objected.

I went to see Dan Ben-Amotz – I was writing a diary piece for the *Listener* – in a lovely house in the harbour wall at Jaffa. It had been an Arab house. Ben-Amotz chatted animatedly about his work, and censorship, forgetting the time. The telephone rang. He looked at his watch and swore. To me, he said: 'That's my weekly radio programme on the line, I'm late at the studio. Come with me. I'm devoting the whole show this week to censorship. Amnon Rubinstein will be on it, and so can you be.' I could not understand how, if Ben-Amotz was banned, it was possible for him to broadcast. It turned out that his show was on the army radio station, not Kol Yisroel, and that on it he was free to say what he liked. I explained how things worked in Britain, citing again the need for more than one outlet, if the censor was to be kept at bay. Israel has free media, under fierce pressure at times. Some of the best people I know work in Israeli broadcasting and journalism. They help make Israel seem worth living in.

Michael Jonathan Isaacs was born in April 1935, the youngest of Sally and Isidore's three sons. Like Raphael, the middle brother, and me, he was evacuated to Kirkcudbrightshire in September 1939, and later attended Glasgow Academy. Like Raphael – who won a major scholarship to Gonville and Caius College, Cambridge – and myself, he went on to one of the older universities, entering Wadham College, Oxford, in 1954. My parents, without fuss, complaint or apparent sacrifice, sent three boys simultaneously to Oxford and Cambridge. They lived unostentatiously, yet, in providing for our education, were generous to a fault. Michael, the quietest and most studious of the three, was much loved by his Oxford friends. Of a conservative disposition, he found work with stockbrokers on the Glasgow Exchange, and later in London. He did not enjoy it, complaining that in Glasgow anti-semitism held him back. In his London years he suffered some sort of breakdown, and for a while underwent analysis. Our parents, I am sure, helped pay for this; they never discussed Michael's illness with me. I may have been part of the cause of it.

Michael and I were long estranged. Something had occurred

between us which he could not forgive. Had I bullied him? Was I just selfish, overbearing, domineering in an unthinking general way? Perhaps, but no one else remarked on it. Was it just that, self-centred and ambitious, I got on with my own life, sidelining him? No; he felt, I know, that I had done him harm. There had been a ghastly episode in his early childhood, in our first home in Roxburgh Street, Hillhead, when he fell into an unguarded nursery fireplace. I can see still the animals my father drew on the walls, and, on this occasion, feathers from a pillow-fight all over the room, and tears. He bore no visible scar, but perhaps an inner one formed. Later, when Michael wrote to me of a grievance, he was unspecific. It was more likely some verbal episode in adolescence that did the damage.

Before he left Glasgow, and in London, living in a flat in Albany Street, his mind ran on going to live in Israel. He learned modern Hebrew, Ivrit. Michael was a practising Jew. His life began to come together round his Jewishness, and in the mid-1960s he took the plunge, sold up in London and made the move to Israel, *aliyah*. It worked. In Israel, Michael at once found a more congenial atmosphere. He made contact with the Michaelsons, and with our family there. He made new friends. He attended synagogue, worked at his Hebrew and began to earn his living as a translator. He had a degree in history, and translated the memoirs of Israel's first ambassador to the United Nations, Eliahu Elath, acknowledged handsomely, but posthumously, in the English edition. He began work on translating a book by an Israeli Cabinet minister, Dov Joseph. He had found himself, and, in the culmination of that process, he found someone to love, and to marry, Ribbie – really Rebecca, or, in Ivrit, Rivka – Soifer.

Ribbie was one of two children of Israel and Margaret Soifer, schoolteachers from Flatbush, Brooklyn. Israel was bookish, Margaret bustling. Now Israeli citizens, they lived at 5 Mapu Street, off Keren Hayesod, near the bottom of the hill. David Soifer, Ribbie's brother, had married an Israeli pianist, Leah, but

stayed in New York; after a year or two of guitar-playing hip-
piedom he became an admired cellular biologist, teaching at
Cornell, running a laboratory on Staten Island. Ribbie came to
Jerusalem and worked in publishing, editing medical journals.
She and Michael met, and fell in love. A happier pair together I
never knew. For Michael, a black cloud had lifted.

In the spring of 1972 the Isaacses set off to Jerusalem for the
wedding. I went to Crete on the way; when I met up with Tamara
and the children in Israel, we hired a car and toured a bit, as well
as attending the ceremony. One day we went to Hebron to visit
Abraham's supposed tomb. We were the only Jews that day in an
Arab town of tens of thousands, except for four Israeli soldiers
manning a machine-gun post in the square. The tomb was closed.
Jews, asserting the memory of the victims of a massacre of Jews by
Arabs there in the 1930s, and claiming the right to visit the patri-
arch's tomb, had established a settlement near Hebron, Kiryat
Arba. It is still there today, a thorn in Palestinian flesh. Of course,
Jews should be free to visit Hebron; but to live so close to it,
defended, at great cost to the Israeli taxpayer, by Israeli military
might, is seen as a provocation. We turned the car round, and
drove out.

Tamara's formidable mother Fay and her sister Rena already
lived in Israel. My parents came there for the wedding, as did
Raphael and Ruth. It was a joyous family occasion. At the *seder*
service at Passover, Jews for centuries had told each other, 'Next
year in Jerusalem.' As sunlight bathed the walls of the Old City, I
could see what they meant. A year later Ribbie gave birth to a boy,
Hillel; when he was a year old they brought the child to Britain to
show him off. Michael was transformed by marriage and fatherhood. Happily, too, he and I now got on well together. A wound
had healed. A year later, when Hillel was nearly two, a second
son, Boaz, was born in late April.

Friday 4 July 1975 was ladies' final day at Wimbledon. (In those
days, the men's final was on the Saturday, the ladies' on Friday.)

Tamara and her sister Avra had tickets; Billie Jean King beat Evonne Cawley 6–0, 6–1. I was at work, and home earlier than usual. In the office, glancing at the lunchtime news, I gathered there had been a PLO bomb in Jerusalem, an unusual event. There had been fifteen casualties. I thought little of it. About six o'clock Sol Margolis, Avra's husband, came to our Chiswick house. My daughter Kate opened the door to him and, when he said he had to talk to me alone, went upstairs again. He found me in the kitchen and gave me the terrible news: although it was not absolutely certain – they could not find body parts to identify – Michael and Ribbie were both believed dead. Kate heard me cry out. Tamara and Avra returned. I rang Jerusalem and got hold of a journalist I knew there, an old Oxford Labour Club friend, Eric Silver, the *Guardian*'s correspondent, and asked him to confirm, if he could, for certain whether or not my brother and his wife were among the dead. He rang back; yes, they were.

With Tamara, I went by train to Hove to break the news to my parents. They were used to our visits on Sundays. When they opened the door this Friday evening, they knew at once why we were there. They too had heard of the explosion in Jerusalem, but not until I told them could they have known that both Michael and his wife were dead. My father, sitting back in an armchair, howled in his grief like an animal in pain. He passed out, momentarily, in shock. My mother, tears running down her cheeks, gripped the arms of her chair and said, 'Isidore, we must go on.' Next day, leaving them to their grief, I flew out to Jerusalem and the funeral on Sunday.

Young men and women, in military uniform, carried the twin coffins covered with Israel's flag. Mere children, they looked stunned, as if they did not know what was happening; familiar, yes, with the cost of war, but unfamiliar with terror in their streets, and dimly aware now, perhaps, of what the future might hold. For Michael and Ribbie's young friends, happy in their lives and the promise of their futures, an idyll had been shattered.

JEWISH ECHO 11th July 1975

14 DIE IN JERUSALEM BOMB BLAST

JERUSALEM

2   JEWISH CHRONICLE July 11 1975

ISRAEL & OVERSEAS

Terror bomb victim was from Britain

From YORAM KESSEL—Jerusalem

First

The first to be buried were Rivka and Michael Ben-Yitzhak (Isaacs) at the Sanhedrin cemetery at a service on Sunday attended by about 100 British and American settlers. Rivka Ben-Yitzhak, an American, whose maiden name was Soifer, came from New York. Her parents live here. Her husband, Michael, was born in Glasgow and came to Israel in 1970. Formerly a stockbroker he worked in Israel as an editor and translator. His brother, Jeremy Isaacs, is a leading British TV producer. Glasgow-born Michael Isaacs and his American wife Rivka leave two orphaned children, Hillel (2) and 10-week-old baby Boaz.

Michael Isaacs was educated at the High School and Glasgow

Esther, a nurse with suffering in her own life – she had a cruelly disabled child; her husband had abandoned them both – unhesitatingly snatched up Boaz, who was ten weeks old, and cared for him as if he were her own. Hillel, aged two, was with his grandparents. I walked him in the park. At nights I sang him to sleep with the lullaby my parents had sung to me:

> If I had a donkey, and he wouldn't go,
> Would I beat him? No, no, no.
> I'd put him in the stable, and give him some corn,
> The best little donkey that ever was born.

I stayed with the Michaelsons in Balfour Street, in a little book-lined room I always had at the back of the flat, next to the kitchen. I am not a believing Jew, but now, religiously, I sat *shiva*. Every morning, waking early, I walked down the hill to Mapu for prayers at the start of the day, saying *kaddish* as principal mourner. One is not strictly supposed to say *kaddish* if one's father is alive;

I explained that in saying it, I was representing him. Most days of the next week I spent entirely at Mapu, slipping out with Hillel to the park. There were prayers again every evening.

The Soifers' friends and fellow worshippers at the synagogue crowded the prayers. You need a *minyan*, a quorum, of at least ten men to pray together; these meetings were over-subscribed. This was a familiar ritual; they came as they always did to a house of mourning. One man was going to London the following week, staying at a new hotel, the Metropole, and asked me what it was like. I found the triviality of this offensive. Could he not see I was thinking of other things? But life, of course, goes on.

Sitting *shiva* involves remaining seated on low chairs much of the day, every day for a week, receiving visits of condolence. These were kindly meant. Israel Soifer, sitting broken beside me, silently acknowledged his visitors. Among them was the Chief Rabbi of Israel, who came to offer comfort: Israel Soifer was a respected man, and the explosion, and the deaths it caused, marked a milestone in the nation's young life.

One day a young man entered, in formal dark clothing, his strong face bearded. He seated himself and announced that he had come with a purpose; then he offered to adopt the children. 'They must be brought up aware of why their parents died. There are too many Arabs in this country. We must get rid of them. We need more Jews. The children must be brought up, and I will ensure they will be, in a settlement on Israel's frontiers, part, one day, of a greater Israel.'

'Excuse me,' I interrupted, 'this is a house of mourning, and you have no business in it. We will not listen to you. The family will see to the children's upbringing.'

'I don't think you know who I am,' he said. 'I am the son of the famous Rabbi Kahane.'

Israel Soifer roused himself, and said quietly over a curled lip, 'I think you mean the infamous Rabbi Kahane.'

The visitor left.

His father Rabbi Meir Kahane, an extremist, advocated expelling Arabs from the land of Israel. He was himself killed, by another Jewish fanatic, some years later.

Israel Soifer's remark has helped me for years. I have never allowed Michael and Ribbie's deaths to cloud my view of Israeli policies and the Israeli state's behaviour, or to affect my belief that Palestinians should have justice, and a Palestinian state.

I had warned Tamara I might have the children with me when I came back, but I returned alone. The family in Israel discussed how and by whom the orphans should be brought up. One perfectly possible and practicable solution – adoption in a kibbutz, and a communal upbringing – was rejected. Ribbie's brother David Soifer and his wife, Leah, had no children; fittingly, gladly, they adopted Hillel and Boaz as their own. The children would be brought up, not in Israel, as some thought essential, but in the United States, though in a home in which Ivrit was for Leah a first and for David a second language. It could not have worked out better.

For my parents there remained the bitter task of visiting their children's grave, to attend the setting of the memorial stone. One tomb in the Sanhedria holds both the 'beloved and lovely' dead. On the double headstone is carved, in Hebrew, the rest of the verse from David's elegy for Saul and Jonathan: 'In life and in death, they were not divided'. I went with my father to the police station in the Russian Compound; a small package of unclaimed belongings, and fragments of belongings, was emptied on to the table in front of us. My father picked out the watch he had given his son.

Michael and Ribbie's friends in Jerusalem devised a living memorial to them. They had both been book-lovers; they left two infant children. The Ben-Yitzhak Award is made every two years in Jerusalem to the best illustrated children's book published in Israel. The competition is supported and administered by the Children's Wing of the Israel Museum. Family and friends gave what they could afford; Vivien Duffield's Clore Foundation made a substantial gift. The standard of work is remarkable. The Ben-Yitzhak Award endures; children benefit.

I have been to Israel several times since Michael died. The Sanhedria cemetery holds many more graves than it did. I never visit Jerusalem without remembering Michael and Ribbie's happiness, their deaths, and our loss.

Sometimes, escaping the embrace of Israeli officialdom, I would stay in the old American Colony Hotel in East Jerusalem. The American Colony, which preserved on its walls and doorways the bullet marks of Israeli incursion in 1967, has tall, cool, Arab-style rooms, all curves and arches; on one visit, all four of us – Tamara and I, John and Kate – spread ourselves in one. Once, I was the guest of the Israeli government in the cultural guesthouse Mishkenot Sha-ananim, in Yemin Moshe, overlooking the Old City; I was showing films then at the Jerusalem Festival. Mostly I have stayed, on one occasion with my daughter Kate, at the Michaelsons'. Claremont, 19 Balfour Street, is a three-storey stone house in Rehaviah, a high, airy, tree-lined district with broad streets. Edna and her architect husband Avram live on the top floor. Isaac and Ora lived below, on the ground. The big, dark room to the left contained the piano, books, paintings, and sober, comfortable old-fashioned furniture; it might have been in Berlin or Glasgow. I used a little narrow room at the back, with a camp bed and a tiled floor. Ora made me welcome always, without question or hesitation. I listened carefully to Isaac's exposition of how things were politically; mild, humorous, optimistic, he was nevertheless patently more and more aware of a sky darkening, and of attitudes to Arabs, and actions, albeit in self-defence, of which he disapproved. Ora was always honest, always courageous. It was inspiring to be with them and, perceiving their lasting love and friendship for Sally and Isidore, to see my parents through their eyes.

I had other family to visit in Jerusalem. Tamara's mother Fay, known as Fanny, had been widowed in middle age and, years later, romantically remarried. Her second husband, Joseph Kahaner, was a widower whom she had rejected long before, when both were young and free and he, a green-fingered agronomist, had come to South Africa from Palestine to study citrus fruit. He attended the agricultural school at Rishon-le-Zion. 'I can't marry you, Joseph,' said Fanny. 'I'm going to marry Johnnie Weinreich.' But forty years later she did marry him, near us, in Uxbridge Register Office. Joseph had been head gardener to the British High Commissioner in Palestine, Sir Harold MacMichael, in the Mandate period. 'At ease, Kahaner,' the High Commissioner would say, stopping to talk on their daily encounters in the grounds. In 1948 Joseph, an Arabic-speaker, was sent up to the north in search of cedars of Lebanon. He checked into an inn on the border and sent out word. Within days there was a tap on a windowpane at night; outside was an Arab, across his donkey's back two young cedars. They were planted on Har Herzl, and are there today. Joseph gardened way into his eighties, crossing limes with lemons, and oranges with grapefruit; he grew a prickly pear without prickles.

Fay lived to ninety-nine. She was a formidably determined woman who survived by facing up to every difficulty, grief or evil, and then, equally firmly, banishing it at once from her mind. Her will – her belief, say, in the diet that kept her healthy – one could only applaud. Her understanding of the rights and wrongs of the Israeli state's behaviour was at best fantasy, at worst an obtuse denial of harsh truths. Fay was a regular attender at synagogue. She edited a parish magazine, the *Adalia Review*, and communed with American Christians who thought the Jewish state wonderful, even if Jews would not convert to Christianity. Fay thought these bible-punchers were representative of world opinion; they probably did reflect the mind of born-again America. Sincerely bent on Arab–Jewish amity and reconciliation, she was convinced that, in law, any Arab who had left a handsome house in West Jerusalem could instantly, on application to its Jewish owner, have it back. When, in November 1977, the Egyptian President Anwar Sadat came at Menachem Begin's invitation to Jerusalem, he gave a press conference. Several hundred journalists from all over the world attended. Thames Television sent a heavyweight reporter, Llew Gardner. The senior figure seated next to him asked him whom he represented. 'Thames Television's *This Week*,' said Llew. 'Ah,' she said, 'you work for my son-in-law, Jeremy Isaacs.' Brandishing her courtesy press pass at the door, Fay had barged her way into history.

On trips to Israel I would escape from family certainties to the liberal scepticism of friends in journalism or broadcasting. Amos Elon was an early source of informed judgement. He had been Washington correspondent for *Ha'aretz* in crucial years, when the Israeli daily was held to be one of six best newspapers in the world. He is known now for fine books, and for his balanced, yet almost despairing, commentaries on Israel in the *New York Review of Books*. Amos lives now with his American wife Beth in Italy. Another hospitable, delightful Israeli was Naomi Shepherd, once the *New Statesman*'s correspondent. Naomi was liberal-realist, and was married to Yehudah Laish, Palestine-born, a civil servant and *bon viveur* with a penchant for large cigars. Yehudah would give me a robust defence of whatever the government was up to. You could not fool Yehudah, and he never tried to fool you.

The best defences of Israeli realpolitik I heard were made in London, by George Weidenfeld, once assistant to Israel's first President, Chaim Weizmann. I was on occasion in the 1970s hospitably reproved by him if Jonathan Dimbleby, say, had reported critically on Israel's conduct or policies for *This Week*. Had George Weidenfeld not preferred London's publishing world to Tel Aviv's Dizengoff and Jerusalem's Hebrew University, what a formidable Israeli foreign minister, or ambassador to Washington or Moscow, he might have made. He never attempted to browbeat me, only to explain Israel's case. Survival, he would argue, justified all, or nearly all. But did it?

When, in 1982, with the excuse of stamping out terrorist bases across the border, Israel invaded Lebanon, it deservedly got a bad press. Critical fury rose to a predictable climax when Israel's troops, commanded by Ariel Sharon, connived in the massacres of hundreds of Palestinian refugees – no doubt some terrorists among them – by Christian militiamen in the camps of Sabra and Shatila. An Israeli judicial commission later held Sharon at least partly responsible for these killings, and recommended his punishment and demotion. British media in Lebanon investigated and reported what they found.

Jews in Britain are by no means unanimous in supporting Israel's government in every action, any more than the Israeli public is, though they usually rally behind it if Israel's existence seems threatened. But the reporting of the Lebanon invasion, and the mindset behind it, provoked controversy. One rule, we were told, was being applied to Israel's conduct; quite another to that of feudalist, authoritarian Arab states responsible, as was Syria's Assad, for massacres within their borders. I agreed to take part in a panel meeting at Chatham House, the Royal Institute of International Affairs, to discuss the British media's treatment of Israel, considered 'biased against' by most of the panel – Melvin Lasky, former editor of *Encounter*, was the leading figure – and all of the audience. Newspaper journalists – Robert Fisk in the *Independent* was particularly singled out – BBC radio and television, ITV's current affairs: all were criticised for double standards. I thought this nonsense, and stood up to say so. It is true that some atrocities are harder to report than others, especially in totalitarian societies. But, I thought, journalists must report Israel's actions accurately, honestly and fearlessly. 'I would like', I added, 'to support an Israel whose actions did not draw critical opprobrium from the world's free press.'

'Change your name,' someone said to me afterwards. 'Be ashamed of yourself.'

One of the best things I know of Israelis is that they are more realistic, less hysterical on these issues than are Jews in the Diaspora. They have fewer illusions. When James Cameron, during the Six-Day War, submitted his copy on Israel's fight for survival to the military censor, it was returned unaltered. 'The sentiments', said the censor, 'are unexceptional, but banal.'

The evenings of talk I would have in Jerusalem discussed complex issues intelligently. In London during the first intifada, Gerald Ronson invited me as his guest to a fund-raising dinner at which Binyamin Netanyahu would speak. Over the salmon, I asked Netanyahu why so many Arab young people and children had been killed. Surely the vast disproportion with Israeli losses was regrettable? He nodded what I thought was agreement; it was hard to explain or defend the gap. In due course he rose to speak. 'Stones,' he said, 'are weapons that kill, just as bullets do. In any case, a thousand Arab dead are not worth one Israeli life.'

Arnon Zukerman was Director General of Israeli Television in the 1970s; tough, shrewd, with a sense of humour, he would tell, with only a touch of exasperation, of the pressure applied by governments, both Ma'arach and Likud, to broadcasters. When Israeli television started, the cameramen's mothers brought their knitting to the studios to keep an eye on how their boys were getting on. Prime ministers, too, sought access to the studio, and thought nothing of personally telephoning a complaint in the middle of the night. Plainly, like any democracy, Israel needed diversity in broadcasting; like others, Israel hesitated to introduce it, for fear of not being able to control it.

In London, many emissaries from foreign broadcasters sought me out. Professor Pappo was chairman of Israel's broadcasting authority. What would I do, he wanted to know, if a programme was put up to me that would certainly displease a neighbouring state, an ally of considerable importance, with a key role in maintaining Israel's security?

'If it was a serious programme,' I said, 'accurate and well

researched, I would certainly broadcast it. Giving diplomatic offence by broadcasting truths that matter is not a proper concern for the journalist in radio or television. Broadcasters in democracies should be seen to be independent of the state.'

He sighed, unimpressed. Later I learned that what concerned my visitor was one of six radio documentaries, already recorded, on the different Christian sects represented in Jerusalem's Holy Places, among them Catholic, Greek Orthodox – and Armenian. The Armenians' account of themselves reflected on the historic trauma that had beset their nation, the massacres of Armenians by Turks early in the twentieth century, which they see as an attempted genocide. Pappo knew well that this would offend Turkey, on which Israel depended for water and other services. He pulled the programme; there was a mild scandal. It was restored to the schedule, as it deserved to be. In an authoritarian society it might never have been made.

In 1980 Brian Wenham, Controller of BBC2, responding to a suggestion from Arnon Zukerman, commissioned a short series based on Moshe Dayan's autobiography. Zukerman was now an independent. The BBC assigned a capable producer. Both Wenham and Zukerman welcomed my involvement. A trip to Israel to meet Dayan? Why not?

Arnon drove us from Jerusalem to a protected enclave northeast of Tel Aviv, set in a luxuriously planted, green and fertile landscape. Israel's greatest soldier, victor of the Six-Day War, liberator of East Jerusalem, received us in his palatial garden. Our piratical host, eyepatch over the lost eye, was surrounded by antiquities – Canaanite, Egyptian, Greek, Roman – he had looted from various archaeological sites. Dayan interviewed well, recounting his military adventures. Politically advanced by Ben Gurion and attached to that stern early generation, he was reputed a moderate. He spoke Arabic and took tea in the tents of the Bedouin. He did not, though, have the weight or political clout himself to strike a deal with the Arabs. Egypt had made peace, and Israel had given back the Sinai; Jordan was friendlier and might yet come to terms; there would be negotiations in the end with Syria. But a glaring omission from his discourse was the word 'Palestine'. 'The Palestinians', Israel's Prime Minister Golda Meir had said, 'do not exist.' What about the occupied West Bank? I asked Dayan. Surely he would not defend annexation, in the world's teeth?

'I don't know about that,' he answered. 'I read my bible; Judea and Samaria were once part of the kingdom of the Jews. They may be again.' I left, disillusioned.

Once, walking in Jerusalem on a summer's evening, I heard through the open windows of every house in the street familiar music: Carl Davis's theme tune for *The World at War*. It meant something to me that the series should be seen here. *The World at War* sold widely round the world. Thames Television, bicycling videotapes from one minor market to another, sold the series to Jordan before Israel. When the tapes reached Israeli Television in Jerusalem, a set of commentary scripts were found attached: the Jordanians had excised from the text every mention of Jews and had, presumably, omitted the episode on Nazi genocide altogether. Many in Jordan, however, could receive Israeli TV.

The World at War, newsreel film and eyewitness testimony, was ripe for imitation. A bright, bouncy, immensely able and likeable young Israeli historian, the producer Yigal Lossin, and his managing colleague Naomi Kaplanski set out to make a history of the birth of Israel, from the origins of Zionism in the nineteenth century to the United Nations declaration of the state's right to exist, and the Israeli proclamation that it did, in May 1948. Yigal came to see me in London. It was clear at once that he understood exactly what was needed; I agreed to see something of work in progress when next I was in Jerusalem. The origins of the state were fairly described; the word Palestine, still unused in official parlance, properly spelled out. The interviews with early pioneers, and those who worked to bring the state into being, were revelatory and moving. *Pillar of Fire* was a major undertaking for Israeli Television, and fulfilled the highest expectations. Every nation should tell its own story.

The bomb that killed fifteen Israelis in Kikar Zion in July 1975 was at the time a rare and unexpected event. For decades *fedayeen* had stalked Israeli settlements or ambushed military vehicles, killing if they could. But the casualties, though every life is precious, were few and far between. Israelis lived surrounded by enemies, they thought, but were scarcely conscious of it; between wars there was a sort of peace. The bomb in Zion Square presaged the end of that; Palestinian fury and frustration, fuelled by the smouldering anger of the refugee camps, inflamed by the winds of bloodthirsty propaganda, would carry terror into Israeli farm settlements, villages, towns, cities. Bombs exploded at bus stations and in supermarkets. The harsh occupation of territories conquered in war brought enemies nearer. Suicide bombers, particularly those who believe they will go straight to paradise, have added a new dimension of horror, penetrating defences like needles piercing flimsy cloth. The Israeli Prime Minister, Yitzhak Rabin, was assassinated by a right-wing Jewish fanatic for daring to contemplate withdrawal to earlier boundaries in the quest for peace. Today, behind a high, oppressive, divisive wall which brings some security, Israelis contemplate a bleak future. Courage, and the will to survive, to defend themselves, of course remain. The optimism of spirit that I breathed when first I went, matching the sunlight, has diminished and disappeared. Idealism is no more; a resigned pragmatism, at best, is left.

It is thirty years since Michael and Ribbie were blown to bits. The man who placed the bomb – he was a member of Fatah, a branch of the PLO – served twenty-eight years in prison, and has been released. Hillel Soifer is now a junior fellow of Harvard, specialising in Latin American socio-economic studies. Boaz is married with three children and instals solar heating in New

Mexico; he called his first child Rebecca, after Ribbie, and his second Isaac, which pleases me. His adoptive parents, the Soifers, real, loving parents in every respect save the genetic, have moved to New Mexico to share their happiness.

Isaac and Ora Michaelson are both dead. After Isaac's death, Ora worked for years for Jerusalem's Blind Society, carrying on his work, bringing to it till she dropped the willpower and desire to serve that always characterised her. Each was honoured as a Citizen of Jerusalem; each has a city street named for them. They were among the very best people I ever knew.

Edna Michaelson and her husband Avram Engel came to London for their daughter's engagement – the wedding was in Jerusalem – and again for their grandson's *bris*. Talking over life in Israel today, they are critical of government policies and actions. But they neither complain nor whinge. We, and you too, have to accept, they seem to be saying, what life brings. 'What would your parents say?' I ask. 'What would Isaac say of Israel now?'

Edna and Avram looked at each other. 'They'd hate it,' said one. 'They'd hate it and be off; they'd have gone by now.'

The other disagreed: 'They'd hate it, and stay.'

16

THE FOURTH BUTTON

In April 1986, while running Channel Four, I had a letter from Malcolm Laver, Highbridge, Somerset, a Romany living in a council house on DHSS unemployment benefit of £29.50 per week. He'd enjoyed Amber Films'

> *Seacoal* (last Monday) whose story and characters I was able to identify with as I spent ten years as an itinerant scrapdealer and car-breaker! (In the Brighton–Newhaven area). Now I seldom leave my council house. A virtual recluse, my friends are Bruckner, Wagner, Sibelius and Mozart, Channel Four, BBC Two (with HTV or BBC One if my favourite channels lack excitement).

Mr Laver hoped he hadn't been 'a bit of a bore'; he only wrote to tell me 'how much I enjoy Channel Four'. I copied that to colleagues, and to Amber, makers of *Seacoal*. Broadcasters pump out utterance into the air; to hear back from anyone is rare. Mr Laver helps explain why Channel Four mattered.

For twenty years there were four buttons to press on the

television set, but only three channels to find on them; the fourth was waiting to happen. Reproachfully, throughout the late sixties and seventies, the fourth button looked at us, saying 'Push Me'. The BBC had argued to the Pilkington Committee on Broadcasting that it needed a second channel to provide a full range of cultural satisfaction, programmes of mass appeal combined with others that suited particular tastes. After a dire start, BBC2 found new audiences who rejoiced at its coming. Pluralism, the notion that there was not just one audience but several, entered the broadcaster's consciousness. But for years, we left it at that. It suited the BBC that the fourth channel was unused; those who wished to see it activated were divided as to what to do with it. Governments, keen to get it right, came and went; action was postponed.

ITV thought itself entitled to own and run the fourth channel, as a matter of equity in its rivalry with the BBC. But ITV, except in London, was a monopoly, and a wealthy one. Advertisers wanted an end to that; they wanted competition, another market to buy in. Others also wanted a market: programme-makers who had nowhere to sell their wares. They argued furiously for access to the airwaves. Others felt they had something to say which was not being heard; they were voices that would not be drowned.

Did the need for a new channel appear urgent to someone like myself, long satisfyingly employed in ITV? Yes; there was a need, and it was apparent. In spite of the creative enlargement that BBC2 conferred on British television generally, in spite of ITV's raising its sights in the 1970s, there was a sameness and smugness about the duopoly that cried out to be challenged. In part, the dispute was between haves and have-nots; yet within the ranks of those in possession, some of us saw the case for change. I ran a documentary department stuffed with talents. Thames's entitlement to airtime only just offered an adequate outlet for their work; we could have contributed very much more – certainly half as much again – without a decrease in quality. How limited, then, were opportunities in the lesser network companies, let alone for talents outside the system altogether? Bombarded with pro-gramme suggestions, I automatically said 'no' – there was no room in the schedule. Some – perhaps without paying themselves a penny – might have scraped together funds to make an inter-esting programme. My budget was committed. I could offer only peanuts to acquire a film which had cost much in dedication, effort, resource; the film Tom Steel and I made for NZTV on the battle for Crete received just such treatment from BBC2. The three extant TV channels were choc-a-bloc; yet much talent, energy, purpose and ambition went untapped. And viewers' choice was limited.

The single most influential suggestion for the fourth channel came from the fertile mind of Anthony Smith, a thinker and a scholar of media with practical experience of programme-making. In an article in the *Guardian* in April 1972, Smith propounded an analogy with publishing as the way forward for broadcasting. An ex-editor of BBC TV's *Twenty-Four Hours*, he saw the hierarchical structures and institutional self-importance of BBC and ITV as restrictions on freedom of expression. These institutions made programmes that said what they thought should be said; they satisfied tastes they determined should be fed. Their range was relatively narrow. Locked in competition for ratings, they imi-tated each other's output; all television tended towards a norm.

Rather than hand the fourth channel to an existing body, or set up another like it, Anthony Smith proposed to bring into being a quite different institution, a National Television Foundation, which would not itself make programmes, not employ pro-gramme-makers, not exercise control editorially, not enunciate an ethos. Instead, the Foundation, as a publishing house, would put its facilities at the service of others, authors with something to say. That way, a thousand flowers might bloom; the talents of varied contributors could be tapped, the public offered a diversity of views and materials. The Foundation would be an editor of last resort – someone has to choose – but would act with a light touch; the programmes it aired would enlarge choice as no conventional channel could ever do.

The Foundation's Achilles heel was funding; who would pay for it? The cost might be borne by different interested parties, Smith thought. But the political parties, vying for office, looked for a more solid financial base from which to proceed, at minimum risk to the Treasury.

Later that year another influential chef entered the kitchen and gave the broth a stir. This was the former Director General of the BBC, Hugh Carleton Greene, in a Granada Guildhall Lecture. Greene had fought the campaign which delivered to the BBC its second channel, and to ITV a trouncing, upon which he remarked: 'They got what was coming to them.' Now he conceded: 'There is a certain elementary fairness in allotting the fourth channel to ITV in one way or another, and that is indeed what Pilkington foresaw under certain conditions.' The IBA was suggesting a complementary service with an enhanced role for itself; this had the attractions, Greene thought, 'of simplicity, finance and availability of studio resources', but was 'just a bit too glib, just a bit too much calculated to safeguard the interests of the existing companies rather than encourage a fresh and experimental output'. Greene reverted admiringly to Smith's Foundation. He proposed that the Foundation should be set up very much as Tony Smith had suggested, 'as a centre for every type of experimental programme'; the IBA should then allocate it a daily block of programme time, some of it in peak. This neatly squared the circle, and made a modified ITV2 respectable.

The ITV companies, meanwhile, led by formidable intellects with considerable political clout, such as LWT's Chairman John Freeman, and Granada's Denis Forman, were lobbying hard for ITV2, *tout court*, no frills, no restrictions. The Minister for Posts and Telecommunications, Sir John Eden, invited other representations. In June 1973 I put forward my view.

A Submission to the Minister of Posts & Telecommunications:

1   The fourth television channel is a public asset which should
     be used and not wasted.
2   ITV has a strong claim to the fourth channel on simple
     grounds of parity with the BBC, and to enable it to provide
     complementary programmes on two channels. But ITV's
     interest is not necessarily the public's interest.
3   The government should only make available a fourth chan-
     nel for use if by doing so it will lead to a wider choice of
     programmes, add to the services which broadcasting pro-
     vides, and offer the possibility of a genuinely new
     experience on British television.
4   All these conditions could be fulfilled by allocating the
     channel not directly to ITV but to the IBA, provided the
     IBA defines more clearly the purposes to which it would
     wish to see a fourth channel put, and provided it can satisfy
     you that it will see those purposes fulfilled in its regulation
     of the channel.
5   The IBA should finance the channel by a levy upon the tele-
     vision companies.
6   The IBA should appoint a Controller of the Channel who,
     while working in harness with the Programme Controllers
     Committee which schedules programmes for ITV-1, would
     nevertheless have sole authority, under the IBA, to schedule
     programmes for ITV-2. It is essential that this authority
     should reside in one person. Only if this condition is ful-
     filled will it be possible to select programmes strictly on
     merit, and to build into the system the flexibility the BBC
     possesses, and which is markedly absent in ITV's schedules
     today.

I thought there would be sufficient advertising available to the
ITV companies to recoup to them the levy they would pay to

finance the channel. And I summed up: 'ITV should have access
to ITV-2, but only on terms that guarantee the public not a mirror-
image of BBC1 and BBC2, but a widening of the range of
broadcasting.'

Having sent this, I got on with making *The World at War*, soon
forgot I had made the submission, and did not follow it up.

In 1974 Labour returned to power. The Ministry for Posts was
abolished, and broadcasting was transferred to the Home Office;
from then on, broadcasting matters would come to Cabinet
backed by the authority and presence of the Secretary of State for
Home Affairs, number three in the pecking order. The Home
Secretary appointed in 1979, after Margaret Thatcher's general
election victory, was William Whitelaw, who has perhaps the best
claim of all to be the father of Channel Four: active in its procre-
ation, present at its birth. In the official history of the channel's
coming into being, Paul Bonner perceptively cites the speeches on
broadcasting Whitelaw made in opposition, as reported by the
IBA Director General to the Authority in August 1979. In them one
can trace how Whitelaw's mind had moved as he responded to
the arguments of the Annan Committee for a new Open Authority
to run a fourth channel, to pressures from the IBA and the ITV
companies, and to the views of would-be independent producers.
The new government's proposals for legislation in other areas
were not yet ready. That autumn Whitelaw would have an opportunity to introduce in Parliament a bill that would bring the fourth
TV channel into being. He took it.

On holiday that summer at Ceibwr in north Pembrokeshire, I
sat down to scribble the lecture I was due to deliver in Edinburgh
at the end of August. The James MacTaggart Memorial Lecture,
bidding to be an event in the television year, was the focal point of
the International Television Festival, a boozy, gossipy adjunct to
the main cultural event. Paul Bonner, a colleague in BBC Features,
for which I was making *Ireland*, chaired it that year; his committee
invited me to speak and, ever fond of the sound of my own voice,

I agreed. I knew that in doing so I would be staking a claim to a role in the fourth channel, when it happened. The lecture I gave was at once dubbed 'The MacTaggart Memorial Job Application'.

Paul Bonner greeted me in Edinburgh on 27 August with the news that Earl Mountbatten had been assassinated by the IRA while on holiday in County Donegal. The lecture would go ahead. I tried to sum up what we knew of the present state of affairs. It was to the IBA, subject to safeguards, that the government had entrusted responsibility for the fourth channel; that meant that it would be ITV2 we would have, and ITV2 it should and would be called. This passage, it turned out, was a dismaying disappointment to the independent lobby, particularly as I added that the independent contribution to the channel's output should start modestly, and grow. But I had long enjoyed my work in ITV; ITV would fund the new channel; the IBA would regulate it. Government had rejected the new Open Broadcasting Authority that the Annan Committee had recommended. It too, at this point, had an ITV2 in mind. The IBA and I were of like mind on another issue: ITV would pay for the channel, but would not control it. A separate body, taking a new view of broadcasting's possibilities, would do that. What sort of fourth channel did we want? I asked. This was my answer:

> We want a fourth channel which extends the choice available to viewers: which extends the range of ITV's programmes; which caters for substantial minorities presently neglected; which builds into its actuality programmes a complete spectrum of political attitude and opinion; which furthers, in a segment of its programming, some broad educational purposes; which encourages worthwhile independent production; which allows the larger regional ITV companies to show us what their programme-makers can do. We want a fourth channel that will neither simply compete with ITV1 nor merely be complementary to it. We want a fourth channel that everyone will watch

some of the time and no one all the time. We want a fourth
channel that will, somehow, be different.

This went down well enough.

Others had also sketched a map of the possible future. In a lecture in June, 'The IBA and Channel Four', the Director General of
the Authority, Brian Young, had set out his thoughtful and appealing wish-list: greater depth in current affairs, arts, sciences,
Europe, experiment and innovation, more of the purely visual; all
featured. 'Our job', he emphasised, 'is to make things possible;
theirs – the producers – to create . . . We must provide the arena in
which many ideas can be tried without having to succeed at once
or appeal constantly to the majority.' This was a fair wind for the
creator indeed; a far cry from regulator-speak. I can scarcely recall
a time when I was not arguing with the IBA's officers about something or other; their contribution to setting up the fourth channel
was exemplary.

How different could the fourth channel be? At Edinburgh, I
said 'different, but not that different'. This remark was derided
there, principally by a film-maker and master of film theory, Peter
Wollen. It came back to haunt me later, at the real job application.
But those five words encapsulated a simple truth. Some radical
spirits hoped for a channel free as the air, on which no restraints
were placed, no prohibitions imposed. But it could never be as
simple as that. The fourth channel would operate under the same
laws, enjoining political impartiality and forbidding material
likely to give offence – whether to all or to anyone was never
specified – as did ITV. It would be ruled by the same regulator, the
IBA, which would bear legal responsibility for what was shown
on screen. It was ridiculous, therefore, to suppose that the new
channel would enjoy the total freedom to utter that Tony Smith's
alternative model, now set aside, was intended to offer. I thought
programme-makers should be under no illusions.

Then again, though this was never writ on tablets, it was the government's plan that ITV, mulched to fund the channel, would recoup the cost from advertisements they sold. The fourth channel would have to pay its way. Licence to fail there might be; there would be no licence to go bust.

The speech that mattered came in Cambridge in September, at the biennial Convention of the Royal Television Society. The Home Secretary, William Whitelaw, began: 'I start from the position that what we are looking for is a fourth channel offering a distinctive service of its own,' and went on: 'There must be programmes appealing to and, we hope, stimulating tastes and interests not adequately provided for on the existing channels.' The extended news the new channel would carry, he stated, 'was clearly a job for ITN'. In a passage of critical importance, the Home Secretary laid down that programmes were to come not just from ITV's network companies and the larger regional companies, but from independent producers; indeed, these should supply 'the largest practicable proportion of programmes'. At Edinburgh, I had argued the independents should make only a modest starting contribution. Whitelaw batted that one aside, and a good thing too. When the Home Secretary sat down, to quote the official history, a buzz ran round the hall: it was clear now to this professional audience 'that the Channel Four Group independent production lobby had won and ITV had lost'.

The Act that would reach the statute book the following year, after further discussion, and much more lobbying, spelled out what was expected. The fourth channel was to 'encourage innovation and experiment', cater for 'interests not served by ITV, provide a distinctive service'. Obligations were laid down to educate, and to carry news; religion, too, was included. Otherwise it would be up to those who ran it to determine what was seen on screen. At Edinburgh I had said, 'If the channel is to have a different flavour, it needs a different chef!' At Cambridge, after Whitelaw's speech, the IBA's Colin Shaw, affirming the need for a single controller, admitted that 'this might be a recipe for megalomania on a scale unparalleled since Diaghilev or Randolph Hearst'. Why not? I thought; but in fact no more responsibility was involved than in editing a newspaper, or having charge of BBC2. It could be done. The IBA, advertising for the team to run the channel, got it, from my point of view, absolutely right; the top job, Chief Executive, would carry responsibility for programmes. Edmund Dell, a former Labour Cabinet minister turned merchant banker, was appointed Chairman, the film-maker Richard Attenborough his deputy.

After a hint or two from the IBA to get on with it, I wrote a short letter of application setting out my priorities. These were:

to encourage innovation across the whole range of pro-
    grammes;
to find audiences for the channel and for all its programmes;
to make programmes of special appeal to particular audiences;
to develop the channel's educational potential to the full;
to provide platforms for the widest possible range of opinion in
    utterance, discussion and debate;
to maintain as flexible a schedule as practicable to enable a
    quick response to changing needs;
to make an opening in the channel for criticism of its own
    output;
to accord a high priority to the arts;
if funds allow, to make, or help make, films of feature length for
    television here, for the cinema abroad.

A chief rival, I gathered later, was John Birt. (Another was Paul Bonner, whom I had encouraged to apply.) Birt submitted fifty pages, including a year's schedule in advance, listing the minorities to be catered for, their numbers backed by the circulation figures of special-interest magazines – canary-fancying, stamp-collecting, model trains, etc. Some board members were aghast at this, though Brian Tesler of LWT defended Birt and the Chairman,

Edmund Dell, impressed himself and lobbied by LWT's Chairman John Freeman, was for choosing him. The risk-averse Tesler, interviewed years later by Paul Bonner for the official history, had patronising doubts as to whether I 'had grown up enough', citing my handing material on Northern Ireland the IBA had stopped to the BBC, which was willing to transmit it. This, he told Bonner, had caused 'a stink'. In fact, there was at least one good precedent for handing on arbitrarily banned material; and in any case, what really caused the stink was the IBA's absurd diktat, over-ruling its own officers' advice. Deference to authority at all times is, *pace* Tesler, no posture for an editor of anything.

Dell didn't want me as Chief Executive. He thought that my Edinburgh speech had been on the timid side and, at interview, found me 'laid back', as if I had already got the job. That was far from my feeling as, one of three, I was summoned to be interviewed a second time. Tamara drove me to Brompton Road, and then to lunch at a pub on the river. Home again, the telephone rang; Edmund Dell offered his congratulations and asked me to see him. A majority of board members – Edmund told me it was unanimous; it was not quite – had held out against his objection. Dell offered me the IBA approved rate, in line with their own salary structure, of £30,000 a year; I asked for and was given £35,000. The job of a lifetime was mine.

The Act was not yet law; the board were still mere consultants; I had other tasks, *Ireland* and *A Sense of Freedom*, to complete. But I started straight away. The board wished me to consider having Paul Bonner as a close colleague. We talked. I was very glad indeed to have him as Channel Controller – not Programme Controller – and said so at once. Edmund Dell, for some reason, later persisted in saying that I resented Paul's joining me. No one who observed our working together could ever have believed that. Paul's post was not advertised; we would not have got on air without him. I at once recruited three senior commissioning editors to begin the process of finding programmes for a start that was only two years away.

Fiction went to David Rose, the BBC's Head of Regional Drama, based in Birmingham, whose track record with the Corporation spoke for itself: *Z-Cars*, *Softly Softly*, Peter Terson's *The Fishing Party*, David Rudkin's *Penda's Fen*, David Hare's *Licking Hitler* were the measure of the man. His production of Malcolm Bradbury's *The History Man* was on our screens at the time. David Rose shared my view we should make films and, as a bonus, fulfilling the need to attract a regular audience, he brought me Phil Redmond's *Brookside*.

Factual programming, in a moment of inspiration, I entrusted to Liz Forgan, the *Guardian*'s women's editor. She had never worked in television, which in this case was just what I wanted: a woman's clear mind taking a fresh view. At Edinburgh I had talked of 'programmes made by women for women, that men would want to watch'. What did I mean by this? she wondered, and came to interview me for the *Guardian*; it was the first time we'd met. I said I had one question to put to her after the interview. It was: Will you take charge of our news and current affairs? She was astonished, but resilient enough, two days later, to say she would. Neither of us ever regretted it.

Education programmes would be a major responsibility; the IBA wanted them to form fifteen per cent of our output. Here we needed a strong leader expert in the politics of education. Naomi Sargant (wife of my Oxford friend Andrew McIntosh), a market researcher, then pro-Vice Chancellor of the Open University, was my choice. She did a terrific job.

The board, the Chairman particularly, were furious with me for acting off my own bat. Having themselves suggested Paul Bonner to me, however, they were in no position to insist on advertising as a condition of recruitment. Other key posts were soon filled. Ellis Griffiths, whom I knew from Thames, was chief engineer – he would install a fully computerised transmission system; Pam Masters, from BBC Presentation, would head up ours. Paul Bonner identified both these stars. The IBA had invited applications for a Finance Controller to work next to, but under, the Chief Executive. Our search stuttered. Eventually we heard that Justin Dukes, an executive at the *FT*, might be interested in coming to a new TV channel – not as financial controller, though; Justin wanted to be Managing Director, in sole charge of the channel's business affairs. This suited. When we met, drinking Pearson's Château Latour at his Islington house, I thought his view of the two roles, on the newspaper analogy, with the editor in sole charge of the paper, exactly right. He found able executives to fill financial, legal, personnel and audience research posts: David Scott, Colin Leventhal, Frank McGettigan, Sue Stoessl. All fitted admirably.

Who would choose the programmes we would broadcast? Well, I would, for a start, and for glorious months before anyone else was around to share the burden I said yea and nay to what I fancied, driven on by the need to fill the ominously blank screen. A television adaptation of the RSC's *Nicholas Nickleby* was commission number 0003 – expensive, but worth every penny. Later, a programme finance committee was put in place to agree cost, stipulate terms, negotiate rights.

Paul Bonner and I needed to bring a programme department into being. Our intention was not to replicate the hierarchical structures of BBC and ITV. A programme-maker I much respected, Norman Swallow, told me once that, as a supposedly key executive in BBC Music and Arts, he had two people above him between him and the channel controller, and two below, between him and the programme-maker. At Channel Four there should be no one, I thought, between the man or woman with an idea for a programme and the executive who gave the commission. This produced a 'flat' management structure, which later raised critical eyebrows. But it was essential to realising the difference we were aiming at; responsive minds, not a committee, would decide what we would show. We advertised for commissioning editors –

Channel 4

Commissioning Editors

Channel 4 is looking for people to help find programmes for the new television service which goes on air in autumn 1982.

Television production experience may be an advantage but is not essential. What is essential is that Channel 4's Commissioning Editors should share a willingness to experiment and a concern to broaden the range of British Television.

You may work in broadcasting, education, journalism, the theatre, modern dance, rock, politics, philosophy, religion. If you think you know a good idea when you see one and could help others realise it on the television screen, write now to Jeremy Isaacs, Chief Executive, Channel 4, IBA, 70 Brompton Road, London SW3.

– and got six thousand replies, and Paul Bonner and I read them.

The key words were 'spot a good idea and help others realize it'. We did not advertise for executive producers who knew what programmes *they* wanted made, and would bid others make them. We invited others to submit suggestions for programmes to us. These colleagues we now recruited would sift, and respond. The core of Tony Smith's publishing proposal is present here. It was to be an absolute rule of the channel's conduct that it did not make its own programmes – the sole exception being *Right to Reply*. And, since I valued programme-makers' own inventiveness, it followed that it would be these others, outside the channel, who would have the ideas, make proposals to us, and seek our backing for them. This was of the essence of what we would set out to do.

The editors we hired were a varied assortment of men and women; not all had worked in television. They had minds of their own, and were not slow to let me know it. They had differing attitudes to their work; some did seek more than others to influence the final shape and texture of what we put on screen. As the ideas poured in it was they, reporting only to me – and, later, to Paul also – who chose, within their budgets, what we would do. They were not to specify to a supplier every detail of what was required, as does M&S or Tesco. What we sought was diversity, and originality. Paul Bonner would construct the schedule.

On 2 November 1982 we went on air. I had agreed to let our Welsh counterpart, Sianel Pedwar Cymru or S4C – whom I wished good luck in Welsh – go first, the evening before. Our opening day's programmes were:

4.45 p.m.	*Countdown*
5.15 p.m.	*Preview Four*
5.30 p.m.	*The Body Show*
6.00 p.m.	*People's Court*
6.30 p.m.	*Book Four*
7.00 p.m.	*Channel Four News*
7.50 p.m.	*Channel Four Comment*
8.00 p.m.	*Brookside*
8.30 p.m.	*The Paul Hogan Show*
9.00 p.m.	*Film on Four – Walter*
10.15 p.m.	*The Comic Strip Presents . . . Five Go Mad in Dorset*
10.45 p.m.	*The Raving Beauties in the Pink*
11.50 p.m.	Closedown

I had convinced myself that to start mid-evening, in high peak, with any one programme, risked identifying the channel's whole point and purpose with that single statement. Since we aimed at plurality of purposes, and would contain multitudes, that would mislead. So I settled instead for an afternoon and an evening's output. *Countdown*, an adaptation of *Des Lettres et des chiffres*, whose appeal in France I had noted in *Le Monde*, and which had had an English trial run on Yorkshire Television, is a participatory game to which viewers play along. It caught on at once, and – bloody hell – is still with us. Its genial presenter Richard Whiteley, the first face on our screen, held his place there for twenty-two years, without interruption, until his death in 2005. He will be missed; *Countdown* continues. *The Body Show* invited viewers to work out together. *People's Court*, an American buy-in, was involving also, I hoped: you guessed the verdict in a small claims court. *Book Four*, a rare regular book programme on British television, was presented by the critic and academic Hermione Lee. *Channel Four News*, at an hour twice as long as ITV's *News at Ten*, came after it. *Comment* and *Brookside* made hesitant starts; after teething troubles, each survived, grew healthily, stayed the course. The Australian comic Paul Hogan, took us up to the nine o'clock watershed.

At 9 p.m. came the real shock of the new. *Walter*, marvellously directed by Stephen Frears from David Cook's script, featured powerful performances by Ian McKellen as a mentally handicapped man struggling to read, write and hold down a mundane job in an unfriendly world, and by Barbara Jefford as his mother. When his mother dies, Walter is committed to a mental hospital; in the final scene, we watched him lose his cherished flock of pigeons. It is strong, compassionate, overwhelming; millions were touched by it. Industry professionals thought *Walter* too gloomy for an opening night; I was sure it was right for us. It should have been the first thing viewers saw.

After it, and after tussles with Enid Blyton's estate, came *The Comic Strip Presents . . . Five Go Mad in Dorset*, a fresh, irreverent, uproarious take-off of a national childhood favourite: the new alternative comedy getting it right in one. To close, we put on one of the best things we ever did, a television version of a revue 'celebrating women's lives', *The Raving Beauties in the Pink*. Devised and performed by three actresses, Anna Carteret, Sue Jones Davies – from Dinas in Pembrokeshire – and Fanny Viner, this was a feast of poetry and song. It remains unique, dammit.

We had started with a mix, not a homogenised blend; everything was different. Our advertising agency, BMP, finding it as hard as we did to find one label for the whole, took space to present a visual jigsaw of a range of programmes. Variety was to be the name of the game – and, for as long as we could manage it, surprise.

The following evening, Jack Rosenthal's *P'Tang Yang Kipperbang*, 'a comedy (with a dash of bitters) about a first kiss', followed *Walter* to the screen – one of twenty *Films on Four* in our first year, and one of six 'First Love' films I bought, at Wheelers in Soho, from David Puttnam. It was directed by Michael Apted. Lovely.

The next evening, Thursday, we put on *The Animals Film*, as unlovely as you can get: a tirade of visually explicit polemic against man's exploitation of animals on a mega-industrial scale. The fanatically committed film-maker Victor Schonfeld fought off libel lawyers, and fought us as we fought the IBA, to get this opinionated monster, almost in its entirety – we, and the IBA, jibbed at incitement to violence – on the air. Preferring not to sit at home and watch it go out, I ensured it was placed against our opening party at Riverside, Hammersmith; thousands came to that, independent producers happiest among them.

On Friday evening, still in the office, I had the blissful shock of watching two programmes' first editions, unseen by me before, which separately bowled me over. *The Tube*, for young music-lovers – when the young were seen as only one of the channel's diverse audiences – was a fluid, riotous, rock-and-roll, in-your-face performance event, the cameras apparently as hepped up as the performers, and the heaving studio of fans. It came from Newcastle; Tyne Tees Television never did better.

The Friday Alternative, which once a week was to divide the news hour with ITN, was supposed to find novel ways of presenting a different take on the news. That it did. Made by David Graham's Diverse Productions, which sent me one of the very few truly original proposals made to the channel, it used graphics, principally, and no presenters, to call our attention to what varying interest groups thought mattered. At first sight, and at second sight too, the style was stronger than the content. Jazzy, colourful, visually brashly compelling, it was making a point all right, and an important one: the news is not the news in any absolute sense; the news is what you make it. Unfortunately, there was less to *The Friday Alternative* than met the eye; you could admire the way they said it, but it was hard to take seriously what was said. *The Friday Alternative* would end in tears. To find out what was going on, Channel Four News itself was always the one to watch. But my week was made.

And my weekend was in the making. On the Saturday evening the Metropolitan Opera, New York, was sending over by satellite Mozart's *Idomeneo*, with Luciano Pavarotti. Leo Kirch had sold me UK rights to four operas a year. We would record *Idomeneo*; Gillian Widdicombe, then a freelance – this was our first meeting – would subtitle overnight; the opera would be broadcast on Sunday afternoon. On the Saturday evening I picked my way across the bare planked floor towards a makeshift editing area. The sound I heard was not Pavarotti, but the commentary on an American football game; someone at White Plains, New York, had touched the wrong switch. They had to send us Act One again. The opera went out live in Germany and Austria; there, viewers rang in to ask the final score.

Willie Whitelaw had lunched with us in Charlotte Street earlier that autumn, on his way to the Tory party conference; 'Castrate the muggers', he told us, was what he feared they'd be shouting at him that year. On our first day on air, he sent round a note wishing me success. On the first Saturday night of our existence, after a busy day outdoors in his Westmorland constituency, he excused himself from the dinner table and went to the television set to see how his creation was getting on. His wife found him there, twenty minutes later, peacefully asleep. This benign tolerance, the attitude all politicians should ideally take to broadcasting, was to be tested in the weeks and months ahead. He remained a bulwark and a lasting supporter.

In the first few weeks – during which disfiguring gaps appeared on our screen, the result of a dispute over commercials between Actors' Equity and advertisers – the press had a field day with us, mocking a media newcomer, as they always do, simply for being there. We were a prime target, though only until

TV-AM came along to distract them from us. The *Sun* led the chase: 'Channel Bore', 'Channel Snore', 'Channel Four-Letter Word' and, persistently, 'The Channel That Nobody Watches'. The *Sun* failed to understand that even zero ratings meant 200,000 viewers – no negligible total; ask, say, the *Independent*. They did not realise that millions watched *Cheers, Brookside, The Tube, American Football, Film Four*. I wrote to the editor, Kelvin MacKenzie, pointing out that he was telling *Sun* readers what they knew were lies. He stopped.

The *Daily Mail*, speaking, it implied, for middle England, launched repeated mean-spirited onslaughts; it disapproved of programmes gays might like, or Northern Ireland republicans, to take two one-off examples. As soon as they had wind of something such in the schedule – they were sent details every week – they would claim to detect a storm of protest breaking over our heads; Storm Over 4, the headlines ran. A rent-a-quote MP, prompted by the *Mail*, would denounce the channel, call for it to close down and demand that I be sacked. One morning in Chiswick, as I was leaving for work, a *Mail* reporter turned up with the paper's front page calling for my sacking, and asked if I would resign. 'No.' He then asked for a lift into town; 'no' again. 'Storm Over . . .', I decided, was when a newspaper reporter told a Member of Parliament something he didn't know, and the MP called for the banning of something he hadn't seen. I have not succeeded in getting this definition into the dictionary.

17

DISTINCTIVELY DIFFERENT

An extract from Channel Four's duty log:

22.15 Pina Bausch: *Bluebeard's Castle*. Gentleman rang to say
that he can't understand why such an inane programme is
being shown and furthermore why he has been watching it for
the past two hours.

What was the Channel Four I helped shape, and launched in
November 1982, actually trying to do? Our purpose was to extend
viewers' choice. Both ITV and BBC, even a BBC with two channels, saw viewers as one audience; their idea was to attract them
early in the evening and hold them till they went to bed. BBC1
might cross-promote BBC2, sending some viewers across at a
common junction. But the notion of a variety of audiences was
still strange to them. The audience, they thought, was a family
audience, comprising several generations; children watched with
their parents. Viewers were passive, regular in their habits, knew
what they wanted, expected more of the same. This unrealistic
stereotype of British society was ripe for challenge; TV viewers,

the public we would serve, were ready for change. For one thing, a fifth of the public were not part of a family audience at all; they had left home, lived alone, viewed alone, might discuss a programme with workmates or friends next day, but consulted no one on what to watch. If Channel Four was aimed at anyone, it was aimed at them. To attract them to tune in to us, our offering would have to be recognisably, and enticingly, different.

Television, I thought, rarely allowed itself ample space to discuss or report complex issues. ITN's main news bulletin, in the early days, when it was showing BBC news a clean pair of heels, ran for eleven and a half minutes. *News at Ten* wrought a transformation; it ran twice as long. Yet even so, I never thought news programmes had space to convey what needed to be conveyed. Their audiences needed to understand economic and social issues, foreign affairs – Cold War confrontation, European integration – and the complexities of Northern Ireland, to say nothing of the arts, science, finance and industry. Television news had too narrow an agenda, was too incident-based. I wanted Channel Four's news to have a different agenda, and to last an hour. A new television channel should offer a new sort of news programme.

Panjandrums at the BBC, conscious perhaps that this was an opportunity BBC2 had missed, were scornfully dismissive; it will never work, they scoffed, and certainly not at 7 p.m., our rumoured start time. ITN said little; there was every chance the opportunity to make it would come to them. That was what the Home Secretary, whom they lobbied, expected, and what the IBA intended. On the Channel Four board, some were not so sure; would ITN deliver what we wanted? One board member, Anthony Smith, was sceptical as to whether we should have news at all. But we were going to have nightly news; a tendering process was put in hand. Liz Forgan was in charge. She told ITN what she was after:

> We wanted an hour-long news programme, a third of the pro-
> gramme to be foreign affairs, a specialist economics
> correspondent, no sport, no stories about the Royal Family, no
> crime, and no pictures of black limousines drawing up outside
> unidentifiable buildings and driving away again. There was a
> sharp intake of breath and then a very senior member of the
> Board said to me, 'Well my dear,' – which was a mistake on his
> part – 'you haven't been in television very long and there's one
> thing you have to understand: the news is the news is the news!'
> I said that if there was one single phrase that most sums up what
> I did not want to do with Channel 4 News, it was that.*

Liz and I suggested to ITN they engage as editor David Watt, a superb journalist and commentator on politics, who might well have edited a national paper. ITN, who in any case resented our interference in attempting to impose an appointment, reckoned he might not be up to the rough and tumble of daily news produc-tion, and proposed to us – we had the right to be consulted – another print journalist, Derrick Mercer. There was broad agree-ment on an extended news agenda, including the arts and sciences – a specialist reporter was to be assigned to each – and a calmer, less breathless approach.

Peter Sissons fronted the programme; able broadsheet

---

* Interviewed by Peter Catterall for *The Making of Channel 4*.

journalists – Elinor Goodman, Godfrey Hodgson, Sarah Hogg – combined an editorial function with reporting on screen. There was much talk of 'news analysis', but little came of it. No one, except John Birt, knew what it meant, but he did know, and his proposal that LWT should supply our news ran ITN close. Liz Forgan again:

Barry Cox and John Birt pitched their vision of his hour-long news to me, and they prepared it immaculately. They described what in many ways would have been the apotheosis of John's vision of broadcasting, but it wasn't mine. It was a long, theoretical and analytical current affairs programme, and I wanted a news programme with brains, I didn't want a lecture with pictures.

It was clear, as we got to air, that since any item on *Channel Four News* could run three times as long as it might do elsewhere, it was possible to convey detail, test statements, prolong discussion. This was good news for Whitehall's press officers. After a difficult first year, the programme got into its stride under a new editor, ITN's Stewart Purvis; our vision was to a large extent fulfilled. Purvis and Forgan deserve the credit. At a lunch to meet Purvis, Channel Four's Chairman Edmund Dell stressed at length the importance of the IMF, Third World debt and other large matters. The Deputy Chairman, Dickie Attenborough, seized Purvis's arm and said, 'Darling, you will remember we are all in showbusiness, won't you?'

Channel Four News, always best in an hour's slot, works well still. I hope it stays that way; for me, it justifies the channel. In Jon Snow, the programme boasts a superb presenter, in another league, I think, from his contemporaries, and not just for his neckwear. Once or twice, though, I have asked myself if we are getting an indication of where his own opinions lie. He is an excellent interviewer, and a reporter too. It will be a pity if he seeks, or is allowed, freedom to editorialise. An attitude permissible in another sort of factual programme will not do in news.

A separate innovation I was bent on, however, was precisely the introduction of unmediated opinion, expressed straight to camera. Newspapers carried both pages of reportage and opinion columns; why should not television also? Plainly, an editorial line of our own was not desirable; the channel had a duty to impartiality. But we should carry, I thought, a spectrum of opinion, not our own. To make the distinction, I wanted ITN's *Channel Four News* to include an item of opinion, nightly, from an extraneous source. ITN was insistent that this should fall outside, not within, the bounds of the news programme. This point prevailed. Organising a nightly *Comment*, immediately after the news, was entrusted to Fiona Maddocks, whom Liz Forgan hired.

I explained to Fiona what I expected: the articulate expression each evening of widely varying points of view on current issues. 'No doubt,' I suggested, 'after a few weeks you will have come across half a dozen or a dozen contributors you can work with, and will simply rotate them.' Fiona preferred to do it the hard way, choosing to find, produce, promote a different novice contributor every single evening. This was a vast labour on her part, and the result a huge success. We had our ears bent rather a lot by zealots, not always on the issue of the day; but *Comment*, under Fiona Maddocks, brought two hundred separate voices to the screen each year – the single most remarkable exercise in pluralism we undertook.

Opinions, another kettle of fish stew, comprised half an hour of eloquent argument addressed to us directly by people with something to say. This notion came to me when the BBC, which once a year invited a figure of stature to deliver the Reith Lectures on radio, and once a year another such to give the Richard Dimbleby Lecture on television, invited the Marxist historian E. P. Thompson to give the Dimbleby Lecture, and then changed its mind and dropped him. Thompson intended to speak in condemnation of the 'military–industrial establishment' and its influence, he thought deleterious, in the world. The BBC Director

General, Ian Trethowan, furiously cancelled his colleagues' invitation, though several well-respected executives were party to it. In doing so, he was saying – what, precisely? These opinions are not to be broadcast? Or these opinions must not be taken to be the view of the BBC? It was the former; Trethowan actively sought the dismissal of the producer Edward Mirzoeff who, after consulting widely – including with Isaiah Berlin – had booked Thompson. It took all Bill Cotton's diplomatic skill to keep Eddie Mirzoeff, a superb documentary-maker, and later the BBC's liaison man with Buckingham Palace, in employment. Trethowan was sure he had detected a Marxist plot.

It was just this broadcasters' refusal to admit pluralism within the whole that I thought fundamentally undemocratic. Charles de Gaulle said famously of Jean-Paul Sartre: *'Il est aussi de la France'*. I wrote to *The Times* to say that when Channel Four came on air, we would be happy to give Thompson a platform. He made good use of it. Other formidable controversialists followed; Paul Johnson on the market economy; Salman Rushdie on racism, British racism; and, in less tendentious vein, Ved Mehta on his blindness and Jeffrey Bernard on life observed through a glass, or several, at the bar of the Coach and Horses. Good talks make good television.

E. P. Thompson's appearance brought rejoicing on the left: 'We never expected to live to see this day.' From such, Paul Johnson brought the opposite response: 'What is he doing on our channel?' It wasn't their channel, I had to tell them; it belonged, and belongs, to us all. I could wish Channel Four still found room for explosive, extensive think-pieces; I may have caught a glimpse of one the other day.

The Broadcasting Act 1980, which brought Channel Four into being, stipulated that 'a suitable proportion of the programmes' must be 'of an educational nature'. The Authority decided to require the channel 'to devote about fifteen percent of its broadcasting time – about an hour a day – to educational material'.

Naomi Sargant was clear that there was a growing need for education that was un-academic in mode, programmes that enabled people to master skills in living and self development. She wanted to help people live more fulfilled lives. The topics she tackled ranged commensurately widely, through the arts and history, literacy and numeracy, the environment, health and family, science and technology, development education, women's studies, media studies, and more. And children's programming besides.

To qualify as educational, each programme series had to achieve 'validation' at the IBA. Naomi Sargant put forward, successfully, 400 hours of programming a year under this rubric. Carol Haslam was Editor, Documentary Series; some of these, too, properly backed up by written material, had evident educational character and worth. Much of it was worth watching, the best lit up the screen. Tom Keating, a skilled faker of great artists' work, now 'going straight', caused mild controversy in *Tom Keating on Painters*; Jancis Robinson came to TV for the first time with *The Wine Programme*; *Take Six Cooks* made our mouths water; *Gardeners' Calendar* held its place; *Plants for Free* gained an enormous audience. In the channel's early days, Norman Tebbit assailed me once for carrying programmes about gays and Northern Ireland rather than golf and yachting; instead of arguing, I should have pointed him to Naomi Sargant's pioneering work. In recent years Channel Four's and BBC2's schedules have groaned under acres of garden and kilos of cooks; the diet we offered was selective and varied, but it recognised that we were consumers and had leisure activities that mattered to us. For children, too, Naomi found alternatives to what was on offer elsewhere; *Everybody Here* celebrated Britain's multicultural society in story, song and rhyme, and with jokes and games; *Chips' Comic*, supposedly made by children and their dog Chips, was aimed specifically at children who were mentally handicapped. Their families, surprised, were grateful.

A memorable single programme was purchased from an

American independent: *Quilts in Women's Lives*. The popular press was scathing. 'Quilts', 'women's lives' – 'why should they matter?' Getting under the skin of the *Daily Mail* is a duty for any broadcaster, but on this the fray was joined by Chris Dunkley, following T. C. Worsley at the *Financial Times*. Dunkley had a total blind spot for programmes he thought targeted minorities, and detected in this 'feminist fascism':

> If you wanted to create the prototypical Channel Four pro-gramme, what would be the requirements? First of all it would have to be made exclusively by women of a certain sort (you know the sort) and second it would have to be about women and would, of course, exclude men. Next it would have to be about a subject of such minor interest that no normal viewer would ever even have noticed this particular minority before, and above all, it would have to involve that sort of religious obsession which brings a crazed gleam to the eyes of its disciples.

This in January 1983; later, at the year's end, he conceded: 'Its saving grace was that in the event it was also quite interesting.' To be provoking, and also quite interesting, is just what the channel was supposed to do.

David Puttnam, in his gallant campaigns to restore life to the British film industry, used always to insist: 'What matters is to get film running through the camera.' Channel Four would make films.

If too much conventional television drama and comedy was hidebound, bricks and mortar played their role. The ITV com-panies had studios, electronic production houses staffed to the gills; expensive overhead which must be kept in use. The BBC, too, was a major in-house production centre, the biggest there was. But Channel Four possessed and would possess no stu-dios, except a tiny one for *Right to Reply*. On Tony Smith's excellent model we would make, with that one exception, none of our own programmes. With one bound, Jack was free! Most of our drama – but we'd call it fiction – would be made not on tape within four walls but, low-budget, out and about on location, on film.

Very soon after I was appointed, I received a delegation of film-makers; led by Simon Relph, it included Richard Eyre, David Hare, Stephen Frears and Ann Scott. They pressed the case not just for film, but for feature film. Films for television were a known entity, both on BBC and, more rarely, on ITV. My visitors wanted something more: that television should fund films for cinema exhibition, in the first instance, which would only later revert to the smaller screen; this was what happened in France, in Germany, in Italy. I was sympathetic, but there were formidable obstacles in the way. The distribution and exhibition elements of the British film industry, terrified at first, and then aghast at the effect of television viewing on cinema attendances, fought to keep new films off the television screen for as long as they possibly could. Their rule was categoric: any film shown in British cinemas could not be seen on TV until three years after its cinema release. Channel Four could not possibly afford to wait three years before that value was returned to it on screen.

The hero of the battle that ensued was Justin Dukes. Justin argued successfully to the Cinema Exhibitors' Association that the three-year embargo should be reduced to one year and, in certain circumstances – a euphemism for doing no business at the box office – to less than that. We were talking not of Bond movies, after all, or *The Sound of Music*, but of films we funded ourselves. That surely gave us a right to decide what to do with them. It was quite wrong for the CEA to play dog-in-the-manger. In the end, common sense prevailed; television would wait for *A Room with a View*, or *My Beautiful Laundrette*, or *Four Weddings and a Funeral*. Much else we made that was seen in cinemas might, fairly promptly thereafter, be available to C4.

David Rose split his fiction budget three ways. There would be a soap opera, Phil Redmond's *Brookside*. Saltier then than other soaps, aimed at a younger audience, *Brookside* would be made in Liverpool where, overshadowed in Granadaland by Manchester, there had been no scope for scousers who wanted to work in TV in their home city. In Redmond's London base, I met one technician working in Dubai; if *Brookside* was commissioned, he could come home. Years later, visiting Liverpool to assess its potential as Europe's Capital of Culture in 2008, I met him again; he thrust into my hand a letter thanking me for changing his life. At first *Brookside* had a bumpy ride; the sound recording in early episodes was poor, and some language that was heard was unacceptable at 8 p.m., let alone for the Sunday afternoon repeat. The IBA Director General, John Whitney, repeatedly urged me to kill the show, not grasping that that was impossible financially. It was partly my fault the language was salty; I had told Redmond, when he asked, that I was prepared to tolerate linguistic rudeness, in the right context. The IBA was not. We adjusted. Ricky Tomlinson and, above all, Sue Johnston, gave great performances. *Brookside* lasted twenty years.

There would be series, too. We showed G. F. Newman's *The Nation's Health*, a fierce onslaught on a stressed National Health Service, from Thames, and bought adaptations of Nadine Gordimer's South African short stories. We couldn't afford to make major drama series, but occasionally, looking for something that would bunk ratings up a bit, we put our toe in the water. We bought into *The Far Pavilions*, a glossy-looking, romantic mini-series set in India. It took off, and for three successive nights we hit over 3 million viewers. This came as no surprise to others, but as a mild shock to me, who hoped we could reach a satisfactory level of audience – a 10 per cent share, I had said – without resorting to too much pap. A bigger shock awaited me. Barbara Taylor Bradford's gutsy tale of feminine ambition, *A Woman of Substance*, took the nation by storm, reaching 7 million viewers an episode. Much more like this, and we'd be in serious default on the obligation to provide 'a distinctive service'; *Woman of Substance* was right up ITV's street. We could, and did, do better. I thought *A Very British Coup* should be a three-parter with cliff-hangers, rather than a one-off. It did well.

But the heart of our fiction would be *Film on Four*. David Rose, assisted by a script editor, Walter Donohue, and by Karin Bamborough, set aside £6 million from his tight budget and set out, in our first year, to make twenty feature-length films at £300,000 each. Some of these had modest top-ups from other sources of funding; none was expensive in film-making terms. Alan Parker's pocket cartoon had a goldfish in a bowl peering out at a camera peering in; 'It's either that Attenborough fellow, or Channel 4 is remaking *Jaws*'. *Film on Four* gave a breath of life to British film. *Walter* on our first night and *P'Tang Yang Kipperbang* on our second each got 3 million viewers. Twenty were broadcast in our first fourteen months, 136 between 1982 and 1991,* each one different from anything else. *Film on Four* encouraged writers as well as directors; it was the antithesis of television fiction off an industrial production line, pre-tested in market research.

Each *Film on Four* was born in an idea, put to us by its creator, and by one man's judgement of it. It was David Rose's proposal alone that went to the programme finance committee, within agreed budgetary limits, for ratification. We trusted David's judgement. It was exhilarating to work with him. Together, we staggered into the Intrepid Fox in Wardour Street after screening Neil Jordan's *Angel*, clearly the work of a major film-maker. Together, we saw Terence Davies's half-completed *Distant Voices*; he had run out of money. It took only a moment, a look and a nod, for us to agree to enable him to finish the job by funding *Still Lives*. David Rose gave me a night to read Hanif Kureishi's screenplay for *My Beautiful Laundrette*; he thought there might be

---

*They are listed and described in *Film on Four* by John Pym, a survey for the BFI, which gives cast and crew; viewing figures; budgets; and C4's financial contribution to each.

concerns; Stephen Frears was waiting. I gave an immediate green light. We both wanted to get Bill Douglas's *Comrades* made, a wonderful account of the Tolpuddle Martyrs in England and Australia, and somehow also of the birth of movie-making. Alex Norton played the Lanternist. David and I both wanted it shorter. Bill was adamant against. It remained long, but powerful with it. Karin Bamborough went to Liverpool to see some film-makers in a pickle, and returned advising we should fund *A Letter to Brezhnev*; we did.

My dear friend Maurice Hatton had made *Long Shot*, a picaresque tale of the impossibility of raising funds to make movies in Britain. It was Maurice who, on being offered a retrospective at the NFT, quipped that 'only in Britain could a film-maker expect to go from première to retrospective without distribution or exhibition intervening'. Bernardo Bertolucci told me he thought *Long Shot* a fine film. I said, 'Bernardo, you only watched twenty minutes of it.' He said, 'A good film is like a good pasta; one forkful, and you know.' Maurice Hatton made two *Films on Four*, *Nelly's Version*, with Eileen Atkins, and *American Roulette*, with Andy Garcia. We were 'enabling' others. This burst of energy, though it did not start a lasting renaissance, mattered in its own right; films that needed to be made got made.

Channel Four saw itself then as part of film culture. (The other day I felt the same thrill of involvement, vicariously, on C4's behalf, watching *The Motorcycle Diaries*). That culture was both British and cosmopolitan. It felt natural to make modest contributions to the budgets of Wim Wenders' *Paris, Texas*, Andrei Tarkovsky's *The Sacrifice*, Theo Angelopoulos's *Voyage to Cythera*. It was only part of our reward to see them on our screen; we supported the exhibition of foreign-language films in Britain by purchasing, say, Werner Herzog's *Fitzcarraldo*, and so enabling Romaine Hart to play it at The Screen on the Hill, or Andi Engel at The Lumière.

It seemed right also to support British animation; we broadcast

John Coates, and Diane Jackson's *The Snowman*, a Christmas favourite, and, also from a book by Raymond Briggs, a vision of nuclear doom, *When the Wind Blows*, with the voices of Peggy Ashcroft and John Mills. We helped animators like Bristol's Nick Park of Aardman, who made *Animated Conversations* for C4, and went on to make *Wallace & Gromit* for BBC, and the Brothers Quay, who made *Street of Crocodiles*. Paul Madden was commissioning editor for animation; nobody has that role today. In Scotland, Lesley Keen, for Naomi Sargant, paid tribute to Paul Klee in *Taking a Line for a Walk*. In Prague, I called in to see Jan Svankmayer at work; we helped commission his *Alice*. Film-making helps television escape the humdrum.

Could comedy on Channel Four be as distinctive? It could, as *The Comic Strip Presents* at once demonstrated. It is true I gave 'entertainment' a low priority in the early stages of planning the schedule; we didn't have enough funding to splash out, and I knew we could acquire entertainment programmes cheaply if I bought repeats. I enjoyed the acts at the Comedy Store in sleaziest Soho, but wondered at first if they would ever get on air, so relentless was the effing and blinding. So I went slow. Cecil Korer found us *Treasure Hunt*, genuinely innovative; in apparent real-time, we watched Anneka Rice climb in and out of helicopters as, on competitors' behalf, she followed clues cross-country, against the clock. In Hollywood, tagging along with the ITV film purchase group, Cecil found us *Cheers*, a Boston bar on which, on Friday nights, British viewers happily dropped in.

At Ascot early in 1983 a panicky programme conference demanded more 'entertainment' in the schedule. The income we received from ITV, 80 per cent of 16 per cent of its revenue, looked likely to grow; we could start to fund comedy without cuts elsewhere. The powerhouse of change was the commissioning editor for youth programmes, Mike Bolland. Mike had delivered *The Tube*, Keith Allen in *Whatever You Want*, and *The Comic Strip Presents*. Given charge of the comedy portfolio, he attracted talent like pollen attracts bees; much honey resulted. *Saturday Live*, and later *Friday Night Live*, presented by Ben Elton, were stand-out successes for stand-up comedy. *Who Dares Wins* you watched on the edge of your seat; it was too rude to go live, we had to pre-record. Today, the performers who made us laugh in the first few years of Channel Four are major stars. Other channels rushed to woo them. What BBC2 had done fifteen years before in new modes of comedy – *Monty Python, Not the Nine O'Clock News* – Channel Four achieved in the eighties, and distinctively so.

I took time, too, to commit to sport. I wasn't sure I had room, or funds. Rights in all major sports were locked up by BBC and ITV, and would be hard to prise away. But sport, which I love, is part of life, after all; I hired Adrian Metcalfe to supply it. We could not persuade the Test and County Cricket Control Board to sell us the one-day competitions; we couldn't tempt the New Zealand Rugby Football Union to let us have rights to NZTV's coverage of Lions tours down under. The BBC made menacing noises in both cases, and frightened the vendors off, though later the TCCCB came to regret it. I first knew the channel was succeeding when an Irish waiter thanked me for broadcasting the finals of the Gaelic Games, football and hurling, from Croke Park. The big new enthusiasms Adrian Metcalfe shared with me were American football and cycling. I had seen the Superbowl live by satellite at the Odeon Leicester Square; I enjoyed reports of the Tour de France. I thought the backgrounds of each – the pzazz, cheerleaders, marching bands, burgers, beer, popcorn in one; the landscapes of France flashing by in the other – would add glamour and a foreign flavour to the screen. Marvellously edited, they did just that; sport with a difference. The British Cycling Federation, grateful for coverage of the Tour, gave me the Percy Bidlake award. I went to Blackpool to receive their handsome pewter plaque; I didn't have the courage to tell them that I can't ride a bicycle.

And we tackled horse-racing in the UK. ITV dropped it; we picked it up. We didn't have to. The board was divided; we could have refused and let others sort out the mess that would have resulted. But for me this was an interest – the horsey interest – that we should cater for. Why not get cameras out and about in the afternoons? The countryside mattered too; Jack Charlton did a series on country sports that predictably rattled tender-hearted dovecotes. The Tory historian Robert Blake was on C4's board; he supported my case for taking over ITV's horse-racing. We did. We did not, however, tamely continue ITV's style of coverage. Adrian Metcalfe insisted on going out to tender, and as a result horse-racing on television got a lively new look.

Channel Four's distinctiveness owed much to material bought in, cheaply, from abroad. The full benefit of this I owed to the enlightened tolerance of the officers of the IBA. ITV was strictly limited in the proportion of imported material it was allowed to show; viewers were entitled, first and foremost, to home cooking. American imports were not allowed to dominate our screens. A strict quota, monitored and reported by each company each week, might be enlarged for some special reason, but only very occasionally.

Channel Four enjoyed a different regulatory regime; we broadcast material acquired abroad, including in the States, virtually without let or hindrance. We showed US series that we cared for – *Cheers, St Elsewhere, Hill Street Blues* – and would have leaped, as the channel has today, at *West Wing, The Sopranos* or even *Desperate Housewives*. We were well within a US quota. But we also showed independent films and programmes, in quantity and variety, from all over the world. However entertaining they were, since they came from foreign parts they were judged educational; so popular drama series in French (*Chateauvallon*), in German (*Schwarzwaldklinik*) and from Brazil (*Isaura Escrava* – *Isaura the Slavegirl*, a soap opera), made it to our screens. Someone claimed to have seen the slogan *Libera Isaura*, 'Free Isaura', on a wall in Kentish Town. David Rose found a series on a policeman against the Sicilian mafia, *La Piovra* – *The Octopus* – that was noticed. In feature films, the world, including the developing world, was our oyster. This was a truly distinguishing feature of Channel Four: not all our programmes were from the UK and the US; not all were in English.

We were bidden to cater to interests other channels neglected; they catered for the family audience, and would not risk offending them. My ITV colleagues at Programme Controllers on Monday morning would speak wistfully of Hollywood movies they'd enjoyed at the cinema on the Saturday before, which could not be shown on TV – *The Last Detail*, for example, or *Shampoo*. I thought there was an audience more tolerant of varied sexual mores and rude language, more prepared for challenge to received ideas, than was the average citizen, and that this audience too should be catered for. The big hits, bowdlerised, went still to BBC and ITV. But we bought feature films, certificated for cinema exhibition, that were not previously thought suitable for screening on television, and showed them. A great hoohah resulted, only partly deflected by the device of inviting a distinguished critic, David Robinson of *The Times*, to introduce each of them on air. The tabloid press was sure the heavens would fall. They did not. Nor did they later, when I marked problematic films with a red triangle which warned: do not allow your children to stay up for this one; if you are easily offended, do not watch yourself. When TV reveals that a film is pushing at the limits, viewing figures go up; some, misled into thinking that pornography is on offer, are disappointed when they find it is art instead. Certain films we showed had homosexual themes. For too long television was reluctant to portray the gay world. C4's *Queer as Folk* has moved us on, as have Alan Hollinghurst's novels, and Lee Hall's and Stephen Daldry's *Billy Elliott*.

We attached a high priority to the arts; we couldn't help but be distinctive in doing so, since no one else did. BBC2 had done once, but had fallen back, though Brian Wenham saluted our coming with a truly bold, imaginative programming coup. On successive Sunday evenings he ran, in ten parts, Wagner's *Der Ring der Nibelungen*, Patrice Chereau's Bayreuth production, an act at a time, the power-struggle soap to end all soaps. But this was a rare event. Art in performance is awkward for channel controllers to handle, coming as it does in odd lengths: nothing runs precisely fifty-nine minutes or, as ITV would prefer, fifty-two minutes, thirty seconds. So ITV, with *The South Bank Show* to boast of, or BBC with *Omnibus* and *Arena*, preferred the weekly magazine to unwieldy events that threaten to take over the evening. If 'weekly' means forty weeks a year rather than twenty, and if the magazine series were broadcast at more accessible hours, this might, just, be acceptable.

For Channel Four, Andy Park, commissioning editor for music, was a dab hand. His taste in music was catholic; his eye for talent keen. Andy brought us wonderful films about fine contemporary musicians I'd never heard of. He found a soap opera written for television by the streetwise John Ashley; a documentary on the record producer Phil Spector in which – unheard-of – contributors told truths; four films by Peter Greenaway on contemporary American composers; and a computerised invention, *Max Headroom*, a robotic character who promptly demanded, and was given, a series of his own. Andy also joined in buying, sorting, screening opera, in which we excelled.

We were guided and aided by Gillian Widdicombe, music critic and subtitler. Gillian had subtitled almost all the BBC's televised opera, live and recorded, for at least ten years. Now she advised us where to look. Gillian knew which of Jean-Pierre Ponnelle's films were most worth screening: Pavarotti in *Rigoletto*, Domingo in *Madama Butterfly*. Andy bought Philip Glass's *Satyagraha*, opera in Sanskrit. I insisted on Schoenberg's *Moses und Aaron*, filmed by Jean-Marie Straub, which a Welsh farmer praised as 'beautiful music, and theology too'. From English National Opera we pushed the boat out financially to secure Dame Janet Baker in Handel's *Julius Caesar* in John Copley's production; Nick Hytner's elegant, witty *Xerxes*; Jonathan Miller's mafioso *Rigoletto*. And Michael Kustow, our editor for the arts, procured, when BBC2 let it drop (though they had commissioned it) the TV première of Harrison Birtwistle's *Yan Tan Tethera*.

Michael Kustow was always one for the big idea; the world was his oyster. We had started high with *Nicholas Nickleby*. He followed that with Peter Hall's masked *Oresteia* from the National Theatre, and with Peter Brook's Hindu saga, *The Mahabharata*. This was, in its way, as bold as you can be in arts programming – made safe of course by Brook's genius; comparable as an 'event' only with Claude Lanzmann's account of the Holocaust, *Shoah*. Each marked the channel as exceptional. Neither would have been possible, had ratings been our principal objective.

We offered a cornucopia of pleasures in the arts, big and small. I think of the poet Tony Harrison's *V*, filmed by Richard Eyre; and of *A Sense of Place*, three fine films on Ulster poets, by a poet of film, David Hammond; and of the collaboration on Dante's *Inferno* between Peter Greenaway and Tom Phillips. High-toned stuff. We showed an opera a month on Sunday afternoons – never matched on British terrestrial television before or since; key to doing so was inexpensive purchase from the marketplaces of the world. Viewers in Penzance and Colwyn Bay, Ballymena and Wick, got to see and hear glories they might never otherwise have encountered.

The world of broadcasting is mapped by acronyms; at the BFI I encountered the IFA, the Independent Film-makers' Association. Denis Forman suggested to me, on my leaving Thames, that I become a Governor of the British Film Institute; the invitation turned out to include being Chairman of the BFI Production Board. This body spent a modest sum annually, £150,000 perhaps, on funding film-makers who worked outside commercial restraints. We administered what had been called the Experimental Film Fund. The money went on inventive, modest, almost invisible projects. I was asked to make the output a little more mainstream, if I could. I became aware of work and of film-makers completely new to me; some were abstractionists, others were into community-based agit-prop. They were not only out-side the system, they never wanted in. They all saw film not just as the art of the twentieth century, but as the hope of the future. They admired revolutionaries like Dziga Vertov, and worshipped Jean-Luc Godard. Some made good films.

Their cause was represented by the IFA. The IFA particularly concerned itself with film-making in communities, a fashionable notion at the time. At Channel Four both Paul Bonner and Mike Bolland had had charge of the BBC's community programmes unit. They knew what the IFA was on about. I thought they could contribute an element to C4's distinctiveness, and gave them a hearing. Our Chairman, Edmund Dell, came too. We were asked to put up £20 million to equip film and video workshops all over the country. This was completely out of the question; we only had £99 million to spend from January 1981 to March 1983. But the proposal was not rejected completely out of hand as, Paul Bonner notes, 'it would have been by any other broadcaster'. The Board agreed a modest input could be made. Alan Fountain got it going. I knew Alan from BFI days; he was fair-minded, calm, per-sistent and, at C4, the most international in outlook of all my colleagues. For a film by Mike Leigh for *Film on Four*, David Rose and I had had to persuade the Board to commit funds though no script was, or would be, available – that was how Leigh worked; but we knew there would be a film to show at the end of it. In the case of the workshops, no guarantee was given that anything worth transmitting would result. We were to invest in process; commissioning was an act of faith. That faith was rewarded. In *The Eleventh Hour*, the late Monday evening slot he programmed with Rod Stoneman and Caroline Fry, Alan Fountain assembled a body of original work, some of it community-based, some femi-nist, some from the Third World, some from Northern Ireland, some gay in content, some grim. And film-makers from Africa,

Asia and South America spoke to us through their work in a strand called *People to People*.

The best of the workshops delivered in spades. To visit them was a humbling experience. I would appear in a decaying pub in North Shields, or a scruffy cubby-hole in Derry, and come away inspired by the commitment to film-making of the men and women who received me, all of them on a minimum wage or wageless. Based in Newcastle upon Tyne, the collective Amber ran a gallery of photography and, tapping local talent like the playwright Tom Haddaway, worked on narrative, feature-length films based on the lives of those they lived among; they played them back to their neighbours as they went along. *Seacoal* showed us folk who made their living scavenging for coal on the seashore. It won a Silver Bear at Berlin (and, when we screened it, caught the eye of my correspondent Malcolm Laver). *Handsworth Songs*, made in Birmingham by the Black Audio Film Collective, said things about race in Britain that only black people could. Skilled as it was in the making, this had a rawness and a passion that were real. So did much else in *People to People* and *The Eleventh Hour*. If C4 was distinctive, as it was asked to be, this was a key part of what made it so. It made sense to tap these strengths; voices with something to say deserve to be heard. Where are they now?

Hence, too, a forum for highbrow argument, *Voices*. George Steiner, Joseph Brodsky and Mary McCarthy debated whether great literature is better forged under oppression and tyranny, for example under communism, or in the freedom of the West; Al Alvarez chaired the discussion. Of this early *Voices*, Claus Moser wrote to me that it was exactly what broadcasting was for. Well, up to a point, dear Claus. A collaboration between two intellectuals, commissioning editor Michael Kustow and producer Udi Eichler, who had made *Something to Say* for me at Thames, *Voices* was aimed at eggheads in the audience. Most TV aims at mass audiences, and rightly so. But why not aim at intellectuals also? Their tastes count too. Future series of *Voices* included dialogues between pairs of thinkers: Umberto Eco and Stuart Hall; Nadine Gordimer and Susan Sontag; Noam Chomsky and Fred Halliday; Günter Grass and Salman Rushdie. And there were series on 'Psychoanalysis Today', presented by Michael Ignatieff, and 'Philosophy Today', presented by John Searle. It is wrong to say you cannot discuss ideas on TV; all you need to do is allow the time.

Before Channel Four started, Mark Boxer had his pocket cartoon characters the Stringfellows, resident in NW3, look forward with apprehension: 'We're worried it's going to be too much our kind of channel.' It never was; *Voices* was way over their heads for a start, and much else, no doubt, beneath their notice. It was, indeed, television with a difference: an hour-long news, unmediated opinions; 'alternative' comedy; new talent in film; music, popular and classical; the arts, high and handsome; broad-based educational initiatives; sports you never saw before; spaces reserved for inner-city clamour; films, programmes from all over the world, broadcast in many languages.

And it worked. Gradually, viewers learned what to expect from the new channel, and found out how to use it to their satisfaction. By 1986 our share of audience regularly stood at 9 per cent of viewing in the UK. ITV now paid a fixed 17 per cent of their revenue in any previous year to fund both C4 and S4C, the Welsh fourth channel; S4C, broadcasting to less than half a million Welsh speakers, got 20 per cent of that 17 per cent; we got the rest. We already gained a higher share of ITV's and C4's combined ratings than we received of ITV's revenues. We were paying our way; we knew our revenue would be higher if we sold our own advertising, nationwide. The argument began: could we go it alone? Alan Budd was commissioned to look at the figures; he concluded that we could. Should we? I was never keen; I knew that as soon as we did so, the temptation to maximise ratings would gain sway, and the choices we afforded viewers would narrow. I was right about that, though I take no pleasure in noting it.

'Stand up for free enterprise, Mr Isaacs, won't you?' Margaret Thatcher called out to me at a reception in 10 Downing Street. I said we would not, but that some of our programmes would. ('Only one did,' she complained to me years later.) But Channel Four did stand up for enterprise. Bidden to take 'the highest practicable' proportion of our programmes from independent producers, we brought into being a new production sector. It now makes programmes not just for C4, but for ITV and BBC too. We encouraged diversity of supply, funding as many individuals as possible. As a result, nobody got rich quick, and few got rich at all. Today it's different; C4 still takes programmes from many makers, but the big boys, with track records of success, doing output deals, delivering bulk, making mergers, begin to dominate the screen. If this goes on, viewers' choice will narrow further.

C4 did good management proud in another area: we kept our overheads low. At the off, we set our face against high living, fat payroll, top-heavy administration. We stayed lean, and mean; at no time in my day did the cost of running the channel reach 10 per cent of expenditure. The money went on programmes. Not one management consultant entered the building; no one was paid to tell us what we could work out for ourselves. The staff, when we started, was 200; five years later, when I left, that had risen to 400. Today, after recent economies, the figure stands at 900, plus freelance contracts. Salaries are higher too.

Were we perfect then? Absolutely not. Some programmes were terrible; some, much criticised – IBT's series on development issues; Ken Loach's attack on trade union leaders, *Questions of Leadership* (which was never shown); *The Greek Civil War,* a one-sided account of the conflict. These were thought, inside and outside the channel, to be politically naïve, tendentious, partial. So they were. If you broadcast 3000 hours of programmes a year for five years, encouraging risk rather than aiming at safety, there are bound to be mistakes of judgement, errors of omission or commission, controversy in plenty. The whole of the controversy that attended these few items noted above is set out in the official history of independent broadcasting, fairly and accurately, at, to me, tedious length. Broadcasting is far, far more than the regulatory issues it generates, though some regulators may disagree.

For the most part, in any case, C4 started and continued with the regulator firmly on its side, smoothing our way, cheering us on, even fighting our battles. When we broadcast the remake of the BBC's banned *Scum*, Mary Whitehouse took the IBA to court; the court saw her off, ruling that the Director General, John Whitney, a Quaker and a prison visitor, who had himself viewed the film and authorised transmission, had acted perfectly properly. When *20/20 Vision* filmed Cathy Massiter, a civil servant whistle-blower who revealed that MI5 illegally tapped telephones, her every syllable was a breach of the Official Secrets Act. By definition, therefore, the programme broke the law. This the Authority refused to let us show, until the Attorney General helpfully indicated he would not prosecute. The *Guardian*'s Hugo Young, advising Liz Forgan and the producer of *20/20 Vision*, Claudia Milne, helped us get Cathy Massiter's testimony heard.

Was the channel too pruriently interested in screening the obscene? Was it, as its Chairman Edmund Dell thought, too left-wing? Edmund's feeling that it was – endlessly insisted on when there was so much else to attend to – soured relations between us. A study of Channel Four and its audience (*Keeping Faith?*, by David Docherty, David E. Morrison and Michael Tracey), has this:

> Perhaps the most interesting and calm judgments on those types of questions come from the person without whose support the channel probably would not exist, certainly not in its present form, William Whitelaw. He comments: 'Of course, I had a running encounter with Mrs Whitehouse who said C4 was obscene. Actually, on the whole it hasn't been, any more than anybody else has from time to time, but it was believed it was going to be a wicked licence for obscenity of one sort or the

other. I think she still thinks it has. I suppose it is marginally more permissive, if that's the right word, than the others. That is again the nature of something that is being rather different – given the trends in our society it is almost inevitable . . . if you do something which is going to cater for minority interests, I don't think it will always be that that minority is on the left, nor do I think that C4 has done that, but I think there will be a tendency for it. For myself I don't think there is anything particularly wrong in that. I think if it had been too left-wing it would have caused me difficulties, but you had to take some risks in this world. I thought it got the name of being left-wing much more than it actually ever was.'

Late in the day, I was glad to see that in print. When, in the channel's early days, storms broke over my head, I asked to see the Home Secretary. Willie Whitelaw asked me to lunch at his club. Over gulls' eggs, we chatted. Willie nodded benignly, said yes, some of his colleagues on the back benches were a bit worked up. He suggested I go carefully, and carry on.

Willie Whitelaw was made Captain of the Royal and Ancient Golf Club at St Andrews. I persuaded colleagues to give him a present, a silver no. 4 iron, as a token of our thanks. Edmund Dell pointed out that gifts, in this price range, to responsible ministers, were completely out of order and strictly forbidden. Years later, after Willie's death in fact, I gathered from someone in his private office that, touched and grateful, he'd managed to hang on to it. He probably paid for it himself.

In 1976 Tamara had found a lump in her breast; she had a mastectomy at Charing Cross Hospital. As the years passed, we more and more dared hope we were safe, but in summer 1984 she was increasingly in pain. At Glasgow, to receive an honorary degree from Strathclyde University, I was cheered loud and long by a hall full of students. In my cousin Esther's home, looking out back into the garden, I grasped that Tamara was again seriously ill. At first the scan showed nothing; another revealed tiny spots in her bones. Secondary cancers had spread. At Charing Cross's excellent oncology department, I was told she would not live a full span. How long? 'Perhaps three years; it is largely a matter of her morale and spirit.' For her, brave, uncomplaining, shadows closed in; for me, life lurched. We tried to make good use of time remaining; we went to Crete, and in January 1985 to her old South African home; together we pottered round Muizenburg in the Cape. A year later the cancer strengthened its grip. I was appointed to the Board of the Royal Opera House; we sat together in the Royal Box. Loved by all her family, short-changed by life, Tamara died on 10 March 1986.

Robert Kee wrote to me, praising her voice and sweet nature; Michael Frayn that, coming into the room, setting eyes on her, 'you knew instantly she was someone you could trust with your life'.

I have worked too hard all my life, and I left her too often lonely and alone. She too worked hard, as a trained social worker, dealing with adoptions in West London. She cared deeply about her work, and so brought others' troubles home. Her innate creativity was too little expressed. We were very happy together; she gave me, more than I always gave her, undeviating love and support. I put on a concert in her memory at St John's Smith Square; the Mozart and Beethoven she loved. Nigel Hawthorne read a Shakespeare sonnet: 'Let me not to the marriage of true minds admit impediment . . .' When he came to supper with us in Chiswick, Eamonn Andrews, who lived down the road, mentioned a poem he was searching for; it was, we guessed, Edward Thomas's 'Adlestrop'. She found it, copied it, gave it to him. At St John's, he took it out of his wallet to show he still carried it with him. I carry memories of her.

It was time to begin again.

In the summer of 1985 Sir Claus Moser asked me to join the Board of the Royal Opera House, Covent Garden, and a year later surprised me by suggesting I allow my name to go forward for the post of General Director, after Sir John Tooley retired. I had been nearly thirty years in broadcasting; why not change course? Channel Four was up and running; I had always said to my colleagues that each of us should only do a turn there, and then leave to give someone else a chance. The challenge at Covent Garden was not just to revitalise the work of the House, but to see through a major redevelopment of the site and the theatre's facilities. I put in for the job, and was offered it, subject to the new Chairman, Sir John Sainsbury (now Lord Sainsbury of Preston Candover) being satisfied that he and I could work together. On the afternoon I was preparing to meet him for the chat that might clinch it, I learned that Alasdair Milne had abruptly left the Director Generalship of the BBC. John Sainsbury and I shook hands in agreement, but all that weekend my telephone rang; friends and fellow broadcasters urged me to apply for the BBC vacancy. I knew, too, that Tamara would have wanted me to do so. The BBC promised a speedy appointment process; Claus Moser allowed a month's grace.

The BBC Governors, chaired by the recently appointed Marmaduke Hussey, had been under evident pressure from government to get rid of Milne. Mrs Thatcher had railed at coverage of the Falklands War, and of Northern Ireland; Norman Tebbit had complained furiously, and unjustifiably, of Kate Adie's reporting of the US bombing of Libya, to which Milne had made a robust response. Embarrassingly, though, when two Conservative MPs sued for libel after a *Panorama* on 'Maggie's Militant Tendency', the BBC first entered a strenuous and prolonged defence, and then, expensively, threw in the towel. Whitehall's view was that change at the top was needed; Hussey shared it. The press had made much, too much, of the coincidence of Granada's *The Jewel in the Crown* on ITV with *The Thorn Birds*, a bought-in pot-boiler, on BBC 1. But programme quality was not the issue; the governors wanted 'a safe pair of hands'.

Rival applicants included Michael Grade, Anthony Smith,

David Dimbleby (Hussey's candidate) and Michael Checkland, the BBC's Director of Resources and Deputy Director General. Only one governor wanted me: the Deputy Chairman, Joel Barnett. The bookmakers offered reasonable odds against me; I made it to the final interview. The executive who received me at Broadcasting House insisted that I be by my telephone from five onwards that evening, and should set aside the next morning for a press conference if successful. The door opened, and in I went.

I explained briefly that the range and quality of the pro- grammes would be my first concern. Money was tight – hence *The Thorn Birds*. I would call a halt to institutional expansion, cutting from the periphery if necessary to secure the broadcasting centre. The Director Generalship, I argued, was actually two jobs in one, editor-in-chief of programmes and managing director over all else: the division of responsibility that had worked so well at C4. I would take charge of output, hands on, and would delegate to another – I suggested Michael Checkland – responsibility for cost- efficient management, and any necessary overhaul of structure and practice. (BBC management has always been, and pretty cer- tainly still is, suffocatingly top-heavy.) My Achilles heel, however, was the same as Alasdair Milne's: I was on the programme- makers' side, and would incur the risks inherent in responsible publishing. One governor, Daphne Park, ex-Foreign Office Intelligence, Principal of Somerville, was scathing: C4's series on the Greek Civil War was disgracefully one-sided; why had I not prevented that? Another, Sir John Boyd, President of the Amalgamated Union of Engineering Workers, a Salvation Army stalwart who played the trombone, delivered the *coup de grâce* in a broad West of Scotland accent. 'Mr Isaacs,' he said, 'you don't look to me like a man who takes kindly to discipline. Now I can see by the smile on your face that you take that as a compliment, but I can assure you that I, and others here, see it as a criticism.' That was that.

'Hope to see you back, Sir,' said the commissionaire as I left; but when the telephone finally rang, after ten, it was Paul Bonner. Had I seen the news? They'd appointed Michael Checkland. Then Duke Hussey rang to tell me personally. 'We much enjoyed what you had to say, Jeremy, but then we enjoyed what everyone had to say. To tell the truth I'm surprised myself at what we've actually done.' He had fought long, hard and alone to appoint David Dimbleby, if not as DG, when that was lost, then as deputy to Checkland, in charge of programmes. The Governors, and Checkland, thought that appointment a matter for Checkland who, when he'd got his feet under the table and consulted, crucially, with Paul Fox, brought in, without advertisement, John Birt.

Would I, a programme-maker first and last, have been effective in overall charge of the BBC colossus, a Glasgow Academical in John Reith's giant footsteps? Myself, I rather doubt it, though I'd have given it my all.

I rang Claus Moser in Zurich and told him I would come, without regrets, to Covent Garden. What I did there is set out in *Never Mind the Moon*. The real change in my life, though, occurred before arriving at the Royal Opera House. In April 1988 I married Gillian Widdicombe, an arts journalist of distinction – former music critic of the *Financial Times*, then Arts Editor of the *Observer*. Was this the best thing that could have happened to me? Of that, then and now, I am very certain.

18

COLD WAR

I was minding my own business, and the nation's, in Covent Garden one day in November 1994 – re-energising, on inadequate funds, one of the world's great opera houses – when, out of the blue the emissary from Ted Turner arrived. Pat Mitchell, President of Turner Original Productions, had come to ask if I would produce a television history of the Cold War. I said I could not. I had a virtually full-time job; there was no way I could do anything like what I did on *The World at War* and combine it with running the Royal Opera House. And I was not prepared to leave ROH prematurely. So, no.

Thinking it over later, I saw that the choice need not be so clear-cut. My understanding with successive ROH chairmen had been that I could devote time to one biggish thing in parallel, to supplement earnings which ROH's straitened finances held down. I had worked on a treatment for a television history of the twentieth century, *Century*; Michael Green, of Carlton, took an option and included it, mentioning my name five times, in his formal bid for the London weekday franchise. Carlton outbid Thames, and took the franchise; but no more was heard of *Century*.

Also while at ROH, I had already been lured briefly back to television, on screen. Udi Eichler had been eager to put forward to BBC2 a proposal I suggested. *Three of a Kind* was studio talk that stressed professional common interest rather than promoted conflict and division. In it I quizzed newspaper editors, football managers, opera directors, psychoanalysts, bringing out what each saw as the job's core purpose and method, before turning to differences between them; light not heat. These programmes had their moments, but I was a novice interviewer, feeling my way and obstinately refusing to wear an earpiece through which a producer's guidance might have been offered. The series was not extended.

Face to Face, interviews with creative figures in the arts, which Michael Jackson commissioned as part of and then as spin-offs from *The Late Show* on BBC2, lasted longer. The title was an act of coat-trailing chutzpah on the BBC's part; John Freeman's *Face to Face* back in the fifties remains a TV landmark for hyper-sensitive but also cruelly targeted interrogation, and for the revelations thus achieved. I was not in that league, and knew it. But Jackson was insistent we keep the title, and I insisted that, if we did, we must also hear again the signature tune, Berlioz's overture *Les Francs Juges*. The format had one huge attraction to me; like Freeman, I would keep out of sight. The camera, over my shoulder, would scrutinise the other participant's countenance, not mine. With an eye to my time, I insisted there should be no editing; we would record live. The programme's length, mooted at first as twenty-eight minutes, was immediately extended to thirty-eight, in effect occupying *The Late Show*'s entire slot. The change was made, without warning to me, in the studio; in full flow, I became aware that the floor manager's next expected timing signal to me (ten minutes to go) was a long time in arriving. Somehow, stretched, I kept going. We stopped and restarted recording only once, when, with a loud crash, someone knocked over some furniture. We did not do so when, mistakenly, I asked the poet James Fenton how he had liked working for the *Daily Telegraph*. 'It would have been interesting to work for the *Telegraph*,' he replied thoughtfully. But he never had. And all my 'ums' and 'ers' stayed in.

Some critics called my interviewing 'wooden'. It was a bit, at times. But producers Julian Birkett and David Herman kept me wonderfully supplied with well-researched material, with suggested lines of questioning, with advice and encouragement. A long line of writers and players took part. People interested in the arts who watched the programmes avidly enjoyed, they told me, their simplicity, and the camera's slow, searching tempo; look quietly at someone's face and physiognomy for forty minutes, and you may feel you get to know them. It was always questions about childhood that yielded most insight: Rod Steiger, wearing a trilby low over his brow, never knew his mother; Bob Monkhouse's mother only hugged him once. Monkhouse and Ken Dodd might get 600,000 viewers, others fewer. Derek Jarman and Paul Eddington, each near death, with courage and dignity brought the screen to life. *Face to Face* was a sort of oasis of seriousness in a frantic, quick-cutting world, and a sign that the BBC still attached value to the arts, before the desert deluge of consumerism overtook all.

The most striking difference between John Freeman's *Face to Face* and mine – our abilities apart – was that each of his memorable interviews was with someone wholly remarkable, never seen on a TV screen, never a caller in our living-rooms before: Carl Jung, Evelyn Waugh, Edith Sitwell, Otto Klemperer. The interview itself, let alone an interview on television, was a rarity. Those conversations were genuine events. Today the interviewer's main preparation for the encounter is to wade through newspaper cuttings; the subject has been interviewed not once and again, but again and again, and again and again and again. He or she is already a celebrity, with answers ready pat to any question to be put. At any rate, recording *Face to Face*, I could leave my office in

Floral Street by taxi, arrive at Television Centre, meet my inter-locutor, sit down, do it, wait for the technical check and clearance, say goodbye, and be back at Covent Garden in under two hours. I doubt I was missed.

When I thought over that first conversation with Pat Mitchell, I realised that the Cold War project she was insistently putting to me could not go into production for nearly a year, and would then take three years to finish, well before which time I would cer-tainly have left the Royal Opera House. Even so, I could not be series producer. What I could do was find someone else to pro-duce the series, and act myself as overseer. Pat Mitchell asked me to go to Atlanta to meet Ted Turner, founder and owner of CNN and other channels. He would be paying the bills.

Earlier that year, in August 1994, Ted Turner had come down to breakfast in St Petersburg at the 'Goodwill Games' – an invention of his, held every four years alternately in the United States and in Russia – with his big idea.

'The Cold War is over,' he told his colleagues.

'Yes, Ted,' they said, unimpressed. 'So?'

'So, we're going to make a documentary series about it. Go and find that fellow who made *The World at War*, Jeremy Irons, and get him to do it.'

I do not look like Jeremy Irons, but Pat Mitchell tracked me down, though she, and Ted, were taken aback to find me running an opera house, two ballet companies and a major redevelopment building programme. Now she was driving me fast along a ring highway outside Atlanta, in the wrong direction, already late to meet Ted who, she said, doesn't like you to be late, at a restaurant called Fifty Seventh Fighter Squadron World War Two, Officers' and NCOs' Mess, Public Admitted. It was next to an airstrip where Ted's jet had landed. There, its walls festooned with US and UK wartime headlines, we met.

Ted, and his wife Jane Fonda, were dressed simply but smartly; they had come by air from his son's wedding – a white witch ceremony – in North Carolina, and were going on to his ranch in New Mexico. They looked handsome, and very together. We sat opposite each other at table; a senior executive of the Turner organisation was also present. Pat warned me Ted would talk a lot, and that he was deaf; and not to look down Jane Fonda's cleavage (she wasn't showing any). We talked for over an hour, Ted keeping one hand on Jane's knee throughout. What was odd, even unique, in the meeting, I still think, was that this man, owner of several TV channels, had had an idea for a series and was himself prodding it into life. I had not met such a hands-on leader since Sidney Bernstein, my first employer, nearly forty years before. Ted Turner, like Sidney, was not interested just in making money. He cared about what his stations broadcast, what he sent to air.

Ted Turner already owned and operated TBS, a cable system and the first US superstation, when in 1980 he had founded CNN, the first 24-hour news channel; he later added a cartoon channel, a movie channel and another broad-based entertainment channel, TNT. His entertainment channels, remarkably, played documentaries in peak, many contributed by the production arm Pat Mitchell headed, Turner Original Productions. Ted loved documentaries, and Pat Mitchell had already made several excellent ones for him; one set of six, narrated by Jane Fonda, was *Women of the Century*, portraits of twentieth-century American women, very politically correct, very Jane, very Ted. *Biker Women* got higher ratings. Now Ted wanted his name on bigger documentary series, as big as they come. TBS already totally funded Jacques Cousteau's underwater explorations, and had co-produced David Attenborough's natural history series made for the BBC. Ted had asked David Puttnam, whom he admired, to make him a series on Nelson, one of his heroes. (The other was Gandhi; he had statuettes of each of them on his desk.) David said it could not be done. And now Ted wanted me to make *Cold War*. As a younger man, Ted had been a sailor. He had spent a fortune to contest, and carry off, the America's Cup. By a delightful coincidence, Gillian Widdicombe's father, Leslie, had made sails for him in Suffolk. He told me what he wanted from *Cold War*.

He wanted to do the subject justice; it must be on a grand scale. There had been two sides to the conflict, and the series must deal fairly with both: he did not want a series solely recounting how the US had triumphed. It must be broader. In the Cold War, he repeated, there were no victors, no losers; humanity had won because humanity had survived. (He kept saying, too, that there would be no more wars, the world was becoming a better place; any counter-example I mentioned – Northern Ireland, Palestine, Bosnia, Rwanda – was brushed aside.) I was listening, I realised, to a visionary whose feet were not wholly on the ground; he was stating hopes, not facts. But I distinguished between his aspirations and what would actually go into the series; we would get as near to objective truths as we could manage.

I was with him completely, though, in not wanting to make a victor's self-celebration, like *Victory at Sea* or *The Churchill Years*. *The World at War* had included the experiences of Germans and Japanese, as well as of Americans and Brits and Russians. In *Cold War* we would present events from at least two viewpoints, Moscow and Washington, calling witnesses from both. We should include China, and Cuba, and the perspectives of those in between; Europe, east and west, bore the brunt of the Cold War and, to a greater extent than the United States, lived in fear of nuclear annihilation. Ted talked a lot, I spoke briefly; but on this essential – a truly international series – we were as one. CNN was seen and heard worldwide too, of course.

How many episodes did he want?

'Forty,' he said, looking at me.

'Not a chance,' I said. 'No one has the stamina to make such a monster, certainly not me; and no one will have the appetite to watch it. In any case, forty episodes will mean abandoning a narrative line; the series will be a compendium; an excuse to let anything in, no reason to leave anything out. We shall have 'Cold War and the Novel', "Cold War and the Universities", "Cold War and Psycho-analysis". Better to be manageable, linear, tight.' I did not want to commit to twenty-six; I suggested twenty. We shook hands. He and Jane left.

I undertook to let Turner Original Productions have a treatment and a budget. When they'd seen those, they would know whether we could work together. It was agreed they'd fund a modest development. I came back to London and reactivated Jeremy Isaacs Productions, JIP.

The Cold War was a prolonged confrontation between two superpowers – one more super than the other – rivals socially, politically, economically, militarily. Since each possessed thermonuclear weapons which they declared they were ready to use, the world lived in fear of the outcome, not just for the survival of peoples and of nation-states, but for the planet's. The confrontation lasted forty-five years and spread to every continent. In Europe an uneasy peace was preserved, but there were major armed conflicts in Korea, Vietnam and Afghanistan, and proxy wars in Angola, Somalia, Nicaragua and El Salvador. The CIA's tentacles stretched to Chile, the Soviets' to Cuba. In the Middle Eastern conflict over Palestine, the superpowers armed both sides.

When, at the end, one side collapsed, the cause was not defeat in a shooting war but the glaring inadequacies of a failed social system; we would need to show the relative prosperity and well-being of the peoples of the US and the USSR over the period. The subject was vast, sprawling, intricate, complex. The Second World War's story was primarily military, with social and political chapters added; it lasted only six years. This was a harder terrain to map and to traverse.

In London, we costed the development and signed the contract for it by Christmas. In January I convened a small group of colleagues; we met weekly on Friday afternoons to talk the thing through. Taylor Downing, Martin Smith, Neal Ascherson were regulars. Isobel Hinshelwood joined. Lawrence Freedman, Head of War Studies at King's College, looked in; he would serve, admirably, as historical consultant. Some subjects suggested themselves: the Marshall Plan; the Berlin airlift; Korea and Vietnam; the Wall; the Cuban Missile Crisis; Nixon in China; Reagan and Gorbachev in Reykjavik. Others were argued in, but seemed natural fits: McCarthyism, US fear of the enemy within; Soviet paranoia, isolating the peoples of the USSR from the West. We thought the hardest thing to recapture might be the pervasive fear of nuclear destruction.

Through January and February 1995 there evolved a shape for a series of twenty episodes; a manageable number which could yet, I thought, do justice to the subject. (It could not quite, but it is where we started.) At the end of April, we would deliver to Atlanta a 20,000-word treatment, a budget and five free-ranging essays, which I commissioned as attachments. In March and over Easter, Taylor Downing wrote most of the twenty-chapter treatment; Isobel Hinshelwood tracked down interviewees, and checked and double-checked facts.

I spotted an article on the Cold War International History Project at the Woodrow Wilson Center, Washington DC. Founded and funded to take advantage of the opening of Soviet and satellite archives barred to the West for decades, the Project tracked down, translated and published documents not read by Western historians. In Washington, Taylor Downing met the project's director, Jim Hershberg, a bright, lively, enthusiastic young historian; he was more than willing to help. So was Thomas Blanton, at the National Security Archive. We would have access to the newest information, and could test oral testimony against documented fact. Did Stalin instruct North Korea's Kim Il Sung to invade the South? Well, he gave permission, the archives revealed, but only after Kim's repeated requests to proceed; more than twenty, in all, were ignored or rejected. It was the right time to make *Cold War*.

In Washington, I too met Jim Hershberg and also, at George

Washington University, Vlad Zubok, a young Russian historian recommended by Cate Haste, who had heard him speak at a conference in Helsinki. He was pleased to help. The big fish we landed was John Lewis Gaddis, then Distinguished Professor of History at Athens, Ohio, probably (I was told) the best US historian of the Cold War. Gaddis, who shortly thereafter moved to Yale, was right for us. Happily we were right for him too; when Taylor Downing approached him in April on my behalf, he said: 'If that's the Jeremy Isaacs who made *The World at War*, the answer's "yes". I use it to teach my students.' I found him searching, wise, fair; a strong support in all we did.

Richard Melman made the budget. I had a rough idea from Pat of what it might be allowed to cost, and within that outline Richard got every detail right; we juggled the single great variable, the relative proportions of original shooting (cheap, except for travel, on tape) and library material (world rights in all media are expensive). I had not had to submit so precise a budget for *The World at War*, or *Ireland: A Television History*; Thames and the BBC took each in its stride. But JIP was an independent production company which could not afford to fail, supplying an American giant which counted every cent. Richard Melman did a thorough job; we were in the ballpark. It helped that we made programmes more cheaply than an independent in the States ever could. But *Cold War* would cost well north of $10 million.

Between Easter and the following weekend, the programme outlines were finalised. Gillian and her former *Observer* colleague John Houston designed and polished what was by now a 100-page booklet; a FedEx van called at Flashback, Taylor Downing's company in Cowcross Street, to take twenty copies to Atlanta. Taylor said to me: 'It could be six months before they make their minds up about that lot!' In less than two weeks word came that *Cold War* was on. In a conference call linking Montana, Atlanta, Los Angeles and London, Ted said: 'We're going to do this, and our grandchildren will be proud of us.'

Ted Turner had spoken, without hesitation or qualification. Pat Mitchell, whose then partner, now husband, Scott Seydel, was part of Ted's extended family, was an expert advocate, but the decision was Ted's alone. Now, however, CNN's bureaucracy intervened; it took five months to negotiate the contract. The London lawyers who examined CNN's draft thought it as heavy-handed as any they'd seen. Atlanta had little regard for the notion of partnership; we would work for them, they thought, on their terms. Gillian Widdicombe, the better half of JIP, refused to sign a lease on premises until she had written assurances indemnifying us if the contract was aborted.* At last, in September 1995, the contract for *Cold War* was signed and sealed, premises at Shelton Street, a quarter of a mile from the Royal Opera House, were taken, staff could be recruited; we started work. CNN had driven a hard bargain – that is what they had lawyers for – particularly as regards end rights; but in managing the series' cashflow, their production executives at every level could not have been more helpful. The budget was in dollars; we were paid in sterling. They, not we, bore the exchange-rate risk. Making *Cold War*, we always had money in the bank.

The key to success was the series producer, Martin Smith. Martin had a fine track record, but it was his character that rang true at every test – honest, hardworking, clear-headed, resolute. He proved an inspiring leader; his style was both collegiate (regular screenings and conferrings) and authoritarian (notices in the tiny kitchen instructed everyone to do their own washing-up – Martin did his). We began with a convivial conference of everyone likely to be involved, including Turner's Pat Mitchell and the far-flung consultants. What was the Cold War? What mattered most in it? Thousands of words were recorded, transcribed – and went, I guess, unread. But the discussion got everyone going, ignited

*On 1 December 1994, after eighteen months of promising negotiation, CNN aborted a contract for a series on the Olympic Games – coming to Atlanta in 1996 – with Taylor Downing's company, Flashback.

enthusiasm, motivated young and old. The project came together. The real work began.

In any long series, time is money. Martin laid down not a template, but an iron grid. Two films only would be editing at any one time – he could not easily supervise more – but each film absolutely must be completed in three months of editing, editing held up and interrupted for a brief few days in each process to allow Pat, my fellow executive producer, guarding CNN's interest wherever she was, to comment on a script, view a fine-cut. The three consultants – Gaddis in New Haven, Zubok in Washington DC, and Lawrence Freedman at King's in the Strand – had the same tight time windows to function in. Without fail, they complied. Martin had to read every thought they uttered, reconciling them, in dialogue if necessary, if they clashed. He managed. Pat and I had to agree on content, personnel, and the overall feel and look. We scarcely knew each other; what if we differed violently? Her first visits to us with her colleagues were awkward, naturally, and provoked apprehension; did they talk sense, are we on the same wavelength? The longer we worked together, the better we got on. Pat Mitchell was always for clarity; she was calm and constructive. Two virtually finished programmes came off the production line every three months. As soon as he saw the first, Ted Turner wrote to congratulate us: 'Keep up the great work – Your pal, Ted.' I pinned that on the notice-board.

Martin Smith assembled a first-class team. We had an excellent production manager and a strong resident camera crew; logging and storing systems were securely in place; the researchers were the very best; fine film editors turned up; the producers knew exactly what they were doing. Following *The World at War*'s precedent, we engaged writers for each episode; some worked on several, among them Neal Ascherson, Hella Pick, Jonathan Steele. I invited Ian Buruma, Mark Frankland, Germaine Greer, Max Hastings, John Lloyd, William Shawcross to contribute also. With these on board, and the consultants, we had no excuse for getting anything wrong.

Carl Davis agreed to write the music; the theme tune was strong. Martin Smith devised a title sequence down a long dark tunnel, with *Cold War* at the end, and a succession of images on the walls at either side: Stalin and Truman; Khrushchev and Kennedy; Brezhnev and LBJ; Mao, Castro, Reagan, Gorbachev. Kenneth Branagh, noted apparently for his Olivier imitations, agreed to narrate. He had already, like Larry, directed and acted in films of *Henry V* and *Hamlet*. Taylor Downing and I were to write a book to accompany the series. All seemed set fair when, in May 1996, Gillian and I arrived in Atlanta to attend CNN World Report, an annual assembly of staff from all over the world, part conference, part party. On this occasion the *Cold War* project was to be introduced to the assembly, perhaps controversially. The series was eventually diverted from Turner Entertainment to CNN itself; not every news-gatherer was happy to see CNN's air-time eaten into by historical compilations.

CNN's Atlanta Headquarters stand apart in a central area of the city; the complex includes a hotel, CNN-owned, where most of us stayed. The day after we arrived Ted gave a dinner for *Cold War* at the Piedmont Driving Club, a grand country club redolent of the Old South. It turned out to be quite a night. A time-bomb was ticking. In stipulating only twenty episodes, I had created a difficulty. Could we squeeze in everything we needed? Seeing a couple of *Cold War* warriors waiting in the lobby, historians

Hershberg and Zubok, Ted, who was driving with Jane to the Piedmont, offered them a lift. In the car he asked how things were going; was everything all right? These two perfectionists mentioned their concern that subject matter that deserved better would get short shrift. Not enough space, in their view, was devoted to proxy wars, involving surrogates for the two power blocs, in different continents; there was no single programme on China, though it was treated *passim* when it claimed attention; most glaring, there was no programme on espionage – what was the Cold War if not a playground for spies? Ted was driving; with one hand he scribbled six (mis-spelled) titles on a scrap of yellow paper, and crumpled it into a pocket.

When the company had assembled in the dining room, he announced he had something to say: *Cold War* was going to be great, but too much was omitted; we needed more episodes. He gave examples. To the amazement of the CNN suits, he announced that six episodes were to be added, and – this is what killed them – that funds for them would be added to the budget. I had known many attempts to cut a project down in size, none previously to enlarge one. Ted was right; we did need more room – at least one more programme for the surrogates, and one on China, and one on spies. I had ducked devoting a programme to China for structural reasons. It was not easy to see where to put it chronologically: put it early, and there's no Cultural Revolution and no Nixon in China; put it late, and it's a long retrospect back to Mao's Long March, and the stand-off with Stalin. (In fact, what is now needed is a series on China.) Espionage is simply a blind spot of mine; I enjoy John le Carré's, and now Alan Furst's, novels, but I do not enjoy documentary films in which – because there are no actual pictures of spying – shadowy reconstructions have to be used to show messages being dropped off in hollow oaks or at deserted telephone boxes. But it was absurd to omit 'Spies'.

Back in London, I rejigged. We rethought two titles we had not yet embarked on; made more space for surrogates, separating Africa, the Middle East and Central America; and inserted China and spies. We ended up with twenty-four episodes instead of twenty; subconsciously I was determined not to go to twenty-six and be judged by something exactly parallel to *The World at War*. (There's one other crucial difference between the two series, in the running times of each episode: *The World at War*, 52 minutes 30 seconds; *Cold War*, 44 minutes 30 seconds.) It cost money to make the change; it added weeks to our schedule, both on location and in editing. Rather than extend, we doubled up. We would still deliver in early summer 1998, for transmission in the fall.

Back in the Piedmont Driving Club – where folks drove a carriage, not an automobile – the night was still young. I had brought with me, not very sensibly – I had forgotten Ted was both deaf and tone deaf – an audiotape of Carl Davis's *Cold War* signature tune, and handed it over, thinking he could take it away with him. He insisted on hearing it at once, and sent for a machine to play it on. It took an age to find a player, and longer to make it work. Eventually, as we stood around in a circle, Carl's theme blasted out from a player on the floor. There was a shocked silence. Few present, the CNN executives certainly not among them, knew much about the series, and the music – suggesting, I hoped, endurance, jolted irregularly by tremors and shocks – meant nothing at all out of context. Into the silence, before anyone tittered, stepped Jane Fonda: 'Wonderful!' she cried. 'I think that's really wonderful!' We heard it again. Conversation re-ignited, and veered elsewhere.

Jane excelled herself that evening. Taylor and I were writing a book to match the series and were having trouble getting Turner Publications to respond, though British publishers were likely to jump at it. Turner Books had first crack at the title; yet, although there was expertise there in marketing TV tie-ins, the executive-in-charge was dismissive. Mentioning at one point that no one read books from cover to cover, he did not want to know. Jane had got wind of this; she sidled up to him, as if to kick him in the shins, glared and said sweetly: 'The book of the series is very important, you know. Some of us can't understand why you are dragging your feet.' He blanched. Later in the evening, after Ted and Jane had departed early to watch basketball – his team, the Atlanta Hawks, were playing – the victim of Jane's assault got up at the dinner table and made an embarrassing speech: he now realised how big *Cold War* was; he wanted us all to know that he and the books division were seriously behind it. The books division did not last long. After Ted Turner backed his TV empire into Time Warner, the book of *Cold War* ended up being published not by Turner Books but by Little, Brown – owned by TimeWarner.

But it was Gillian's encounter with Jane Fonda that was the high point. 'You know, Gillian,' said Jane, 'you and I have a lot in common. We're married to very similar men. Look at 'em over there, talking to each other. They're so alike. It's our task,' Jane said firmly, 'to keep 'em rooted.'

In Shelton Street, the production team crewed up to take account of four additional programmes, and slogged on. The material we needed flowed in. Alison McAllan, in charge of film research, spent time in Moscow, pushing at archive doors now, for a fee, half-open; some tapes she got her hands on fell off the back of a KGB lorry. Steve Bergson and Miriam Walsh were just as perceptive and assiduous. Miriam searched out images of life in Soviet-dominated Eastern Europe; she would dance with gleeful excitement as the best of it was first viewed in the editing suite. In Russia, we advertised for home movies, got more than we hoped for, and put them to use.

More than 500 interviews were recorded for *Cold War*. We talked to US Presidents Jimmy Carter, Gerald Ford, George Bush Senior; and to Gorbachev, and his foreign minister Eduard Shevardnadze. Alas, Alzheimer's took Reagan; we could not interview the extraordinary figure who denounced the Soviet Union as the 'evil empire', yet so hated the thought of nuclear war that he was prepared at Reykjavik to go the last mile in negotiation to achieve total nuclear disarmament – though he would not surrender the final card he held: the plan to build a safety umbrella for the United States, an anti-ballistic missile system, ABM, that would serve as a shield. I interviewed his Secretary of State, George Schultz, in Bechtel's offices at San Francisco. He told how, at the critical moment, Reagan had passed him a note: 'George, am I right?' Schultz scribbled back: 'Absolutely.' It was the threat, rather than the reality of the ABM system, 'Star Wars', that broke the Soviet camel's back. If the US, which might or might not have been able to afford it, installed it, the USSR must do likewise. But the Russians could not possibly fund the vast hike in defence expenditure this would have entailed. To raise his people's standard of living – as they now demanded – Gorbachev had to cut military expenditure, not increase it. He needed to disarm.

Margaret Thatcher, who had concerns that total nuclear disarmament would leave the UK exposed while the US was protected by the ABM, would not talk to us, in spite of every intercessor – Charles Powell, Bernard Ingham – I could bring to bear. She preferred always to be sole mistress of her own record, rather than a participant with others in a general account. Charles Powell spoke for her, immaculately; we found out afterwards he had come straight to the camera from a briefing lunch with her and Bernard Ingham at Wilton's. Thatcher made an impact personally all the same, telling the news camera that she could do business with Mr Gorbachev, and electrifying a Moscow studio, and the airwaves, by lecturing Russian interlocutors on what democracy meant.

Fidel Castro also played hard to get, keeping our crew waiting for weeks in Havana on the half-promise of an interview. After several visits, at last he said yes, making himself available to Pat Mitchell and Martin Smith at ten o'clock one evening. Pat asked him twelve questions; he talked for five hours. CNN got a special programme out of it – interviews with Castro were rare. Fidel Castro confirmed that, during the Cuban Missile Crisis, Soviet troops on Cuba had deployed tactical nuclear weapons which would certainly have been used had the US invaded, as some urged they should. That would have meant nuclear war. It was Ted Turner's friendship with Fidel – they went duck-shooting together – that most roused neo-conservative anger and criticism.

Other key figures – Henry Kissinger, James Baker, Helmut Schmidt, Vaclav Havel – agreed to talk, to go on the record, to have their words made available to future scholars in the archive, and on the web. CNN Interactive put the full text of every interview we did on their *Cold War* website, marking a new high in access to television's working process. Students could read all of it.

Not all the interviewees were contemporary big shots. Taylor Downing interviewed Sir Frank Roberts, UK ambassador in Moscow during the Second World War, in March 1995, before we sent the treatment to CNN. He was wise and spry, and very old. In February 1946 George Kennan sent the 'Long Telegram' to the State Department, warning of the USSR's nature and intentions, and setting out what the West would need to do about it; John Gaddis, his biographer, managed to interview him. We questioned Giulio Andreotti, the Italian Christian Democrat, later many times Prime Minister, about the dollars the CIA provided to help clinch the 1948 election for the right, rendering Italy eligible for Marshall Plan aid. Andreotti said he knew nothing, but you can tell from his expression that he understood exactly what we were getting at. In Berlin we talked to airmen who had flown in supplies during the Berlin airlift, tank crews who had confronted each other in the city centre, men and women who had escaped across the Wall – and some who had seen others die in the attempt.

The men and women who talked to us trusted our researchers, first among them Isobel Hinshelwood* and Svetlana Palmer. Later, in Washington for the series launch, I encountered grizzled, elderly former CIA veterans who would enquire after Miss Hinshelwood, and ask to be remembered to her. Svetlana, a Russian, now married in England, had the hard task of persuading KGB officers to talk and, when it came to it, to tell the truth. Even harder was to get young Soviet soldiers who had fought in Afghanistan, experiencing horrors and inflicting them, to speak of what they saw and did. For years they had kept silent; their friends and families, and the veterans' associations, urged them to keep their mouths shut; but the knowledge of evil was eating them up inside. Svetlana took a bottle of vodka to a building site at night to unlock the tongue of one young ex-squaddie. He told her his nightmares; they were real.

It is to researchers, diligent, passionate for accuracy, tough and wily, that twentieth-century television history owes its strength and authority. *Cold War* was well served.

---

*Isobel Hinshelwood, who worked with me on *The World at War* and on *Cold War*, and on other major series, died in 2003. She was special.

Martin Smith's commitment to getting every fact right was reinforced by the scrutiny of our consultants, who saw every fine-cut, read initial outlines and commentary script. That surveillance was supplemented by a fusillade of constructive niggles from Bill Burr of the National Security Archive in Washington. He and the Director, Tom Blanton, appointed themselves extra watchdogs; they criticised, encouraged, cheered us on.

The BBC, too, took a hand. At Pat Mitchell's prompting, Michael Jackson, Controller BBC2, agreed to buy UK rights in *Cold War* and screen the series as soon as CNN did – indeed, he had to be restrained from going first. He was buying in at a fraction of the total series cost; CNN was the sole funder, in fact. But the convention in such cases is that the rights purchaser is credited as co-producer, the purchase represented as a co-production. In this case, the modest price BBC Acquisitions paid – a substantial sum, however, over twenty-four episodes – was topped up by raiding an internal budget, that of BBC News and Current Affairs. Senior news executives, nominated as 'executive producer for the BBC', turned up in Shelton Street to cast a critical glance over our work.

Tim Gardam, the first assessor, liked what he saw; his notes were a model of what comment at the fine-cut stage should be. When he left the BBC for Channel Five, he asked to stay in touch. Mark Damazer, who came after, was as informed and as acute a critic. He saw at once that the no-frills combination of visual record and trustworthy testimony was simply an extension of what news and current affairs, at its best, should be; journalism is, after all, the first draft of history. He thought *Cold War* an important offering for BBC News; he did not say it might properly have originated at the BBC.

The man who did finally catch us out in error was Ted Turner himself. In an early episode, which we made late, we said that 'Roosevelt declared war on Japan'. 'No, he did not,' Ted wrote to me. 'Congress, not the President, declares war.' Good for him, I thought, keeping an eagle eye. When he came once to Shelton Street to see us, he went round the room shaking hands, 'leaving an impression' on everyone he met.

The *Cold War* team of producers boasted its highly capable regulars, James Barker, Richard Melman, Taylor Downing, Cate Haste; there were also visiting firemen. Three of these stuck out a little. Ken Kirby made a film on Afghanistan, 'Mujaheddin', that had great power: it included a startling sequence of the ambush of a Soviet convoy, shot by an intrepid freelance; the terrible aftermath of an assault on a mountain village; and news footage of the US National Security Adviser, Zbigniew Brzezinski, in Pakistan, telling a group of turbaned tribesmen to get back over the border into Afghanistan and fight: 'Your cause is just. You will prevail; God is on your side.' Among these were members of the Taleban.

In 'America's Backyard', on wars, civil and colonial, in Central America, the distinguished anthropological film-maker Brian Moser, maker of *Disappearing World*, worked with writer Hugh O'Shaughnessy to unravel the recent past. Moser had been in Bolivia, on the scene, when Che Guevara was captured and shot; his still photographs form part of the world's record of Che's death. This film, brutal horror compressed, was a powerful one, yet complex; at the end of Nicaragua's bloody wars, Violetta Chamorro, for the right, won election victory. It was surely in its own backyard, though, that the United States – through US-trained death squads, the Contras – came nearest in moral equivalence to the murderous KGB.

'Spies', by Jonathan Lewis, was one of the very best films of the series. The interviewees included Ted Hall, the young physicist at Los Alamos who passed information to the USSR at the same time as Klaus Fuchs. Fuchs was caught; Hall escaped detection. The KGB had more agents on the atomic bomb site than the West knew. Why engage in espionage? At the Cold War's beginning, spies were moved to act by ideological conviction; at the end, by mere greed. Ted Hall, at Los Alamos, thought 'the right thing to do was to act to break the American monopoly' (on nuclear weaponry). Aldrich Ames, unmasked in 1994, told us his reasons were 'personal, banal, and amounted really to greed and folly'. In prison, Ames reflected on the mess he'd made of his life; he made no mention of the men he sent to their deaths to put a fur coat on his ambitious wife's back. Jonathan Lewis showed us a fine-cut that had not a frame out of place. I blushed to watch it.

Cold War took a broad panoramic sweep over forty-five years of history. It is the details that stand out: Missouri mules, sent under the Marshall Plan to work for Greek mountain farmers, three times as big and unruly as the locals to which they'd be yoked; a US pilot who parachuted chocolate for kids on to Berlin streets during the airlift; the horrible accident during a Soviet missile-launch at Baikunur, concealed from the public and, until our series, from the world, in which 180 died; a picnic in a Russian home movie, a conga-line of summer happiness lighting up the humanity of a bleak and hungry world.

If Berlin was the centre of the Cold War, Checkpoint Charlie was its epicentre. Here, on 27 October 1962, tension ratcheted up as US and Soviet tanks confronted each other, 20 metres apart. 'Holy Christ,' one US tank commander told us he called up his base, 'the Soviets are coming right in here. Defecation is about to hit the fan.' You can motivate the US cavalry to kill, and to risk their lives in war; you cannot get them to say 'shit' on prime-time TV.

In *Cold War* we saw Robert McNamara begin, repentantly, to rethink his posture on Vietnam, while still asserting confidently, and correctly, that 'mutually assured destruction, MAD, was not mad, but the essential core of effective deterrence'; we watched, too, as the promising young State Department aide, Condoleezza Rice, recalling the Bush–Gorbachev summit at Malta, made her debut on the diplomatist's stage.

Henry Kissinger, when I interviewed him in his Manhattan office, confident that he and Nixon had made history in China, raised an eyebrow when I asked about West Germany's and Willy Brandt's Ostpolitik: 'I can see you've been talking to Egon Bahr,' he said. Bahr, Brandt's foreign policy adviser, had told him, not consulted him, about this major initiative; Kissinger had had to go along. Brandt himself gave the history of post-war Europe its most resonant moment when, in front of the Memorial to the Fighters of the Warsaw Ghetto, he sank to his knees in tribute, and in contrition for Nazi crimes.

I asked a friend who was in Berlin the night the Wall came down what he felt. He said only that there was a lot of noise. The sounds that distracted him were of an epoch ending. The journalist Timothy Garton Ash contrived in that *annus mirabilis* to be in Warsaw, Budapest, Leipzig, East Berlin and, later, in Prague, at just the critical moment. He watched brave men and women flood into the streets to demonstrate against the hated regimes that oppressed their lives, not knowing whether or not police or army, confronting them, would shoot, as the Chinese did in Tiananmen Square. Garton Ash reckoned they were, literally, making history, the history of the present. Cate Haste, who made five fine *Cold War* films, used the pictures to show how it ended.

The young Prime Minister of Hungary, Miklos Nemeth, told how he had asked Gorbachev directly: 'If in the coming election the Hungarian people vote the communists out, will you repeat the 'fifty-six exercise, and forcibly overturn the result?' Gorbachev replied unhesitatingly: 'There will be no such instruction, no order to act.' In the most chilling account we had of post-Stalinist brutality, Nemeth told us that after the 1956 rising was put down with tanks in the streets of Budapest, prisoners were taken, and shot; but some freedom-fighters were as young as fourteen or fifteen. So: 'The gaolers waited till the teenagers reached their eighteenth birthdays. And then they killed them.'

A history of the present impinges on the politics of the present. The US neo-con right did not admire our series, and said so, vehemently; one critic, in an article in *Commentary*, accused us of telling 'Twenty Four Lies about the Cold War'. There were no lies, and scarcely an error of fact. 'Comrades', the first episode, was inevitably a too-compressed account of the pre-Second World War period; although it spelled out the evil of Stalin's show trials, his engineered famines, his murderous purges, it made rather less of Lenin's terror, and rather more of Western intervention against the young Bolshevik state, than the right might have wished. 'Comrades' brought US and Soviet troops together in 1945 at Torgau on the Elbe. Many young Americans today have no idea who Adolf Hitler, Joseph Stalin, Winston Churchill and Harry Truman were, and are not aware that the USSR and the US were allies, comrades in arms, against Nazi Germany.

The programme that provoked most neo-con antipathy was episode six, 'Reds'. This dealt with the fear that the threat of nuclear conflict nurtured in both parties: a fear of enemies within. Playing on two uses of the word 'reds', we compared and, as we hoped, contrasted the United States' succumbing to a bout of anti-communist paranoid hysteria, led by Senator Joe McCarthy, in which thousands lost their jobs and two spies, the Rosenbergs, were sent to the electric chair, with the all-pervasive apparatus of prolonged state oppression, under Stalin and after him, in the Soviet Union: a spasm that stained a democracy, contrasted with the murderous system that characterised an authoritarian regime. The distinction was clear in our narration, and quite explicit in the book of the series Taylor Downing and I co-authored. (He wrote most.) But to no avail; dealing with the two societies in the same film caused offence. If 'Reds' was a hostage to fortune, it was my doing.

The neo-conservative right wanted a series they knew they were never going to get from Ted Turner; a series which portrayed a heroic US victor and a slain Soviet villain. But that would have been to substitute cartoon for complex reality. It couldn't allow for the contrasting moods of US statesmen, sometimes high on the ideology of freedom and the evil of totalitarianism, at other times pragmatists dealing matter-of-factly with the enemy to achieve specific ends. It couldn't explain how a red-baiting Nixon later made history by going to China, or how the Reagan who backed the Contras and denounced the Soviet's 'evil empire' sat down to negotiate with Gorbachev, and strolled through Red Square to tea in the Kremlin. Both sides are pragmatists when it suits them; a narrative to which both sides contribute does not imply their moral equivalence. What the neo-con right perhaps wants, and should certainly get, is a series on the crimes of communism.

It is true that the US faced down the USSR; but Reagan did not end the Cold War on his own. Gorbachev played a key role. Other First Secretaries of the Communist Party of the USSR might well have adopted a far more belligerent stance. Gorbachev, though he did not envisage the end of communism in the USSR, did will an end to nuclear confrontation. At the Cold War's end, he helped engineer a soft landing. The verdict of the historian and former State Department analyst Raymond L. Gartoff will stand: 'What happened would not have happened without him; that cannot be said of anyone else.'

In spite of Ted Turner's strictures to me at the beginning, the series made quite clear who won the Cold War. The United States was rich enough to spend on defence and yet still grow the economy: a liberal democracy running a market economy won out; the command economies lost. The Soviet Union denied its peoples consumer goods for decades, bankrupting itself to stay in an arms race it could not win. At the end, Gorbachev could not afford to keep up defence expenditure, let alone raise it. And *perestroika* unleashed forces he could not control, leading both to the fall of communism and to the break-up of the USSR. Marxism–Leninism, the system which did not deliver, was the clear loser in the Cold War.

The brunt of Cold War suffering was borne not in the Kremlin, nor in the White House, but in homes and workplaces in Eastern Europe, in the gulags and bread queues of the Soviet Union, in the villages and jungles of Angola and El Salvador. The Cold War preserved peace in Europe for nearly fifty years, but at a price. I gave the last word to Vaclav Havel, placed under house arrest for years in Soviet-dominated Czechoslovakia, freed in time to help engineer a velvet revolution that brought down a regime, and to become his country's President. He told Cate Haste:

> Communism as a system went against life, against man's fundamental needs, against the need for freedom, the need to be enterprising, to associate freely. Against the will of the nation, it suppressed national identity. Something that goes against life may last a long time, but sooner or later it will collapse.

Cold War won a Peabody award; John Gaddis, who used fine-cuts to teach students at Yale, saw his classes triple in number – he had to change lecture rooms twice. Another winner was Ted Turner; *Cold War* will go on being watched, used, consulted. Ted Turner had the idea, and saw it through to fruition. I am glad and grateful he sent for Jeremy Irons.

19

MILLENNIUM ... AND AFTER

'*Millennium*: a thousand years of history, ten hours of television.' Had anyone told me, at any other time in my working life, that I should embark on a project so fantastic, I would have laughed them out of the room. But in the mid-nineties the media world was falling victim to severe bouts of millennium fever. There was no escape.

Halfway through making *Cold War*, Pat Mitchell told me Ted wanted 'a millennium project'. He did not say what it should be. She did not know what he meant. I had no idea what he was after either. I ignored the hints and nudges, and got on with *Cold War*. Pat returned to the subject, still not able to specify. Eventually it turned out that what Ted Turner wanted was a world history of the last thousand years, to be ready by 2000. Now I grasped the idea, but had not the faintest notion of how to realise it. I could conceive of a history of Christianity over a thousand years, or of sail, or of painting. But the world? I did not know where to start, and mentioned the dilemma to the publishers who were bringing out a book from me on my time at the Opera House, *Never Mind the Moon*, and the book of the *Cold War* series. 'But I have just the book for you,' said the publisher Ursula Mackenzie, 'it is called *Millennium*, by one of our authors, Felipe Fernández-Armesto. It is a history of the last thousand years.' Gillian and I were going abroad for a few days' break. Ursula sent it out to us. Fernández-Armesto's book made all things possible.

Millennium is an extraordinary book by a remarkable historian. Felipe Fernández-Armesto writes about the world with elegance and verve, as if he knows everything, and perhaps he does. The book is 800 pages long, full of meat, crammed with vivid detail. I started at once to read it and soon saw, long before I had finished, how the text might prompt a television series into being.

I did not know of a single theme that strikingly explained world history over those ten centuries. Others might well have done; the triumph of the West, perhaps. But John Roberts, Warden of my old college, Merton, had done just such a series for BBC TV. What Fernández-Armesto's book showed me, as I devoured succulent pages on the Afghan court and gardens at Herat in the eleventh century, or the bustling fifteenth-century prosperity of the Chinese city Kaifeng, was that the detail itself was revelatory and exciting. We would not need a single grand theme or thesis; we would not paint a single picture, but offer a sequence of vignettes, telling, particular, diverse.

Secondly – and surely this would appeal to Ted Turner's internationalist spirit, his sense of all of us in one world – Fernández-Armesto's *Millennium* was a history not of any one continent, nor even of a world seen from one continent, from a European, Atlanticist or American point of view. It was a history of the world seen from space. Fernández-Armesto envisaged himself writing, not at a desk in Oxford, but out in space as a 'galactic observer', like Spock in *Star Trek*. He had written more of the riches of the East, India and China, than of Europe; more of Africa than of the Americas; as much of Islam as of Christianity. With this *Millennium* to guide us, we could make a series work.

MillenniuM
A thousand years of history

I sent the book to Atlanta, and promised that a treatment would follow. In London, I met the author and discussed what his role might be. Felipe was overjoyed there might be a TV series, eager to write and present it. I did not think he could do that on screen; his bespectacled presence and elegant diction were indeed compelling, but not what CNN would think right for the US audience, or for sales worldwide. Besides, every page he had written suggested imagery; whatever difficulties doing without a presenter to camera might pose, this surely was an opportunity for pictures to tell the story. I urged CNN to option the book. We agreed Felipe would write a treatment, outlines and, eventually, scripts.

Our working relationship with Felipe Fernández-Armesto would be bumpy, but I always found him formidable in intellect and energy. Formally suited, with collar and tie, poplin shirts and bright-hued braces, shined shoes, and powerful spectacles behind which keen eyes gleamed, he had a slightly old-fashioned bearing, as if George V or Alfonso XIII were still on the throne. But he was anything but pompous, rasping out a biting commentary on events and personalities in resonant, nasal tones. He was never short of an idea, or of the words to express it. He had made a reputation as a scholar with concise early books, his biography *Columbus* a most readable example. Now he aspired to the world view.

In our collaboration, he never quite took on board the distance between print and video. Any treatment he wrote was always in the prose he wrote naturally, a shorter version of his book's narrative, but not much shorter; too wordy for TV. Still, his text was a starting point, and always an inspiration.

What proposal should we now send to Atlanta? How shape it? The obvious format for organising subject matter was one programme per century. Gillian came up with a further formative idea; instead of a continuous narrative flow – to be interrupted in any case by US commercial breaks six or seven times in the hour – why not create several short films on disparate topics, shot in different continents, and leave them unconnected, within the same hour? This was what we did. After all, we began from Felipe's perception of history as an aggregate of detail, rather than a broad sweep or defining line. We would give each hour a semblance of coherence with a title; Century of the Sword, of the Stirrup, of the Telescope. But the content would be diverse.

In the treatment sent to Atlanta we suggested twelve hours of television, including an hour to paint the scene, the world in 1000; and, post-2000, an hour of futurology. But the bookends dropped off. The kernel was: 'a thousand years of history in ten hours of television'.

When David Attenborough discussed with Kenneth Clark the television series he might make for BBC2, it was the word 'civilisation' that caught K's interest. And *Civilisation* is what he made; European civilisation. There is no mention of Africa, little of any other continent than Europe in those luminous thirteen hours. What was needed now, I thought, *mutatis* very much *mutandis*, was not *Civilisation*, but *Civilisations*.

Pat Mitchell had reported to me that Ted had read Felipe's book when I sent it to him. I did not believe it; I had not finished it myself. It would be a shorter text and pictures that would clinch it. Gillian cut Felipe ruthlessly, raided SOAS for dazzling images, and worked through the night to create an enticing sales brochure. I wrote a foreword, and a sentence I hoped might prove irresistible: 'This project has been developed for R. E. Turner, who always takes the global view and has the vision to inspire.'

In the week before Easter 1997, FedEx conveyed another bulky box to Atlanta. Pat told me she had a meeting fixed in Ted's diary at 4 p.m. on the Friday – Good Friday, by which time in Britain offices were empty, and most executives off already for the holiday weekend. She would be seeing him again, socially, for Sunday lunch. We were in Suffolk for Easter. At 7 p.m. that Easter day, 2 p.m. in Atlanta, the telephone rang. Ted had said 'Yes'. *Millennium* was on.

By this time, JIP had a good relationship with CNN's executive team. It was short work to settle on ten episodes, not twelve; easier, therefore, to agree the hefty budget per hour that would enable us to film in thirty-two countries around the globe. We included a substantial sum for computer graphics. These, used sparingly because so expensive, brought noble ruins back to their earlier glory at Pueblo Bonito in Chaco Canyon, New Mexico, and at Medinat az-Zahrat outside Córdoba; they re-created the Aztec city of Tenochtitlan, and rebuilt the vast wooden naval vessels with which, in the fifteenth century, the Chinese Admiral Zheng He ruled the ocean waves. JIP's contract with CNN for *Millennium* was swiftly finalised. Ted and I met for dinner at the Ritz-Carlton on Central Park South. Larry King was dining there also. On his way to the table, Ted bellowed to him across the room: 'How do you like your shares now, then? Didn't I tell you they'd go up?' He had sold Turner Broadcasting to Time Warner. Ted liked to say that he and I were partners. Seated, I asked what he would do to make that partnership good – improve JIP's end rights? He grunted non-committally. In the end, our share of still distant rights was marginally adjusted; but the basic fee, JIP's margin on production, was generous. Coming in on time and budget could markedly improve our finances. Easier said than done; *Millennium* was the most complicated production I have ever been involved with.

The first six months of production were a nightmare. The line-producer we initially appointed was defeated, as well he might have been, by the complexity of the project. We had to stop and start again. More difficult was making a schedule to film six segments for each hour in all five continents; at last I saw the light, and cut six to five. From then on, the sums worked. We could send crews where we needed, and get them back again. We shot on digi-beta video, not celluloid.

David Wallace, a master film-maker, went to Ethiopia to film Christian churches hewn out of solid bedrock at Lalibela in the twelfth century – 'Century of the Axe'. From the moment he came back, it was clear we would succeed. There, at the famous churches, was today's congregation, topped up with pilgrims, celebrating Lalibela, their ancient king, his magic powers and their faith. These pictures told the story. After Ethiopia, a globe would turn – in the US there'd be commercials – then something totally different, Tuscany; San Gimignano, with the forest of slim towers that once distinguished its skyline restored by the computer. I recruited directors of high repute, who would accept working on a small scale – eight minutes only for a take on the Renaissance. The premium was on invention; *Millennium* was a chance to show off. Dave Wallace, Mike Dibb, Murray Grigor, Marc Kidel contributed. 'You've got all the talents there,' the BBC's Managing Director Television, Will Wyatt, said to me. He knew how grudgingly others made space for film-makers of that generation. And we recruited younger bright sparks, including Henry Chancellor and Richard Curson Smith. Neil Cameron and Emma De'Ath – line producers – filmed, co-ordinated, made graphics happen. We had a fine graphic artist at Framestore, Bernard Heyes; Richard Blackford wrote a signature tune to accompany Bernard's main title. Glenn Keiles worked with Richard Blackford to provide apt, ethnically diverse music, segment by segment. Recording with the BBC Concert Orchestra – the lady first trumpet sensational – was a joy. Ben Kingsley, not the easiest man to work with, recorded commentary in Chipping Norton, near his Cotswold home, and in Los Angeles.

All came together in the end.

At Glasgow Academy I had enticed sixth-form friends to St

Andrew's Halls to hear Mozart and Beethoven; when the trumpets sounded for the finale of the Fifth Symphony, they sat up with a jerk. Now *Millennium* was pointing millions to the marvels of the world's past. Did you know, we asked, that in the fifteenth century China looked outwards, commanded the oceans? We met Admiral Zheng He. And Timur, and Baibars. We gazed at the green-blue cupolas of the mosques of Samarkand, and – to me, the most stunning sight of all – the brick-built mosque at Mali's capital, Djenne, where in the fourteenth century, while Europe languished in war, ruin, plague and desolation, a great African civilisation traded gold for salt.

Others responded. Ted Turner had taken his broadcasting empire into a vaster conglomerate, Time Warner, and surrendered his independence in doing so; projects costing over $1 million now had to be approved by the board. Time Warner's CEO, Gerald Levin, was a cultured man, with a degree in Arabic. Pat Mitchell and I discussed *Millennium* with him; he approved. As it happened, Pat and I were due to make a presentation on *Cold War* to the Time Warner main board. Richard Parsons, then Director of Public Affairs, now Chairman and CEO, conducted a rehearsal the day before; you enter here, speak there, take questions at the table. He admired my neckwear – the sort Jon Snow wears on C4 News – designed by Gene Meyer, and sold at MOMA. 'Whatever you do tomorrow,' said Dick Parsons, 'wear that tie.' On the way back to the hotel, Pat suggested we call in at a restaurant, Le Cirque, to book a table. All the waiters were wearing Gene Meyer ties. Next day at the board meeting, there were tough *Cold War* questions:

'Did you get to interview in China?'

'Er . . . No.'

Someone admired the tie.

'Well, thank you,' I said, with English self-deprecation, 'but at Le Cirque, where we ate last night, all the waiters were wearing one.'

'Hell of a good restaurant.'

In London, Mark Thompson snapped up *Millennium* for BBC2; he saw it, I guess, as accessible high culture. And inexpensive, too. When it came to 2000, BBC TV was happy to include *Millennium* in its publicised range of offerings to mark the occasion on television. They had little of their own making to put forward, though radio had done some goodish things. BBC TV's trump card was the hugely expensive, and hugely popular, *Walking with Dinosaurs*. At a dinner chaired by the Chairman, Christopher Bland, I asked the man who'd produced *Dinosaurs* what that had to do with the millennium. He replied: 'Why this fuss over a thousand years of history? Dinosaurs ruled the earth for thirty-seven million years!' There was no answer to that.

Controller BBC2, Jane Root, wondering what to do with a classy series that had no internal advocates, scheduled *Millennium* at five o'clock on Saturdays. I protested; another slot was found at seven o'clock on Monday evenings. At that early hour *Millennium* reached and held over 2 million viewers a week. Mothers, we gathered, watched it with their children. It was truly popular history. The historian Eric Hobsbawm came to the London preview, and was, to my surprise, complimentary; so was John Roberts, to Gillian. *Millennium* opened eyes to the richness of our world.

And the whole, in the end, was greater than the sum of its parts. Felipe Fernández-Armesto's view of the world from space, from outside history, was revealing. Three over-arching themes stood out as the series came to its conclusion in the present. In the first five centuries of the millennium we began by marvelling at what Africa, the Americas and the cultures of the East achieved; how inventive was China, how influential Islam, how rich India. In the millennium's second half, however, we watched European, Western culture, at first overshadowed by the East, begin to assert itself, reaching, by conquest and colonisation, for world hegemony. Second, we noted the rise of science alongside religion, and the growth in the minds of men and women of scientific explanations of the universe. We have answers now to questions to which, a thousand years ago, there was no response. Third, while *Millennium* celebrated diversity, it also showed that today humanity inhabits one world; we can photograph it from space, circle it by satellite in an hour, send messages round it in a second. Is it possible that, at the end of another thousand years, humankind will contemplate, not this planet's, but the universe's diversity? Meanwhile, we have much to learn from the past.

Fifteen months before the Millennium Dome was due to open there was still no announcement of what it would contain. I went to see the Director, Jenny Page, to ask if the wonders we were accumulating in our image-store might not, translated into three dimensions, furnish a pavilion displaying a history of the past thousand years. Jenny Page had with her a marketing man, formerly at J. Walter Thompson. She stated categorically, and he said their research confirmed, that no one was interested in history.

Among those advising on the contents of the Millennium Dome were Michael Grade and Alan Yentob. Ted Turner could teach them a thing or two.

Was there life for JIP after *Millennium*? Ted Turner thought so, inviting proposals for a third series from us. I cobbled together an outline for *The Neutrals*, the subject *The World at War* left out. What did the neutrals get up to in the Second World War; whose side were they on? Sweden sold iron ore to Germany; Swiss banks impounded Jewish assets; Ireland sent fire-engines from Dublin when Belfast burned, but De Valera signed the German Embassy's book of condolences on Hitler's death. And British and German agents drank next to each other in the bars of Lisbon and Madrid. Fascinating stuff, I thought. Ted went off the idea, announcing, in a corridor of the Waldorf Astoria, that we should leave the past and tackle the future.

We came up with *Twenty Twenty*, a guess at what life might be like in the year 2020. We canvassed futurological opinion, sketched out six possible films and got another prompt go-ahead. A bright producer, new to us, Ian Holt, pulled the programmes into shape; something presentable, I thought at first, resulted. Or maybe not. You can predict the future in fantasy, as did Kubrick in *2001 – A Space Odyssey*. You cannot do it in factual mode; stuff happens, and proves you wrong. How would the skyline of Manhattan look in 2020? Subtly, we thought, in an expensive computer graphic for the title sequence, we added a third to the two Trade Towers. On 11 September 2001 our guesses were blown away.

By now, Ted Turner was not the power he had been within the Time Warner conglomerate, enlarged to gargantuan size by the disastrous merger Gerald Levin engineered with AOL. Pat Mitchell, too, was moving on, onwards and upwards. In 2000 she became President of PBS. In the life of JIP a tectonic plate had shifted.

As Director of Programmes, I had once assembled Thames's producers and directors in a viewing theatre at Euston. There were well over a hundred present. 'Our average age in this room', I told them, 'is thirty-eight. How many of you think you'll be doing roughly the same job in ten or fifteen years' time?' Nearly everyone put their hand up. 'You won't, you know,' I said. 'The industry we're in demands new blood, new ideas. Some of you should think of changing. If anyone here has ever thought' – I plucked it from the air – 'of keeping a chicken farm, it may soon be time to make the move.' In ITV, the pensionable retirement age was mostly set low, at sixty; earlier retirement at fifty-five grew common. In 2000 I was sixty-eight. 'The whirligig of time brings in his revenges': Ted Turner had been inviting, but in the UK, whatever programme proposals I put forward, no one wanted to know.

Tom Courtenay, born at Fishdock in Hull, kept the letters his mother wrote him at RADA, and made a touching book of them. The publisher, Ursula Mackenzie again, sent it to me; a loving family portrait and emblem of his mother's frustrated cultural longings, her talent unrealised, except vicariously, through her son. *Dear Tom* was skilfully adapted, on spec, by Alan Plater, a neighbour of the Courtenays' in Hull's poorest quarter, responsible for much television drama of high quality. It was warm-hearted, touching, and said something that mattered. No one at the BBC, in ITV or at Channel Four, had any interest in it. Alan Plater may well re-write it one day, and have it do the rounds again.

I was sure that in 2005 TV should commemorate, in a big way, Nelson's death at Trafalgar on 21 October 1805, the two-hundredth anniversary of a victory that gave Britain command of the seas for a century. Channel Four was willing to fund a script; successive chief executives, and a director of programmes, gave the nod. I commissioned Charles Wood, a screenwriter with a passion for battle and a loathing of the consequences of war – *Charge of the Light Brigade, Tumbledown* – to write it. 'What is the relevance of this today, Jeremy?' I was asked. It has not got made. Perhaps it was not bold enough in finding a 'new, contemporary take on Nelson's character'. I had thought, after *Longitude* and *Shackleton*, that every so often C4 would want to make something in period, if the subject was of sufficient interest. But other priorities swept *Nelson* aside. 'We fucked you up, Jeremy,' Tim Gardam, Director of Programmes, told me. 'When we commissioned the development, we did not really know what we were doing.'

A German independent production company, part of Bavaria Film in Munich, asked me to work with them in making a series on communist terror, based on *The Black Book of Communism*, a thorough, if partisan, catalogue of crimes that cost tens of millions of lives. For some reason, there is more interest in Hitler and Nazism as a subject for television history than in Stalin and Marxism–Leninism. Yet Stalin (and Mao) ordered more deaths than Hitler, and it is a close call whose regime was the more evil. I would say Nazism, myself. But can one differentiate between such horrors in meaningful terms? There have been superb books on Stalin's crimes, Robert Conquest's *The Great Terror* for a start. And there has been much good television. But nothing on TV has taken an overview and looked at the cost in lives of communist terror worldwide. I hawked this proposal round too, in the UK and, notably to WNET, PBS's New York flagship – to no avail. Two years' effort went for nothing. Large projects happen only when someone who thinks big has the financial clout to go it alone and, preferably, owns the media outlet that will present the result.

The Gulag, the Lubianka, man-made famine, deportation and death depress the spirit. Handel, Mozart and Rossini lift mine. As the conventional broadcasters – foreheads worn villainous low – sidelined the arts to the margins of their output, or banished them altogether, a thought took hold. Now that digital is with us, why not a channel devoted to the arts? We called it Artsworld.

The first suggestion that this could happen was put to me at the Royal Opera House. Rupert Murdoch sent Andrew Knight to see me; he wanted advice on how it might be done. Murdoch was well ahead of the game in spotting that a multiplicity of digital channels, delivered by satellite, would make all sorts of specialist provision possible. It is notable, though, that he should specify an arts channel. Was it his personal taste? I doubt it. Perhaps he thought that pleasing arts-lovers, and one supposed arts-lover at 10 Downing Street, would buy his empire upmarket respectability and weaken the BBC's claim, as a public service broadcaster, to the licence fee.

Weighed down by the difficulty of getting opera and ballet on to terrestrial TV, I gave Andrew Knight unhelpful answers. I saw the problem then as how television could help the arts. It mattered enormously at Covent Garden when we put back in place an agreement to relay a dozen operas a year on BBC radio. For TV, the expense of this was much greater. I thought first of television's responsibilities to the arts; not of its power to exploit them.

The right answer, staring me in the face, was the one I'd seized on at Channel Four; buy the world's back catalogue, cheaply.

When David Elstein had had charge of Sky's programming, Gillian and I had told him of our eagerness to help if he ever wanted an arts channel. Now another ex-Thames colleague came to see me. He was working, with John Hambley, on a proposal for an arts channel; would I work with them? This was Richard Dunn.

Richard had been an executive under me at Thames. He had caught Howard Thomas's eye when running a community cable service at Windsor. In time, after Bryan Cowgill moved out, he took over as Managing Director and, bravely and wisely, appointed David Elstein as Director of Programmes. Thames kept its lead in ITV's profitability stakes and its high reputation, but lost its franchise, outbid by Michael Green's Carlton in an auction substituted for qualitative judgement as the key to winning. A clause in the Act gave the Authority the right to take 'special circumstances' into account. It did not exercise it. Richard sought and found employment elsewhere. When he came to see me during *Cold War*, I agreed to collaborate in making an arts channel happen.

Richard Dunn was tall, with a friendly countenance. He was also thoughtful, resolute and honest; the sort of man you could not fail to admire. In August 1998 he was found dead in his swimming pool in Berkshire. He had suffered a heart attack. Next time John Hambley and I talked, we knew we owed it to Richard to go on together.

I was Artworld's Chairman. John Hambley was Chief Executive, and did the work; with Christopher Turner, ex-LWT, he spent a year raising the necessary capital. There were two lead institutional investors; individuals with an interest in the arts invested also, as did a family trust. Sky was pleased to see us: 'just what we are looking for'. Artsworld would be a stand-alone subscription channel, £5.99 a month to subscribers, who would also need a satellite dish and a basic Sky package. The business plan called for us to attract 1.5 per cent of their vast subscriber base – 'You'll reach that easily,' they said. Someone reported I was 'taking Murdoch's shilling'. Not so; Sky was to benefit, it was supposed, from our energies and the investors' capital commitment.

We appointed Richard Melman as Programme Director, and prepared to launch in December 2000. We had undertaken in the contract with Sky – after hard, prolonged negotiations – to spend an agreed sum on programming, and splashed out a bit at the beginning. JIP made some of the opening schedule: a documentary with the amazing Lesley Garrett (we took her back to her Yorkshire roots); Michael Nyman's band; BRB's performance of David Bintley's ballet *Such Sweet Thunder*, Shakespeare to the music of Duke Ellington. The schedule also boasted, comparatively expensively and, as it turned out, mistakenly, a topical arts magazine. Budgets were very tight, less than a tenth of what is now available to BBC4. There was little profit to JIP in programme-making; but it kept our hand in.

For Artsworld Gillian made programmes with musicians, mainly, simple half-hour recitals: with Paco Peña the guitarist, in Córdoba; soprano Amanda Roocroft; James Crabb, an astonishing virtuoso on the classical accordion; and others. The organist Simon Preston, an old friend, pulled out all the stops on the new organ in the chapel of Tonbridge School, perhaps the UK's finest. At Goodwood, in the sculpture park made by Wilfred and Jeanette Cass, she made three films, *Walking with Sculptors*.

I dabbled happily in the visual arts. The film-maker Diane Tammes – cameraperson, at a pinch recordist, writer/director – took just one day to film each *Artist at Work*. Twelve half-hour films resulted. Lucy Jones is physically disabled, but a bold, vibrant painter, lugging canvasses bigger than herself across the studio; 'I was never going to be a ballet dancer,' she explained. Our pal Bert Irvin, who paints abstracts, was the subject of the first film we made. Eighty years old, he waited long for recognition. Then it came.

'Bert,' friends told him, 'you're an overnight success.'

'In that case,' said Bert, 'it's been a bloody long night.'

Aged eighty-five, Terry Frost, another colourful abstractionist, was the star of a very jolly film, made, as it turned out, shortly before he died. Other production companies, on equally frugal budgets, chipped in to good effect.

While we made these little beauties on a shoestring, the BBC, except for showcasing Rolf Harris, was doing virtually nothing in the arts on either of its channels. They needed the slots for low-brow entertainment, cookery, gardening and sundry makeover shows.

On a bigger scale, Artsworld dazzled. We bought in a fresh cycle of Beethoven symphonies, conducted by Claudio Abbado, frail but still commanding. And we showed, from Bayreuth, Wagner's *Der Ring des Nibelungen*, conducted by Barenboim, with Lancashire's John Tomlinson as Wotan, and Wales's Anne Evans as Brunnhilde. Stephen Fry emailed me to thank us for the joy their long scene together had given him, making him 'as happy', he wrote, 'as a pig in sherry'.

ARTSWORLD

We were all of us over-optimistic; making the arts channel grow was far harder than we, or Sky, anticipated. The marketing budget was limited. We tried to sell Artsworld to the arts community – people who went to the V&A, Tate, ENO or the National Theatre – but they needed to have a dish, a set-top box and a basic Sky subscription before they could receive it. If we aimed instead at Sky subscribers, there was, it turned out, no way cold-calling call-centre staff could know which of the millions on Sky's list had any interest in the arts. The subscriber base grew very slowly. When we were able to ask Artsworld subscribers, eighteen months in, what they wanted of us, their answer was clear: arts programming across the board, but principally classical music, opera and dance. They didn't want a topical magazine; they wanted major performance. They were an older audience, at home in the afternoons; one couple thanked us for 'making our retirement worthwhile'. For some we were a source of deep pleasure, of cultural riches, a constant solace. They did not want us to dumb down in any way.

When Artsworld made a second call for funds, our lead investors – one was the Guardian Media Group – unwilling to incur further loss, refused, and plunged us into crisis. Others stood by and, indeed, came to the rescue. On 31 July 2003, having already told subscribers we could not continue to broadcast, we put on a boozy farewell party – a wake, in fact – in a West End pub. When I arrived, John Hambley told me we would not close after all: 'That man standing there [Julian Simmonds, a substantial shareholder who cared] has put up the cash to keep us on air.' We are still there. I never knew a paying audience more loyal than Artsworld's. By telephone, letter, email, they begged us to keep going. For the next year, though we spent nothing on marketing, the subscriber base remained level. Today, the station is in Sky's sole ownership. It will cease to depend on stand-alone subscription, and will be offered instead as part of a more general package. May it flourish.

Gillian did make a film for BBC2 – on the composer Francis Poulenc, marking the centenary of his birth. We filmed it at Noizay, in Touraine, amid the Vouvray vineyards where, not far from the Loire, his country house still stands. Graham Johnson, of *Song-Makers' Almanac*, masterly accompanist and programme-planner, helped devise the structure. At Noizay, he played Poulenc's piano. Dame Felicity Lott lent her sunny soprano and perfect French diction to the songs; Denise Duval, for whom Poulenc wrote, came out of her Swiss retirement, looking good, touched to be involved in a programme on the composer with whom she had loved working; she had given the première of *La Voix Humaine*. The film was simple yet revealing; it gave pleasure, and told truths. The *Sunday Telegraph*'s critic, Michael Kennedy, thought it 'a gem'.

Obvious variations on this theme – a composer's songs, in a house he knew – suggested themselves. Gillian, prompted by Graham Johnson, mentioned the likeliest to the BBC: Richard Strauss at Garmisch; Hugo Wolf at Perchtoldsdorf; Edvard Grieg at his house in the woods near Bergen; Manuel de Falla at the Alhambra in Granada. BBC TV said 'No, thank you.'

Charter renewal is upon us, with an attendant flurry of renewed attachment to the arts. But so long as that attitude persists – it's not trendy; we don't want it – there will be a need for Artsworld.

20

JAMIE KISSED ME

There will be only one mention by me in this book of a golden age of television, and that was it. I respect programme-makers who came before me, rejoice in those with whom I worked, admire the best of those at work today, as good as any there ever were. Whether this age is gold, platinum, silver or bronze is still uncertain. What is certain is that the world we live in has changed, almost out of recognition, over fifty years, and we have changed with it.

Peter Black, in *The Mirror in the Corner: People's Television*, one of the best books to be written on the medium, stated a truth that lasts: television reflects the society it serves. When I left school, there were still gas lamps in the streets; horses pulled brewers' drays; cricketers were either players or gentlemen; footballers earned £5 a week, the same as their supporters on the terracing, and wore suits and overcoats and hats. Pop music was just about to be born, rock and roll not yet upon us; I can still feel Bill Haley and his Comets' first impact on my eardrums. I used to enjoy listening to Jack Jackson's *Record Round Up*: Pee Wee Hunt playing *Twelfth Street Rag*, Phil Harris's throaty patter, Theresa Brewer belting out ballads. But rock never captured me; I was by then immersed in classical music, theatre, painting, film and, above all, books. The popular culture which was to give boundless pleasure to massed millions was on its way – an irresistible force, as Tim Gardam has put it, occupying space once reserved for other, quieter, pleasures.

In technology, too, all is changed utterly. I am writing this in longhand; I seldom use a mobile phone. When, as President of the Royal Television Society, I received Prince Charles, our patron, at a conference at St James's Palace, clusters of lively, with-it young people in media confidently discussed the future. At one session I sat beside him. He turned to me: 'What is Yahoo, Jeremy?' I told him: 'A character in Jonathan Swift, I think.' That did not seem quite right. I removed myself, and enquired. By the time I got back, he'd found out from the chap on his left. I console myself for this by remembering that at least I did attend, on a blissfully sunny afternoon at Claremont Campus, UCLA, the graduation ceremony – strawberries, a bagpiper, the Governor of California – of a bright young man who is now somebody in Google.

Since I started in 1958, television channels in the UK have changed, most noticeably in number. We learned to count them on the fingers of one hand: 1, 3, 2, 4, 5. At Granada and, at first, at Rediffusion, anything I produced competed only with one other programme, on BBC1. Then came BBC2. When ITV broadcast from Glyndebourne Monteverdi's *Il Ritorno d'Ulisse in Patria*, the audience might desert it; the advertisers could not. They had nowhere else to go. The principle of not requiring rival broadcasters to compete for revenue from the same source was observed in the setting up of Channel Four. It served as the root promoter of excellence in British broadcasting for decades. Framework matters. The BBC still has a monopoly of the licence-fee billions; ITV's hold on advertising is now broken by competition with Channels Four and Five, and with satellite, cable, the internet and others. Yet, I insist, the dispensation under which we work does not govern what programming we do. We are free to choose.

In a free market, the law of the jungle prevails: kill or be killed, eat or be eaten. In a system of broadcasting dedicated only to the pursuit of ratings and profits, participants fight each other all the way to the bank. But even in rampantly commercial ecologies, in the US, in Australia, where public corporations are on the sidelines, good broadcasters have other obligations than simply to feed at the trough. Systems are impersonal, broadcasters human; systems determine, broadcasters follow judgement, hunch, predilection, risk, taste. They want to stand out from the crowd, even if only to promote their own financial advantage. All broadcasting, Tony Smith stated, tends towards a norm. But who wants to personify a norm?

In the UK, broadcasters still have public service obligations. ITV, now under single ownership, may try to slough them off, but has not yet succeeded entirely. Channel Five appears undecided. For the BBC, for Channel Four, the issue of doing so does not even arise, as Channel Four, after flirting, incredibly, with the notion of a merger with Five, has now reaffirmed.

How serious are Channel Four and the BBC in renewing pledges of faith to high ideals? A dog is not for Christmas; a commitment to public service not just for Charter renewal. Michael Grade, the BBC's Chairman, once a commercial broadcaster to his fingertips, has clearly perceived that BBC TV, and particularly BBC1 under Greg Dyke, went too near the cliff's edge in pursuit of ratings: *Panorama* on Sunday evenings at 10.15, no other current affairs on BBC1, the arts banished almost altogether, no science, hardly a documentary to be seen. Four *Eastenders* weekly, *Holby City* and *Casualty* the year round, pushed BBC1's ratings, for the first time ever, ahead of ITV. Controller BBC1, now departed, explained that she couldn't play *Panorama* in peak time; ratings would fall. So what? someone asked. Is that the star public broadcasters sail by? Is that what we pay our licence fee for?

Popular programmes are, properly, the main component of any mainstream schedule. Ratings matter; but not all of the time. Critics of channel controllers who aim only at mass audiences are sometimes dismissed with the charge that we want to marginalise the BBC, leaving it as the poor relation to the commercial sector. Not at all; the alternative to obsession with ratings is not to neglect them, but simply not to allow their pursuit to govern every scheduling and commissioning decision.

Television that matters aims at viewers, not at ratings, and acknowledges that different viewers have different tastes. *Crossroads*, *Eastenders*, *Brookside* and *Coronation Street* meant and mean much to millions. Yet, in the mind of its creator, it is for this or that individual that a programme is broadcast: I'm talking to you; can I interest you in what I'm saying? The trouble is that ratings are powerful drugs, and most channel controllers are hooked on them, addicted to numbers. If you are addicted, choosing to broadcast something that will get fewer viewers is hard, the temptation to do the same again irresistible, as every drinker knows.

'Another?'

'No thanks, I've had enough.'

'Sure?'

'Oh, all right then, why not?'

Channel controllers rarely wean themselves off ratings – not for Lent, not through January, not one day a week. But the best broadcasters have other ends.

In 1965, after a wobbly start and a reshuffle, Huw Wheldon asked David Attenborough to give up furry beasties for a while, and take over BBC2. Michael Peacock had chosen to give each evening of the week its own character – *Seven Faces of the Week* – and seen that notion die the death. He had commissioned some fine programmes and established, for instance, that BBC2 would treat music seriously. Attenborough discovered that he could book the great American jazz and swing bands and regale himself, at the end of a day's work, with Duke Ellington or Louis Armstrong in the studio downstairs. 'But', he tells us in his autobiography *Life on Air*,

> classical music remained paramount in the network's sched-
> ules. BBC2's second Christmas – the first under my charge –
> was coming up. I asked the Music Department to arrange a
> performance of Berlioz's *L'Enfance du Christ*. At that time,
> Berlioz's music was rarely performed, either at Christmas or at
> any other time. This charming short oratorio would certainly be
> unfamiliar to most of the television audience, but its appropri-
> ateness was obvious. Colin Davis, who was already renowned
> as a champion of Berlioz's music, would conduct and we would
> stage the performance in Ely Cathedral. It would bring real dis-
> tinction and innovation to BBC2's Christmas.

Attenborough went on to offer viewers the 83-year-old Igor Stravinsky conducting *Firebird*. 'With proper attention to Britain's pre-eminent composer of the time', he put on Benjamin Britten's *The Burning Fiery Furnace* from Orford Church, and a full-scale studio production of *Billy Budd*, Peter Pears as Captain Vere, Charles Mackerras conducting; BBC2 commissioned from Britten a new opera, *Owen Wingrave*. 'Proper attention', David Herman has pointed out, 'tells us everything about the values that inspired Attenborough and his channel.' He brought to the screen the archaeological series *Chronicle*; when colour became possible, he lit up our lives with Kenneth Clark's *Civilisation*, and snooker's *Pot Black*.

David Herman, who writes cogently on television for *Prospect*, believes passionately that there was a golden age, from the 1960s to the 1980s. The test, he says, is the specific programmes; in let-ters to me, he lists cornucopias of them on the BBC, and to a lesser extent on ITV also. He is surely right to argue that quiz shows, sit-coms and soap operas, though staple fare, are neither the greatest achievements nor the only tests of a healthy television culture, such as that which British broadcasting, admired worldwide, is held to exhibit. Writers – Troy Kennedy Martin, John Hopkins, David Mercer, Trevor Griffiths, Jack Rosenthal, Alan Bleasdale – and directors – Ken Loach, Philip Saville, Peter Watkins, Richard Eyre, Leslie Woodhead – and maybe even executives, count too.

One high-water mark we owe to David Attenborough, the most gifted and persuasive TV communicator of our time. What was he up to in 1964, in putting his choice of the best before us? He was following his nose. Michael Grade, a new broom at the BBC's top, has threatened sanctions against executives who default on public service obligations. He would do better to insist on the BBC's appointing only those who value them in the first place.

If everything else changes, though, can 'public service' escape redefinition? Is 'high culture' still on that menu? It should be. The arts speak to us, searchingly, of things that matter and raise the spirit. Jennifer Lopez's bum may be culture, low culture; it is not art. Reithians – though I never once heard a colleague claim Reith as mentor – believe in giving everyone a chance to sample what they believe to be best: in the arts and the sciences, in drama and in thought. David Attenborough saw that as BBC2's particular role, that role part of the BBC's natural function. But he acted before the digital age was born.

At Banff, in the summer of 2000, Mark Thompson, then Director of BBC Television, since Chief Executive of C4, now Director General of the BBC, spelled out the difference various new digital outlets could make to mainstream BBC output. He suggested that BBC TV should address mass audiences on BBC1 and BBC2, and treat subject matter of interest principally to limited audiences on digital; niche subjects for niche audiences on niche channels. Classical music, he went out of his way to say, was just such a niche item; classical music-lovers, a niche audience. Prepare to take your place, he indicated, in a long queue. The intellectual Thompson put the argument forcibly into the public arena. Greg Dyke was right behind him. They went too fast – not everyone yet had digital – and too far; it's the function of public service to display greatness boldly in the mainstream, not stash it away in a corner.

There has already been a change of heart; the outcry against dumbing down has put pressure on the Governors to restore the arts and current affairs to BBC1's and BBC2's peak-time schedule. They will continue to feature there, at least until the Charter is renewed and a new licence fee set. Mark Thompson, in the BBC's *Annual Report for 2004/5*, led off with 'Beethoven Week', a change of tack indeed, and a success. But the BBC used not to have to invent a 'Week' to give us Beethoven. *Bleak House*, though, was a triumph.

We are all consumers now. Once factual programmes looked outwards, to shared aims and ends; today much of the time it's me, me, me that TV caters for in peak time. Media, in print and on the airwaves, devote acres of space to personal material satisfaction: food and drink we imbibe, clothes we wear, bodies we inhabit, homes we live in, cars we drive, holidays we take, properties we acquire. This leaves little room for poetry, for religion, for medieval church architecture, for books, for ideas. And the 'same again please' syndrome has done its work, so that cook succeeds cook, and gardener gardener, on our screens. For years this pandering to consumer appetites has passed for factual programming. Jane Root, the Controller BBC2 principally responsible for her channel's part in the deluge, explains that all this works as entertainment, and is half a million pounds an hour cheaper than drama or comedy. So BBC2 and C4 played a ghastly game of 'anything you can do, I can do more of'. Some of us turned of an evening to a good book.

The misnomer of the age is 'reality' television. In the last year of Rediffusion we made documentaries supposedly 'inside' great institutions. The Vatican was one; the British Foreign Office another. A hand-held camera followed the Foreign Secretary, George Brown, from his official residence in Carlton Gardens down the steps, past Horse Guards Parade, into the Foreign Office and up in the lift to his vast room. He strode across it, positioned himself behind his desk, and stood there. The camera kept running; nothing happened. A gaggle of civil servants were watching from the door. Was this a convincing view of an institution at work? George Brown didn't think so, and called out to them, petulantly, 'Come over here, some of you, and make it real.'

It never was, nor ever could be. The television camera intervenes. Nowadays, TV no longer observes or describes; we must learn, or teach others, by being involved. Some claim that watching personality, appearance or marriage being made over is genuinely revelatory. Perhaps. But peering into what should be private to satisfy prurient curiosity is no way for public media to behave. C4's *Big Brother*, a huge, lucrative phenomenon – appreciated, it has to be said, in its early years at least, by millions – is tacky, and getting tackier. But C4 is stuck with it for some years yet, so large a part of its revenues does this voyeur's charter deliver – revenues, the argument goes, that pay for better things. The very opposite of closely, objectively, observed behaviour – as in, say, *Badger Watch* by infra-red camera – these goings-on are contrived, manipulated, incited, distorted to suit commercial ends. The problem for C4 is that it has risked being known better for this cynical money-spinner than for anything else. If C4 were a gutter tabloid, bent on maximising profit, there would be no problem. But C4 claims still to be a public service broadcaster.

From the moment the channel sold its own advertising, it became harder to sustain the remit to innovate, to take creative risk. In a sense, C4 was too successful at selling advertising. Its revenues boomed; but instead of relaxing, and aiming pricklier, more austere insights at diverse audiences, the channel stepped on the gas. On marketing's advice, it devoted itself to pursuing and pleasing one lucrative demographic target primarily – and secondarily, and thirdly: the 16–34-year-olds. One documentary-maker I know was advised not to use three-syllable words in commentary. Another colleague, pitching a series taking another look at the Falklands War, through the eyes of its official historian, was asked by a junior commissioning editor: 'What's in this for a woman under the age of thirty-five?' And the Falklands, by the way, was the only war in English history since the time of Elizabeth I when the commander-in-chief was a woman. Senior channel executives shudder at this true anecdote, and wave it away: 'Surely not.' But that is what happens when programmers, ambitious to do well, are drilled by the marketing department to respect advertisers' targets – three million viewers, please, next time – and rewarded for doing so.

Channel Four, my baby, is not a baby any more. But I want to hear it praised for doing right, not sneered at for programmes that would make a tabloid blush. The best C4 does is better than ever. I caught *Why Men Wear Frocks*, a stylish piece on transvestites by Turner Prize-winning potter Grayson Perry. Perry was adept at coaxing others to talk sensibly about themselves, at ease discussing gender issues with articulate young men. And all out in the open, to camera. I thought at once of *This Week*'s tentative steps forty years ago, interviewing gays and lesbians in silhouette. And I thought of *The Naked Civil Servant* with John Hurt. Grayson Perry should play himself in the movie.

Under Kevin Lygo, C4's programme department, as the BAFTA awards attest, makes many excellent one-offs each year; yet it will always need to reaffirm basic qualitative goals. It must sustain *Channel Four News* and current affairs; cherish single documentaries; and keep pushing the boat out in drama and entertainment. It could also favour the arts, cut down on the sex, add something to its great strengths in history and archaeology. Something for the choosiest of highbrows would not go amiss; instead of *Eurotrash*, how about European life, politics, languages, culture?

Channel Four, like the BBC, has taken the digital route; a new channel, More4, caters, we are told, for older, more intelligent viewers. Confusingly, and depressingly, it was marketed at the launch as 'adult entertainment'. Its Controller promised that

More4 would be more '*Wifeswap* than Wagner, not po-faced or elitist'. Shame; he has this the wrong way round, surely? And where does this leave C4? Will it be more Wagner than *Wifeswap*? I still hope for riches on both.

There's a suggestion that, if ratings fall, C4 may make a call on public funds, distributed, perhaps, through Ofcom. If it does, it would be fatal to say: '*Big Brother* pays the bills; if you want us to keep the news, and do more current affairs, pay up.' C4's only possible further claim on public funds is: 'Look at the range of programmes we make, and the marvels we display. Will you ease the cost of spectrum for us, one way or the other, to see us through?' We who love C4 will go on urging it to renew its commitment to public purposes, aiming to please disparate audiences, acknowledging the unapologetically neo-Reithian role of stretching minds.

The best book on broadcasting of recent years is Georgina Born's perceptive and severe study, *Uncertain Vision: Birt, Dyke and the Reinvention of the BBC*. Responding to it in the *London Review of Books*, the playwright David Edgar reminds us, in a fine piece, that 'there is also the responsibility of a public service to give a voice to those who aren't heard'. He may have Channel Four, as well as the BBC, in mind when he writes:

> Providing a service which meets people's needs as well as their wants, which seeks to expand as well as echo the experience of its users, which is prepared to jolt and disturb as well as confirm or sustain, which provides a site for public conversation and which acknowledges and articulates our collective as well as our individual affinities and identities, is a pretty good mission statement for a public realm communicator. Ofcom is right to define public service in terms of purpose and function rather than institutions, but it is the purpose of institutions to provide conditions in which such purposes can be best pursued.

I say ditto to all that. But promoting public conversation is a function of the mainstream. Digital channels, each a niche, do not talk to each other.

'Journalism', George Ffitch, my colleague on *This Week*, used to say, 'is written on the sands, washed away by the tide. Television journalism, even more ephemeral, is written on the wind.' Writing this book has been an act as much of reconstruction as of memory. It all seems now a very long time ago. Yet traces of what I did, and encouraged others to do, remain. I was never bored, and often happy. I was fortunate to be working when the BBC set standards for others to emulate; when ITV companies contended to excel; when Channel Four was waiting to burst into life; when Ted Turner and Sidney Bernstein said 'Go for it', and I did.

As President of the Royal Television Society, at the Cambridge biennial convention, I was asked to tell delegates: 'Be sure to be prompt in the hall next morning to view the largest television screen in the world.' It would be blank – nothing on it. But it was, I was told to say, a must-see. After dinner in King's Great Hall, I rose to make this 'housekeeping' announcement, and couldn't; the words would not pass my lips. I had a fit of the giggles. I remembered what I had to say, but my mind would not let me. An empty screen? I knew this was nonsense; what on earth was the point of looking at an empty screen? The giggles persisted; tears streamed down my cheeks. At the back of the hall, voices demanded to know: 'What's he on, then? Can we have some too?' Next morning came references, unjust but unsurprising, to my making an unsteady way across the quad to bed.

It is what is on the screen that matters, all the same.

This tale ends, as it began, at a prizegiving. Three times a year I shook hands with prizewinners at assorted RTS award ceremonies. At one, the highlight came in a shoot-out between cooks for a documentary prize. The winner erupted at his table and strode towards me in high, jaunty style, plainly ecstatic. Arriving at the platform, bubbling over, Jamie Oliver looked me in the eye and left an impression; he planted a fat wet kiss on both my cheeks.

What would John Reith have made of that?

ACKNOWLEDGEMENTS

In this book I have tried to dispel a myth: talented individuals, given their heads, do make the best television programmes, but they do not make them alone. Team-work made *The World at War*; every producer is dependent on the skills and commitment of others. So in these pages, they speak too.

Since I ran programme departments, and even a channel, much of what I take pride in was actually created by my colleagues; they know, I hope, that I know how much I owe them, and that applies also to those I do not mention. The Romans, praying to particular gods after favours received or yet to be granted, used to name Jove or Venus, and then add, for safety's sake, 'and all the gods and goddesses'. So I thank all those I name, and also all those I don't have room to.

This book was put together on the novel plan of writing it first – 'Don't just sit about, write!' – and researching it afterwards. I am grateful to all those who helpfully, and at times critically, jogged my memory: Roy Addison, Andy Allan, Jack Andrews, Mike Bolland, Kevin Brownlow, Jacqueline Davis, Taylor Downing, John Edwards, David Elstein, Liz Forgan, Alan Fountain, Murray Grigor, John Hambley, David Hammond, Ralph Isaacs, Michael Kustow, Verity Lambert, Pat Mitchell, Chris Palmer, David Rose, Bob Rowland, Naomi Sargant, Naomi Shepherd, Martin Smith, Liz Sutherland, Vicki Wegg-Prosser, Phillip Whitehead, Joyce Wooller, and others.

I have relied much on the official history of ITV, *Independent Television in Britain*, and particularly the admirable volume by Paul Bonner (with Lesley Aston) that deals with Channel Four. Iain MacLeod, deputy-rector and archivist of Glasgow Academy, found the text of John Reith's 1950 prize-giving speech. The BBC's Written Archive at Caversham found *Panorama* scripts of my day; an access enquiry, under the Data Protection Act 1988, enabled me to read my BBC personnel file and relevant extracts from the Board of Governors minutes on *Panorama* in 1966. Roger Cull kindly allowed me to consult his copies of *Fusion*, Associated Rediffusion's house magazine; Vicki Wegg-Prosser showed me her archival dossier on *This Week*. Kevin Brownlow has allowed me to quote extracts from his diary, on the run-up to *Hollywood – the Silent Years*. I have used Patrick Leigh Fermor's vivid description of George Psychoundakis, taken from his introduction to *The Cretan Runner*, which he translated, and, generously, he has permitted me to include the sketch of George he made at the time.

Jimmy Boyle has allowed me to use an extract from *A Sense of Freedom*, and Robert Kee from *Ireland, a History*. I am ever grateful to both. Extracts from *The World at War* are reproduced courtesy of Thames Television, part of the FremantleMedia group. I have quoted liberally, with their permission, from colleagues' accounts of their working methods on the programme. I thank each and all.

Readers will find a lengthier personal account of my time and role at Channel 4 in *Storm Over 4*, Weidenfeld, 1989, and a critique, and subsequent discussion, in *The Making of Channel 4*, edited by Peter Catterall.

David Herman and Anthony Howard took time and trouble to read the manuscript at fuller length, and offered blunt and sage advice. I thank them for it; we remain friends. John Hambley, Pat Mitchell and Peter Taylor have kindly read and commented on portions of the text. Louise Stein checked facts, names, dates, corroborating some guesses, eliminating some howlers; for any that remain, I am responsible. Nini Aldridge deciphered my scribbles and committed them to disk; she remained cheerful doing it, which helped too.

Charles Walker, at Peters, Fraser & Dunlop, encouraged me, and pushed the book on. At Time Warner Books, Ursula Mackenzie gave the lead; Tim Whiting and Vivien Redman carried the project forward. Linda Silverman did the picture research. Gillian Somerscales made an immaculate job of copy-editing the text.

First and lastly, I owe thanks to Gillian Widdicombe for setting me to work, and keeping me at it. The book has occupied a great space in our life together, like a pile of storage boxes in a living room. Now that it is finished, we shall see more of each other. Hooray!

Jeremy Isaacs
Greshornish, Isle of Skye
Castelvecchio, Umbria
2003–5

BIBLIOGRAPHY

Afriat, Alan and Elstein, Farr, Kuehl, McConachy, *Journal of the Society of Film and Television Arts, The World at War*, Vol. 2, Nos 9–10, SFTA, 1971

Arnold-Forster, Mark, *The World at War*, with an introduction by Richard Overy, Pimlico, 2001

Attenborough, David, *Life on Air*, BBC, 2002

Beevor, Anthony, *Crete, the Battle and the Resistance*, John Murray, 1991

Black, Peter, *The Mirror in the Corner*, Hutchinson, 1960

Bonner, Paul (with Lesley Aston), *Independent Television in Britain*, Vol. 6 *(New Developments in Independent Television, 1981–92)*, Palgrave Macmillan, 2003

Born, Georgina, *Uncertain Vision: Birt, Dyke and the Reinvention of the BBC*, Vintage, 2005

Boyle, Jimmy, *A Sense of Freedom*, Canongate Publishing and Pan Books, 1977

Brownlow, Kevin, *Napoleon, Abel Gance's Classic Film*, Jonathan Cape, 1983

Cannadine, David (ed.), *History and the Media*, Palgrave Macmillan, 2004

Catterall, Peter (ed.), *The Making of Channel 4*, Frank Cass, 1999

Darlow, Michael, *Independents Struggle*, Quartet Books, 2004

Docherty, Morrison and Tracey (eds) *Keeping Faith? Channel Four and Its Audience*, John Libbery, 1988

Fenández-Armesto, Felipe, *Millennium*, Black Swan, 1996

Finch, Cox and Giles (eds), *Granada Television, the First Generation*, Manchester University Press, 2003

Forman, Denis, *Persona Granada*, André Deutsch, 1997

Frankland, Noble, *History at War*, Giles de la Mare, 1998

Franklin, Bob (ed.) *Television Policy, the MacTaggart Lectures*, Edinburgh University Press, 2005

Holland, Patricia, *The Angry Buzz: This Week and Current Affairs Television*, I. B. Taurus, 2006

Isaacs, Jeremy, *Storm Over 4*, Weidenfeld & Nicholson, 1989

Isaacs, Jeremy with Taylor Downing, *Cold War*, Transworld, 1998

Isaacs, Jeremy, *Never Mind the Moon*, Bantam Press, 1999

Kee, Robert, *The Green Flag*, Quartet Books, 1976

Kee, Robert, *Ireland, a History*, Abacus, 2003

Lindley, Richard, *Panorama*, Politico, 2002

McIntyre, Ian, *The Expense of Glory: The Life of John Reith*, HarperCollins, 1994

Michaelson, Isaac and Ora, *Memoirs*, Jerusalem (privately printed), 1982

Milne, Alasdair, *DG, the Memoirs of a British Broadcaster*, Hodder & Stoughton, 1988

Potter, Jeremy, *Independent Television in Britain*, Vol. 3 (*Politics and Control 1968–80*); Vol. 4 (*Companies and Programmes 1968–80*), Macmillan, 1989–90

Psychoundakis, George, *The Cretan Runner*, (translated and with an introduction by Patrick Leigh Fermor) Penguin Books, 1998

Purser, Philip, *Done Viewing*, Quartet Books, 1992

Pym, John, *Film on Four, A Survey*, British Film Institute, 1992

Sendall, Bernard, *Independent Television in Britain*, Vol. 2 (*Expansion and Change, 1958–1968*), Macmillan, 1983

Whitelaw, William, *The Whitelaw Memoirs*, Aurum Press, 1993

INDEX